Introduction to Opera

"GÖTTERDÄMMERUNG," ACT II, WITH HELEN TRAUBEL AND LAURITZ MELCHIOR

By courtesy of Louis Mélançon

Introduction to Opera

Mary Ellis Peltz, Editor

A Guidebook Sponsored by
THE METROPOLITAN OPERA GUILD

Based on *Opera Lover's Companion* and *Opera News*, both publications of The Metropolitan Opera Guild, with adaptations for this volume by Carol Ann Luten and C. J. Luten and annotated list of recordings by C. J. Luten.

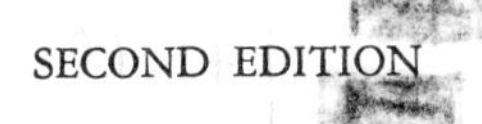

SECOND EDITION

BARNES & NOBLE, INC., NEW YORK
PUBLISHERS · BOOKSELLERS · SINCE 1873

Fifth Printing, 1962

Based on *Opera Lover's Companion*
Copyright, 1948
By The Metropolitan Opera Guild, Inc.
and selected issues of *Opera News*

L. C. Catalogue Card Number: 62-8353

Printed in the United States of America

Contributors to This Volume

Bruce Archibald
William Ashbrook
Lilian E. Foerster
John W. Freeman
Ernest Gold
Paul Jaretzki
Robert Lawrence
C. J. Luten
Katherine Griffith McDonald
Frank Merkling
Paul Nettl
Herbert F. Peyser
Max de Schauensee

Contents

INTRODUCTION TO OPERA

Introduction to the First Edition

Introduction to Opera, sponsored by The Metropolitan Opera Guild, will help you develop an appreciation and understanding of opera. This is true whether you already have an interest in opera and want to expand your knowledge of it or whether you are approaching this magical medium for the first time. Because of space limitations, the operas covered are limited to forty rather standard repertory works. Since repertory changes as public taste fluctuates and as singers capable of assuming certain roles come and go, there will undoubtedly be some who will question at least a few of the works presented. Our aim, however, has been to select hardy perennials (e.g., *Aïda, Carmen*), works that are revived with some measure of regularity (e.g., *Norma, Orfeo ed Euridice*), and works that are currently enjoying some degree of popularity (e.g., *Così fan tutte*)—with special emphasis on what has been presented in the major American operatic theaters during the last five years. Another consideration has been the reader's likelihood of hearing performances of the works outside cities with resident opera companies—either on radio and TV broadcasts or in presentation by local amateur or semiprofessional groups. (Hence the omission of such operas as well known by name as *Parsifal* and *Wozzeck.*) An exception to our general criteria is the inclusion of all four operas of Wagner's *Der Ring des Nibelungen* even though *Die Walküre* is the only portion regularly presented. The *Ring* is a unit; and it seemed impossible to pull one section of it out of context for independent discussion.

When listening to operas, you must remember that opera is a special kind of *theater.* Just as ability to understand the spoken word is necessary if you are to comprehend a play, you cannot fail to profit by knowledge of the words of an opera. It is inconceivable that one should attend a performance of a Shakespearean tragedy, for example, simply for a view of the stage pictures and the beauty of the sound of the actors' voices. It is also unlikely that one should want to attend an opera without any knowledge of the text. If opera is theater and the words are important, what part, then, does music play? Music in an opera adds a new dimension to the word. It begins where the word ends to communicate expression beyond the power of words.

As you will discover, there are various operatic forms, but you are apt to find that the greatest difference among operas is that some employ set pieces (individual arias or ensembles) and some do not. In the first type (e.g., *Carmen, Don Giovanni, Il Barbiere di Siviglia*) the composer uses spoken words, accompanied recitative, or bridge passages of somewhat neutral expression to carry his plot forward to the point where music is necessary to expand one or more characters' thoughts and feelings. In the latter type, the creative artist aims for more realism and attempts a continuous dramatic fabric with a continuity similar to that of a play (e.g., *Pelléas et Mélisande, Tristan und Isolde*). Further differences in operatic forms and styles are pointed out in the articles relating to the selected works.

For the reader's convenience we have divided the book into two sections. In Part I the forty operas are presented in alphabetical order in their original title (with the exception that the operas of the *Ring* are grouped together in order of sequence). Next there are listed the opera's composer and librettist, the date and place of its first performance, and its principal characters (in order of appearance) with the type of voice sung by each. An act-by-act plot summary follows. (All of the plot summaries are adapted from the official publication of The Metropolitan Opera Guild, *Opera News*, edited by Mary Ellis Peltz.) Here important set pieces (or pivotal first lines in those operas that don't employ set pieces) and the character who sings them are identified in brackets. Each key line is in its original language and in translation. Most of the translations have been done expressly for this book; they are usually literal, though sometimes they try merely to capture the spirit of the original. They are *not* designed for singing. However, in three operas—*Boris Godunov, Così fan tutte*, and *Die Zauberflöte*—which are currently sung in English at the Metropolitan Opera House, the English versions, as they are sung (rather than the literal translations), are given. When you are hearing an opera, you should listen carefully for the first line so that you will know where you are in an act. (Eventually you should try to acquire librettos for your favorite operas; no matter how detailed the summary, it does not compare with having every word in front of you.* As your interest develops still further, you may want to learn to read a vocal score and to add some scores to your music library.)

After the plot summary of each opera, there is a discussion of the work's musical and dramatic content and style. All of these discussions were written by specialists. Most of them were re-

* Most libraries have collections of librettos. They are on sale at many music stores. They are usually included in complete recordings of an opera. And members of The Metropolitan Opera Guild may purchase from the Guild for a nominal fee librettos of operas to be heard on Saturday afternoon broadcasts.

printed in *Opera Lover's Companion,* a volume edited by Mary Ellis Peltz, comprising articles selected from *Opera News.* The article on *Don Pasquale* was especially prepared for this Guidebook.

In the Guide at the end of the book the operas are again listed in alphabetical order, and here each complete long-playing recording of the opera is listed and the performance evaluated. With so many recordings to choose from, it seemed that such a section would be particularly helpful to the readers of this book, most of whom will not have an opportunity to compare performances before making a purchase.

We are grateful to many friends and acquaintances for suggestions and help in preparing this edition for publication by Barnes & Noble. Those who co-operated to make possible the *Guide to 40 Operas on Long-playing Records* are listed at the end of the introduction to that section; here we must single out for special thanks Claudio Fantino, who translated the first lines of the Italian operas.

1956

CAROL ANN LUTEN
and C. J. LUTEN

Introduction to the Second Edition

Since the original edition of these pages, the operagoing public's appetite for a broader repertory has increased. To satisfy this demand, American opera companies are staging more frequent revivals of a number of works which were formerly heard only seldom.

In the light of this trend, we have added to this new edition eight operas, each of which has been produced at the Metropolitan Opera in the very recent past. The new operas have been accorded the same treatment as the forty covered in the first edition.

C. J. LUTEN

GIUSEPPE VERDI (1813–1901)

Aïda

Libretto by Antonio Ghislanzoni and Verdi, based on a book by Camille du Locle and a sketch by the Egyptologist Mariette Bey. First performance in Cairo, December 24, 1871.

Characters

Ramfis, High Priest of Isis	Bass
Radames, captain of the Egyptian guards	Tenor
Amneris, daughter of the King of Egypt	Contralto
Aïda, slave to Amneris	Soprano
The King of Egypt	Bass
A messenger	Tenor
A priestess	Soprano
Amonasro, King of Ethiopia (Aïda's father)	Baritone

The Story

ACT I. In a hall of the royal palace at Memphis, Radames learns from the High Priest, Ramfis, that the Ethiopians are threatening the Nile Valley and that the goddess Isis has decreed a new commander for Egypt. Radames longs to be chosen in order to win the hand of the slave girl Aïda (**Radames:** *Celeste Aïda*—Heavenly Aïda). The King's daughter, Amneris, interrupts his revery (**Amneris:** *Quale insolita gioia*—What unaccustomed joy) and questions him shrewdly. Her suspicions that he does not respond to her own affections are increased at the entrance of her slave Aïda, of whom she is mortally jealous (**Amneris:** *Vieni, o diletta*—Come here, dear one—with **Aïda** and **Radames**). At the conclusion of their trio, the King of Egypt and his train enter to give audience to a messenger from the front, who reports that the Ethiopians are marching on Thebes. The King announces the appointment of Radames to command the Egyptian army, and the rapturous crowd leads the young officer away (**Chorus:** *Su! del Nilo al sacro lido*—Let us go to sacred banks of the Nile). Aïda remains, regretting that she, too, has cheered him to victory (**Aïda:** *Ritorna vincitor*—Return victorious), for the enemy are her own people; the King of Ethiopia is her father. Torn by inner conflict, Aïda prays for mercy (**Aïda:** *Numi, pietà*—Gods, pity my suffering).

Through the dim columns of the temple of Phthà, a priestess is heard addressing the god (**Priestess:** *Possente Phthà*—Hail, mighty Phthà). Ceremonial dances are performed while Radames receives the sacred arms from Ramfis (**Ramfis:** *Nume, custode e vindice*—God, guardian and avenger).

ACT II. On her luxurious terrace Amneris sighs for the return of Radames (**Amneris:** *Ah! vieni amor mio*—Ah, come my love). Dismissing the little blackamoors who have been dancing for her pleasure, Amneris summons Aïda, cajoles her into admitting that she, too, loves the warrior (**Amneris:** *Fu la sorte dell' armi a' tuoi funesta*—The army's fate was deadly to your people), and threatens her with humiliation at his triumph (**Aïda, Amneris:** *Ah! Pietà ti prenda*—Ah, take pity).

At the gate of Thebes a mighty procession crowds about the King's throne to welcome the victorious Radames (**Chorus:** *Gloria all' Egitto, ad Iside*—Glory to Egypt and Isis). The King offers the hand of his daughter as a reward to the young warrior. The Ethiopian captives stagger forward in chains. Their leader, Amonasro, whispers to his daughter Aïda that she must not disclose his rank, then, turning to the King of Egypt, implores his mercy (**Amonasro:** *Ma tu, re*—But you, King). Amonasro is retained as a hostage; the other captives are freed, and as Radames is led off by Amneris, Aïda falls weeping into her father's arms.

ACT III. On the moonlit banks of the Nile, the High Priest leads Amneris to the temple of Isis for a vigil on the eve of her wedding. Aïda enters for a farewell tryst with her lover and mourns her lost country (**Aïda:** *O patria mia*—Oh, my homeland). Her father has followed her and begs her to draw from her lover his plans for the new campaign (**Amonasro:** *Rivedrai le foreste*—Once again you shall see the forests). Aïda protests against such treachery but finally succumbs under the weight of her father's impassioned pleas (**Amonasro:** *Su, dunque! sorgete*—Well then, rise). He hides as she greets the ardent Radames, begs him to flee with her (**Aïda:** *Fuggiam gli ardori inospiti*—Ah, let us fly from the unkind heat), and finally learns his tactics. When Amonasro triumphantly emerges and tries to win Radames to his side, Amneris suddenly appears and accuses them of treachery. Ramfis summons the guard and arrests Radames as Aïda and her father rush away.

ACT IV. Crouching at a portal of the palace judgment hall, Amneris bewails the treachery of Radames (**Amneris:** *L'abborrita rivale*—The hated rival), but when he is led in by his guards, vainly urges him to flee. He will not live without Aïda. Despairingly (**Amneris:** *Ohimè! morir mi sento*—Alas! I feel as if I were dying), she listens to the verdict of the priests echoing the word *traditor* ("traitor") from the judgment hall.

Radames has been sealed in a gloomy vault beneath the temple of Vulcan. Here he finds Aïda, who has hidden herself to die with him (**Radames:** *Morir! Si pura e bella*—To die! So pure and lovely). Peacefully the two lovers bid farewell to earth (**Radames, Aïda:** *O terra addio*—Farewell, oh earth).

AÏDA fulfills the specifications of conventional opera in the fullest degree, but its clarity of form, ideal proportion, freedom from every excess of bulk, and general "rightness" and inevitability set it on a totally different plane which its immediate predecessors [*Don Carlo* and *La Forza del Destino*], in their patchiness and incongruities of style, never achieve. Without *Aïda* Verdi would have presented an enigma to the world. But with *Aïda* his significance would have been largely solved even without *Otello* and *Falstaff*.

Arrigo Boïto [composer of *Mefistofele* and librettist of *Falstaff* and *Otello*] once said that the brief prelude that opens *Aïda* was really meant for an interlude and "is simply thrown away where it now stands." Yet it is hard to think of a more perfect introduction to *Aïda*, one of the most poetic and exquisite pages Verdi ever composed. . . .

There are several representative themes in *Aïda*, though they are not utilized in the Wagnerian manner. Two of them are heard in the short prelude and constitute its thematic substance. The first is the lovely theme of Aïda and her love, woven with delicate polyphony; the second, the heavy bass phrase of the priests, treated fugally. The prelude comes to a brief but vigorous climax after a soft recall of the Aïda motif, then melts away in a vaporous and enchanting close.

The short opening dialogue of Radames and the High Priest, Ramfis, is carried on above a simple but telling theme progressing in tranquil imitations. At the exit of Ramfis a change comes over the music. A brief but vigorous recitative of Radames, punctuated by martial fanfares, brings the most celebrated air of the opera, the romanza, *Celeste Aïda*. It has always been the writer's belief that the instrumentation of this air (which is in three-part song form, with a coda) is of more interest than the melody itself. In any case, the poetic close prescribed by the composer with the singer uttering a high B-flat pianissimo and *morendo*, is invariably ruined by tenors who bawl the last tone at the top of their lungs, presumably because they are technically incapable of taking it as prescribed.

With the appearance of Amneris we meet the character whom Verdi loved above all others in this opera, on whom he conferred a humanity surpassing almost any figure in the whole range of his works. At first a pair of insinuating orchestral melodies indicates a nature outwardly alluring; but almost at once an agitated phrase, carried on at some length, paints her deep-seated jealousy, and is recalled for this purpose a number of times through the opera.

Lovely, but breathing falsehood, is her address to Aïda, *Vieni, o diletta, appressati,* followed by a swift recurrence of the music of jealousy. A fine trio, built over it, leads to the appearance of the king and to an animated, concerted piece. The words of the Pharaoh are uttered over a simple octave bass, but the orchestra grows more agitated as the messenger tells of the hostile invasion and priests and people furiously demand war. Then comes that magnificent, foursquare march melody, *Su! del Nilo al sacro lido,* which hostile criticism has tried in vain to belittle. Ramfis interjects a middle section, *Gloria ai numi,* and after a *reprise* of the melody we hear it in a curious duet form, by Radames and Aïda. The young warrior delivers the tune, *grandioso,* while against it the heartbroken Aïda sings a kind of emotional counterpoint, in tearful, syncopated phrases that subtly express her anguish. A superb resumption of the march, with powerful orchestral sonorities, culminates in the exclamation, in which even Aïda, momentarily carried away, joins—*Ritorna vincitor.* One more recall of the march, as the throng leaves the stage, leaves the scene free for the soprano.

Repeating the words *Ritorna vincitor,* in horrified self-reproach, Aïda launches on her first great dramatic *scena.* The hearer should pay especial attention to the section *L'insana parola,* with its agitated syncopations and melody in the lower strings; the return of the Aïda theme; the sorrowful melody, *I sacri nomi;* and particularly the lachrymose closing *cantabile, Numi, pietà.*

What most people regard as local color in *Aïda* is really more Verdi's imaginative inspiration than some tangible element of music. However, one detail of the lovely, mysterious hymn of the unseen priestess of Phthà, beginning the next scene, invariably evokes the Orient. That is the interval of the lowered second, a melodic step which lends this song its exotic character, more even than do the broken chords of the accompanying harps. Directly after this invocation comes the sacred dance of the priestesses, perhaps the best ballet music Verdi ever wrote. The dance in question is lovely, no less for the exotic nature of its melody than for its use of flutes and oboes. The consecration that follows in broad, *cantabile* melodic phrases is grand opera at its finest.

Rapturous phrases for Amneris and a charmingly capricious dance for little Negro slaves bring us to the fine and vigorously dramatic scene in which the daughter of Pharaoh first affects sympathy toward the captive Aïda, then, in an access of jealous triumph, turns on her apparently defeated rival. Let no one overlook Aïda's touching *Ah! Pietà ti prenda* or the jubilant phrases of Amneris as the music of *Su! del Nilo* sounds from without.

The triumph scene is spectacular, full-panoplied opera in the Meyerbeerian sense, though musically it towers above any artifice of Meyerbeer. The first great chorus, *Gloria all' Egitto*, was adopted by the Egyptian government for the national hymn of Egypt soon after the work was first given. There is a beautiful contrasting lyrical melody for the women, *S'intreci il loto al lauro*, while the priests enter to their ponderous bass theme, which may suggest the composer's lifelong violent dislike for priests and priestcraft.

We cannot, of course, overlook the march of the long trumpets. Verdi did not employ these instruments for their Egyptian authenticity but because of their festal sonorities. The march tune itself is familiar the world over. The sudden change from A-flat to B at one point is always a striking effect. The ballet music again rises to Verdi's best.

Pomp gives place to drama only with the advent of Amonasro, whose vigorous declamatory phrases and beautiful appeal, *Ma tu, re*, are the emotional high point of the scene. The pealing ensemble which grows out of it is one of the grandest moments of the opera. Toward the close a conjunction of two great melodies, among Verdi's most considerable feats of counterpoint, is often lost in the sonorities of the stage band.

The opening page of the Nile scene is the tonal embodiment of the enchantment, at once bewitching and menacing, of an African night. Verdi wanted the scene to be impregnated with the sight, the sound, the smell of Africa. By the magic of his instrumentation, he has conjured up the whole tropical atmosphere: the hum of insects, the scent of embalsamed airs, the vegetation almost throbbing in its luxuriance. Aïda's romanza, *O patria mia*, with sinuous oboe *obbligati*, is as beautiful as anything in the literature of the Italian aria.

The finest moments in the third act, however, are to be found in the matchless colloquy of Amonasro and Aïda. In the briefest span we have the appeal of the Ethiopian chieftain to his daughter's love of her native land—*Rivedrai le foreste imbalsamate*—her reply, *Ah! ben rammento,* then the sudden outburst of savage fury as she refuses to wrest from the enamored Radames the secret of his battle plans and that piteous appeal, *Padre a costoro schiava non sono,* together with those longspun, wondering phrases of Amonasro's *Pensa che un popolo,* and Aïda's nostalgic cry, *O patria, oh patria, quanti mi costi!*

What wonder that, after this, the meeting of Aïda and her lover should lapse somewhat, fine as it is? Even Verdi complained to Ghislanzoni that the scene was somewhat commonplace. Yet it has many fine pages, too, particularly Aïda's *La tra foreste vergini* and Radames' answering *Sovra una terra.* To finer tastes the impassioned trio of Radames, Aïda, and Amonasro after the betrayal may appeal even more than the showy and operatic duet, *Si fuggiam.*

The first scene of the fourth act belongs magnificently to Amneris. It is a flawless masterpiece, dramatic, somber, passionate, even if the great, sweeping phrase, *Ah, tu dei vivere,* might conceivably come out of Gounod or Bizet. In the whole opera, furthermore, there is little so moving as those ten bars of Radames' *Gli dei l'adducano,* whose value Verdi so appreciated that he was very specific to Ghislanzoni about the text. The trial scene deserves a chapter to itself; but we must at least call attention to that heart-shaking, thrice repeated cry of Amneris, *Ah pietà,* with its broken exclamations, *Numi pietà,* which Verdi recalled from the tower scene in *Trovatore.* Her shrill curses against the implacable priests and the turbulent orchestral postlude bring down the curtain in a fury of sound.

For the closing scene Verdi warned his librettist against any suggestions of physical suffering or death pangs. With rare psychological insight he wished the atmosphere to be lyrical and elegiac throughout. In the entire scene there is nothing more literal than those eight bars of reiterated low D's which picture the act of sealing the fatal stone above the vault in which the lovers are entombed. Unearthly in its beauty is Radames' *Morir, si pura e bella,* interrupted by that wondrous passage in which Aïda fancies she sees the Angel of Death. This music, which Francis Toye [foremost biographer of Verdi] has finely called "lightheaded," was for its time so novel in its scoring (muted violins *legato* in the upper registers, the other strings *arco, pizzicato, tremolando,* harp, flute, two clarinets, bassoon, and horn) that Verdi entreated the conductor, Bottesini, to inform him how it sounded. At the last, against the songs of priests and priestesses and echoes of the sacred dance, comes O *terra, addio,* one of the most ethereal canticles to death ever hymned by a soul on the threshold of release.

HERBERT F. PEYSER

GIUSEPPE VERDI (1813–1901)

Un Ballo in Maschera

Libretto by Antonio Somma. First performance in Rome, February 17, 1859.

Characters

Samuele	Bass
Tommaso	Bass
Oscar, a page	Soprano
Riccardo	Tenor
Renato, the King's secretary	Baritone
The Judge	Tenor
Ulrica, an astrologer	Mezzo-soprano
Silvano	Baritone
Amelia, Renato's wife	Soprano
Amelia's servant	Tenor

The Story

ACT I. The friends and adherents of the King of Sweden (referred to in the opera as Riccardo, or the Count) await him in his audience chamber, together with a group of conspirators under the leadership of Samuele and Tommaso. As the king enters, his page Oscar hands him various documents, including the list of guests for a forthcoming masked ball. Here the king finds the names of Renato, confidant to the throne, and his beautiful wife Amelia, with whom the monarch is secretly in love. The sight of her name prompts an ecstatic outburst in which he anticipates the joy of seeing her again (**Riccardo:** *La rivedrà nell' estasi*—I will see her again in ecstasy). As Oscar and the others leave, the page admits Renato, who wonders why the king appears disturbed. When Riccardo confesses to a secret concern, the guileless Renato warns him that his fears are justified: a conspiracy is afoot against the crown. Considerably relieved, the king deprecates the danger, but his secretary tells him that he must continue to live for the sake of Sweden's glory and destiny (**Renato:** *Alla vita che t'arride*—To the life which smiles upon you). A magistrate enters with a decree banishing an ancient soothsayer, Ulrica, who is accused of evil practices. Before signing it, Riccardo asks Oscar about Ulrica and is told of the woman's prowess at reading fortunes in the stars (**Oscar:** *Volta la terrea*—She turns her face toward the stars). The king resolves to see her for himself and, over the objections of Renato and the judge, cheerfully invites the reassembled courtiers to join him in an incognito visit to the witch's lair.

Muttering fearsome incantations over her caldron (**Ulrica:** *Re dell' abisso, affretati*—Hasten, oh king of the abyss), Ulrica awes the visitors to her hut by prophesying that one of them, a sailor named Silvano, will find money in his pocket, which he does with the help of the disguised Riccardo. When the wretched Amelia enters, seeking a magic herb to free her of her illicit love for the king, Ulrica advises her that the plant is to be found at the foot of the gallows. After Amelia leaves, Riccardo, who has overheard, begs the sorceress to read his hand (**Riccardo:** *Di' tu se fidele* [Barcarolle]—Tell me if the sea waits for me faithfully). Although the monarch laughs off her prophecy that he is soon to die by the friendly hand he will next shake, Ulrica repeats it while glaring at Samuele and Tommaso, who fear that their plot is known (**Riccardo [Quintet]:** *E scherzo od è follia*—Is it a joke or a folly?). Greeted by a handclasp from the entering Renato, Riccardo is recognized by the crowd and hailed as king by all save Ulrica and the conspirators (**Chorus:** *O figlio d'Inghilterra*—O son of England).

ACT II. To the lonely gallows field Amelia comes trembling in search of the herb that will obliterate her passion (**Amelia:** *Ma dall' arido stelo*—But as I will have plucked that herb from the dry stem with my own hand). Her royal lover, however, has followed her and urges his suit. As Amelia confesses her own love (**Riccardo, Amelia:** *O qual soave brivido*—Like a sweet shudder, it cools the burning heart), she and Riccardo are joined by Renato, seeking to protect his master from the pursuing conspirators. The secretary urges the king to flee for his life, but only Amelia's desperate threat to raise her veil moves Riccardo to leave her and give thought to his own safety (**Amelia, Riccardo, Renato:** *Odi tu come sonano*—Hear how muffled are the sounds of death). Procuring Renato's promise to conduct the lady in silence back to the capital, the monarch rushes off just before Samuele and Tommaso enter with their henchmen. When the conspirators make insolent remarks concerning the veiled woman, Renato draws his sword; in the confusion Amelia's veil falls, revealing to the astonished husband his own wife. While Amelia bemoans her dishonor, Renato bitterly deserts the king in favor of Samuele and Tommaso, who are amused by the ironic turn of events and retreat with cynical laughter (**Samuele, Tommaso, Chorus:** *Ve' se di notte*—See if during the night).

ACT III. In his own house Renato prepares to kill his wife for her supposed faithlessness. Amelia pleads for mercy, asking that she be allowed to embrace their son once more before she dies (**Amelia:** *Morrò, ma prima in grazia*—I die, but allow me first to embrace my only child). Relenting, Renato orders her from the room and turns to vent his wrath instead on his monarch, whose portrait is on the wall (**Renato:** *Eri tu che macchiavi*—It was you who were soiling that soul). Samuele and Tommaso enter and dispute with their new adherent the privilege of stabbing the king. As they prepare to draw lots, Amelia returns with Oscar, who brings an invitation to Riccardo's masked ball. Forcing his wife to draw one name, Renato finds that he is chosen to murder the king. Led by the page, who does not know what is afoot, the five anticipate the festivities with the most mixed feelings (**Oscar [Quintet]:** *Ah, di che fulgor*—Ah, what splendor).

Alone in his private apartments, Riccardo resolves to give up Amelia and send her and Renato abroad, even though he fears that his heart will be broken (**Riccardo:** *Ma se m'è forza perderti*—But if I am forced to lose you).

The curtain rises on the ballroom, where the court is assembled in masks and dominos. Oscar hesitates to divulge his master's disguise to Renato but finally confesses (**Oscar:** *Saper vorreste*—Would you want to know). As the dancing continues (**Ballet**), the king refuses to leave in spite of Amelia's repeated warnings (**Amelia, Riccardo:** *T'amo, sì, t'amo e in lagrime*—I love you, yes, I love you, and in tears I throw myself at your feet). The lovers bid each other a furtive farewell; Renato stabs the king, learns too late of his wife's innocence, and remorsefully accepts forgiveness from the dying monarch.

BOTH humor and courtly elegance help to give *A Masked Ball* a place of its own in its composer's output. The elegance of Gustave III of Sweden (or Riccardo, Governor of Boston, if you prefer*) is something perceptibly different and certainly more

* There has always been a deal of confusion about what names to give the characters and where to place the locale of *A Masked Ball* because of the censorship forced upon Verdi at the time of the original production. Italian authorities made so many demands upon the composer and his librettist that the final result is a hodgepodge. Riccardo was intended to be King Gustave of Sweden; Renato, to be Count Anckar-

genteel than the free and easy manner of the conscienceless Duke of Mantua. Neither is this well-bred fun in any way related to the rough humors of Brother Melitone, let alone to the world-shaking laughter of Sir John Falstaff. It is a solitary note, one which Verdi had not struck before and was not to strike again. But there is also another kind of mirth in this opera—the sinister, mocking, sardonic chuckles of the conspirators, maliciously delighted at the prospects of savory scandal growing out of the abasement of Amelia, entrusted for safe conduct to her own unwitting husband after her assignation with his king and—incidentally—his friend.

There are other conceits and felicities of characterization in *A Masked Ball* which are lacking in earlier Verdi operas. There is, particularly, Oscar, the royal page, a trousered soprano like Siébel, like Urbain, like dozens of other operatic youths with male attire and female voice. Yet Oscar, pert, lighthearted, irrepressible, is practically unique in the Verdian gallery. Conceivably Verdi shaped him in the image of another royal page, Urbain in *Les Huguenots*. Actually he seems more of a blood relation to Cherubino, though much shallower than Mozart's glorious adolescent. Yet, with any one of the three arias which Oscar blithely chirps, Verdi rivalled Mozart to the degree in which he successfully hits off a character with but a few strokes of the pen.

In sheer copiousness of musical invention *A Masked Ball* ranks with almost any other opera of its composer. The brief but fascinating prelude furnishes only a faint idea of the melodic abundance which piles up undiminished throughout the three acts of the piece. Yet the materials it exposes are of a consistently high order. First come detached, staccato octaves with a little rhythmic figure punctuating them and serving presently a minor contrapuntal function. Directly, then, we hear *sotto voce* a fine, warm melody which at the rise of the curtain courtiers and populace sing to the words *Posa in pace*. It is followed, as it is in chorus, by a stealthy staccato subject in octaves which, throughout the work, is associated with the conspirators and their dark designs. This subject, plastic and rhythmically shaped as it is,

ström, his secretary; Samuele, to be Count Horn; Tommaso, to be Count Wartung, etc. At various times and in diverse productions Riccardo has been Governor of Boston, Governor of Naples, and sometimes King of Sweden—with corresponding changes in the rest of the cast. The best policy for the listener seems to be to forget locale and names insofar as possible and concentrate instead on the music and basic themes of the story—love *vs.* duty, thwarted love, secret ambition, etc.—C. A. L.

seems conceived first of all for the purposes of counterpoint; and it is as a deft *fugato* of some ten bars' length that Verdi treats it. It will recur repeatedly in the course of the opera. Another tender *cantabile*—the king's subsequent love song, *La rivedrà nell' estasi*—expanded to some length, ornamented with transparent polyphony, brings us to a recall of the *fugato* episode and some tender lyric measures rounding off the delicate preface, which is fashioned, it is true, on the lines of the conventional potpourri overture, though without the disturbing impression of formlessness.

If the first scene is comparatively short, it is, however, richly stocked with music. Gustave's (or Riccardo's—everyone to his own taste) love melody develops to a finely sonorous ensemble, *Con nostro bene,* with the mutterings of the conspirators making part of the musical texture. Immediately afterwards *Il cenno mio,* the sinister motif, appears again, with unmistakable significance. And presently it is Renato who, having come upon the scene, is the object of Verdi's solicitude and receives his first air, a bravely expansive *andante* melody, terminating with a short cadenza.

The short scene of the king's talk with the judges is likely to be overlooked amidst the more pressing business of this interesting act but in its easy dignity it will repay attention. Presently, however, it is Oscar who assumes prominence in the picture with his first air, *ballata, Volta la terrea,* in two strophes—a light brilliant *allegretto,* spiced with coloratura and directed to be sung dashingly, *con slancio,* with the full joy of the thing.

The ensemble—or *stretta*—bringing to a close the opening scene is delightful. Delicate staccato melodies, bright and laughing, form its substance and build up a whirling close. One step further and the border line of operetta would be crossed. But with the instinct of a master craftsman Verdi created this effect of brightness the better to set off the somber opening of the scene that follows.

The opening—the broad and powerful but fundamentally lyrical invocation of the sorceress, Ulrica—begins with slashing, detached chords that sting like a lash. One detail of the introduction is peculiar to Verdi—the way he employs certain of the deeper colors of the clarinet to evoke a sinister or eerie effect. Ulrica's summons, *Re dell' abisso,* has about it something grandiose, like the conjuration of a prophetess inspired. And still in the grand manner is her scene *E lui!,* to be delivered with exaltation.

We must pass over the brief fortunetelling episode of Silvano to arrive the more quickly at the scene of Amelia's anxious inquiries, which builds up to a fine trio by the tormented lady, her lover (half-concealed behind curtains), and the clairvoyant Ulrica. One feature exacting notice is Ulrica's 3–8 *cantabile, Della città all' occaso,* not one of Verdi's most sweeping inspirations, perhaps, yet in its more intimate way as admirable as anything in the score. Then, when Amelia has gone and the throng of courtiers and peasant folk has urged the sibyl to exercise once more her gifts of prophecy, the disguised monarch himself entreats her once more in a lighthearted barcarolle, *Di' tu se fedele*—a strophic song in lilting 6–8 with a light staccato chromatic transition *Sollecita, esplora* to the very hearty refrain, *La morte, l'amor,* designated like so much else in this opera to be sung *con slancio,* which is equal to saying "with relish."

Unwillingly enough at first, Ulrica prophesies death to the king by the first friendly hand he may grasp. For a moment the music grows somber, almost frightening. Then the easy humor of Riccardo gains the upper hand. With a kind of elegant abandon he sings one of the most famous passages in the opera, the laughing song *E scherzo od è follia,* with chuckling phrases of detached and staccato notes. A quintet develops with conflicting rhythms of the laughing song and of Oscar's melody, *E talfia dunque il fato.*

The appearance of Renato, who innocently grasps the king's outstretched hand, brings a dramatic thrust which gives the great ensemble a poignant significance. Yet, when the king makes known his identity, Verdi closes the act on a smashing chorus of acclamation, *O figlio d'Inghilterra,* robust and somewhat goodnaturedly blatant—a tune with the unmistakable trade-mark of Meyerbeer on it. Let us admit at this point that the cloven hoof of the composer of *Les Huguenots* shows its traces several times between the bar lines of *A Masked Ball.* We discern it again—to anticipate a little—in that vengeance trio which Renato and his fellow plotters fulminate after their resolve to dispatch their king at his own masked ball.

The second act offers us one of the most evenly sustained flights of Verdi's creative genius. Practically from first to last the lyrical trajectory of the music traces a great arch of unbroken line. After agitated introductory measures portraying at once the soul state of the distraught Amelia and the terror of her midnight tryst by the gallows, the orchestra develops a warm and lovely *cantabile* characterized by that melodic turn frequent in Wagner but in Verdi flowering principally in his transition period.

After a recitative of some length and complexity Amelia embarks upon her searchingly beautiful and expressive air, *Ma dall' arido stelo divulsa,* preceded by four bars of oboe solo which, though they are dissimilar, inevitably call to mind those oboe traceries in the Nile scene of *Aïda.* The aria itself falls into three parts—a long but by no means unvaried *andante,* a terrified *allegro,* and a curtailed but impassioned recall of the first tempo, ending on a slow, expressive *cadenza.* The subsequent elaborate duet of the lovers is uncommonly rich even for Verdi in its abundance of dynamic melody.

One may call attention to a few of its purple patches, such as Riccardo's *Non sai tu che se l'anima mia,* expanding and gaining in passion from page to page; the jubilant frenzy of the king as he draws from Amelia the admission that she loves him; and then the ecstatic and winged melody, *O qual soave brivido,* presently caught up by Amelia and swinging into a duet of superb impetuosity, peppered with brave sequential figures and dotted rhythms.

The arrival of Renato alters somewhat the complexion of the music but does not check its exuberant flow. Not till we hear in the distance the approaching conspirators muttering—unaccompanied—their fugal motive is the lyrical course of the act arrested.

Then, with the fateful duel and the humiliating exposure of Amelia, Verdi achieves something of a master stroke and, without losing artistic caste, crosses the thin line which divides the sublime from the ridiculous. The conspirators are overcome with the monstrous fun of the bitter situation. They have their own laughing chorus of merciless, ribald mockery. Like diminutive Mephistos they fill the shadowy countryside with their venomous guffaws. Renato leaves the place with murder in his heart, Amelia goes bowed beneath a weight of her tragedy and shame.

The first scene of the last act moves on a musical plane almost as high. There is room here only to cite a few outstanding features. First, the implacable music of the vengeful Renato, then Amelia's dolorous plea for a last look at the child she fancies she must leave, *Morrò, ma prima in grazia*—music of subduing pathos and closing with a *cadenza* which takes the soprano from high C to low A and up again above the staff. Hard upon Amelia's appeal comes a fine recitative for Renato and then the most celebrated number in the opera, the aria, *Eri tu,* beginning sternly upon a kind of bolero rhythm and with a stark bass figure in octaves. But the harsh mood presently melts and gives way to a tender flute *cantabile* sustained by harp arpeggios. Renato takes up the moving orchestral melody, *O dolcezze perdute,* even to the ornamental turns. With his bitter reflection, *E finità*, the music once more grows inflexible. Yet it is on a softer sentiment that the air comes to its close.

Once more the conspirators and again heralded by their *fugato!* Presently Renato intones that martial and Meyerbeerian tune, *Dunque l'onta di tutti sol una,* to which reference was made above and which enlarges into a trio. A finer moment, musically, is that ferocious orchestral passage that accompanies Amelia's fateful business of drawing the name of her lover's appointed murderer from an urn. Another ensemble, a quintet, opens with a second typical song by the page, Oscar—an *allegro brillante,* with exuberant trills, *staccati,* and bright vocal leaps—and brings the scene to a sufficiently lively and effervescent conclusion.

The finale of the act, the episode of the masked ball itself, does not, perhaps, preserve the same levels of inspiration as the foregoing. The best part of it is the opening, the king's nostalgic *romanza,* which reverts passingly to some of his earlier melodies. Its sentimental kernel is the C minor *andante, Ma se m'è forza perderti,* simple but curiously affecting. After this solo number it is dance music for the most part which serves as dramatic background. These dances are not much better or much worse than most ballet music Verdi wrote, apart from that in *Aïda.* The village band seems in such cases never to have been far from Verdi's mind. However, the number does not depend for its effect on the melodies of the ballet. That piece is Oscar's third solo, a charming *scherzando, Saper vorreste,* with a simple but quaint harmonization and an exuberant *Tra-la-la* refrain. Of the page's various utterances this *canzone* is perhaps the best.

The actual murder scene, with a stage minuet as a musical and visual background, is restrained, one might even say decorous, in its cruelty. The fatal stroke is violence at low tension, the more so as the doomed monarch can be said to have frankly expected it. Death comes to him in music that is more elegiac than poignant or heart-searching, and final dissolution is not half so protracted as in numerous other Verdi operas. A somewhat unusual touch is the conceit which causes the royal victim to expire in the middle of a word!

HERBERT F. PEYSER

GIOACCHINO ROSSINI (1792–1868)

Il Barbiere di Siviglia

Libretto by Cesare Sterbini, based on the play by Beaumarchais. First performance in Rome, February 20, 1816.

Characters

Fiorello, the Count's servant	Baritone
Count Almaviva	Tenor
Figaro, a barber	Baritone
Dr. Bartolo, Rosina's guardian	Bass
Rosina	Soprano
Basilio, a music teacher	Bass
Berta, a maid in Bartolo's house	Soprano
A sergeant	Tenor

*The Story**

ACT I. With his hired band of musicians, Count Almaviva comes at dawn to serenade Rosina, whom he has seen but once in the Prado (**Almaviva:** *Ecco ridente in cielo*—Lo, the radiant sky). Rosina, ward of Dr. Bartolo, who keeps her a virtual prisoner in hope of marrying her himself, does not answer him, so Almaviva dismisses the musicians and resolves to wait until day in order to see her again. The barber Figaro then arrives and describes his busy life (**Figaro:** *Largo al factotum*—Make room for the factotum). Figaro promises to help Almaviva win Rosina, reassuring the Count with information that he is in Dr. Bartolo's employ. Suddenly the doors of Rosina's balcony open, and Rosina emerges from her room, followed by Dr. Bartolo. In spite of his precautions, she drops Almaviva a note advising him that she is aware of his interest in her and that she would like to know his name and rank. When Dr. Bartolo hobbles from the house, Almaviva sings a second serenade (**Almaviva:** *Se il mio nome saper voi bramate*—If you are anxious to know my name), telling Rosina that he is Lindoro, a poor creature who can offer her nothing but love. She passes his test, answering him that she will love him for himself alone, but suddenly she is pulled from the window by a duenna. The barber then suggests that the Count disguise himself as a drunken soldier in order to gain ac-

* The story of *The Barber* is here broken into three acts. The opera was originally written in two acts, however (Acts I and II being combined), and is still sometimes thus presented.

cess to the house and hints that such a capital idea should be rewarded with gold (**Figaro:** *All' idea di quel metallo*—At the thought of that gold). When Almaviva promises to reward him adequately, Figaro gives the Count his address while the latter reiterates his devotion for Rosina (**Almaviva:** *Ah! che d'amore la fiamma io sento*—Ah! I feel the flame of love).

ACT II. Alone in the doctor's drawing room, Rosina dreams of the voice that has touched her heart (**Rosina:** *Una voce poco fà*—A voice, a little while ago). She leaves at the arrival of Dr. Bartolo and the music master, Basilio. The doctor is worried by Almaviva's address to his ward, so he agrees to Basilio's plan to blacken the Count's reputation with Rosina (**Basilio:** *La calunnia*—Calumny). Figaro, who has overheard the plot, warns Rosina and promises to give her letter to the Count (**Rosina, Figaro:** *Dunque io son*—So, I am fortunate?). In vain Bartolo tries to prove that Rosina has been guilty of writing to her lover: the girl is too smart for him. Furious at Rosina's indifference, Bartolo threatens her with his authority (**Bartolo:** *A un dottor' della mia sorte*—To a doctor of my rank). Later, when Almaviva arrives disguised as a drunken soldier, she manages to hide the answering note which he slips to her. The maid Berta arrives on the scene followed by Basilio and by Figaro; the latter informs them that a crowd of townspeople is outside in the street, attracted by the confusion of the scene within. A knock at the door announces the police, who have come to restore order. Convinced that Almaviva is responsible for the uproar, the police captain informs him that he is under arrest, whereupon the Count reveals his identity to the officer. Almaviva is instantly released; Bartolo is astounded at this turn of events. The act closes with a noisy ensemble of comments on the events of the day (**Rosina [Sextet]:** *Freddo ed immobile*—Cold and immovable).

ACT III. In the same room, Bartolo is congratulating himself on finally having gotten rid of the soldier when the Count enters, this time in the guise of an unctuous music teacher (**Almaviva, Bartolo:** *Pace e gioia*—Peace and joy). He pretends to be a pupil of Basilio, who he says is ill. Bartolo brings Rosina in for her lesson (**Rosina:** *Lesson Scene*—interpolated aria). To assure the young people of a moment together Figaro now proposes to shave the doctor, but Bartolo refuses to leave the room. His face is covered with lather when Basilio appears, in perfect health. Persuaded by the Count that he is really ill, Basilio departs, accompanied by a farewell sung by all (**Almaviva [Quintet]:** *Buona sera*—Good evening). Bartolo's suspicions are now fully aroused;

he calls in his servant Berta, who complains that confusion is driving her mad (**Berta:** *Il vecchietto cerca moglie*—The old man seeks a wife).

As night falls, a thunderstorm begins. In the midst of it the Count, accompanied by Figaro, climbs through the window to elope with Rosina. At first she refuses to go with them, believing Basilio's slanderous tales about her suitor who, he tells her, wants to sell her to Almaviva. Radiant with happiness, the Count reveals his identity. After a joyous moment (**Rosina, Almaviva, Figaro:** *Ah, qual colpo inaspettato*—Ah, what an unexpected blow), they prepare to escape (**Rosina, Figaro, Almaviva:** *Zitti, zitti, piano, piano*—Quiet, soft). Figaro discovers, however, that the ladder has been taken from the window and that intruders are coming. When Don Basilio and the notary appear, prepared to marry Dr. Bartolo and his ward, they are persuaded to marry Rosina to the Count. Bartolo, rushing in too late to stop the wedding, bestows his blessing on the pair.

WHEN Rossini, accompanied by the poet Carpani, visited Beethoven in 1822, the creator of the Ninth Symphony greeted him with the exclamation: "Ah, Rossini, so you're the composer of *The Barber of Seville.* I congratulate you! It is an excellent *opera buffa* which I have read with great pleasure. It will be played as long as Italian opera exists . . ."

. . . . .

Here is a score which from first to last speaks for itself. Yet it is not amiss to call the listener's attention to certain recurrent devices which are hallmarks of *The Barber*. There is, for instance, the famous "Rossini *crescendo*," an effect that is perhaps less the invention of this master than is generally supposed, since it may be found in the composers of the Mannheim school, in Mozart, and even Beethoven. Rossini merely repeats a phrase or a figure with increasing dynamics and augments the instrumentation with every reiteration of the passage.

In the orchestral accompaniments the melodic construction should be noted, based on the *staccato* repetitions of the same notes (eighths, sixteenths, thirty-seconds) in ascending and descending movements. Also, the untiring use of that Italian operatic stereotype, the harmonization by thirds and sixths. When *The Barber* was first give in France, one of the charges brought against the work concerned its scarcity of *cantabile* melody. The reason lies much less in Rossini's inability to write such melody than in the nature of the work itself, whose humor and frequent irony demand a mercurial *scherzando* style, primarily rhythmic in its elements.

No need to speak in this place of the overture, an established classic. . . . Another number, adapted from an earlier Rossini work, is Almaviva's richly ornamented *aubade, Ecco ridente,* in the opening scene, which originated in *Ciro in Babilonia.* One wonders whether the *allegro* portion (*Oh sorte!*) also derived from that source. The next air, however, Figaro's entrance *cavatina,* the rollicking *Largo al factotum,* is no borrowed plumage. Rightly or wrongly it is the most famous song in the entire opera, a kind of whirlwind *tarantella,* more remarkable for its rhythm, its fun, its infectious *brio* than for any definite melodic quality.

Each section of the engaging Figaro-Almaviva duet which concludes the opening scene, beginning with *All' idea di qual metallo* and culminating with Figaro's D major waltz, *Numero quindici,* will repay the most careful attention. Rosina's ornate yet aristocratic *cavatina, Una voce poco fà,* which opens the second scene [or second act] paints us a picture of the spirited, artful, ebullient Rosina, full in the round. The delicious, mocking moderato, beginning *Io sono docile,* is simply beyond price as a piece of characterization with the simplest of harmonic and rhythmic means and the brightest, most expressive sparkle of coloratura. Incidentally, it is well to remind the listener that we rarely hear Rosina sung as Rossini first planned her—not as a soprano soubrette but a mezzo with a sumptuous lower range.

As a specimen of the "Rossini *crescendo*" at its most robust and dramatic, the opera offers nothing quite so masterfully built as Basilio's great air about the powers of calumny. Melodically there is hardly anything to this song but a rising and falling phrase in thirds and sixths to support a comparatively simple vocal part. Yet its total effect is explosive, indeed cyclonic.

We are lucky today in the restoration of Dr. Bartolo's fine aria, A *un dottor della mia sorte,* formerly omitted or else replaced by a very inferior air by one Pietro Romani. It is regrettable, on the other hand, that no operatic establishment has seen fit to restore, in place of the habitual "lesson scene" (in which sopranos, without regard to musical fitness or style, interpolate almost any extraneous song which enables them to parade their particular vocal excellences), the aria in D major which stands in the score at this point. There is a legend to the effect that a trio meant to be heard in the lesson scene was lost. Yet Rosina's fine air, *Con-*

tro un cor, is there, black on white, to serve as the young woman's vocal exercise. . . .

Two further numbers in the last act must be briefly mentioned —the aria of the servant, Berta, *Il vecchietto cerca moglie*, and the trio, *Zitti, zitti*. The first, a so-called *aria del sorbetto* or ice-cream air (thus qualified because the Italians of the day ate ice cream while it was being sung and hence paid little attention to it), is a sprightly tune . . . [and] individualizes capitally the fragile old woman who sings it. The trio, *Zitti, zitti*, commands attention for the reason that its opening bars are almost identical with the beginning of the song of the ploughman, Simon, in Haydn's oratorio *The Seasons*. But considering Rossini's adoration of Haydn, there is no ground for surprise in this venial plagiarism.

A passing word as to the so-called *secco* recitatives which, supported by simple piano chords, fill a large part of *The Barber*. Like those of Mozart's Italian operas, they are so wholly a by-product of the Italian language that their association with another tongue is almost unthinkable. It is therefore in obedience to a sound artistic instinct that in France and in Central Europe, where operas are heard in translated versions, these recitatives are always replaced in performances of *The Barber* by spoken dialogue.

HERBERT F. PEYSER

GIACOMO PUCCINI (1858–1924)

La Bohème

Libretto by Giuseppe Giacosa and Luigi Illica, based on *Scènes de la vie de Bohème* by Henri Murger. First performance in Turin, February 1, 1896.

Characters

Marcello, a painter .... Baritone
Rodolfo, a poet .... Tenor
Colline, a philosopher .... Bass
Schaunard, a musician .... Baritone
Benoit, a landlord .... Bass
Mimi .... Soprano
Parpignol, a toy vendor .... Tenor
Musetta .... Soprano
Alcindoro, a councilor of state .... Bass
A customhouse sergeant .... Bass

The Story

ACT I. In their cheerless attic in the Latin Quarter Marcello and Rodolfo try to keep warm among the smoking chimneys of 1830 Paris. In lieu of logs, the poet feeds the stove with pages of his play. Colline and Schaunard join them, the latter bringing with him food, fuel, and funds. When Benoit, the landlord, interrupts their Christmas Eve gaiety with a bill, the four friends ply him with wine and then evict him for his indiscretions. Rodolfo, who remains to write when his companions go off to a café, is surprised by a knock and admits his young neighbor, Mimi, who has come for a light for her candle. About to leave, she drops her key; as they search for it, both candles blow out. In the darkness the poet tries to warm the delicate girl's shivering hands and tells her of his dreams (**Rodolfo:** *Che gelida manina*—What a frozen little hand). She responds by giving him *her* story, that of a lonely creature who embroiders flowers and loves sunlight and spring (**Mimi:** *Mi chiamano Mimi*—They call me Mimi). Rodolfo's friends are heard calling for him from the street below. Ignoring them, he gazes rapturously at Mimi and kisses her (**Rodolfo, Mimi:** *O soave fanciulla*—Oh, sweet maiden) but on her suggestion agrees to join the others and take her with him. The young couple go off arm in arm singing of their new love.

ACT II. Rodolfo and Mimi join their friends in an animated scene at the Café Momus. Hawkers shout their wares; the toy-vendor Parpignol passes by with a train of eager children (**Children's Chorus:** *Ecco Parpignol!*—Here is Parpignol). Here Marcello's fickle sweetheart Musetta, in spite of the presence of her rich and elderly admirer Alcindoro, tries once more to regain the affections of her former lover, singing to him of the attention she attracts wherever she goes (**Musetta:** *Quando m'en vò*—When I am going down the street). Marcello promptly succumbs; Musetta feigns that her shoe hurts and sends Alcindoro to have it repaired. Then when a detachment of soldiers marches by the café, Marcello and the other Bohemians fall in behind it, bearing Musetta aloft and leaving the bill for Alcindoro to pay on his return.

ACT III. At dawn on a snowy morning Mimi comes to a tavern at a Paris tollgate where late merrymakers can still be heard clinking beer glasses. She wants help from Marcello, who is living there with Musetta. Workers and market women pass through the gate while the sleepy guards try to warm themselves. When Marcello emerges, Mimi confesses to him that she is distraught over Rodolfo's jealousy and wishes to leave the poet. She hides as Rodolfo appears from the tavern to tell Marcello of his jealousy (**Rodolfo:** *Mimi è una civetta*—Mimi is a flirt) and of his fears for poor Mimi's health: she coughs incessantly. Mimi overhears him. Reassured of her lover's affection but aware that she has not long to live, she comes forth to bid him farewell, with no regrets (**Mimi:** *Donde lieta usci*—From where she happily came). As Mimi and Rodolfo review the joys they will no longer share, Musetta runs from the tavern quarreling with Marcello, who has caught her flirting (**Rodolfo, Mimi, Marcello, Musetta:** *Dunque è proprio finita!*—So it is really all over). The contrast is too much for romantic Rodolfo and Mimi, who decide to reunite their fortunes at least until spring comes.

ACT IV. The lonely poet and painter have returned to their attic to bewail the absence of the fickle Musetta and the apparently faithless Mimi, who has been seen riding in a carriage (**Rodolfo, Marcello:** *O Mimi tu più non torni*—Oh Mimi, you will not return). Schaunard and Colline join them, bringing a little food, and they all dance gaily to keep up their spirits. In the middle of a mock duel which follows, the door bursts open, and Musetta enters in the utmost agitation, announcing that Mimi waits below with hardly enough strength to climb the stairs. All four Bohemians help the fragile, half-frozen girl to a chair. In order to buy medicine and a muff to ease Mimi's last moments, Musetta leaves to sell her earrings and Colline prepares to pawn the overcoat that has served him so faithfully and so long (**Colline:** *Vecchia zimarra, senti*—Old cloak, listen). When they are alone, Mimi wistfully reminds Rodolfo of their first happy days together (**Mimi, Rodolfo:** *Sono andati? Fingevo di dormire*—Have they left us? I only pretended to sleep). The others return as she is seized with a violent fit of coughing. Given the muff, Mimi exclaims with delight that at last her hands will be warm and then seems to fall peacefully asleep. Musetta and Marcello are reunited by the touching scene. Suddenly Schaunard whispers to Marcello that Mimi is dead. Rodolfo, aware of what has happened by the looks on his friends' faces, throws himself despairingly on her body.

TO SEE *La Bohème* in the clearest light, it is desirable to approach the work through its characters. In Murger they are thinly disguised portraits of real denizens of the *Quartier Latin.* Puccini, in a masterly bit of surgery, has excised the specific and left us the universal residue of these people, their pathos and tragedy immortalized in his music. These more somber qualities, clothed in exterior gaiety, provided Puccini with just the bittersweet combination that appealed to him. It is the mark of his genius that he completely exploited these characters, subtly making them his own.

Mimi is the exception among the heroines of which Puccini was so fond, and for her he lavished much time, care, and sympathy as his letters so markedly bear out. He has drawn Mimi, albeit always in pastel colors, with remarkable variety and completeness. Even in her moments of expansion she conveys a pathetic rather than a tragic mood. Yet the tragedy is all there, but underneath . . . implied. By emphasizing Mimi's [inner qualities of] gentleness and helplessness in the face of an inexorable fate, Puccini exploits the inherent pathos of her situation to the utmost.

There is not a phrase for Mimi which does not, in some way, explain or develop her character. Puccini has made no waste strokes. For example, the expansive *Ma quando vien lo sgelo* episode of her first-act aria gives us an important key to her personality . . . her ability to accept a rigorous present by dreaming of a more pleasant future. Her little phrases in the enchanting duet which concludes the first act express to perfection the traits that drive her to seek the only kind of security she knows, an attachment.

The crisis for Mimi is, of course, the scene behind the tree in the third act where Rodolfo, not believing her within earshot, describes her fatal malady to Marcello. The tragic implications of this scene are almost unendurable, but the tenderness and sympathy of Puccini's treatment carry us irresistibly along. A little later, the mournful way the *Mi chiamano Mimi* theme steals out at the beginning of her *Addio* is just one of many exquisite touches in this scene. And, again, in the same aria, the extraordinary change of tint achieved by the modulation from the key of D-flat to A major heightens the pathos of the moment in a way not apparently possible from such a simple device. And how the emotional tension is increased in the return to the original key in one of those highly charged phrases so characteristic of Puccini!

In the final act, Puccini has given Mimi, with the exception of one or two passages, little new music to sing. The effect achieved by this mass quotation from the first act is that of the dying Mimi, deprived of future, dreaming of the past. The simplicity of means by which Puccini secures his effects in this final scene has seldom been approached. Nothing more poignant could be imagined than Mimi's last words *Qui amor . . . sempre con te . . . Le mani . . . al caldo e . . . dormire . . .*, sung on a reiterated A-flat with the theme associated with Rodolfo's taking her hand sighed by the orchestra.

Musetta, on the other hand, presents a different and more difficult problem. In the second and third acts she is drawn as flirtatious and capricious in the extreme, while in the last act she is subdued, solicitous, and religious, traits not previously in evidence in her personality. Hence it is no easy task to encompass these separately manifested qualities in a single embodiment. From Musetta's entrance we should feel her hoydenisms arise from good humor rather than petulance. The best-known music for Musetta is her infectious waltz in the second act, especially interesting because at the *reprise* of the original melody, Mimi sings a counter theme expressive of her very different nature. In the beginning of the third act, through that chilly scene which expresses the winter of the heart, we hear Musetta again in the measures of her waltz, but how different the effect of these phrases without the original accompaniment and without the bustle of the Café Momus scene! In the final act, the relationship between the goodhearted and the more flamboyant aspects of Musetta can be more readily appreciated if Puccini's carefully worked-out stage directions are more closely observed than is the prevailing custom. For example, Musetta's little prayer, *Madonna benedetta,* is to be "unconsciously murmured as she heats the medicine over the spirit lamp"; and then, again, as the curtain falls slowly the directions read, "Terror-stricken, Musetta rushes to the bed, utters a piercing cry of grief." If these directions were more strictly adhered to, as well as the excellent custom employed by the Opéra Comique of casting a dramatic soprano in the role, the varied aspects of Musetta's personality would more readily emerge as a unit.

Puccini has sketched Rodolfo in less detail than either of the girls. That he is ardent is corroborated by the phrases of the *O soave fanciulla* duet. His charm is at its most persuasive in his first words to Mimi. He shares the carefree sense of humor of his Bohemian comrades. The composer has created in him the perfect foil for Mimi. It is a curious fact that Rodolfo's first phrases, *Nei cieli bigi,* were originally to be found among the sketches for an opera on the subject of Verga's *La Lupa* which Puccini discarded in favor of the Murger story. The famous narrative, *Che gelida manina,* is replete with all the charm and appeal that explain so well the poet's attraction for Mimi. In the third act Rodolfo's emotional instability is brought out in that curiously sarcastic passage, *Mimi è una civetta,* and then genuinely affecting is his account of Mimi's illness and their poverty. In the last act, the duet with Marcello expresses the amorous nostalgia that is such a Puccini specialty. And to Rodolfo is accorded the most heartbreakingly poignant moment in the work: his discovery that Mimi is dead, as the orchestra thunders out the theme of their *Sono andati* duet in the somber key of C-sharp minor.

Marcello is an especially appealing character. It is his tragedy to be the realist of the group, and, at the same time, to be susceptible to Musetta's unstable affections. He is the one, however, who is aware of the inevitable conclusion of the affair between Mimi and Rodolfo. There is an unmistakable parallel between the positions of Sharpless [American consul in *Madama Butterfly*] and Marcello because of their wider vision and their acute sense of helplessness to avert the tragedy. In the aforementioned scene behind the tree in the third act, it is Marcello who is aware that Mimi is overhearing Rodolfo's too candid diagnosis and who vainly tries to drag him away. At the end of the opera, Marcello's choked *Coraggio,* which in effect informs Rodolfo of Mimi's death, sketches in a single word Marcello's relation to the tragedy.

In the rest of his characters, Puccini has filled in his canvas with a healthy restraint. Schaunard and Colline contribute to establishing the Bohemian atmosphere with its *joie de vivre* designed to cloak a barren living. Colline's famous song on the pawning of his coat is so skillfully introduced, and so undeniably effective, that only the most sanguine would condemn it as padding the score.

In the quartet which concludes the third act Puccini acknowledges his debt to Verdi by adapting the principle of the famous *Rigoletto* ensemble to his needs. In welding into a single unit the emotions of the two who despair and the two who laugh, Puccini does not achieve the marked individuality of expression that is Verdi's but, rather, utilizes his material in free fashion in order to wring the utmost from the pathos of the lovers' situation. It is rare, however, that passages of *La Bohème* lend themselves to such comparison. Puccini's approach to opera is different from that of his predecessors. His music grows as much from the characters as from the situations. His feeling is for characterization at the personal rather than the detached heroic level, and this is one of Puccini's greatest holds on the public affection.

WILLIAM ASHBROOK

MODEST MUSSORGSKY (1839–1881)

Boris Godunov

Libretto by the composer, based on a play by Alexander Pushkin. First performance in St. Petersburg, January 27, 1874.

Characters

Nikitich, a guard	Bass
Mityukh	Baritone
A woman	Soprano
Shchelkalov, Secretary of the Duma	Baritone
Prince Shuiski	Tenor
Boris Godunov, Tsar of Russia	Bass
Brother Pimen	Bass
Grigori, later Dimitri	Tenor
Innkeeper	Mezzo-soprano
Missail	Tenor
Varlaam	Bass
An officer of the frontier guard	Baritone
Xenia, daughter of Boris	Soprano
Fyodor, son of Boris	Mezzo-soprano
Nurse	Mezzo-soprano
Boyar	Tenor
Marina Mnishek, a Polish noblewoman	Mezzo-soprano
Rangoni, a Jesuit	Baritone
Simpleton	Tenor

The Story *

ACT I. Goaded by a police official, a crowd of Russian peasants, assembled in the courtyard of a monastery near Moscow, is praying for a successor to the dead tsar. Shchelkalov, clerk of the Duma, announces that Boris declines the throne but suggests that the people petition him anew. A procession of pilgrims advances, praying for their country.

In the square in the Kremlin, Prince Shuiski hails the new Tsar

* The current Metropolitan Opera production (1955–56) utilizes Mussorgsky's original score and his final order of scenes. In the past one has far more often encountered the Rimsky-Korsakoff adaptation. Rimsky-Korsakoff made many changes in the original instrumentation, rhythms, and harmonies. He also omitted the first scene of Act IV and transposed the coronation and monastery scenes of Act I and the revolutionary and Boris' death scenes of Act IV.—C. A. L.

Boris to the acclamations of the people. Boris, followed by his children, admits his uneasiness (**Boris:** My heart is sad *).

The aged monk Pimen is recording the history of Russia in his dim monastery cell. The young novice Grigori awakes from a nightmare and questions Pimen on the rightful heir, Dimitri, whom Boris is thought to have murdered. Pimen describes seeing the slain child, who would have been the same age as Grigori. The novice cries that Boris will be punished by God.

The innkeeper of a tavern near the Lithuanian border sings a ballad to herself (**Innkeeper:** In a pond quite near) and then welcomes Grigori, who is accompanied on his way to liberty across the border by two drunken friars, Varlaam and Missail. Varlaam entertains them with a song (**Varlaam:** Near Kazan). A police official enters in search of the renegade Grigori, but is eluded by the novice, who first alters the warrant, then escapes through a window.

ACT II. In the apartments of the tsar in the Kremlin, the princess Xenia bewails her betrothed. To cheer her the nurse sings (**Nurse:** Gnat and bug were friends), then joins the young tsarevitch in a duet (**Nurse, Fyodor:** Owl thinks that is wrong). Boris enters and studies a map of Russia with his son. Alone, he ponders his problems as monarch (**Boris:** Mine is the highest power). A boyar reports a conspiracy. Fyodor returns to tell how a parrot had caused an uproar among the servants and is praised by his father. Prince Shuiski is summoned to describe the insurrection of Grigori, the pretender, but assures Boris that Dimitri is long since dead. A clock striking nearby unsettles the guilty Boris (**Boris:** I'm suffocating here).

ACT III. Four maidens entertain the proud princess Marina Mnishek, in the Polish castle of Sandomir. The Jesuit Rangoni urges Marina to influence the pretender Dimitri to bring Russia under the dominion of the Roman church.

In the castle gardens Rangoni tells Dimitri (Grigori) of Marina's love for him. Guests emerge from the castle to dance a polonaise but leave Marina alone with Dimitri, whom she accepts provided he will make her empress of Russia (**Marina:** My tsarevitch).

* Because of the difficulty of assembling a cast who can sing Russian, *Boris* is customarily given in translation in the United States. In years past it was most often sung in Italian. It is now presented in English. The English translations quoted here are taken from material copyrighted by John Gutman and are used with his permission.

ACT IV. Outside a convent near Moscow the peasants are discussing the claims of Grigori, the Pretender. A group of boys is tormenting a simpleton. Boris and his retinue enter, distributing alms. Though the simpleton refers to Boris' murder of Dimitri, the monarch protects him.

Assembled in the hall of the Duma, the boyars discuss the fate of the country. Shuiski tells of the hysteria of the Tsar Boris, who interrupts the description, denying his guilt. The ancient Pimen is introduced and announces a miracle: a blind shepherd has been healed at the grave of the murdered Dimitri. Overwhelmed by this omen, Boris dismisses the company, sends for his son, and bids him farewell (**Boris:** Farewell, my son). To the tolling of bells and the chanting of the returning boyars, the emperor dies, insisting that his son is the rightful heir.

A crowd of revolutionary peasants drag a boyar through the Forest of Kromy and jeer at his rank, pretending that he is Boris. Varlaam and Missail stagger in to rouse the populace to the cause of Dimitri. Two Jesuit priests also plead the cause of Dimitri but are attacked by the mob. Dimitri is led on in triumph by a torchlight procession and claims the throne (**Dimitri:** Dimitri Ivanovich). The simpleton is left alone to bewail the woes of Russia.

IT IS one of the extraordinary properties of *Boris* to be at once the supreme specimen of national opera and at the same time to possess a validity and an appeal which are to the last degree universal. There are episodic details about the text which Mussorgsky drew from Pushkin, from the historian Karamzin, and from his own stores of invention. Yet the magnificent canvas, with its multiplicity of figures and its seemingly unrelated cross currents of incident, is no more a patchwork than *Macbeth* or *Richard III*. A tremendous and awe-inspiring compendium of the soul of the Russian people, it sets against each other two dominating characters: the spiritually tortured Tsar and, now oppressed, now seething, the Folk. The music—even denatured by Rimsky-Korsakoff as you may think it*—is in almost every page of such transcendent greatness that it is difficult to speak of it with moderation.

Of all nations on earth Russia is probably richest in its marvelous plenitude of folk song. The music of *Boris* is supersaturated with this element. This is not to say that Mussorgsky has filled

* See footnote, p. 27.

his score with actual folk tunes. Rather, he has so steeped himself in the spirit of his native folk song that his melodies are sometimes indistinguishable from the genuine wild flowers of native music. The very first phrases of the orchestral introduction to the prologue make this point instantly clear. The choruses of appeal, supplication, and wild lament which fill the scene and the solemn canticles of pilgrims that bring down the curtain carry it further.

Let it be noted that thematic labels, or leading motifs, are not few in *Boris*. But if they fill a significant dramatic purpose, they are not employed in Wagner's symphonic manner and are rarely the subject of expansion or development. What one does repeatedly encounter is that extraordinary dramatic element of so much Russian music, the *ostinato*—the repetition, usually in the bass, of a rhythm or a figure of piercing emotional effect.

The somber, cloistral atmosphere of Pimen's cell is instantly established by a slow, monotonous weaving in sixteenth notes that sounds like a monastic variant of Wagner's *Waldweben*. Modal harmony and melody color the greater part of this scene (as they do so much else in the opera). One of the important motifs of the work is that solemn, two-bar phrase associated with the monk Pimen and his labors over an historic chronicle of the Russian tsars; another, that fine, flashing phrase portraying the future pretender, young Dimitri—a phrase magnificently expanded in the Polish and revolutionary scenes. Like a blinding shaft of light it flames up momentarily from the trumpet when Dimitri learns that the murdered tsarevitch would now be about his age and thus becomes filled with his adventurous plan.

The Coronation scene is one of the glories of the work. How those pealing dissonances, that clash of larger and smaller cathedral bells must have shocked the conservatives in Mussorgsky's day! There is probably nothing like them in all music, except in a funeral ode of Bach. And before Boris appears, the assembled people burst into the Glory chorus—*Slava*—a real folk melody, which Beethoven used in the *scherzo* of his second Rasoumowsky Quartet and Rimsky-Korsakoff in his fine opera, *The Tsar's Bride*. The musical idiom in which the words of the anguished Tsar are couched is the innermost accent of one grievously sick of soul.

The picture in the frontier inn . . . enables us to perceive some of that realism to which the more finicky in the 'seventies took such vigorous exception. The brief introduction paints the pair of besotted friars, the threatening police agents (a powerful *ostinato*), the escaping Dimitri. The lusty song of the duck, trolled by the innkeeper at the start, is quite in the folk vein. In momentary counterpoint with the chorale of the friars it furnishes a little master stroke of characterization. Varlaam's drunken, turbulent ballad about the bloody siege of Kazan, with Tartar hordes dynamited sky high, is absolutely irresistible in its impetuous dash and furious whirl. There is much else of musical inspiration in this scene—too much, indeed, for detailed scrutiny.

The scene in the apartments of Boris, one of the most grandiose in all opera, opens with a lament of Xenia for her dead lover with her fresh, touching theme. Two light, filmy folklike songs follow—little nursery diversions, one by the nurse, the other a duet by her and Fyodor to an *obbligato* of clapping hands. With the entrance of the heart-heavy Boris and the great air in which he deplores his guilt we hear that gorgeous melody which lifts us like a great wave (*Mine Is the Highest Power*) and suddenly melts into weird chromatics. The stormy and agonized scene of Boris and Shuiski has at least one absolutely incomparable passage in ascending and descending thirds as the crafty boyar discloses the details of the murder of the prince and sets Boris' soul on the rack.

Hard upon this narrative follows the grisly scene of the conscience-stricken monarch's hallucination and wild fit of terror. Musically, this scene is built on three elements—an *ostinato*, based on the interval of the raised fourth, eerie scales in the strings, and grisly sounds in woodwinds and brass. And when Boris, regaining mastery of himself, prays for mercy, the music regains, as it were, its own composure.

The Polish act begins charmingly in the apartments of Marina Mnishek. Her maids sing a graceful chorus, in Krakowiak rhythm. Her own words presently take the shape of a *mazurka*. The episode with the Jesuit, Rangoni, is, perhaps, the least nationally colored in the whole work.

The action shifts to the garden, bathed in blue shadows. After a romantic song of longing, by the enamored Dimitri, comes the grand *polonaise*, which forms the central point of the act. It is known that Mussorgsky planned to score this dance almost exclusively for strings. Rimsky has orchestrated it with such flaming color and jewelled brilliancy that it is hard to imagine it otherwise. . . . The love duet of Marina and the Pretender has been reproached as "operatic." Yet if so, it is operatic in the very finest sense—a magnificent tune of superb effect, especially in the grandiose conclusion which Rimsky-Korsakoff has supplied.

The frenzied fear of the haunted Boris, the calm narrative of

Pimen, which recalls the earlier scene in his cell, the breakdown and death of the Tsar—these are the chief ingredients of the Death scene. The tenderness of the hapless ruler's devotion to his children sounds again as it did in the second act. But in the twinkling of an eye the bitter agony of death invades the music, heightened by the churchly canticles of the black-clad priests. . . .

Nowhere in the entire work has Mussorgsky been fired by such flaming inspiration, particularly in his choral writing, as in the Forest of Kromy. The terrific impact of these ensembles voices the Russian folk. The gorgeous moment of the arrival of the Pretender—with the thud of drums resounding like distant cannon, with the fierce skirling of woodwinds, the bardic sweep of harps, the scarlet blare of trumpets—adds poignancy to that indescribably desolate lamentation which follows when the forsaken, but momentarily inspired, simpleton bewails the misery which all these happenings portend to unhappy Russia.

HERBERT F. PEYSER

GEORGES BIZET (1838–1875)

Carmen

Libretto by Henri Meilhac and Ludovic Halévy, based on the novelette by Prosper Mérimée. First performance in Paris, March 3, 1875.

Characters

Morales	Baritone
Micaela, José's village sweetheart	Soprano
Don José, a corporal	Tenor
Zuniga, a captain	Bass
Carmen, a gypsy	Mezzo-soprano
Frasquita, a companion of Carmen	Soprano
Mercédès, a companion of Carmen	Mezzo-soprano
Escamillo, a toreador	Baritone
Remendado	Tenor
Dancaire	Baritone

The Story

ACT I. A company of dragoons lounges at a street corner outside their post in nineteenth-century Seville. The officer on guard, Morales, tries to flirt with Micaela, a shy young country girl who has come to ask for Don José, but the girl retreats. Followed by a squad of urchins, the relief guard marches in, among them Don José (**Urchins' Chorus:** *Avec la garde montante*—With the mounting guard). The cigarette girls saunter out of their factory. Carmen, a gypsy, appears last and is surrounded by her admirers, to whom she sings of the ficklessness of love (**Carmen:** *L'amour est un oiseau rebelle* [Habanera]—Love is a rebellious bird). Piqued by the indifference of Don José, she throws a flower in his face and then retires with her companions to the factory. Micaela returns to give José a message of affection from his mother (**José, Micaela:** *Parle-moi de ma mère!*—Tell me about my mother). When she modestly withdraws, José vows to marry her as his mother wishes. Suddenly the girls pour out of the factory, crying that Carmen has wounded a worker. Brought before Zuniga, Don José's captain, the gypsy defiantly resists arrest. Now held by José before imprisonment, she induces him to loosen her bonds by promising him a rendezvous (**Carmen:** *Près des remparts de Séville* [Seguidilla]—Near Seville's ramparts), and as the soldiers lead her off to prison, she breaks away.

ACT II. In Lillas Pastia's tavern near the walls of Seville, Carmen and her friends Frasquita and Mercédès describe the joys of gypsy life (**Carmen, Gypsies:** *Les tringles des sistres*—The jingles of the tambourines). The toreador Escamillo arrives with a party and recounts his adventures in the bull ring (**Escamillo:** *Votre toast—je peux vous le rendre*—Your toast—I can return it); he is soon enamored by Carmen. All leave save the gypsy and her friends, who are persuaded by the smugglers Remendado and Dancaire to join them on a mountain expedition (**Quintet:** *Nous avons en tête une affaire*—We have a scheme in mind). Don José hurries in, free at last from the guardhouse where he has been disciplined for letting Carmen escape (**José:** *Halte-là! Qui va là?*—Stop! Who goes there?). Carmen dances for him; but when retreat sounds and José prepares to return to camp, she is furious. He feebly clings to his military loyalties but protests his passion, showing her the flower she once threw him (**José:** *La fleur que tu m'avais jetée*—The flower that you threw to me). Carmen insists that if he loved her he would follow her to the mountains (**Carmen:** *Là-bas, là-bas, dans la montagne*—There, there in the mountains). José refuses to desert; but when Zuniga enters and orders him back to the barracks, he disobeys. The two men are about to fight when the gypsies rush in and disarm Zuniga, forcing Don José to throw in his lot with them.

ACT III. The smugglers and gypsies pause in a mountain pass (**Smugglers' Chorus:** *Écoute, écoute, compagnon*—Listen, comrade, fortune waits below). Despite his shame, José still adores Carmen, but she is tiring of him. Frasquita and Mercédès read their fortunes in the cards; when Carmen deals the pack, she finds only death (**Gypsies, Carmen:** *Mêlons! Coupons!*—Shuffle! Cut!). As the gypsies carry their bales away, the terrified Micaela approaches in search of Don José (**Micaela:** *Je dis que rien ne m'épouvante*—I say that nothing is going to frighten me . . . but . . .). She hides as Escamillo arrives, looking for Carmen. He and the jealous José speedily come to blows, but their duel is stopped by Carmen herself. The toreador leaves after issuing an invitation to the bullfights in Seville, and the others are about to resume their march when Micaela is discovered. José agrees to go with her when she reveals that his mother is dying, but he warns Carmen that they will meet again.

ACT IV. In a festive Seville square a gay Sunday crowd gathers for the bullfight. Guests in a loggia overlooking the square are entertained by dancers (**Chorus:** *Dansez, dansez! Tournez,*

tournez!—Dance! Twirl around!), after which they crowd the rail to watch the colorful procession entering the arena.*

The loggia disappears, disclosing the bullfighter's quarters, where preparations have been made for a feast of victory. Escamillo arrives with Carmen and, certain of her affection, goes off to the contest. Carmen bravely meets Don José, who is lurking nearby. Though wretched and dishonored, he pleads with her to return to him (**José:** *Carmen, il est temps encore*—Carmen, there's still time), but her heart is elsewhere. When Escamillo's triumph echoes from the arena, Carmen rushes toward the entrance with a cry of delight. Maddened, Don José plunges his knife into her breast.

CARMEN in its original form is an *opéra comique* and thus includes quantities of spoken dialogue. At the Opéra Comique it is always heard with this dialogue, which is often more telling than the recitatives employed in most theaters and which elucidates certain dramatic points otherwise in some degree obscure. . . . The recitatives that we hear, expertly made as they are, are not Bizet's at all, but the handiwork of his devoted friend, Guiraud. . . .

Let us consider for a moment some outstanding pages of a score which has enthralled millions, divergent as they may be in tastes and temperaments. Several things strike us throughout—Bizet's virtually Mozartean gift of characterization; the faultless balance he maintains between voice and orchestra; the transparence, the sensitiveness, and the color of instrumentation; the

* Traditionally Act IV takes place in a public square, at the back of which is an entrance to the bull arena. Spectators, toreadors and picadors (some mounted on horseback), and others parade across the stage during the chorus *Dansez, dansez* and enter the arena. Sometimes even a ballet is introduced to interpolated Bizet music (e.g., to music from *L'Arlésienne* or *La Jolie Fille de Perth*). It is in the deserted square that Carmen and José have their last meeting.

When the Metropolitan Opera remounted *Carmen* several years ago, it changed the scene of Act IV to that described in the summary. Many persons have objected to the change on the ground that a girl so resourceful as Carmen could never have been murdered inside Escamillo's dressing room where there were so many ways of defending herself, so many avenues of escape, and undoubtedly people nearby to whom she could cry for help. Those supporting the change say that Carmen was superstitious, had read her fate in the cards, and was prepared to accept her death.—C. A. L.

tingling rhythm; the ceaseless diversity of expression, ranging from the sentimental, the blithe, mercurial, and humorous to the sensual, the vulgarly swaggering, the starkly shattering, and tragic! The score is a microcosm of all this and more.

The short prelude has the impact of a blow between the eyes. It starts brilliantly with that crashing tune to which, in the fourth act, the chief actors in the sanguine sport of the bull ring arrive on the scene. Then comes the refrain of the Toreador Song—blatant, common, if you will, but irresistible; a picture of the dashing, insensitive roughneck whom it paints. Directly on its heels and beneath a shuddersome tremolo comes that marvellous, fate-laden theme marked by the interval of the raised second. Twice it mounts and falls, then rears itself to a climax and abruptly breaks off. We shall hear this inspired phrase a number of times during the work with an ingenious modification or two. For one thing, it heralds Carmen's entrance in the first act in an impudent rhythmic transformation. . . .

The introductory chorus at the rise of the curtain communicates something of the warm, lazy atmosphere of the Sevillian square. The instrumentation is delicious, not the least in the economy with which its characteristic color is obtained. The arrival of Micaela and her few words with the soldier, Morales, form a brief interlude before the resumption of the chorus. A fanfare brings the changing of the guard and a chorus of street urchins—a musical plaything, if there ever was one, with little effects by flutes, piccolos, cornets, and *pizzicato* strings that most composers could not imitate with an entire instrumental battery at their disposal.

From beneath a bridge stream the working girls on their way to the neighboring cigarette factory. Their appearance is heralded by a melting little ensemble, enchantingly colored by the orchestra. Suddenly the scoring takes on a richer hue; and, to an accompaniment of string and harps, the woodwinds trace a swaying, sinuous melody—the delicious cigarette chorus. Carmen's appearance, preceded by the diminution of the fate theme, brings us to the *Habanera*, an expression of Carmen's philosophy of life and a number which deserves a special word, familiar the world over as it is.

Originally, it is said, Bizet had written for Carmen's entrance song a piece in 6–8 time with the chorus. But Galli-Marié, the first exponent of the gypsy baggage, did not find it to her taste and promptly let her feelings be known. Bizet, like more than one sensitive dramatist, had trust in that astonishing instinct of an actor which is sometimes the safest guide a theatrical author can have. He rewrote the piece, once, twice, six times, twelve times, but always without gaining her approval. Finally, at his wits' end, and with the première only a short time off, he tried a thirteenth time and apparently succeeded. The rhythm of the *Habanera* is of Cuban or, at any rate, of Spanish-American origin. For melodic ideas Bizet had recourse at this late hour to a collection of Spanish songs by the popular composer, Sebastian Yradier, in whose music he found something which dimly resembled the *Habanera* he finally produced. The words of the Yradier tune—"My Chiquita come to me, don't you see that I am dying for you?"—were the customary idiocies of the popular ballad type. Apparently Galli-Marié this time was won over—for the melody, which strikes us as inevitable as a sunrise, remained in the score.

With the entrance of Micaela and her duet with José, a complete change comes over the sultry, sensuous idiom of the music. Actually, this duet and Micaela herself have come in for some rather absurd abuse. The music itself, if sugared, is lovely. Micaela, blond of hair and blue of eyes, was an invention of the librettists, who made her out of a suggestion in Mérimée to the effect that the only women Carmen's lover had hitherto known were those in his village who wore blue dresses and pigtails.

Even Bizet was amused at the Sunday school virtues of the pretty little doll Meilhac and Halévy fashioned for him. *Une petite perfection,* he mockingly called her and then proceeded to put into her mouth music that brought her to life. Let us refer, since we are on the Micaela subject, to her big aria in the third act. It is suavely effective with some telling instrumentation, in which 'cello and horns are conspicuous. It is claimed that Bizet originally wrote the air for Sardou's *Grisélidis,* others say for the unfinished *Noé,* by his father-in-law Halévy. The high B-flat with which so many sopranos like to end it is not, it is only fair to say, an inspiration of Bizet's, and is never sung at the Paris Opéra Comique.

The lively quarrel chorus of the cigarette girls and notably Carmen's provocative and irresistible *Seguidilla* are other high spots of the first act. The listener should notice particularly that feeling of savage triumph which the simple accompaniment exudes as José loosens Carmen's bonds and, sure of her power, the irresistible creature proceeds to her conquest. The appearance of the soldiery to lead Carmen off to jail is prefaced by a *fugato* based on the theme of the chattering quarrel ensemble, the act ending in a lively chorus after a brief, insinuating instrumental recall of a phrase of the *Habanera* melody.

Before the curtain rises on the next act we have the melody of the song *Dragon d'Alcalà,* which José will presently sing off stage. The contrapuntal ornaments with which Bizet has here embroidered this melody are especially fascinating. More memorable still is the gypsy song and dance with which the act opens. As the music progresses it assumes a wildness, a delirious quality which appears more fiercely African than Spanish. Then comes Escamillo with his Toreador Song. Of this vigorous though vulgar effusion little need be said beyond the fact that Bizet himself is understood to have exclaimed angrily: "If they want *ordure,* let them have it!" But trash or not, the effect of the song is unfailing.

Vastly finer and, indeed, one of the most precious jewels of the score in point of characterization, brightness, and delicious workmanship is the quintet of Carmen, the smugglers, and their two female companions. Carmen's song as she dances before the liberated José becomes a counterpoint to the fanfare of the call to retreat. Possibly it was composed, as has been surmised, with this object before the composer's eye. But it is no less good for that reason. José's subsequent Flower Song, even with its somewhat farfetched modulation at the close, which so frequently sends the singer off pitch, scarcely needs description. It is simply one of the great arias of operatic literature.

The third act opens with an exquisite prelude which, however, has more the style and color of the *Arlésienne* music than of *Carmen* and appears to have been composed for the former work. The ensuing smugglers' march is a unique page full of somber premonitions and harmonic effects that once struck listeners as extraordinarily daring. The little fortunetelling duet of Frasquita and Mercédès is delicate enough to have been written by Mendelssohn. Quite another matter is Carmen's air on reading her prophecy of death in the cards. The workings of somber destiny and inescapable doom sound in the solemn trombone harmonies toward the close and proclaim Bizet one of the great tragic tone poets of the theater.

There is little space left to consider the violently dramatic finale of the third act or the brilliant, festive music which ushers in the fourth. It may be true, as so many Spanish musicians have insisted, that *Carmen* is not truly Hispanic. Yet if the prelude to the fourth act is not authentically Spanish, it surely comes as near to that condition as the non-Spanish listener is likely to demand. . . . it embodies all the life, the brilliancy, the glare, the color, the sinister undertones which we instinctively feel to be essentially of Spain.

And now, after Escamillo and Carmen have sung their sensuous love duet and the glittering throng has withdrawn to the bull ring, there begins that never-to-be-forgotten and terrible scene, hardly matched in its concentration and awful intensity, and in which the whole drama of Carmen is epitomized. José grows in tragic stature from moment to moment; Carmen becomes the tracked, defiant animal. The pathos and agony of the scene are almost intolerable.

If *Parsifal* is the highest expression of spiritual suffering in music, here, assuredly, is the most poignant tonal expression of physical anguish. The music is now stark and magnificently denuded of every ornament. The scene is lyric tragedy in its grandest manifestation. And as José yields himself to the officers with the heartbroken words, "You may arrest me, it is I who have killed her. Oh! Carmen, my adored Carmen!" the music suggests an uncanny similarity to the supreme phrase of Isolde's Love Death.

HERBERT F. PEYSER

PIETRO MASCAGNI (1863–1945)

Cavalleria Rusticana

Libretto by G. Targioni-Tozzetti and G. Menasci, based on a story by Giovanni Verga. First performance in Rome, May 17, 1890.

Characters

Santuzza	Soprano
Mamma Lucia	Contralto
Alfio, a teamster	Baritone
Turiddu, son of Lucia	Tenor
Lola, wife of Alfio	Mezzo-soprano

The Story

After a brief offstage prologue in which Turiddu sings of his undying love for Lola (**Turiddu:** *O Lola*—Oh Lola in your milk-white nightgown), a small Sicilian village comes to life, as a cheerful crowd of villagers prepares for Easter Mass. The young peasant Santuzza anxiously knocks at the tavern door to ask the aged innkeeper Lucia for news of her son, the girl's former lover, Turiddu. The teamster Alfio now enters gaily, singing of his beloved horses and his new wife, Lola (**Alfio:** *Il cavallo scalpita*—The horses' clopping). Alfio admits that Turiddu has been seen near his house. After the Easter hymn (**Chorus:** *Inneggiamo*—Rejoice), Santuzza, now abandoned by Turiddu, confesses to Mamma Lucia that her son has deserted her for the teamster's wife, Lola, whom he loved in his youth (**Santuzza:** *Voi lo sapete*—You know, dear mother). Forbidden by excommunication to enter the church with her friends, Santuzza accosts the returning Turiddu and detains him while Lola minces in, singing (**Lola:** *Fior di giaggiolo*—Blossom of the lily), and throws him a flower on her way to church. Santuzza vainly begs Turiddu to return to her (**Santuzza:** *Rimani ancora*—Stay a while). He hurls her to the ground and goes off to join Lola. Desperate with jealousy, Santuzza blurts out the truth to Alfio, who vows vengeance and rushes away, with Santuzza, torn by guilt, running after him. The orchestra blends with the organ in the famous *Intermezzo*, denoting the exaltation of Easter. The congregation assembles in the square, and Turiddu leads them in a health to Lola (**Turiddu:** *Viva il vino spumeggiante*—Hail, the sparkling wine). The infuriated teamster breaks in and bites Turiddu's ear as a challenge to fight him. The crowd disappears, leaving Turiddu alone with his mother, Lucia, to whom he bids farewell (**Turiddu:** *Mamma, quel vino*—Mother, that wine). As he goes off, Santuzza rushes in to embrace Lucia. A distant murmur is heard outside, and a woman runs in with the news: Alfio has slain Turiddu.

CAVALLERIA opens with a prelude which brings us several of the chief melodies of the opera. . . . The beginning of the prelude, a sweet, tender, and peaceably flowing *andante sostenuto,* sounds like a foretaste of the famous *Intermezzo* which divides the two parts of the work. The pace of the music presently quickens, and one hears the broad strains in which later Santuzza entreats the love of Turiddu despite his infidelities to her. A transition then leads to the sentimental *Siciliana, O Lola, bianca come fior,* which concludes with a sort of dying fall on the lovelorn sighs of "Ah! Ah!" A repetition and intensification of music previously heard brings one of the most important tunes of the work, a 6–8 measure, *andante un poco di moto,* the melody of the impassioned duet of Santuzza and Turiddu: she pleading for his love, he scorning and rejecting her. Broadly sustained and repeated with bombastic orchestration, it culminates in a mighty crash and a recurrence of Santuzza's song of appeal. Then the prelude terminates in a tranquil but sorrowful *diminuendo,* colored by the harp.

As the curtain rises, church bells provide a foundation for the vigorous melodies which follow. The orchestra has fairly protracted passages while the peasant folk assemble. A striking characteristic of the music is the melodic triplet, one of the native devices of Italian folk music. The prolonged chorus is at once unified and varied, the menfolk supplying in their *In mezzo al campo* a bustling contrast to the springtime songs of the women. With the actual dramatic business of the piece it all has little to do. This begins somewhat hesitantly with the nervous entrance of Santuzza and her despairing inquiries about the whereabouts of Turiddu. A somber, tortured phrase beneath syncopated harmonies paints the agitation of the unhappy woman. But the colloquy is brief.

Crackling whips and jingling bells announce the arrival of the teamster, Alfio. His boisterous song, *Il cavallo scalpita,* celebrating his calling, and echoed by the villagers, is cheap and common stuff, but it furnishes padding and contrast. Then, after another few words, this time between Alfio and Mamma Lucia, comes another elaborate ensemble, having only indirectly to do with the case—the *Regina Coeli,* an *a cappella* canticle heard from within the church and, sung by the throng on the village square, the swelling Resurrection Hymn.

After a short organ interlude Santuzza joins in the passionately devotional *Inneggiamo il Signor non è morto.* Syncopated chords and powerfully striding basses support her soaring voice. Shouts of "Alleluia" come from the worshippers in the church, while outside the song rolls in a mighty flood of devotional ecstasy, with pealing organ tones and great orchestral surges. It is one of those things in the work which subdue even the least susceptible.

Now, and only now, does the dramatic conflict really begin. When the crowd has withdrawn, Santuzza, left alone with Mamma Lucia, opens her heart to the old woman and in the romanza, *Voi lo sapete,* makes known her bitter torment. The aria is a true soul picture, perhaps the finest page in the entire opera, a really poignant expression of anguish. Here again we meet that melodic triplet found in the opening chorus, but in this case more genuinely emotional. Santuzza's repeated protestations, *l'amai*—"I love him"—amount to far more than those vain word repetitions found in numberless operas. They are followed by a passionate phrase in octaves which gives way to a contrasting section, *Quell' invida,* the accompaniment being those syncopations and dark phrases we heard upon Santuzza's first appearance. Then follow some simple but pitiful measures, *Priva dell' onor,* and another *crescendo* of passionate despair as she reflects that Turiddu loves not her but her rival, Lola. Pathetically she explains that, being an excommunicate, she cannot implore God in church to save her.

Turiddu arrives, and we are at the heart of the play. Santuzza entreats, abases herself. Listen to her music—some of the best in the score—of her *Battimi, insultami,* thrice repeated. Lola appears, singing her blithe, typically Italian *stornello, Fior di giaggiolo.* When, after a scene of bitter irony between her and Santuzza, Lola leaves, the great duet of the heartsick woman and her betrayer (whose melodies we recall from the prelude) brings us to the climax of the piece. This climax closes on an episode of sickening violence, and in a manner that makes the furious outbursts and defiance of Alfio, when he learns of Turiddu's perfidy, become the more terrible.

It is upon the heels of these baleful oaths of vengeance that the orchestra plays, while the stage is deserted, the famous *Intermezzo.* There is no need to describe this ten-times familiar page. It has no dramatic, no delineative office. Its function is clearly to supply a soothing contrast between the violence that has gone before and that which is presently to come.

The opera as such resumes with a chorus of villagers which, though different, reminds one of that which opened the piece. Turiddu's succeeding drinking song, *Viva il vino*—merely a song hit of no dramatic significance—is musically about as bad as Alfio's entrance number. But the scarcity of incident unquestionably compelled the composer to spin his web very thin. Drama reappears with the sinister challenge to Turiddu by the darkly determined teamster. Turiddu's leave-taking from his mother, his appeal to her to protect the woman he wronged (*Voi dovrete fare*), seems like the appeal of a frightened child and is the most moving page of the second part of the opera. The end is terrible in its swiftness. A recall, *fortissimo,* of a phrase from the *Voi lo sapete;* a shriek, "They have killed neighbor Turiddu"; a piercing cry from Santuzza; and a precipitous rush of octaves bring the work to its finish.

HERBERT F. PEYSER

JACQUES OFFENBACH (1819–1880)

Les Contes d'Hoffmann

Libretto by Jules Barbier, based upon three tales by E. T. A. Hoffmann. First performance in Paris, February 10, 1881.

Characters

Lindorf, a councilor of Nuremberg	Baritone
Andrès, a servant	Tenor
Luther, an innkeeper	Baritone
Nathaniel and Hermann, students	Tenor and Baritone
Nicklausse, Hoffman's friend	Mezzo-soprano
Hoffmann, a poet	Tenor
Spalanzani, an inventor	Tenor
Cochenille, a servant	Tenor
Coppélius, rival to Spalanzani	Bass-baritone
Olympia, a mechanical doll	Soprano
Giulietta, a courtesan	Mezzo-soprano
Schlemil	Baritone
Dappertutto, a magician	Baritone
Pitichinaccio	Tenor
Antonia, a singer	Soprano
Crespel, a councilor of Munich	Bass
Franz, a servant	Tenor
Dr. Miracle	Bass
Voice of Antonia's mother	Mezzo-soprano

The Story

PROLOGUE. The evil councilor Lindorf beckons the servant Andrès to follow him into the dark wine cellar of Luther's Tavern and bribes the stammering waiter to give up a letter which he is bearing from the actress Stella to the young poet Hoffmann. The sinister magistrate goes off to gloat in a corner (**Lindorf:** *Voyons: "pour Hoffmann"*—Let's see: "For Hoffmann") as a band of students, led by Nathaniel and Hermann, invades the tavern. They are joined by Nicklausse and his friend Hoffmann, who is persuaded to sing a spirited ballad of the dwarf Kleinzach (**Hoffmann:** *Il était une fois à la cour*—There was once at the court). In spite of the applause of his friends, Hoffmann's thoughts stray to his mistress, Stella, who combines the fascinations of three women in his past. The students ask their story. "The first," exclaims the poet, "was Olympia!"

ACT I. The inventor Spalanzani paces his richly furnished ballroom, rejoicing in his triumphs over his rival Coppélius, who is actually responsible for his latest success, the mechanical doll, Olympia. Hoffmann applies for admission as a pupil and promptly falls in love with the sleeping Olympia. In vain Nicklausse warns him of possible dupery (**Nicklausse:** *Une poupée aux yeux d'émail*—A doll with china eyes); the ingenuous poet even buys some magic spectacles from the rival inventor Coppélius (**Coppélius:** *Je me nomme Coppélius*—My name is Coppélius; *J'ai des yeux*—I have eyes), who has come to extract more money from Spalanzani and is put off with a note. The servant Cochenille announces a company of guests, to whom Spalanzani introduces Olympia. The doll is wound up and sings (**Olympia:** *Les oiseaux dans la charmille*—The birds in the bushes). When the guests depart for supper, Hoffmann passionately addresses Olympia (**Hoffmann:** *Doux aveu*—Sweet avowal), but she rebuffs him. Coppélius returns, furious at having learned the note to be valueless. The guests come back to dance. Olympia whirls Hoffmann about till he falls in a faint and she is removed by Cochenille. A crash is heard in the adjacent cabinet. Coppélius has destroyed the doll. The inventors hurl curses at each other. "An automaton," murmurs Hoffmann, "she was only an automaton."

ACT II. In her sumptuous palace on the Grand Canal in Venice, the courtesan Giulietta sings a barcarolle with young Nicklausse (**Giulietta, Nicklausse:** *Belle nuit*—O beautiful night), while her guests recline at their ease. As they retire to the card tables, the magician Dappertutto invokes the power of a magnificent diamond ring to lure Giulietta to steal Hoffmann's reflection (**Dappertutto:** *Scintille, diamant*—Sparkle, diamond). He leaves her to ensnare the poet, who proves an easy prey (**Hoffmann:** *Extase! ivresse inassouvie*—Ecstasy! Unsatiated intoxication). The revelers return and two of Giulietta's admirers, Schlemil and Pitichinaccio, plot with Dappertutto to destroy the poet (**Hoffmann, Giulietta, Dappertutto, Schlemil, Pitichinaccio:** *Hélas, mon cœur*—Alas, my heart). Hoffmann begs Schlemil for the key to Giulietta's room to look for his image which he no longer sees in the mirror. It is refused. Seizing Dappertutto's sword, he mortally wounds Schlemil, only to find that Giulietta is gliding off in a gondola with Pitichinaccio.

ACT III. The wistful young singer Antonia sits at her clavichord in the dark living room of her father, Councilor Crespel, of Munich. She bewails the loss of her pet dove (**Antonia:** *Elle a fui*—

She has fled). Crespel begs her not to sing, since he knows she has little strength, and tells his deaf servant Franz to admit no one. Franz muses on his hard lot (**Franz:** *Eh bien! Quoi!*—Well! What!). Hoffmann and Nicklausse manage to gain entrance, and the poet joins Antonia in a rapturous duet (**Hoffmann, Antonia:** *Ah! j'ai le bonheur*—Ah, I am happy). He accompanies her at the clavichord in another love song (**Antonia:** *C'est une chanson d'amour*—'Tis a song of love). Hoffmann hides when Crespel reappears, followed by the sinister Dr. Miracle, who proceeds to give absent treatment to the unfortunate girl. He encourages Antonia to sing—despite Crespel's protests that he is sure singing will hasten the girl's death. When the doctor is finally dismissed by Crespel, Hoffmann promises Antonia to come again the following day; and the girl is left to the temptations of the returning Dr. Miracle (**Miracle:** *Tu ne chanteras plus*—You're no longer singing?). The voice of her dead mother as it echoes from a portrait on the wall cannot save her (**Ghost of mother:** *Chère enfant*—Dear child). Antonia's song rises above the doctor's crazy violin playing, till she falls dying beside the sofa, as the horrified Hoffmann rushes in to gather her in his arms.

EPILOGUE. Hoffman has finished the story he has been telling to his gay companions in Luther's Tavern. The students continue their carousal and then leave him in a stupor. Suddenly in the distance a vision of the Muse appears to offer him the serenity of art instead of earthly passion. In an ecstasy he falls fainting, just as Lindorf enters with Stella to find him, as they think, dead drunk. The students clink their glasses, ready to sing until morning.

IN *The Tales of Hoffmann* we find a unique work of the modern repertory. It is of the French school of romantic opera, but not a part of it. Its antecedents are to be found in *Faust*, for example; its effects are peculiar to Jacques Offenbach.

The elements of satire and burlesque in the opera, coupled with the hero's repeated disillusionments, offer evidence of Offenbach's rejection of superficial libretto-drama and his striving for a symbolic significance. What better vehicle for this biting commentary than the Gothic romances of E. T. A. Hoffmann? Yet far more effective than any single tale is the unity with which Jules Barbier, Offenbach's librettist, juxtaposed the several episodes and set them off with prologue and epilogue.

The significance of the bitter satire is far more apparent when a single soprano essays the three heroines with one baritone arrayed against her in the evil characters of Coppélius, Dappertutto, and Dr. Miracle, since this admirably underscores the repeated fate of Hoffmann. It is a rare thing, however, to find a singer capable of the widely varying vocal demands of, first, the frigid and technically difficult coloratura of the doll, Olympia, then the alternating flowing and dramatic measures of Giulietta, climaxed by the fragile humanity and expansiveness of Antonia's phrases. Likewise, few baritones are capable of encompassing all the varied villains in a single performance, particularly since Dr. Miracle is in reality a bass part.

Offenbach's experience as a writer of innumerable *opéras-bouffes* had given him an intimate knowledge of the exigencies of the stage. And in this posthumously produced work which occupied his last years, the practical exploitation of his experience is evidenced not only in the skillful apportionment and juxtaposition of the airs, but in the basic musical architecture of each scene and the consistently accruing sense of climax.

His skillful use of the famous Barcarolle, framing as it does the Venetian scene, demonstrates most vividly Offenbach's canny sense for the stage. After the brittle waltzes and *fioriture* of the Olympia episode, the languors of the Barcarolle form a perfect contrast*: externally to the rest of the opera and internally to the viciousness and sorcery of the Venetian scene itself. A similar effect is achieved by Dappertutto's suave air, *Scintille, diamant,* with its almost hypnotic evocation of the forces of evil. And again at the end of the scene we find the greatest sense of contrast of all, where the duel is fought after an exciting spoken dialogue, all against the seductive measures of the Barcarolle. This episode is one of Offenbach's most effective, because of the striking employment of the contrast between speech and song and between the lulling melody in the background and the bloody scene enacted upon the stage.

In the episode of Hoffmann's blind love for the mechanical doll, Offenbach's biting wit has free rein. The revenge of Coppélius, the destruction of the automaton, first embodies the implacable and frustrating element in Hoffmann's romances. The

* For some unknown reason it has lately been the custom at most opera houses to transpose the Antonia and Giulietta scenes. The Metropolitan Opera, for example, has long put Giulietta first, even though Offenbach directed that Antonia come before Giulietta. Recordings of *The Tales of Hoffmann* also observe this now almost traditional transposition.—C. A. L.

character of Olympia is surely one of the most novel in all opera. The devices employed by Offenbach, such as causing her to run down in her air and have to be wound up again, are little masterpieces. The brilliance and unabashed coloratura of her music are entirely in keeping with her mechanical personality.

The Munich or Antonia scene is the finest part of the opera. Although certain of its elements, such as the Mephistophelean character of Dr. Miracle and the extended trio in several keys, remind us of Gounod's *Faust*, there are, nevertheless, many moments of originality and charm. The scene opens with Antonia's restrained *Elle a fui, la tourterelle*, the finest bit of musical portraiture in the opera. Not the least attractive thing about this scene is the fact that the *ingénue* Antonia, after the scenes of the automaton and the courtesan, is a completely sympathetic character. And nowhere is this more apparent than in the lilting love duet, *C'est une chanson d'amour*. It is a pathetically brief *reprise* of this duet that she sings as she dies. If it were not for the sincerity of this passage, it could be hazarded that Offenbach was laughing up his sleeve when he caused her to succumb after a protracted trill.

Hoffmann shares the fate of Don José and des Grieux, but to a worse degree, in that he is overshadowed by not one heroine but three. Although the consistent recurrence of misfortune makes for a certain inelasticity in his character, he is not without interest. And, as if to compensate for his poor luck with the ladies, Offenbach has given him much grateful music to sing. The *Légende de Kleinzach* in the prologue, with its opening passages of *grotesquerie* and subsequent drifting off into amorous cantilena, gives us the index of Hoffmann's character, particularly when he has to be reminded of the thread of the *Légende*. The constant companion to Hoffmann, Nicklausse, is one of those boy-mezzo-soprano rôles that recur so often in French romantic opera. And to Nicklausse is allotted the most perfect ironical commentary when he quotes Leporello's *Notte e giorno* (I work night and day). For what could be further from [this] than Hoffmann's continually frustrating experience [with Nicklausse]?

Charming as are many of the more obviously melodic pages of this brilliant score, *The Tales of Hoffmann* exists today as a masterly satire, not only of the school from which it sprang, but of a whole period. Its ironies and witticisms are still as keen and barbed for us as they were sixty-odd years ago when *Hoffmann* was first performed.

WILLIAM ASHBROOK

WOLFGANG AMADEUS MOZART (1756–1791)

Così Fan Tutte

Libretto by Lorenzo da Ponte. First performance in Vienna, January 26, 1790.

Characters

Ferrando .... Tenor
Guglielmo .... Baritone
Don Alfonso .... Baritone
Fiordiligi, engaged to Guglielmo .... Soprano
Dorabella, engaged to Ferrando ...... Mezzo-soprano
Despina, maid to Fiordiligi and Dorabella ... Soprano

The Story *

ACT I. Don Alfonso, elderly cynic of eighteenth-century Naples, is seated in a café, discussing the constancy of women with Guglielmo and Ferrando. These lovesick young bachelors insist that their respective fiancées, Fiordiligi and Dorabella, are paragons of virtue and gladly accept a wager to let Alfonso put the girls to any test he chooses. They even plan how they will spend the hundred sovereigns they will win from him (**Ferrando, Guglielmo:** *Una bella serenata*—I shall serenade my goddess).

In their seaside garden Fiordiligi and Dorabella praise their absent lovers, but are interrupted by Don Alfonso, who starts his plot by reporting that the youths have been ordered to the front. Guglielmo and Ferrando come to bid the girls farewell. The girls say they would rather die than see their lovers go. Soldiers and villagers join the officers (**Chorus:** *Bella vita militar*—On to glory). The lovers continue their leave-takings; then the men depart. The women wave till their ship is out of sight, while Alfonso laughs at his joke: he is sure he will win the bet (**Fiordiligi, Dorabella, Alfonso:** *Soave sia il vento*—May breezes blow lightly).

The pert maid, Despina, brings breakfast to the weeping ladies in their boudoir. Dorabella's grief is hysterical (**Dorabella:** *Smania implacabile*—Implacable compulsion). Both resent Despina's cynical advice (**Despina:** *In uomini, in soldati*—Stability in a soldier!). Alfonso now bribes the maid to further his plans;

* The aria translations of *Così fan tutte* are those of the English version now sung at the Metropolitan. Copyright, 1951, by G. Schirmer, Inc., and printed by permission.

he wants her to help him introduce Ferrando and Guglielmo, who come in disguised as Albanians, to the unsuspecting girls (**Alfonso:** *Alla bella Despinetta*—I present Miss Despinetta).

Fiordiligi and Dorabella, unaware of the deception, are at first implacable. Fiordiligi dismisses the strangers, boasting her own faithfulness (**Fiordiligi:** *Come scoglio*—Strongly founded). Guglielmo gently pleads the new suitors' case (**Guglielmo:** *Non siate ritrosi*—How can you refuse us?). But the ladies walk out in high dudgeon, leaving the youths delighted by their failure to lure the girls from the memory of their former lovers. Alfonso insists that they are but innocent babes, that the women will eventually relent. Ferrando reiterates his devotion (**Ferrando:** *Un aura amorosa*—My love is a flower).

Alone in their garden the sisters unite in grief (**Fiordiligi, Dorabella:** *Ah, che tutta in un momento*—Ah, how sad and unrelenting). Guglielmo and Ferrando now stagger in, still disguised, and fall on the grass, apparently poisoned, in the throes of hopeless passion. The girls show signs of softening. Despina, disguised as a doctor, restores their inanimate bodies to life with a giant magnet.

ACT II. In the privacy of their room Despina urges the girls to relent (**Despina:** *Una donna a quindici anni*—Any girl, fifteen or over). The sisters finally decide that there will be no harm in a little flirting since their financés are away at war; they must merely choose between the two Albanians. Dorabella picks first and selects Guglielmo—the dark one—because he's the smarter (**Dorabella:** *Prenderò quel brunettino*—I will choose the handsome dark one). This is all right with Fiordiligi who thinks Ferrando—the fair one—would be great fun.

The youths have gathered a band of musicians in the garden to serenade the girls (**Ferrando, Guglielmo, Chorus:** *Secondate, aurette amiche*—Forward a little). Because the men are so slow in their approach, Alfonso speaks for them, and because the women are equally reticent, Despina answers for them (**Alfonso, Ferrando, Guglielmo, Despina:** *La mano a me date*—Give me your hand). Guglielmo now woos Dorabella in earnest, and Ferrando strolls affectionately off with Fiordiligi. Guglielmo soon persuades Dorabella to accept a heart as a gift from him. Fiordiligi fights harder to resist Ferrando and orders him to leave; left alone, however, she guiltily admits her new love (**Fiordiligi:** *Per pietà, ben mio*—Dearest love, I beg your pardon). The men meet to compare their luck with the other's girl; when he hears of Dorabella's behavior, Ferrando has to be restrained from accosting her. Guglielmo admits the waywardness of the entire sex (**Guglielmo:** *Donne mie la fate*—Lovely women) but is quite proud that it wasn't *his* sweetheart who "fell." Alfonso warns him not to count his chickens before they've hatched.

On their terrace Dorabella and Fiordiligi both admit to Despina that they have followed her advice. Dorabella candidly confesses the power of love, but Fiordiligi still hesitates. It would be better to dress up in the uniforms the men have left behind, she says, and join them at the front. The three men have been watching through a crack in the door, and Ferrando now rushes forward swearing he will die of despair should she leave him. Fiordiligi resists a moment longer, then passionately surrenders. Now Guglielmo is ready for the devil to strangle both him and Fiordiligi; but when Ferrando returns, Alfonso points out that they both still love their shattered idols and advises them to take the girls as they are, for they would be no better off with anyone else because "they all [women] do it" (**Alfonso:** *Tutti accusan le donne*—Women cannot be faithful).

Despina comes to announce that the ladies are ready to marry the Albanians; she and Alfonso quickly prepare a festival hall for the double wedding. A large company greets the couples, while Alfonso brings on the notary: it is Despina, in wig and gown. Just as the contract is signed, Alfonso announces the arrival of the former sweethearts. General confusion. The girls push their Albanian lovers into another room. Ferrando and Guglielmo now reappear in uniform and accept the apologies of their sweethearts, who lay all blame on Alfonso. All unite in a philosophic finale (**All the principals:** *Fortunato l'uom*—Happy is the man of reason).

THREE special talents are common to the greatest operatic composers: they know a good libretto when they see it, they can individualize their characters through music, and they can somehow combine beauty of musical design with dramatic excitement.

By the time Mozart wrote *Così fan tutte,* more than twenty years of experience with the theater had developed his natural gifts and had added a musical sense of gesture and a consideration for stage timing unusual among even the finest composers. . . .

A most interesting shift in emphasis can be seen in Mozart's libretti as he reaches maturity: the displacement of the aria in favor of the ensemble. Many of the early works use the texts of Metastasio, the most popular operatic poet of the century; others are constructed according to his standards by lesser poets. These libretti are particularly kind to soloists. The aria depicts an emotion in graceful verse, and an occasional ensemble provides variety. If action takes place at all, it is in recitative.

In Mozart's later works, the proportion changes considerably. A glance at three operas, spaced at equal intervals, shows about equal attention to the aria in all three (a necessity if the composer is to be on friendly terms with the singers) but a sharp rise in the number of ensembles.

The earliest, *The Abduction from the Seraglio,* contains 13 arias, 4 duets, a quartet and a "vaudeville"—a lightweight finale which bears no resemblance to the dramatic finales of the Italian works.

Four years and four operas later, *The Marriage of Figaro* shows 14 arias, 6 duets, 2 trios, the wonderful sextet, and 3 action-filled finales, each a series of ensembles in itself.

After another four-year interval, we find in *Così fan tutte* 13 arias, 6 duets, 5 trios, a quartet, 2 quintets, a sextet, and 2 finales. The total:

Abduction (1782): 13 arias, 7 ensembles.
Figaro (1786): 14 arias, 12 ensembles.
Così (1790): 13 arias, 17 ensembles.

. . . . .

It is easy to see why Mozart finds the ensemble increasingly preferable to the aria. First of all, it is possible to contrast two or more characters—always more fruitful than a single portrait, however lovely the portrait may be. Second, action can be carried on, giving scope for the composer's gesture-and-motion sense. Third, between the beginning and the end of an ensemble the situation may change considerably, and this affords a chance for a change in musical form as well. This is possible in a soliloquy, but not common; in the ensemble, the reaction of one character to another brings it about quite naturally.

The composer has a variety of resources for characterizing persons or situations. A contrast in rhythms is a useful device; just as a man's pulse responds immediately to his psychological state, a rhythmic pattern can reflect his emotions with great subtlety.

The first ensemble of the opera demonstrates this technique. The curtain rises in the middle of an argument: Alfonso has exploded his favorite conversational bomb, and the two lovers declare their scorn in a teasing dotted rhythm.

Don Alfonso, older and more realistic, speaks in a rhythmic pattern which sounds matter-of-fact in contrast: "I'm well over sixty. I know what I'm saying."

But Ferrando and Guglielmo are deep in the argument now; if Alfonso deals in facts, let him prove them! It is in Alfonso's own rhythm that they answer this time. As they cry "Choose your weapon!" two swift ascending scales in the orchestra tell us that their own swords are already in hand.

A few bars later, all three men sing together in identical rhythmic patterns, but Alfonso is slightly out of step with the others, rhythmically as well as psychologically.

A broken rhythmic pattern is always a sign of breathlessness, whatever the cause may be. Perhaps it indicates little gasping sighs of lovesickness or that the characters are overcome by tears or that they are pretending to be; or they may be overcome by laughter, as the merry syncopations of the men's trio show a little later. Again, we see Alfonso out of step with the others; he laughs for a different reason!

Characterization can often be accomplished by using a distinctive musical line which is echoed in some form over and over. Fiordiligi has her heroic vocal leaps; Ferrando prefers a lyrical curving line; and Despina is always recognizable by her bright patter of repeated notes.

Harmony is another effective indication of psychological state, and in *Così fan tutte* we hear the harmonies of dramatic tension used just as if the situation were quite serious. In the first quintet, for example, listen to the sudden darkening into the minor key, flavored by one well-placed diminished seventh, as the ladies beg their lovers to kill them rather than leave them! The chord itself is the stab of the dagger.

A little later, Alfonso and the two sisters pray that the sea may be kind to the travelers. Even the cynical old man (evidently a first-rate actor!) seems serious for the moment, and gently moving harmonies in a whispering string accompaniment make the trio one of extraordinary beauty. The contrapuntal handling of the lines seems effortless, as all excellent music should, but it is a marvelously calculated piece of vocal writing. Listen particularly for the moment when the flutes, in a high register, join in a diminished seventh chord over a dominant pedal point—a harmonic and instrumental color of heavenly quality!

The finale of the first act gives Mozart another opportunity to clarify situation through harmony. At first the ladies, melancholy but unconscious of danger, comment on their plight with comparative serenity. We hear the fluttering of the two flutes which often accompany them, but only momentarily does a chromatic harmony disturb them—when they sing "I shall die of dark despair." The quiet orchestra assures us that they haven't seen anything yet.

The emotional picture changes as the lovers rush in with their bottles of poison. An ominous tremolo in the strings, rapidly changing harmonies, the tension of augmented sixth and diminished seventh chords contribute to the agitation. The tonality has shifted from a clear D major to a stormy G minor, Mozart's key of pathos and passion. "You have disdained our wooing, brought on our sad undoing," the strangers moan, while the harmonies writhe.

Alfonso's advice to show some pity seems to calm the wild harmonies for a moment, and a quieter orchestra reflects his presence of mind. When the ladies are left alone with their victims, however, the tonality begins to wander as their virtuous intentions begin to weaken. "Are they suffering?" they ask each other. In the orchestra, two brief musical motifs are being developed, moving hesitantly from key to key and instrument to instrument. Indecision is evident. Should they leave? Should they go closer? Do they dare to touch the poor men? Should they be in C minor or G minor or F minor, or perhaps A-flat major or B-flat minor? In another neat bit of counterpoint, heavily colored with chromatic tones, the men express their amusement at the ladies' confusion.

Despina's entrance as the doctor brightens the tonality again —G major—but the unexpected reaction of the patients brings an unexpected modulation into B-flat. Renewed vigor carries them back to D major; but here the ladies are on their home ground, and cannot be swayed. Mozart must have smiled to himself as he gave a slowly rising chromatic line to their words, "The more my fury rises."

It is somewhat surprising that for many of the ensembles of *Così fan tutte* Mozart uses the most static of musical forms, the *da capo*. Here the composition is divided into three clearly articulated sections, the second contrasting with the first, the third an approximate repetition of the first. The form is described in academic shorthand as "A, B, A."

A ridiculous form to choose for showing progress in drama, is it not? The characters sing the same words again, to the same music; the idea is essentially undramatic. Mozart sees, however. that the repetition of a text always carries a slightly different emotional color from the first statement—added assurance, perhaps, or added passion. Accordingly, though he returns to the original musical material, quite recognizably, he makes enough difference in the musical repetition to point out the difference in the dramatic situation.

A good example is the duet of Fiordiligi and Dorabella in Act II. Persuaded by Despina, the ladies agree to play along with their strange suitors, and they decide who shall take whom. Their melody is appropriately light-hearted and graceful. The whole affair is a joke, after all!

In the central section, they imagine how their new lovers will behave—"Mine will say, My soul is burning"—and a sudden little agitation in the orchestra tells us that the ladies may not see things as objectively as they claim. By the time the first theme returns, after a long and luxuriant cadenza, they have worked themselves into such a state of enthusiasm that they cannot wait for each other to finish, but sing the melody in a gleeful canon.

Now the composer takes a new turn and develops a motif from the first section into a coda. And what a coda! Time after time the ladies seem about to reach a cadence; time after time it is delayed, and they sing on in a sort of intoxication with their own idea. While subtly burlesquing the endless cadences of operatic convention, Mozart tells us that their joke is running away with them.

From the beginning, Dorabella and Fiordiligi have been differentiated through their music. Sisters, yes; and sisters who agree enough to sing in thirds and sixths a great deal of the time. Mozart makes a running joke of doubling the "free" moments of song, the cadenza and the recitative; at one point the two men declare their devotion in a long recitative in parallel thirds—well-rehearsed spontaneity, indeed!

But the sisters are not temperamentally identical. Fiordiligi is relatively cool-headed; we hear her first in a calm vocal line supported by smooth, undulating strings or clarinets. The mind rules the heart here, and the mind is an imaginative one; Fiordiligi is inclined to idealize and dramatize everything.

Dorabella, more earthbound in thought and vocalism, is at the same time more volatile in emotion. Her vocal line in the first duet is much like her sister's, but a palpitating orchestra, with staccato violins like a quick heartbeat, betrays her true character.

It is not surprising, therefore, to find Dorabella yielding to her new lover rather early in the second act—the first time she is left without her sister's support. The music of her duet with Guglielmo shows amusingly how easily she is won. She has agreed to accept his gift of a heart-shaped jewel; now he pleads that she give him her own heart. She tries to be sensible: "The heart that you ask for is not here to give." The music follows the most logical of forms, so far: his request, tonic to dominant; her refusal, dominant to tonic. The rhythmic motion is stately, in well-considered eighth notes. If the duet should end here, in the area of polite conversation, Dorabella would be safe.

Guglielmo is not willing to leave matters there. A new theme appears with his new idea: if her heart is gone, why does it beat so? Here Dorabella makes her mistake: she tries to answer in his own terms—to the same melody—and staccato heartbeats in sixteenth notes show that danger is near. Guglielmo has discovered the weakest spot in her defense.

As he persuades her to wear his heart in place of Ferrando's portrait, there is another quickening of note-values, and little sighing phrases in the violins show her state of mind. Now their union is inevitable; they will live happily ever after, singing in parallel thirds. Once, indeed, their lines move in contrary motion—the moment when Guglielmo remembers the unpleasant part of a pleasant assignment: "Ferrando, poor fellow! His future looks dire!"

Fiordiligi is not so easily swayed; to all appearances she is, as she describes herself, "a marble tower." To herself, however, she admits that she is weakening and wisely resolves to leave the scene of temptation. In what appears to be the beginning of a conventional aria, she tells us her purpose: in disguise, she will go to the battlefield and find her beloved. Beginning in A major, the music takes the predictable turn to the dominant, E major, as she anticipates the joy of seeing Guglielmo again.

Now comes an unexpected development: Ferrando appears from his hiding place, and there is a sudden modulation to the minor key. Fiordiligi is not the woman to surrender without a fight, and pulling the harmony violently into C major, she orders him to leave. He agrees with her key, but he stays; suddenly we hear her echoing his own theme, and, a few bars later, singing in the dangerous thirds and sixths with him! Is she lost already? The text proves what the music has told us: "My resistance starts to weaken!"

Pressing the advantage, Ferrando tries to lead her back to A, the key of her love. She resists, pulling away into D minor, but the struggle is useless. In an ingratiating *larghetto*, now firmly established in A major, he makes his final plea. His ardor melts the rock; and an exquisitely tender phrase from the oboe marks the moment of her surrender.

Now we hear unashamed thirds and sixths, and another evidence of her capitulation: canonic phrases in which she, not he, leads the way!

Guglielmo, understandably, is bitter about Fiordiligi's faithlessness, especially since he has boasted so confidently of her strength! The moment comes, however, when he must join the others in toasting the marriage and singing a round, the favorite after-dinner sport of the century. The round is a charming one, like so many that Mozart himself left us; Fiordiligi, Ferrando, and Dorabella enter in turn, yet Guglielmo cannot bring himself to take part. Here a purely practical reason guided the composer: the melody lies too high for the baritone voice. As always, musical design must coincide with dramatic design; musical necessity must appear motivated by dramatic necessity. Thus Guglielmo sings—in a staccato line which cuts easily through the smoothly flowing ensemble—"Just to think of their dishonesty makes me wish there had been poison in their tea." In the same moment, we are shown the absurdity and the pity of the situation.

Every musical resource has been used to point up the drama in all its delightful artificiality, laughing at operatic convention even while observing its rules. The musical humor is sometimes obvious, usually more subtle, and always an illumination of the text. The wonder is that the technique is not obvious. In the charming make-believe of *Così fan tutte*, composer, librettist, singers, and orchestra speak with perfect spontaneity, take on fantastic disguises with equal ease, and poke fun at one another with the same good-natured mockery.

KATHERINE GRIFFITH McDONALD

WOLFGANG AMADEUS MOZART (1756–1791)

Don Giovanni

Libretto by Lorenzo da Ponte. First performance in Prague, October 29, 1787.

Characters

Leporello, servant of Don Giovanni	Bass
Donna Anna	Soprano
Don Giovanni	Bass or Baritone
The Commendatore, Donna Anna's father	Bass
Don Ottavio, Donna Anna's fiancé	Tenor
Donna Elvira, a noble lady of Burgos	Soprano
Zerlina, a peasant girl	Soprano
Masetto, Zerlina's fiancé	Bass

The Story

ACT I. On a terrace of the Castilian palace of Don Pedro, Commander of the Knights of Malta, Leporello bewails his fate as servant to the dissolute nobleman Don Giovanni (**Leporello:** *Notte e giorno faticar*—I work night and day). From the palace emerges Donna Anna, daughter of the Commendatore, frantically struggling from Don Giovanni's embrace. When her father rushes out in response to her cries, Giovanni kills the old man with his sword and escapes with his servant. Donna Anna, who had momentarily fled, now returns with her fiancé, Don Ottavio. He tries to console her, but in her anguish she bids him leave (**Anna:** *Fuggi, crudele*—Leave me, cruel one).

Roaming the neighborhood in quest of other quarry, Giovanni and Leporello withdraw as Donna Elvira, a former sweetheart of the Don, comes in search of the man she still loves (**Elvira:** *Ah! chi mi dice mai*—Ah, who will tell me). At first not recognizing her, the Don approaches to console her; then he slips away as Leporello tries to discourage Elvira by reciting his master's many conquests (**Leporello:** *Madamina! Il catologo è questo*—Little lady, the catalogue is this).

The peasants Masetto and Zerlina dance in with their friends to celebrate their approaching wedding. Giovanni, joining the merrymakers with Leporello, is attracted by Zerlina and, bidding his servant attend to Masetto, who reluctantly leaves (**Masetto:** *Ho capito, signor sì!*—I understand, yes, sir!), invites the bride to his villa (**Giovanni, Zerlina:** *Là ci darem la mano*—There we

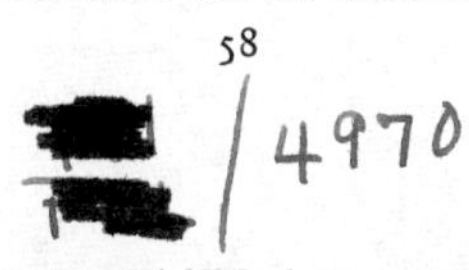

will hold hands). Their idyll is interrupted by Elvira, who warns the girl against her new suitor (**Elvira:** *Ah, fuggi il traditore*—Ah, fly from the traitor).

Meeting unexpectedly with Anna and Ottavio, Giovanni drags Elvira away lest she disclose his identity to Donna Anna. But the orphaned daughter of the Commendatore has already recognized Giovanni, and calling on Ottavio for vengeance, she describes to him the attack she suffered before her father's death (**Anna:** *Or sai chi l'onore*—Now you know who stole my honor). Left alone, Ottavio dwells on his love for her (**Ottavio:** *Dalla sua pace*—My peace depends on hers).

With Leporello, Don Giovanni now prepares for a feast in honor of Zerlina (**Giovanni:** *Finch'han dal vino* [Champagne Aria]—Until the wine goes to their heads).

As Zerlina and Masetto approach the gate of the mansion, the girl begs forgiveness for her apparent neglect of her rustic swain (**Zerlina:** *Batti, batti, o bel Masetto*—Chide me, good Masetto). When Giovanni has led the couple away, Elvira, Anna, and Ottavio, masked and robed in dominos, gather to the music of the minuet, vowing to punish the Don.

The peasants crowd Giovanni's terrace from which the host entices Zerlina to a neighboring apartment. The avenging maskers burst open the door at Zerlina's cry for help and denounce the Don, who barely escapes with Leporello.

ACT II. Giovanni and Leporello again approach Elvira's house. The Don forces Leporello to change cloaks with him, then coaches him in wooing, so that Leporello can, disguised as the Don, simulate a reconciliation with Elvira. Left free, Giovanni then serenades Elvira's maid (**Giovanni:** *Deh vieni alla finestra*—Come to the window). Masetto, leading a band of peasants to punish Giovanni, is disarmed by a ruse of the Don, badly beaten, and then consoled by Zerlina, who is attracted by his lamentations (**Zerlina:** *Vedrai, carino*—You will see, my dear).

Elvira, still believing Leporello to be her beloved Giovanni, leads him to a cloister where Ottavio and Anna also gather. Zerlina and Masetto follow them, unmasking Leporello, who, to protect himself, likewise vows vengeance on his master (**Leporello:** *Ah pietà signori miei*—Ah, mercy, my dear sirs), and then escapes. After the distraught Donna Anna leaves, Don Ottavio sings of his love for her and his desire to take vengeance on the Don (**Ottavio:** *Il mio tesoro*—Go and console my treasure). Now alone, Elvira rehearses the perfidies of the man she still loves (**Elvira:** *Mi tradì*—That unfaithful soul betrayed me).

Giovanni and Leporello hide in the cemetery, where they find themselves in the shadow of the equestrian statue of the Commendatore. The statue warns them their mirth shall soon end; but the Don impudently invites him to supper (**Leporello, Giovanni:** *O statua gentilissima*—Oh, most noble statue), an invitation which the statue accepts, much to Leporello's horror.

In her home Don Ottavio urges his suit on Donna Anna, but she begs him for a seemly delay till her father's death is avenged (**Anna:** *Non mi dir, bell' idol mio*—Don't say, my handsome idol).

Don Giovanni gives directions to Leporello for the banquet he has planned for the Stone Guest (**Giovanni, Leporello:** *Già la mensa*—The supper is ready). Elvira enters and again implores the Don to reform his behavior, but he waves her aside. Rushing from the hall, she exclaims in terror. The frightened Leporello hides under a table. Giovanni, going to investigate, meets the statue of the Commendatore in the doorway and is summoned to hell (**Commendatore:** *Don Giovanni! a cenar teco m'invitasti*—Don Giovanni! You invited me to supper and I have come). Giovanni resists to the end; then flames burst around him, and he is dragged below.

At the close of the opera the other principals assemble at the front of the stage and deliver the moral: sad is the fate that awaits all libertines.

A FEW days after the first performance of *Don Giovanni* the Prague *Oberpostamtszeitung* published a review which probably excels anything written about the work. It read simply: "Connoisseurs and musicians say that nothing like it has ever been produced in Prague"!

. . . For Prague substitute the world and you have an appraisal which is fully as sound today as it was in November, 1787. There is literally nothing like Mozart's *Don Giovanni* either among its composer's creations or elsewhere.

. . . . .

"What is more perfect than *every* number in *Don Giovanni?*" asked Richard Wagner. "Where else has music won so infinitely rich an individuality, been able to characterize so surely, so definitely and in such exuberant plenitude as here?"

Figaro is, if you will, the more perfect artistic entity of the two—*Don Giovanni* is looser, less consistent, on the surface even grossly illogical. But so, too, is human nature. If ever there was in opera a *comédie humaine* it is most surely *Don Giovanni.*

In a larger sense the author's designation, *dramma giocoso,* could scarcely be more apt. If all the world's a stage, what more than a *dramma giocoso* is the experience of life? Whatever the narrow intent of Lorenzo da Ponte, when he carpentered the book out of well-known odds and ends, it was with a profound knowledge of the sorrows and absurdities of humankind that Mozart breathed into it an abiding soul.

. . . . .

It is with awesome tones that the overture begins. Those D minor chords, subsequently associated with the marble statue of the murdered Commendatore, smite the listener with the full force of the orchestra. A somber echo from the double basses continues momentarily. Pulsing harmonies beneath nervous phrases lead us to scale passages fraught with menace. Directly on the heels of this portentous *andante* there sets in the main body of the overture, an *allegro assai,* with a subject that may be said to paint the reckless, insatiate passion of Don Giovanni. Subsidiary themes assert themselves, one of them a descent of octaves in close imitations. An inconclusive coda leads into the first scene proper.

The famous opening phrases of Leporello's *Notte e giorno faticar* introduce the air itself, which with a few strokes sets the discontented creature before us. Mozart continues to draw him in the round as the escaping Don Giovanni and the incensed Donna Anna rush out of the house, struggling violently, while the ignoble groom continues to babble.

The entrance of the Commendatore speedily precipitates a mortal duel. A few trenchant scales paint the flash of rapiers. The old man falls, hurt to death (we almost feel his strength ebbing away in the sighing phrases that summon help). There is a magnificently passionate outburst of grief and terror as Donna Anna, returning with Ottavio and the servants, catches sight of the bloody work. She swoons, revives, laments, then fervently exacts of her lover an oath of vengeance. Ottavio, in consolatory phrases (*Lascia, o cara*), strives to comfort her.

Next, Elvira confronts us. We are instantly made aware of her disquiet through the troubled syncopations and the wide melodic leaps of her aria, *Ah! chi mi dice mai.* By contrast, how suave and lovely are those orchestral phrases with which Don Giovanni, ignorant at first of Elvira's identity, seeks to cajole a supposedly new victim!

One of the supreme buffo arias of all opera presently follows —Leporello's *Catalogue Song,* enumerating his master's conquests. Note that scurrilous, mocking laugh in the flute and bassoon! Note, as well, the melting *cantilena* of the contrasting part of the air, the *andante con moto, Nella bionda!*

It is impossible, unfortunately, to do more than signalize the delicious, tripping duet and chorus in which we first encounter Zerlina, Masetto, and their rustic friends; or the bumptious *Ho capito* of Masetto, aware of his helplessness against the wily amorist. But we should pause to cite that intoxicating *duettino, Là ci darem la mano,* perhaps the most famous melody in the opera and, assuredly, one of the most persuasive. It characterizes the self-assured philanderer and the hesitant but wholly feminine coquette as no verbal description could paint them.

The return of Elvira, thwarting Don Giovanni's seductive design, brings us to the so-called Handelian aria, *Ah! fuggi il traditore.* Accompanied by strings alone, the air is a D major page of unadorned beauty. Those who are aware of Mozart's preoccupation with Handel and Bach need not be surprised at the imprint their work occasionally left upon his own music till the end of his life. Quite different, but in its way as noteworthy, is the quartet, *Non ti fidar, o misera,* one of those masterpieces of ensemble writing with four characters expressing (or intimating) contrasted feelings yet preserving the most harmonious effect. . . .

As Don Giovanni and Elvira depart, leaving Donna Anna and Ottavio alone, we reach one of the stupendous peaks of the score —the formidable accompanied recitative, *Don Ottavio, son morta* and the ensuing Vengeance air, *Or sai chi l'onore.* The dreadful certainty which has forced itself on Donna Anna that, in her attempted seducer, she has seen the murderer of her father, finds vent in a page of terrific violence and explosive energy. Wagner himself paid the G-flat passage of the recitative, *Era già alquanta avanzata la notte,* the compliment of imitation when he wrote Telramund's *Dank König, dir* in the first act of *Lohengrin.* A contrasting pathetic middle part, *Rammenta la piaga,* leads to a magnificent reprise of the first portion of the air.

It is a tribute to the tender beauty of Ottavio's love song, *Dalla sua pace,* that it does not produce an effect of anticlimax after Anna's furious cry for revenge. Like Elvira's splendid *Mi tradì* it was added to the original score by the composer for the Viennese Ottavio, who had his troubles with the more exacting *Il mio tesoro.*

Don Giovanni himself has relatively few solos in the opera

which revolves about him. The so-called *Champagne Song, Finch'han dal vino,* is his outstanding opportunity for dizzy *bravura,* a sparkling *presto,* wholly impossible to articulate except to da Ponte's Italian text. The flute and violins, two octaves above the voice, add to its heady excitement.

To Zerlina falls the next jewel of the score, the aria *Batti batti,* with which she cajoles Masetto into pardoning her attempted flirtation. The hearer is as helpless as Masetto against this melodic flattery, and it is with something like a certainty of triumph that the minx launches forth on the coda, the passage *Pace, pace, o vita mia* with its adorable, weaving 'cello designs.

The first finale ranges over two scenes. Its gems include the encounter of Don Giovanni and Zerlina, with the lovely phrase accompanying *Tra quest' arbori celata*—which Gounod was later to remember in the garden scene of *Faust;* the first appearance of the famous minuet—and the trio of Masks, a romantic melody over a beautiful accompaniment of woodwinds and horns alone. In the brilliantly lighted ballroom of Don Giovanni's palace the host has been careful to suit the entertainment to the customs of his guests. No less than three stage orchestras, soon all playing at once, provide the proper music for the respective diversions. There is a minuet for the folks of quality; a contradance, for the rustic beauty, Zerlina, with whom Don Giovanni momentarily dances; finally, a *Teutsch* or rapid waltz, into which Leporello forces Masetto to divert his attention from the nobleman's designs. And we presently hear a counterpoint of duple and triple rhythms, proceeding with the utmost smoothness.

This frolic, however, is short-lived. A shriek from Zerlina leads to the discovery of Don Giovanni's perfidy. In a magnificent ensemble, with rushing scales and stormy tremolos, the act moves to a tumultuous close.

It is not easy to follow the arguments of those who maintain that the second act of the opera falls below the level of the first. Such flaws as dramatic structure or logic may reveal are not duplicated in the music, as boundlessly rich, as varied, as ingenious as ever. For all the buffoonery which accompanies it, the A major trio of Elvira, Leporello, and Don Giovanni is as tender as anything in the work. A particularly subtle moment is that melodic presage of the Serenade when Don Giovanni addresses to her the words, *Discendi, o gioia bella.* The Serenade proper, with its delicate accompaniment of mandolin and plucked strings, is another lifelong friend.

We must neglect several fine numbers in order to note—however casually—such landmarks of the closing half of the masterpiece as Zerlina's consolatory air sung to the manhandled Masetto, *Vedrai, carino*—a sweetly solacing balm to broken heads and wounded hearts. Not the least precious part of it is the twenty-bar-long postlude. The wonderfully organized sextet, beginning with Elvira's *Sola, sola in buio loco,* excels even the quartet in the first act. Mark that simple but inspired change from B-flat to D two measures before Ottavio's *Tergi il ciglio;* the rapturous lyric line of Donna Anna's *Lascia almen alla mia pena;* that chromatic figure of eighths and sixteenths that buoys up many of Elvira's words and also sustains the phrases of all six characters before the music launches upon the ensuing *molto allegro!* What an incredible commingling of lofty sorrow, touching entreaty, and buffoonery!

Ottavio's great air, *Il mio tesoro,* constructed in readily recognizable three-part form, is as heartbreakingly difficult as it is beautiful. Woe to the singer who attempts it without extraordinary length and well-schooled control of breath; all that such a vocalist will accomplish is to shatter the far-flung arch of Mozart's exquisitely sculptured phrases. Small wonder that nine artists out of ten quail before such a cruel obstacle!

In a churchyard, by night, Don Giovanni listens, unshaken, to the sepulchral tones of the Commendatore's stone statue warning him against mocking the dead with his shallow presence. The spectral words, emphasized by solemn harmonies, set Leporello a-quake. In quavering accents he vainly tries to answer as his master bids him. Finally the libertine takes it on himself to challenge the powers beyond the grave. The statue accepts his defiant bid to come as dinner guest. . . .

Before passing on to the catastrophe with the terrific music of the Stone Guest and the chastisement of the unrepentant libertine, it will be advisable to observe Donna Anna's so-called letter air, the rondo, *Non mi dir.* Its noble, prefatory recitative, *Crudele? Ah no, mio bene,* allows us to hear two of the themes of the aria proper. The chief subject of the rondo is a twining *larghetto* phrase in F. A lovable episode in thirds and sixths asserts itself. Following a recall of the principal theme and a supplementary one, Mozart provides, *allegro moderato,* a lengthy and taxing *cabaletta,* with *bravura* of great exaction. The air terminates with a brilliant coda, after deftly postponing a full cadence.

Like every eighteenth-century nobleman Don Giovanni has his household musicians to entertain him at mealtime. In this instance [at the beginning of the supper scene as Leporello serves his master] they play extracts from operas popular at the moment—a tune from Martin's *Cosa rara,* another—*come un agnello*—from Paisiello's *Fra i due litiganti il terzo gode* and, finally, *Non più andrai,* from Mozart's own *Nozze di Figaro.* Hearing the latter Leporello exclaims: "This music I know only too well"—a sally that must have awakened an instant response among Prague operagoers in 1787, and which even today never fails to arouse a warm-hearted laugh.

Elvira once more breaks in upon the mood of the moment with one of her impassioned pleas to her betrayer. Then, after she turns away with a sudden shriek of terror, doom stalks across the threshold. Those portentous chords we heard at the beginning of the overture now threaten the very underpinnings of the universe. The Stone Guest has taken his host in dreadful earnest. Terrible is that succession of C naturals with which the affrighted Leporello describes the tread of the supernatural visitor (*Ta, ta, ta, ta*). No words can describe that unearthly music with which Mozart has contrived to paint the very ecstasy of terror. Yet even against these implacable harmonies the resolute defiance of Don Giovanni maintains itself, and there is a kind of satanic grandeur in that cutting phrase *Ho fermo il core in petto.* The dread splendor of the music grows, swells, and at length culminates in a stupendous D major. After this there should be nothing but the release of silence!

There should not be, but there is! In recent years it has become the fashion to retain that pretty but platitudinous epilogue which Mozart may or may not have included at the Prague première but which he certainly eliminated at the first production of the opera in Vienna. Whether or not it is justified by the classification of the piece as a *dramma giocoso* is of small consequence.

HERBERT F. PEYSER

GAETANO DONIZETTI (1797–1848)

Don Pasquale

Libretto adapted by Donizetti from Salvatore Cammarano's opera *Ser Marc' Antonio*. First performance in Paris, January 3, 1843.

Characters

Don Pasquale .... Bass
Dr. Malatesta .... Baritone
Ernesto .... Tenor
Norina .... Soprano
Notary .... Tenor

The Story

ACT I. The crabbed bachelor Don Pasquale wishes to marry and provide himself with an heir in order to punish his rebellious nephew Ernesto, who will not give up his beloved—the young widow Norina—to take a bride of Don Pasquale's choosing. Pasquale's old crony, Dr. Malatesta, suggests his beautiful sister as a bride (**Malatesta:** *Bella siccome un angelo*—Beautiful as an angel). Pasquale urges Malatesta to bring the girl quickly or he shall die outright; left alone, he sings with delight at the thought of his impending marriage (**Pasquale:** *Un foco insolito*—A strange fire). Ernesto, who arrives shortly, is once again offered the bride of Pasquale's choosing and again refuses. Pasquale then announces his impending marriage and his disinheritance of Ernesto. Realizing he cannot support Norina without his allowance and expected inheritance, Ernesto resolves never to see his love again (**Ernesto:** *Sogno soave e casto*—A sweet and chaste dream). He makes one last effort to save his happiness, though; consult the wise Malatesta before taking such a step, he pleads, and is overwhelmed to discover that not only has Pasquale done so but that it is Malatesta's own sister whom Pasquale is marrying.

Norina is in the garden laughing over a book of romance (**Norina:** *Quel guardo il cavaliere*—What a glance the cavalier). As she lays the book aside, she reflects on how well she knows the techniques of coquetry (**Norina:** *So anch' io la virtù magica*—I also know the magic merits). A messenger brings Ernesto's note of farewell; crushed by the news, she is cheered by Dr. Malatesta, who promises that she won't lose Ernesto and explains to her his scheme to save their love: she will impersonate his sister, marry Pasquale in a mock ceremony, and drive him to such desperation that he will be at her mercy. Norina is delighted by the plot (**Norina:** *Pronta son*—I am ready); together the two sing of the end their scheme will effect (**Norina, Malatesta:** *Vado corro*—I'll go running).

ACT II. In Pasquale's luxurious library Ernesto bewails the prospective loss of his beloved (**Ernesto:** *Cercherò lontana terra*—I will look for a faraway land), exiting hastily to avoid seeing his uncle, who arrives to instruct the servant. Malatesta enters with the veiled Norina, who quickly captures Pasquale's heart. A fake notary is brought in to prepare the wedding contract according to Pasquale's instructions. Just as Norina is signing, Ernesto breaks into the room to bid his uncle good-by, furious at having originally been denied admission. He starts in horror at finding Norina Pasquale's bride, but Malatesta is able to draw him aside and explain that the ceremony is a fake. No sooner has the notary sealed the marriage and Pasquale bequeathed his fortune to his wife than Norina turns from the demure role she has first assumed to an extravagant hussy. In vain Pasquale protests his fate, while Malatesta, Ernesto, and Norina delight in the success of the ruse (**Pasquale:** *Son tradito*—I am betrayed).

ACT III. Servants bustle about carrying out the new mistress' orders. Pasquale is horrified by the bills of his "wife," which are brought to his library. Pasquale attempts to stop Norina from going to the theater, and the two argue violently. Norina wins, however, and impudently ends the argument with a mocking waltz (**Norina:** *Via, caro sposino*—My dear little husband, don't be a tyrant), as Pasquale mutters "divorce." In leaving the room Norina carefully drops a letter which Pasquale picks up and reads; it is a note setting a rendezvous for that very evening! Enraged, Pasquale sends for Malatesta. The servants are appalled by the new confusion in the house (**Servants:** *Che interminabile andare*—What eternal goings-on). Meanwhile Malatesta and Ernesto set plans for the rendezvous which the young man has arranged with Norina. The upset Pasquale pours out his troubles to Malatesta and agrees to accompany the doctor to the garden that evening (**Pasquale,** then **Malatesta:** *Cheti, cheti*—Gently, gently).

In the starlit garden Ernesto serenades Norina (**Ernesto:** *Com' è gentil*—How gentle); she responds warmly, and Ernesto joins her in a rapturous duet (**Norina, Ernesto:** *Tornami a dir*—

Tell me again). Malatesta and Pasquale arrive too late to catch the young man.

The doctor now plays a new trick. He announces that Ernesto is about to introduce his own bride, Norina, into the house. Pasquale's "wife" with mock fury threatens to leave; and since her antics have thoroughly disgusted the old gentleman, she exacts his permission to let the young couple marry with a handsome dowry. Malatesta then gives away the secret: Pasquale's wedding was a farce, his "wife" is in fact the beloved of Ernesto. After a moment's hesitation, the bewildered Don gives his blessing to the young couple to the delight of all (**Malatesta, Norina, Ernesto:** *Bravo, bravo, Don Pasquale*).

ERNEST NEWMAN has remarked that "of the enormous repertory of Italian comic operas in the last quarter of the eighteenth century and the first half of the nineteenth only three works still keep the boards intact . . . admired as masterpieces that seem . . . to be perennially young. These three works are Rossini's *The Barber of Seville* (1816), Donizetti's *L'Elisir d'Amore* (1832), and his *Don Pasquale* (1843)."

The three operas Newman mentions have proven so hardy, perhaps, because they are strong enough to withstand less than ideal performances (for Donizetti, not to mention Rossini, undeniably wrote for singers of a quality not often found today—Sontag, Ungher, Stolz, Lind, Rubini, Lablache, Duprez, Mario, to cite but a few).

Don Pasquale certainly appears to be virtually foolproof. For one thing it has an abundance of graceful melodies that beautifully display the human voice. Then there is the warm good will with which Donizetti approaches each of the four major characters. No matter what the situation—how seemingly real or unreal—each character behaves in a believable, convincing manner. None loses his basic humanity—not even Don Pasquale during his most outrageous behavior. This sweet, compassionate view of life is especially welcome in our theaters today.

Moreover, the libretto, which has provoked all manner of jokes about its verisimilitude (some apt ones, but mostly poor ones that reveal little understanding of the work) is more valuable than one would imagine it to be. As Walter Kerr suggests in his recent book *How Not to Write a Play*, our recent theater has been too much concerned with actuality. Actuality invariably slows any theater piece to a laggard pace. To get but two hours of life from two hours in the theater is not much entertainment no matter how you slice it. It puts value on identity instead of on general recognition and disregards the proven tenet that any theater art is the selecting and heightening of experience. The libretto of *Don Pasquale* is then actually a strength in that it serves as a perfect springboard for various musical elaborations, it maintains a trust in the shorthand of artistic conventions, and it combines with the music to produce a speech that is economical and richly evocative.

The overture to *Don Pasquale* is, frankly, a potpourri and incapable of sustaining one's interest as an independent musical structure. In spite of this, it serves its purpose well enough. It prepares its audience for much of what is to follow. The opening bars with their bright colors and sprightly rhythms indicate that the opera will be a comedy. The melody which follows, and the way it is handled (it is Ernesto's serenade in the final act), foreshadows the elegance and tenderness with which Donizetti will treat his characters. A bit of Norina's aria *So anch' io la virtù* shows that sophistication and wit will be part of the evening's entertainment. Next there is a Rossini-like crescendo which pegs the time of the opera's composition and displays Donizetti's professional admiration for the master of Pesaro's skill. A tune associated with the relation of Don Pasquale and Dr. Malatesta then emerges, followed by more stylized dramatic gestures. There is a return to Norina's aria—now gentle and then finally elaborated with spirited flourishes.

As the curtain rises, we hear a quiet, genial, flowing melody in the low strings occasionally interrupted by the bright tones of the flutes and oboes. All this underlines Don Pasquale's calm assurance that he can outwit his nephew and points up his jumpy anticipation of Malatesta's arrival. Malatesta enters and quickly comes to the point: "I've found you a wife," he exclaims. The music here is jubilant as Don Pasquale rejoices and Malatesta mutters, "What a blockhead." So that he can glowingly extol the beauty and virtue of his find, Donizetti has given the doctor an aria (*Bella siccome un angelo*) with a warm and graceful melody that allows for delighted interruptions by Don Pasquale. The aria has an appropriate "unfinished" shape as if Don Pasquale were too excited to allow the music to take a conventional close. The old man is, to be sure, as his further questioning tells us. The music accompanies this action, attends Malatesta's hasty exit, and hurries without formal hint into Don Pasquale's delightfully giddy *Un foco insolito*, a waltz surcharged with the comic and humane characteristics of the old man about tc take a young bride.

A tune of lightness and elegance announces the entrance of Ernesto. An accompanied conversation in which Don Pasquale gives Ernesto the choice of giving up Norina or being disinherited is important only for its indication of Ernesto's serious intentions and real love—*Amo Norina, la mia fede è impegnata.* As the astonished Ernesto learns of his uncle's impending marriage, there is a duet in which Don Pasquale's confidence and assurance are heard in the steady rhythm articulated by the low strings and Ernesto's acceptance of his fate is felt in his lovely revery upon his blighted plans, *Sogno soave e casto.* During this romanza, Don Pasquale lets us know that he feels sorry for his nephew but that the young man has brought the situation on himself.

The scene in Norina's garden provides our first meeting with the charming heroine. She enters reading a passage from a most romantic, knightly tale, *Quel guardo il cavaliere.* So soft, so feminine, so docile does she appear—until she throws the book aside and sings in a most brilliant aria, *So anch' io la virtù magica,* that she has learned the secrets of coquetry and intends to put them to good use. She bubbles with wit, high spirits, and insouciance. Donizetti has here put in his debt every lyric soprano with the flexibility to handle his *tessitura*—the aria is a perfectly adorable piece of character study and an enchanting and brilliant musical creation. At this point Malatesta arrives, and after Donizetti tightens the screws on his plot, he launches the doctor and Norina into a superlative duet which begins with Norina's heartfelt *Pronta son, purch' io non manchi* and jumps quickly into her relish of the trap set for Don Pasquale. Malatesta's feelings are similarly revealed—first, his sympathetic response, then his delight in the comedy. The climax of the duet is the rollicking *Vado corro* in which the two contemplate what their executed plans will accomplish, expressing themselves in an exhilarating vocal manner with all kinds of bravura skips, runs, and ornamentations. It concludes the first act with desirable dash and éclat.

The second act opens with a comparatively uninspired recitative and aria for Ernesto as he ponders his plight. The scene is useful only in that it preserves Ernesto as a serious character to serve at least temporarily as a foil to Don Pasquale. After Ernesto exits, Don Pasquale enters proud as a peacock. "Really, for a man near seventy . . ." he boasts. The bassoons chuckle as Norina is led in by Malatesta, and the subsequent little ensemble *Mosse, voce, portamento* catches the gaiety of the two and the excited anticipation of Don Pasquale. Donizetti uses music sparingly while he makes his next plot step. Then with the fake notary at hand he has a good time with legal language (*et cetera, et cetera*) as Don Pasquale recites the marriage contract. A good-humored tune hangs in the background during this episode, while flutes and pizzicato strings accompany Malatesta's and Norina's mock-ironic comments on Don Pasquale's generosity. The mood changes as the distraught Ernesto arrives with his tones of consternation on first being denied entrance, then on his seeing Norina. There follows an ensemble in which Donizetti employs the simplest means to maintain musical and dramatic equilibrium: he alternates rapid and slow sections—rapid for Pasquale's protests and Norina's demands; slow for the old man's withdrawals to lick his wounded pride and for Norina, Ernesto, and Malatesta to tell us privately that they really feel sorry for Pasquale's situation and pity his stubbornness. The climax of this act's finale is the brilliant patter-singing of all the principals beginning with Don Pasquale's bumbling *Son tradito, calpestato,* accompanied by chirping trumpets and chortling woodwinds.

The third act likewise contains its share of musical and dramatic treasures. The tonal brilliance and rhythmic bustle of Donizetti's orchestra accompanies the *presto, presto* of the household chorus filling their new mistress' demands, as the act opens. After Don Pasquale enters and has worked himself up by counting through the bills Norina has incurred, the composer gives us a duet which is high comedy indeed. Donizetti mirrors in his music at each point the emotions of Don Pasquale and the real and feigned ones of Norina. The duet opens with Pasquale's quiet and dignified *Dove corre* (Where are you going so fast?). When he gets his answer, he is outraged (*A non mettermi,* Don't push me too far). Norina promptly boxes the old gentleman's ear. Then we get the comic self-pity of Don Pasquale's *E finita* with its broken phrases and the real pity of Norina's *E' duretta la lezione* (The lesson has been a severe one). The conclusion of the duet is Norina's impudent waltz *Via, caro sposino* punctuated by Pasquale's protests of *Divorzio! Divorzio!*

The lively chorus which follows with its *din, din, don, don* (describing servants' bells ringing) reminds one briefly of the Susanna-Figaro duet in the first act of Mozart's *The Marriage of Figaro.* After Malatesta and Ernesto get their signals straight, the doctor and Don Pasquale participate in a madcap duet in which they plan to catch Norina at her tryst, *Cheti, cheti immantinente.* Note here the saucy colors in the instrumentation and, toward the end of the duet, the composer's device of having the singers accelerate their words on one note, another style of patter-singing so loved by nineteenth-century audiences.

The final scene, laid in a garden, opens with Ernesto's moonlight-drenched serenata *Com' è gentil,* an irresistible melody redolent of Italian warmth, tenderness, and passion, accompanied by guitar, tambourine, and chorus. This is followed by another set piece, the ravishing duet of Ernesto and Norina, *Tornami a dir che m'ami,* in bewitching three-quarter time. Here one revels in the pure simplicity of the liquid thirds and sixths so characteristic of Donizetti and other Italian operatic composers of the day and still so sweetly mellifluous to us in the mid-twentieth century. An enchanting number!

After so many riches, how can there be anything left except a good-humored conclusion to our story and the jolly but somewhat conventional final ensemble *Bravo, bravo Don Pasquale?* In truth, that is all there is, because that is exactly what is needed to fill out to the satisfaction of all a most pleasing form. Donizetti would doubtless have been one of the first to agree with Debussy's dictum *Pas de trop!*

C. J. Luten

GIUSEPPE VERDI (1813–1901)

Falstaff

Libretto by Arrigo Boïto, based upon Shakespeare's *The Merry Wives of Windsor* and *King Henry IV*. First performance in Milan, February 9, 1893.

Characters

Dr. Caius, a physician .... Tenor
Sir John Falstaff .... Baritone
Bardolph .... Tenor
Pistol .... Bass
Mistress Alice Ford .... Soprano
Anne or Nannetta, Alice's daughter .... Soprano
Mistress Meg Page .... Mezzo-soprano
Dame Quickly .... Contralto
Fenton, a young gentleman in love with Anne . Tenor
Ford, a wealthy burgher .... Baritone

The Story

ACT I. Sir John Falstaff, a portly, good-humored rascal of fifteenth-century Windsor, sips his sherry in his comfortable armchair at the Garter Inn, surrounded by his knavish cronies Pistol and Bardolph. Unruffled by the accusations of Dr. Caius, the town physician, that the fat knight's friends have robbed him, Falstaff—in debt as usual—seeks to better his fortunes. He will woo two lovely ladies at once and then steal their gold. His henchmen defiantly refuse to carry his missives and protest that their honor is at stake. Sir John gives the notes to a page and retorts that such talk of honor is humbug (**Falstaff:** *Puo l'onore riempirvi la pancia?*—Can honor fill a belly?)

Mistress Ford and her daughter Anne meet their neighbors Mistress Page and elderly Dame Quickly in a sunny garden and rapidly compare the notes which Sir John has sent them. He has sent the same passionate message to both Mistress Ford and Mistress Page (**Alice, Meg:** *E il viso tuo*—And your face). They decide to punish Falstaff's impudence. Meanwhile Master Ford arrives with Caius, Pistol, and Bardolph who hasten to apprize the ordinarily jealous husband of Falstaff's intentions. With them comes the young gentleman Fenton, who seeks to woo Anne Ford and remains to snatch a kiss from his beloved (**Fenton, Anne:** *Labbra di foco*—Lips that are burning). They are interrupted by the return of the three ladies who have decided to let Dame Quickly invite Falstaff to visit Mistress Ford; she in turn will confront him with Mistress Page. Independently the men have agreed that Ford shall go to Falstaff, under another name, to encourage the knight in his courtship.

ACT II. Back at the Garter Inn Bardolph and Pistol feign penitence for their former mutiny and announce Dame Quickly. With mock reverence (**Dame Quickly:** *Reverenza*—O most honored sir) she gives Sir John Alice Ford's promise of a rendezvous (**Dame Quickly:** *Dalle due alle tre*—From two to three). Hearing that Mistress Page also favors his suit, Falstaff preens himself on his success (**Falstaff:** *Va, vecchio John*—Go, good old John). Bardolph then announces the arrival of Ford (under the name of Signor Fontana, Master Brook), who tells the knight that he is hopelessly in love with Alice and suggests that his money may tempt Falstaff into breaking down her scruples. While Sir John is arraying himself for the amorous adventure, Ford laments his equivocal position: perhaps his wife is going to deceive him (**Ford:** *E sogno?*—Am I dreaming?). The two men go off together.

In a flutter of excitement the four women prepare for Alice to receive Sir John, hide him in a laundry basket when Meg appears, and dump him unceremoniously in the river. They retire to leave Alice alone with her plump suitor. He boasts of his fascinations as a youth (**Falstaff:** *Quand' ero paggio*—When I was page to the Duke of Norfolk). Suddenly Ford and his companions arrive, to the surprise of the women and Falstaff. When Ford first breaks in to search the room, he empties the laundry basket, but Sir John is safe behind a screen. At the second invasion Ford discovers Fenton and Anne behind the screen: Falstaff has climbed into the basket, which is emptied into the Thames.

ACT III. Thoroughly soaked by his bath in the river, Falstaff, back at the Garter, calls for a beaker of mulled sherry (**Falstaff:** *Ehi! Taverniere!*—Hey, Innkeeper), and is consoling himself at a table in front of the inn when Quickly again greets him, apologizing for his rough treatment and inviting him to Herne's Oak in Windsor Forest, where she promises that Mistress Ford will be waiting at midnight. As Quickly and Falstaff enter the inn, the three Fords arrive with Mistress Page to plan how they will mock the knight in an impromptu masque. Ford then promises Dr. Caius that he will bless his wedding to Anne. But he is overheard by Quickly from the inn, and the women subsequently hint at a plan to upset Ford's.

Just before midnight Fenton arrives at the oak, dreaming of his beloved Anne (**Fenton:** *Dal labbro il canto*—From lips the song flies ecstatically). No sooner does she arrive than the merry wives carry the lovers off to dress up for the masque. The clock strikes just as Falstaff ambles in, ready to woo Mistress Ford, but his flirtation is interrupted by a throng of witches, goblins, and fairies, led by Anne, veiled in white (**Anne:** *Sul fil d'un soffio etesio*—Play, dreams, on the threads blown by a fresh wind). One and all give Falstaff a thorough thrashing. When he realizes that he has been shamed before all of Windsor, the fat knight promises to mend his ways. Dr. Caius brings in his bride for Ford's blessing, but "she" turns out to be red-nosed Bardolph in disguise, so Anne is now free to wed Fenton. The whole assemblage joins in praise of mirth (**Entire cast:** *Tutto nel mondo*—Everything in the world is a joke).

EVEN those whose adoration for *Falstaff* is the keenest seem always to have felt that some explanation of its basic paradox—the singular public reaction to a work of its admitted perfections—was in order. These explanations have been various. It is claimed, for instance, that the opera is too fine, too aristocratic for the more insensitive palates of the multitude. No doubt for some it is. But is *Falstaff* so much more fine and patrician an art product than, let us say, *Le Nozze di Figaro?* A comedy, it has been judged less human in its appeal than the greatest of its composer's tragic works. Yet Rossini's *Barber* is also a comedy and a highly artificial one at that.

It is to Verdi himself that we should, in a more or less roundabout way, look for an answer to the main paradox of *Falstaff*. When he gave the public what many will continue to esteem his grandest work he sighed: "I feel that with *Otello* I have fired off my last cartridge." After all, he had reached seventy-four! To be sure he exclaimed shortly afterwards: "If I were thirty years younger I should like to begin a new opera tomorrow on condition that Boïto provided the libretto." He was to keep his word, though not literally on the morrow. He had not become "thirty years younger" when at length he did so, but about six years older.

Age both helped and hindered him. It sharpened his perceptions of the comic aspects of life in the way a young blood can never apprehend them. It filed and lent edge to his resources of wit, of humor, of innuendo. What it diminished in him at the same time that it enhanced his technique and imagination were his gifts of melodic invention. And in this diminution we have the solution of the *Falstaff* anomaly. For the melodic flesh-pots of *Aïda* and *Trovatore* allure the operagoer as all the fine art of *Falstaff* does not.

This point of view has been more or less adroitly contested. We have been told that what makes the melodic content of this opera appear thin is the brevity of the tunes and the circumstance that they flash by before the ear has a real chance to seize and retain them; in plainer words, that the ordinary listener is unable to see the forest for the trees. These are at best half-truths. In point of fact there is something strangely tenuous, even bloodless, about the melodic idiom of *Falstaff* as a whole. The composer takes refuge again and again in cadential melodic formation—notice, for instance, things like Dame Quickly's reiterated mock-obsequious *Reverenza*, the pert *Dalle due alle tre*, the artificial dolefulness of *Povera donna*, Mrs. Ford's *O soave Sir John*, and Falstaff's *Non so far lo svenevole*. The list might be extended if there were any point in it. Of broadly developed melodies there are few. The love music of Fenton and Nannetta —several times recurring—is one of the exceptional pages of its lyrical kind which the score offers and worthy of Verdi's more luxuriant inspiration. (Observe, though, with what amusing abruptness the composer breaks it off in the forest scene and sternly discourages applause by having the swelling but truncated duet shatter into a bit of trifling declamation!)

Perhaps the best known independent number in the opera is the Fat Knight's little *allegro con brio*, *Quand' ero paggio*—a tiny *arietta*, barely twenty-five bars long, over almost before one realizes it has begun, and instantly absorbed in the mercurial current of the music. Inevitably the listener will be attracted to another tripping tune—the light, *staccato* melody in D major to which Alice Ford in the first part of the third act sings the words *Avrò con me dei putti* and which recurs at the close of the scene as darkness falls and the little company makes for Windsor Forest.

To a single claim of those who idolize *Falstaff* one can cheerfully subscribe that nowhere else is there such perfection in the treatment of the word or such matchless equilibrium of music and text. The composer has found for the communication of the dialogue a wonderfully fluid medium, an idiom which seems like an outgrowth of Mozart and Rossini.

Falstaff is an opera of details rather than of long, sweeping lines, of ensembles than of lyrical solo effusions. If this grows to a degree out of the nature of Boïto's book (a condensation and concentration of Shakespeare's rowdy and sprawling farce), it arises scarcely less from a recognizable depletion of the composer's melodic capital. These details—strokes of genius, practically every one in their now witty, now pictorial connotations—point and season the monologues which in *Falstaff* supplant the great arias of the older Verdi works. Yet the monologues themselves have their roots in much older scores (one has but to think of those in *Rigoletto* or *Don Carlo*).

Probably the most famous of the *Falstaff* monologues is the Fat Knight's discourse on honor, toward the end of the opening scene. It is easy, listening to the orchestral part, to appreciate what relish Verdi must have found in the composition of this page. No one is likely to overlook that *staccato* D of the bassoon (with its prefatory *appoggiatura*) which underlines the Fat Knight's answer, "No," as he asks, "Can honor mend a leg? Can honor fill a paunch that is empty?" and so on through the Shakespearian list.

Another purple patch is found in the course of the ruminations of the Knight at the beginning of the third act, where, following his misadventures with the merry wives, he rails against the world and reverts to thoughts of wine and its consolatory uses. Here the orchestra underscores his reflections with a gigantic trill that begins softly and expands into a mighty *crescendo* that grows and bursts into something like a paean of bibulous triumph.

But Falstaff himself does not have a monopoly on soliloquies. The jealous tirade of Ford, *E sogno? O realtà?* is one of the high points of the opera. And in the preceding encounter of Falstaff and *Signor Fontana* (Shakespeare's Master Brook) Verdi accepted at once the suggestion offered by the talk about the money bags the disguised Ford presents to his host. One need not see the actual contents of the sacks; one hears the coins jingling in the orchestra. Characterization in Verdi's last opera is sharply and unmistakably achieved, though a system of representative phrases or leading motifs in even a remotely Wagnerian sense is not the method employed. The means, however, are unmistakable.

The Fat Knight is pictured in music which could belong to no one else in the piece. So, too, is the jealous Ford, whose violent utterances in his monologue could be associated with no other. The merry wives can be identified whenever they come into question—whether in their chattering, *scherzando* idiom or by things like the mock litany they intone in the final act. The two lovers are mirrored in the sweet lyrical measures which convey their feelings. As for definite melodic associations and recurrent motifs of one sort or another, there is here even less utilization than there was in operas like *Aïda* or *Otello*. Perhaps the nearest approach to a thematic label is that blustering phrase at the beginning of the opera, with its falling sixteenth notes and short, detached chords. Obviously it refers to the hero himself. But after a number of diversified repetitions in the first scene, it is heard no more. Three bars of it, however, furnish as much introduction as the piece offers, and the curtain rises without musical preliminaries as in *Otello*. In fact, about the only orchestral preface in all *Falstaff*, barring the sounds of horns that depict Windsor Park at midnight, is the *staccato* music swelling in agitated *crescendo* before the curtain rises on the Garter Inn in the third act—music already heard in the scene of Falstaff's discomfiture in the house of Mistress Ford.

At the first performance of the work at La Scala the third act was received with rather less enthusiasm than the first two. The scene in Windsor Forest especially failed to stir many of its hearers as might have been expected. There is, indeed, a certain artificiality about it, as there might be in a masque or a *commedia dell' arte*. To sensitively cultivated tastes this touch of artifice, one might even say of stylization, heightens the fascination of the piece. Yet obviously one section of the public remains cold to the scene. As the curtain rises, Verdi has undoubtedly captured with rare poetry of mood the sense and spirit of the nocturnal woodland. The delicate picture is such a one as Watteau might have painted. Yet it may be questioned whether the composer has altogether equalled the lovely tones with which Otto Nicolai, in his *Merry Wives of Windsor*, has delineated the same sylvan haunt. Inevitably one thinks of Weber and Mendelssohn in the music of the simulated elves. For all its gossamer charm it has a fragility and a quality of artifice that removes it from the romantic sphere which was second nature, even reality itself, to these earlier masters.

One of the details which must have struck earlier *Falstaff* audiences as extraordinary and which, even in these days of harmonic adventure, preserves its atmospheric poetry, is that passage of thirteen bars heard as the Windsor bell strikes midnight. Absurdly disguised in a heavy cloak, his head crowned with antlers, Falstaff enters, pausing to count the strokes of the bell. Slowly he enumerates each chime, while a wonderful and mysterious succession of slow, shifting seventh chords supplies a magical basis to the repeated naturals of the bell and of Falstaff's count.

But the most celebrated number of the closing scene has always been the great fugue which, built on a text declaring in substance that "All the world's a stage," constitutes a sort of massive epilogue. It is said that Verdi obtained the subject of the fugue from a tune sung by a crowd of children. The ensemble itself is, in fact, a kind of *vaudeville*, such as terminates Mozart's *Entführung aus dem Serail*, though more complex and certainly more boisterous. For a long time musicians were lost in wonder that an Italian composer should introduce the learned form with such skill and constructive adroitness into an opera. Yet those who knew their Verdi might have realized that the *Falstaff* fugue was not his first operatic use of counterpoint, or that the composer of the *Requiem* did not lack the technical knowledge to write fugue as pure as Bach's.

Falstaff is, as we have indicated, a superlatively aristocratic work. Shakespeare's *Merry Wives of Windsor* is anything but aristocratic. In fact the poet wrote few plays so brawling and farcical in tone, so wholly plebeian, so loosely built. What Boïto furnished Verdi was a refined, purified, and concentrated version, with suggestions borrowed from those scenes of *Henry IV* where Falstaff is vastly more his incomparable self than he is the slapdash entertainment Shakespeare carpentered in a couple of weeks to please a whim of the Virgin Queen. That the Italian poet did not aim to retain the typical English, or rather Elizabethan, flavor of the original piece is obvious. In the operatic transmutation the characters surround themselves with an aura appreciably more Italian than Shakespearian. Yet it is a question whether the music of a composer so fundamentally Latin as Verdi could have been any more English or Shakespearian had Boïto followed the *Merry Wives of Windsor* with more slavish fidelity.

HERBERT F. PEYSER

CHARLES GOUNOD (1818–1893)

Faust

Libretto by Jules Barbier and Michel Carré, based upon Part I of Goethe's poem. First performance in Paris, March 19, 1859.

Characters

Faust	Tenor
Méphistophélès	Bass
Wagner	Bass
Valentin	Baritone
Siébel	Mezzo-soprano
Marguerite, Valentin's sister	Soprano
Dame Marthe Schwertlein	Soprano

The Story

ACT I. The aged philosopher Faust sits in his library lamenting his wasted life (**Faust:** *Rien! En vain j'interroge*—Nothing! I've questioned and studied in vain). Twice he resolves to put an end to his life by drinking poison, and twice his hand is stayed by the sound of Easter merrymakers singing outside (**Chorus:** *Paresseuse fille*—Lazy girl). Tormented, he calls the devil before him. Faust reveals his longing for youth and pleasure (**Faust:** *A moi les plaisirs*—I want pleasure, young mistresses), and Méphistophélès assures him they can be his—if he will sell his soul. When the philosopher hesitates, the devil conjures up a vision of Marguerite. Enthralled, Faust agrees to the bargain, drinks a potion, and is transformed into a handsome young student. The two go off together.*

A Kermesse, or town fair, is in progress. Valentin, a young army officer, grasps a medal given him by his sister Marguerite, the subject of his touching farewell (**Valentin:** *Avant de quitter ces lieux*—Before leaving this place). A students' chorus is interrupted by Méphistophélès, who offers an impudent song in praise of greed and gold (**Méphistophélès:** *Le veau d'or*—Calf of gold). He infuriates Valentin with an insulting toast to Marguerite. When the soldier draws his sword, it breaks, prompting the others to ward off evil by holding their sword handles like

* *Faust* was originally presented in five acts, Act I being completed here and the scene following—the Kermesse episode—comprising Act II. Occasionally *Faust* is still given in five acts.

so many crosses before Méphistophélès. As the crowd joins in a waltz (**Chorus:** *Ainsi que la brise légère*—Even as the gentle breeze), Faust enters. He accosts Marguerite on her way toward church, but she charmingly refuses his offer to escort her. Méphistophélès prevents Siébel, another suitor, from reaching her while Faust declares his love.

ACT II. Siébel brings flowers to Marguerite's garden, where he leaves them, hoping that she may learn his devotion (**Siébel:** *Faites-lui mes aveux*—Bear to her my confession of love). Faust, brought to the garden by Méphistophélès, serenades Marguerite's dwelling (**Faust:** *Salut! demeure* [Cavatina]—Greetings, chaste and pure abode). With the devil's help, he leaves a casket of jewels to win Marguerite. The two men withdraw as the girl enters the garden and seats herself at her wheel, singing a ballad while she begins to spin (**Marguerite:** *Il était un roi de Thulé*—There was a king of Thule). She interrupts the verses with reflections on the handsome stranger who has spoken to her. When she discovers the jewel casket, she exclaims with delight on seeing herself decked in the precious gems (**Marguerite:** *Ah! je ris de me voir si belle* [Jewel Song]—Ah, I smile at seeing myself so beautiful). Méphistophélès leads Marthe, a middle-aged neighbor, into the garden, pretending to woo her, so that Faust may again declare his love for Marguerite (**Faust, Marguerite:** *Laisse-moi, laisse-moi*—Let me, let me gaze upon your face). Méphistophélès finally rids himself of Marthe; then observes the young lovers (**Méphistophélès:** *Il était temps!*—It was time!). As night falls, Marguerite admits that she returns Faust's ardor but, still overcome with maidenly scruple, begs him to leave. He agrees, but is urged to return by Méphistophélès, who laughs derisively as Marguerite, after singing of her joy to the skies (**Marguerite:** *Il m'aime*—He loves me), yields to the returning Faust's embrace.

ACT III. Marguerite, oppressed with fear over her guilty love, seeks refuge in church, where she is pursued by the relentless Méphistophélès, who curses her and torments her with damnation.

In the square of the city, Valentin and his fellow soldiers return triumphantly, singing of the glory of those slain in battle (**Soldiers' Chorus:** *Gloire immortelle*—Immortal glory). Valentin questions Siébel concerning Marguerite, but the youth replies evasively. Valentin's fears are realized when Méphistophélès arrives with Faust and serenades Marguerite with an improper song (**Méphistophélès:** *Vous qui faites l'endormie*—You who are shamming sleep). The serenade drives the brother to defend his sister's honor; he fights a duel with Faust, who, under Méphistophélès' protection, wounds him fatally. Dying, Valentin curses Marguerite for all to hear, swearing that he dies by her hand alone (**Valentin:** *Écoute-moi bien, Marguerite*—Listen to me carefully, Marguerite).

ACT IV. It is Walpurgis Night; Faust and Méphistophélès repair to a barren spot where the most beautiful women of history are brought before Faust in an effort to make him forget the hapless Marguerite.*

Marguerite is in prison, condemned to die for the murder of her illegitimate child. Faust and Méphistophélès enter her cell, bent on spiriting her away. At first the distracted girl is overjoyed to see her lover, but she refuses to leave, insisting on recalling their first meetings. When she spies Méphistophélès in a corner urging them to leave while there is still time (**Méphistophélès** [**Trio**]: *Alerte, alerte ou vous êtes perdus*—Be quick or you are lost), she calls on the angels to save her (**Marguerite:** *Anges purs, anges radieux*—Pure, radiant angels). As she dies, Méphistophélès pronounces her condemned, but angel choirs are heard proclaiming her salvation. An unearthly radiance transforms the cell as Marguerite's soul rises to heaven.

IF THERE really is such a thing as the most popular opera in the world, *Faust* comes about as close to it as anything else in lyric drama. It has no problems today, however it may once have suffered. It seems incredible to us that once upon a time George Eliot should have put herself on record as believing that the love scene, with all its charms, could never brook comparison with the one in *Les Huguenots*. In common with works like *Trovatore, Rigoletto,* Rossini's *Barber*, and a few others of their stripe, *Faust* has an iron constitution. Even the poorest of performances cannot kill it. And if the description is at all permissible *Faust* might be characterized as the most operatic of operas. It contains about every feature, every specialty the average taste looks for in the entertainment furnished by the lyric theater. From the first it has been assailed because it was not the *Faust*

* The Walpurgis Night scene is frequently omitted from productions of *Faust* because it requires a ballet, which some opera companies are unwilling or unable to provide.

of Goethe. Of course it is not the *Faust* of Goethe—neither is any other of the myriad *Faust* operas. If it were, it would—depend on it!—be vastly less popular.

Exactly because the work is so little problematic, so full of operatic effects and stunts and features, so copiously supplied with dramatic, romantic, and melodic attractions of one sort or another, we may pass directly to a survey of the musical rewards which, in such plethoric measure, it offers us. This is not to say that all of its music is equally good. Far from it! A good deal is merely sweetly sentimental, some pages are affected with a kind of sugared religiosity; others, again, are an offense to cultured taste. Yet as so often happens in music some of the commonest things in it maintain an astonishing vitality.

It is really a pity that listeners ordinarily pay so little attention to the first two pages of the orchestral introduction, for these somber, brooding measures are worthy of the best man who ever ventured to approach Goethe's poem with musical intentions. Actually, they capture something essential of it. Unfortunately, after a dark, creeping, sinuous *fugato* of great promise, a platitudinous modulation and a few thin measures of harp scales introduce the melody of one of the numberless song hits of the opera, the tune sung afterwards by Valentin to the words *Avant de quitter ces lieux*, ending in a typical Gounod cadence. Faust's gloomy monologue at the curtain rise is, like the first part of the overture, another inspiration that deserves a more careful hearing than it usually gets—particularly the phrase *J'ai langui, triste et solitaire*. Then, the pretty 6–8 melody of the solo oboe which breaks in upon Faust's meditations is almost certain to linger in the ear, the more so as it is shortly repeated by a soprano chorus outside (*Paresseuse fille*). And the listener is almost certain to be challenged by Faust's resolute *Salut! ô mon dernier matin*, which, along with his utterances that immediately follow, are melodically very typical of what one might call Gounod's *Faust* style.

The appearance of Méphistophélès is musically none too striking, for the composer has not at this point endeavored to portray the devil in very striking tones. He sets him before us chiefly as a gallant swaggerer in a red (or black) cloak with a sweeping feather in his cap—in brief, as he himself says, "a real gentleman."* Then, after the devil has interrogated Faust as to his wishes and received the reply that more than all else the philosopher desires youth, the latter breaks into the fine, swinging

* In the current Metropolitan Opera production, the devil appears in top hat and tails!—C. A. L.

tune *A moi les plaisirs,* which afterwards becomes the basis of a duet. But before the act ends we have a lovely episode, the vision of Marguerite at the spinning wheel, the horns singing beneath a murmuring spinning figure of violins and harp a melody which we will hear more fully developed in the nocturnal duet between the lovers in Marguerite's garden.

The scene of the *Kermesse* is heaped with gaudy and richly varied melodic merchandise. There are, first of all, the lively and popular choruses—or rather one big chorus made up of half a dozen successive ones of burghers, students, soldiers, young girls, old men, matrons; all of them with jaunty melodies of their own, the rousing ensemble ending as it began. Then, to solemn, religious harmonies, appears Valentin, who presently delivers his song of farewell remembered from the overture. This air, incidentally, was added to the opera after its first hearing and to an Italian text (*Dio possente*). It appears here in three-part form, with a rather martial middle section not heard in the overture. The next considerable signpost is Méphistophélès' vigorous Song of the Golden Calf—a number with a dash that carries all before it.

A subsequent detail which ought not be overlooked is that downward chromatic rush of strings as Méphistophélès calls upon Bacchus to fill the cups of the crowd with fresh wine—a capital bit of musical description. It is scarcely necessary to direct the hearer's attention to the chorale of the swords—a number in Gounod's unmistakable churchly vein—in which the men, suddenly conscious of the evil identity of their strange visitor, exorcise him with the crosses on their swords. But this cloud is quickly dissipated by a wholly irresistible waltz. It is in reality not one waltz but four, the chorus singing a sort of counter-melody against the main one and the melodies following. It might be argued that this waltz is too elegant for these burghers and peasants, yet who can resist the spirit and sweep of it? Suddenly a change comes over the music and, as Marguerite appears and, after a few words, quickly vanishes, we hear the graceful, adorable melody of the lovers' first meeting. Thereafter the waltz measures return, bringing the act to its close in a whirlwind of animation.

Deeper tones underlie the introduction to the second act. A rhythmic motif is followed by a meditative, weaving figure of violins, which spins its course in sixteenth notes. After a short, sweet clarinet phrase the orchestra announces Siébel's gracious Flower Song, almost too familiar a melody to require comment. The appearance of Faust and Méphistophélès brings us in short order to the tenor cavatina, *Salut! demeure,* a song of tenderest sentiment and a delicacy of instrumental color (notice particularly the lovely orchestral prelude and postlude), which suggests Gounod's preoccupation with Mozart. The air is fashioned in ternary form, with a contrasting middle section, *O nature, c'est là que tu la fis si belle.*

The chain of gems sparkles steadily with other bright inspirations—Marguerite's song of the King of Thule, with its touch of northern mystery and the brief interrupting phrases as the maiden pauses in her spinning to meditate on the handsome cavalier who seems to love her; her startled surprise at discovering the casket of jewels; finally the Jewel Song itself—a *valse brillante,* seemingly a trifle incongruous for a girl of such simplicity as Marguerite, until we recall that the Marguerite which the librettists Barbier and Carré invented for Gounod is not the Gretchen of Goethe.

The fine quartet which grows out of the presence of Faust, Marguerite, Marthe, and Méphistophélès, is one of the high spots of the opera and a notable piece of collective characterization as well. But finer still is the love scene, exquisite in its melodic fragrance of the phrase, *Laisse-moi contempler ton visage* and the manner in which another ravishing inspiration, *O nuit d'amour,* becomes by the simple process of inversion that wondrous phrase, *Je veux t'aimer,* which we heard in the momentary vision of Marguerite in the first act.

It is not possible, unfortunately, to signalize the various other beauties of the garden scene, though one cannot avoid mentioning Méphistophélès' broad invocation and the melting passage which Berlioz, at the first performance of the work, cited as the finest thing in the entire opera, *Il m'aime, quel trouble en mon cœur.* And, as the curtain descends, this passage swells to a passionate and grandiose outburst.

The ensuing cathedral scene of the third act is one of the finest in the work. Contrasting with the devout chantings of priests and choir boys we catch the satanic utterances of Méphistophélès which are like the afflicting voices of conscience in Marguerite's ears. Amid the scourging dotted rhythm of the orchestra with the snarls of stopped horns, the unhappy woman hears the accusing words of the fiend till, with a prodigious effort, she wrests her spirit from the diabolical torments in a paroxysm of supplication. The song in which she finds release, *Seigneur, accueillez la prière,* is perhaps not the loftiest type of musical inspiration, but rather a tune related to such religious outpourings as *The Palms* or as Adam's *Holy Night.* Yet for all its sweet obviousness, it is the right thing in this place and has a surging uplift which carries away the least susceptible.

The following scene opens with the universally familiar Soldiers' Chorus, a thoroughly blatant, rowdy, and vulgar tune, which one excuses for better or worse as a piece of musical rubbish. But in a short time, as a French critic wrote, "the music fades into the distance, for the relief of our ears," and better things assert themselves—particularly Méphistophélès' sardonic Serenade, with its cynical accompaniment and the devilish laugh at the close with the malicious "Ha! Ha! Ha!" through two falling octaves. The big ensemble of the curse and death of Valentin, as the flame of insanity begins to burn athwart Marguerite's distraught features—this ensemble ending with the whispered choral prayer, *Que le Seigneur aît son âme,* achieves something of the pity and terror of the scene conceived by Goethe.

Of the prison scene, which closes the opera, not much need be said. Marguerite's momentary recall of the melodies associated with her happier days—the waltz, the love music—is touchingly reminiscent. But the climax of this act is the trio, with its interesting orchestral details (like the beating of horses' hoofs as Méphistophélès mentions his impatient steeds) and Marguerite's soaring, ecstatic melody, *Anges purs, anges radieux,* thrice repeated, each time a tone higher, and gleaming with a kind of supernal light. Marguerite's pardon and her redemption are proclaimed in a somewhat theatrical apotheosis to the Easter hymn, *Christ Is Risen,* while angels bear her spirit heavenward.

Herbert F. Peyser

LUDWIG VAN BEETHOVEN (1770–1827)

Fidelio

Libretto by Joseph Sonnleithner and Georg Friedrich Treitschke, based on a play by Jean Nicolas Bouilly. First performance in Vienna, November 20, 1805.

Characters

Jacquino, a turnkey .... Tenor
Marzelline, Rocco's daughter .... Soprano
Rocco, a jailer .... Bass
Leonore, wife of Florestan (Fidelio) .... Soprano
Don Pizarro, governor of the prison .... Baritone
First and second prisoners ...... Tenor and Baritone
Florestan, state prisoner .... Tenor
Don Fernando, Minister of State .... Bass

The Story

ACT I. In the gatehouse of a state prison in eighteenth-century Spain, young Marzelline, daughter of the jailer Rocco, turns from the unwelcome attentions of the turnkey, Jacquino. Her heart is set on the new errand boy, Fidelio (**Marzelline:** *O wär ich schon*—Oh were I already united with him!). The hard-working lad—actually Leonore, the wife of Florestan, disguised as a boy to learn the whereabouts of her husband—arrives with a basket of provisions and is horrified by Marzelline's interest, especially since it has the blessing of Rocco. The four unite in the Canon Quartet (**Marzelline, Leonore, Rocco, Jacquino:** *Mir ist so wunderbar*—I feel so wonderful). Rocco then warns the young couple that a marriage cannot succeed on love alone (**Rocco:** *Hat man nicht auch Gold daneben*—If one doesn't also have money). When Rocco describes a political prisoner, dying in the vaults beneath them, Leonore suspects that he must be her husband and summons courage to visit him, heartened by the jailer and his daughter (**Rocco, Leonore, Marzelline:** *Gut, Söhnchen*—Good, my son).

Pizarro, the prison's cruel governor, orders his men to guard the courtyard and learns from dispatches brought by Rocco that Don Fernando, the benign Minister of State, is on his way to inspect the fortress. Pizarro vows to murder Florestan before the Minister's arrival (**Pizarro:** *Ha! welch' ein Augenblick!*—Ha, what a moment!). He orders the jailer to prepare a grave (**Pi-**

zarro, Rocco: *Jetzt, Alter, hat es Eile*—Now, old man, hurry up) and is overheard by Leonore, who forces herself to new hope for Florestan's release (**Leonore:** *Abscheulicher!*—Monster). Leonore interrupts a brief flirtation between Marzelline and Jacquino, begging Rocco to allow her to accompany him to Florestan's cell and persuading him to give the prisoners a few moments of exercise and fresh air in the courtyard. The prisoners murmur their gratitude (**Chorus:** *O welche Lust!*—Oh, what delight to breathe fresh air) but are soon ordered back by Pizarro, who hurries Rocco off to dig the grave.

ACT II. Haggard and chained, Florestan sits in his cell (**Florestan:** *Gott! welch' ein Dunkel hier!*—God! How dark it is!), contemplates his fate, and envisions Leonore (**Florestan:** *In des Lebens Frühlingstagen*—In the days of my spring). Exhausted by emotion, he fails to recognize his wife, who enters with Rocco. Leonore and Rocco begin to dig the grave (**Rocco, Leonore:** *Nur hurtig fort und frisch gegraben*—Now dig quickly). The jailer, moved by Florestan's cry of thirst, gives him some wine (**Florestan, Rocco, Leonore:** *Euch werde Lohn in bessern Welten*—You will be rewarded in a better world), then resumes his digging and blows his whistle as a signal to Pizarro that all is ready. The governor advances with drawn dagger (**Pizarro,** then **Florestan, Leonore, Rocco:** *Er sterbe*—He dies), but the fearless Leonore intercepts him with a pistol she has concealed. At this moment a trumpet call from the prison tower announces the arrival of the Minister. Rocco and Pizarro hurry out to face the dignitary, leaving Florestan and Leonore in each other's arms (**Florestan, Leonore:** *O namenlose Freude*—Oh, indescribable joy).

The humane Don Fernando summons the prisoners to the castle yard (**Fernando:** *Des besten Königs*—Our sovereign King), where Rocco pleads for mercy for Florestan and describes the courage of Leonore. Populace and prisoners rejoice as the faithful wife ecstatically removes her husband's fetters (**Leonore:** *O Gott, welch' ein Augenblick*—Oh God, what a moment) and is hailed as the noblest of women.

OF THE three *Leonore* Overtures, the third is the most famous, the second, in some ways the most audacious, dramatic, and original; the first, the most unfamiliar and tentative. The *Fidelio* Overture proper, which introduces all performances of the opera, is a product of the 1814 revision and avoids the problems posed by the others. Far from an empty piece, it stands in much more balanced relation to the opening scene and to its surface moods than those other independent poems which distill the quintessence of the inner and outer section and, in a sense, make the rest of the opera a superfluity. But it is much too easy to underestimate the importance of the E major Overture, even if this is matter of no such charge as the *Leonore* trilogy.

. . . . .

Much nonsense has been prattled concerning the two numbers which begin the opera proper, the duet of Marzelline and Jacquino and Marzelline's E-flat aria, *O wär ich schon* (which appeared in reverse order in the original versions). . . . If they are not Beethoven at his loftiest they capture to perfection that homespun, middle-class world which, for the moment, was the composer's concern. The same thing holds true of Rocco's song about money, with its contrasting sections in 2–4 and 6–8, and to a certain extent of the trio of Leonore, Marzelline, and Rocco. In melodically pleasant but unpretentious style they paint the little bourgeois joys and troubles of the kindly jailer and his young folk.

It is Leonore's entrance into the action which brings a change and a sympathetic enhancement over the scene. Marx has pointed out that her very presence "lifts the work to a higher level, the conversation of the three becomes finer, the range of thought more elevated." The Canon Quartet, *Mir ist so wunderbar,* is the first manifestation of this new element, the first disclosure of the composer's aims. This quartet takes rank among the great ensemble pieces of operatic literature. The eight introductory bars, *andante sostenuto,* stand in their profound religious feeling beside Beethoven's most exalted slow movements in the sonatas, concertos, and quartets. The ensemble as a whole might profitably be studied beside the antithetical *Rigoletto* quartet. There each of the personages is sharply characterized by the music he or she sings. Here, there is no dramatic purpose or differentiation as such; yet with the four persons in profound communion of spirit, Beethoven, by the simplest of means, evokes an elevated mood which has unfailingly exercised its spell since the opera was first performed.

Beethoven did not possess that instant and mercurial gift of characterization which was the priceless birthright of Mozart. But nothing would be further from the truth than to imagine him incapable of musical portraiture. *Fidelio* reveals this gift in the most persuasive fashion. The trio which follows the Canon Quartet depicts the differing personalities of Rocco, Marzelline, and Leonore in the liveliest, most unmistakable strokes. Paternal kindliness, gentle anxiety, and high resolve disengage themselves with the utmost eloquence of effect.

Villainy of the blackest dye courses like a deadly poison through the vengeful fury of Pizarro's entrance air. The ferocious pace of this *allegro agitato* never relaxes its breathlessness. Terrorizing *sforzandi* alternate with writhing, serpentine triplet figures in the accompaniment. Greater and more convincing still, the succeeding duet between Pizarro and Rocco offers us a magnificent study of contrasting characters—the benign if vacillating jailer on the one hand, the impatient, cunning but overbearing tyrant on the other. A rapacious beast of prey, Pizarro is still clever enough to try to make himself appear as Rocco's benefactor. After a furtive disclosure of his sinister intention, he gradually reveals the full enormity of his plan and his idea of making the old man his accomplice. There is scarcely anything more vivid in the whole score than that marrow-chilling unison, *Nun eile rasch und munter* and, shortly afterwards, that harrowing *fortissimo* chord which like a flash of lightning lights up the words: "One blow and he is silent!"

The volcanic recitative which introduces Leonore's tremendous *scena* did not exist in the earlier versions of *Fidelio*. For it we have to thank the shrewd stage instincts of Treitschke [co-librettist] and Beethoven's sense in replacing the earlier pathetic E minor recitative, *Ach, brich noch nicht, du mattes Herz.* Wonderful is the ease and felicity with which the composer takes us in a few bars from the impetuous upsurge of violence to the feeling of hope which irradiates Leonore's soul like a rainbow of promise. From the orchestra rises the hymnlike song of three horns. This *adagio* bridge passage leads to the superb *allegro con brio* body of the air. Here we find some of those vocal obstacles which have pained generations of singers obliged to leap from G-sharp above the staff to B-sharp below it and then to struggle with a *cadenza* taking the soprano from a high G-sharp down a tenth and thence up the scale of E major clean up to a top B.

The first chorus of prisoners (an earlier inspiration than the subsequent ensemble) is one of those compassionate outpourings which has not its equal in what one might in Wagnerian phrase term the "purely human." Never has the inhumanity of man to man been the object of such a sermon in tone. Two incomparable solos briefly interrupt the melodic course of the choral song. No listener should fail to remark in the second one (for bass) those ten measures of chromatic harmony, as modern as if they had come out of Wagner. We must refrain, unfortunately, from pointing out the somber splendors of the first finale, which unquestionably owes something to the parallel ensemble in *Don Giovanni*. It is impossible, however, to remain insensible to the momentary spiritual uplift of Leonore's inspired cry, *Noch heute*, as Rocco promises she shall visit the dungeon this very day.

The portentous orchestral introduction to the second act is a picture (if one may permit himself the paradoxical figure) of looming darkness grown visible. Beethoven paints in grim strokes an F minor scene of horror that might be an episode out of Dante's Hell. Presently the mood softens, and we hear Florestan's *adagio cantabile* air, whose melody everyone knows from the *Leonore* Overtures. Almost greater than this air is the *poco allegro* with which it ends. This miraculous page, which "seems like the last flicker of life's flame before its extinction," is another detail we owe primarily to Treitschke. The original prison air ended in a manner to whose artifice Treitschke took exception on the score of dramatic literalism.

Those who innocently believe that the spoken dialogue of the German *Singspiel* or the French *opéra comique* is incompatible with realism and artistic balance are herewith recommended to study the carefully planned distribution of song and speech in *Fidelio*. Nowhere in this masterpiece is there less a question of artificiality, or an effect of a hybrid species, than in the so-called melodrama of the arrival of Leonore and Rocco in the dungeon. The orchestral part, alone, is an astounding repository of devices of literal tone painting, of which, for that matter, Beethoven has given us such an abundance throughout *Fidelio*. The eerie tones of the double-bassoon evoke the grave-digging operation, a vivid instrumental passage suggests the disengagement of the heavy stone which blocks the spade.

No greater example of stupendous theatrical and emotional effect in all opera than the prison scene lies in my experience. The whole scene is a cumulative masterpiece of dramatic excitement and psychological truth. Each number seems greater than the one preceding—the A major trio than the A minor duet, the murder and rescue quartet, with its thrilling double *dénouement* of Leonore's pistol threat and the simultaneous fanfare of salvation. It is hard to imagine that such things as the frenetic duet should ever be questioned on grounds of purely theatrical value! They vindicate *Fidelio's* place among the supreme operas of the world.

On the heels of the shattering prison scene virtually all modern opera houses give us the Third *Leonore* Overture. Beethoven did not intend it so, of course, nor did he design this monumental conception as an *intermezzo*. But a *Fidelio* audience deprived of the *Leonore* Overture might justly feel moved to demand its money back. There is no more logical place for this titanic page than between the two scenes of the second act. Gustav Mahler appreciated this fact long ago, Arturo Toscanini followed in his footsteps, and practically every *Fidelio* conductor now does the same. . . .

Despite the grandeur of what has gone before there are glorious pages in this sunlit picture. The first chorus of rejoicing does not rise to a pitch so high that it loses by comparison with the superhuman coda of the great overture. But the two chief other numbers in the scene are reached late enough not to be crushed by what might otherwise be an uncomfortable proximity. These numbers are the devout and exalted *sostenuto assai, O Gott, welch' ein Augenblick*, and the intoxicating finale in praise of wifely devotion. Even as the rapturous duet which ends the prison scene was originally sketched by Beethoven for an opera on an antique subject, which was never carried out, so this prayerful F major hymn originally formed part of a funeral cantata which he wrote nearly fifteen years before *Fidelio* upon the death of the Emperor Joseph II. Just as little as the duet melody did it actually suffer by transplantation into the opera. As for the closing celebration of conjugal love, there breathes through it that same heaven-firing exultation which, in the *Ninth Symphony*, fills the *Hymn to Joy*.

HERBERT F. PEYSER

GIUSEPPE VERDI (1813–1901)

La Forza del Destino

Libretto by Francesco Maria Piave, based on the Duke of Rivas' *Don Alvaro o La Fuerza del Sino*. First performance in St. Petersburg, November 10, 1862.

Characters

Marquis of Calatrava	Bass
Donna Leonora, daughter of the Marquis	Soprano
Curra, Leonora's maid	Soprano
Don Alvaro	Tenor
Friar Melitone	Bass
Padre Guardiano, an abbot	Bass
Don Carlo of Vargas	Baritone
A surgeon	Baritone
Trabucco	Tenor
Preziosilla	Mezzo-soprano

The Story

ACT I. In his palace the Marquis of Calatrava warns his daughter Leonora against her suitor Alvaro, son of an Inca mother and a disloyal Spanish Viceroy. Hardly has the elderly nobleman retired when Leonora's maid Curra prepares her mistress for her elopement. Leonora reflects on her love (**Leonora:** *Me pellegrina ed orfana*—I, a wandering orphan). Alvaro now enters through a balcony window. The Marquis interrupts the lovers as they are about to leave to be married and is accidentally shot to death as Alvaro throws down his pistol to permit the Marquis to assassinate him and vindicate his daughter's honor. Seeing that the Marquis is dead, the lovers run away.*

The second scene of the act opens at the monastery of the Madonna of the Angels in the mountains of Spain. Leonora, who has become separated from Don Alvaro in their flight, has

* *La Forza* was originally presented in four acts, this scene ending Act I. A village scene which begins Act II and a scene in which a student relates how he and Don Carlo, Leonora's brother, vainly sought the elopers are customarily omitted from American productions. The monastery scene, here described as scene 2 of Act I, originally formed the end of Act II. Also missing from many productions are a scene between Alvaro and Carlo following Carlo's discovery of Leonora's miniature and the Trabucco and Melitone scenes before Preziosilla's *Rataplan*.

dressed herself as a boy for safety and now seeks refuge and spiritual help (**Leonora:** *Madre, pietosa Vergine*—Merciful Virgin Mother). The peevish Friar Melitone takes her to Padre Guardiano. Hearing Leonora's story, the Abbot urges her to embrace the cross for strength, gives her the habit of a friar to wear, and offers her sanctuary in a nearby cave, where, as a hermit, she will spend the rest of her days in solitude and penitence (**Guardiano:** *Sull' alba il piede all' eremo*—At dawn you will go to the hermitage). Guardiano calls for heavenly blessing (**Guardiano, Leonora, Chorus:** *La Vergine degl' Angeli*—The Virgin of the angels).

ACT II. Believing Leonora to be dead, Alvaro has wandered into Italy, where he has joined the army in the War of the Austrian Succession. Lingering near a deserted battlefield, he remembers his beloved (**Alvaro:** *O tu che in seno agli angeli*—O you, who amongst the angels). Suddenly he hears voices raised in a quarrel and rescues an officer in trouble. It is Don Carlo di Vargas, Leonora's brother, who—never guessing the identity of his rescuer—swears undying friendship with Alvaro. Both men are called to fight, but soon return, Alvaro badly wounded. Before the surgeons carry him away, Alvaro makes Carlo swear to burn a sealed packet which he will find in Alvaro's valise (**Alvaro, Carlo:** *Solenne in quest' ora*—In this solemn hour, you must swear that you will fulfill my pledge). The surgeons carry Alvaro away as Carlo discovers the package. Torn by doubt and suspicion that Alvaro may be the lover of Leonora and the murderer of his father, Carlo opens the seal. Seeing a miniature of Leonora, he exclaims with ferocious joy that Alvaro is finally in his grasp (**Don Carlo:** *Egli è salvo! . . . gioia immensa*—He is saved! . . . great joy). As gypsies and beggars invade the camp, Preziosilla leads vivandières and soldiers in a rousing chorus in praise of war (**Preziosilla:** *Rataplan, Rataplan*).

ACT III. In the monastery court, Friar Melitone distributes soup to beggars while Padre Guardiano, reading his breviary, admonishes the monk about the charitable duties of the Church. Carlo enters, in search of Alvaro, whom he has traced to this place of refuge. Summoned by Melitone, Alvaro enters, dressed in a religious habit. He refuses to enter a duel with Carlo, pleading his monastic vows (**Alvaro, then Carlo:** *Le minaccie, i fieri accenti*—The threats in fiery words), but, infuriated by Carlo's taunts, he finally takes up a sword. Both men rush away to fight.

In the inaccessible valley near the monastery where she has taken up a hermit's existence, Leonora prays that her tormented soul may find peace at last, admitting her love for Alvaro and begging God for death (**Leonora:** *Pace, pace, mio Dio*—Grant me peace, God). Her prayer is interrupted by sounds of the duel, which is taking place nearby. Alvaro rushes in, crying desperately that he has again shed the blood of a Vargas. The voice of Carlo is heard in the distance, calling for absolution in the hour of his death. Alvaro begs Leonora, whom he thinks to be a hermit, to give final blessing to the dying Carlo. As she emerges from the cave, she and Alvaro recognize each other. Realizing that Alvaro has mortally wounded her brother, Leonora rushes away to find him. A shout is heard, and Leonora returns, fatally wounded by the dying Carlo and supported by Padre Guardiano, who exhorts them all to turn to God for salvation (**Guardiano,** then **Leonora** and **Alvaro:** *Non imprecare, umiliati*—Don't curse, humble yourself).

LA FORZA *del Destino* is not a work which confronts the hearer with problems. The overture practically epitomizes the score even if it does not consider its lighter aspects. It is less a presage of dramatic incidents than of musical contents and as such furnishes a bird's-eye glance over some of the most characteristic inspirations of the score. It begins with six bars of vigorous strokes, half a dozen iterations of E-natural in strong octaves. Then appears, *allegro agitato e presto,* a kind of motto which might be termed the most important theme in the whole work, a dramatic, agitated, somber phrase which is associated in the composer's mind with the workings of that destiny which brings to their downfall the principal characters of the dark melodrama. Again and again this motto recurs during the progress of the opera, now in the tragic accents in which we first hear it, now lengthened, developed, and altered, now as an effective counterpoint of dramatic significance against other melodies.

A little further, after an expressive tender *andante,* beneath which are heard the mutterings of the destiny theme, appears (*andante mosso*) above tremolo harmonies what is, perhaps, the outstanding melody of the whole work, the broad, passionate tune of Leonora's prayer to the Virgin, *Deh! non m'abbandonar, pietà, pietà di me,* contrasted with the growlings of that fate theme which presently invades the picture in a *presto* elaboration. Once more a fragment of the sorrowful *andante* appears, only to give place to an *allegro brilliante,* one of the most ecstatic melodies that Verdi has written—the melody which, in the convent scene, Leonora sings to the words *Tua grazia, O Dio!* More dramatic accents, in which destiny rages, are softened briefly by some consolatory religious harmonies—the monastic element plays a vital role in this opera. A grandiose phrase of Leonora's prayer, again, given out full force by the orchestra, a recall of the exuberant, ecstatic melody (this time as a kind of variation in *staccato* eighth notes), and a forceful *coda* bring the energetic preface to a smashing close.

Those six E-naturals which began the overture sound *pianissimo* as the curtain rises on the first act. The orchestral part, far richer than those of Verdi's operas of ten years before, makes plainer than words how far the composer has travelled in a decade and how, technically at any rate, he has transcended his earlier efforts. One might point out many details of interest in this first scene. One must, however, pause an instant to signalize the duet of Leonora and Don Alvaro, with its fine, principal melody, *Ah! seguirti fino agli' ultimi confini della terra,* which, in common with all of Verdi's love music, is soaring but not erotic.

The lively folk scenes of the ensuing act, the choruses acclaiming the impending war, give place in striking fashion to the prayer intoned by pilgrims. Taken up by the rest of the throng this forms an ensemble built up with all of Verdi's cunning and theater sense, the pilgrims singing in minor, the rest in major. The scene continues, a bright canvas of motley episodes.*

The ensuing one takes us into the mountains and a monastic vicinity. With the arrival of the hapless Leonora, fate once more makes its presence felt. Leonora's prayer, *Madre, pietosa Vergine,* furnishes one of the peaks of Verdi's score. . . . The effect of the lovely prayer is enhanced when the monks, singing against it a hymn, *Venite adoremus,* provide the melody with a warmly felt tonal background. The entire ensuing episode, with duets between Leonora and the Father Guardian, culminating in the melody remembered from the overture, *Tua grazia, O Dio,* is possibly the finest sustained inspiration of the opera. Magnificent, likewise, is the great finale, with still another great melody—indeed, one of Verdi's noblest, *La Vergine degl' Angeli.*

A word as to Friar Melitone, a delightful comic character to whom falls later in the opera a mock sermon. Melitone, like Preziosilla, was one of the means Verdi adopted to shed some light athwart the tragic shadows of the play. His music is couched in an idiom which we can recognize as the forerunner

* The scenes described in this paragraph are those often cut in current productions of *La Forza.*—C. A. L.

of the style that came to such astounding fruition in *Falstaff* many years later. Melitone is, in any case, one of the really priceless individualities in *La Forza.*

The second act brings us, along with much else, a fine orchestral interlude; . . . a battle scene; and the duet for tenor and baritone, *Solenne in quest' ora,* which rightly or wrongly, is perhaps the best known and most popular number in the opera. The later portion of the act offers us attractive numbers in abundance—jubilant choruses, dances, . . . and Preziosilla's *Rataplan.* . . . The remaining popular number of the opera and one in which Verdi has risen indisputably to his fullest stature is Leonora's affecting air, in elegiac vein, the *Pace, pace, mio Dio,* one of those inspirations of the composer which was world famous long before the rest of *La Forza* and which is still, in some ways, the touching crown of the entire work.

HERBERT F. PEYSER

AMILCARE PONCHIELLI (1834–1886)

La Gioconda

Libretto by Tobio Gorria (pseudonym for Arrigo Boïto), based upon Victor Hugo's *Angelo, tyran de Padoue.* First performance in Milan, April 8, 1876.

Characters

Barnaba, a spy of the Inquisition .... Baritone
Gioconda, a ballad singer .... Soprano
La Cieca, Gioconda's blind mother .... Contralto
Zuane .... Baritone
Isepo .... Tenor
Enzo Grimaldo, a Genoese nobleman .... Tenor
Laura Adorno, Alvise's wife .... Mezzo-soprano
Alvise Badoero, leader of the Inquisition .... Bass

The Story

ACT I. The Lion's Mouth. Barnaba, spy for the Inquisition, observes the throng of gay Venetians who gather in the courtyard of the Ducal Palace to celebrate a regatta on the Grand Canal, whither they presently repair. Left alone, Barnaba cynically reflects that the Venetians have been dancing on their tombs—i.e., the gratings of the subterranean prisons (**Barnaba:** *E danzan su lor tomba*—And they danced on their tomb). Then he muses on his passion for the beautiful ballad singer La Gioconda. Gioconda now appears with her blind mother, La Cieca, who expresses her gratitude for her daughter's loving care (**Cieca,** then **Gioconda** and **Barnaba:** *Figlia, che reggi*—Daughter, who supports the trembling steps). In order to get Gioconda in his power, the spy persuades the returning populace that La Cieca is a witch and has caused the gondolier Zuane to lose the boat race. Not even the presence of Gioconda or the appearance of the sea captain Enzo, whom she loves, can protect the old woman from the angry crowd, which threatens to burn her at the stake. Alvise Badoero, leader of the Inquisition, and his wife Laura, masked, arrive just in time to save La Cieca, who turns to the kindly voice and thanks Laura by giving her her cherished rosary (**Cieca:** *Voce di donna*—The voice of a lady). The sly Barnaba, realizing that Enzo is actually a proscribed Genoese nobleman formerly in love with Laura, thinks he can win Gioconda's affection if he proves her lover to be faithless. Accordingly he tells

Enzo that he can arrange for Laura to visit Enzo's ship that very evening (**Barnaba, Enzo:** *Enzo Grimaldo*). Overjoyed, Enzo has no sooner rushed away than Barnaba dictates news of Laura's impending desertion to the public scribe Isepo; from behind a column Gioconda and La Cieca overhear, then enter church to pray. Exulting in his power, Barnaba thrusts the accusation into the bronze Lion's Mouth, repository for such missives (**Barnaba:** *O monumento!*—Oh, monument!). Maskers enter and dance; and as the sound of vespers (**Chorus:** *Angele Dei*—Angel of God) issues from St. Mark's, Gioconda departs, bewailing Enzo's betrayal of her love (**Gioconda:** *O Dio! Cuore! dono funesto*—O God! Heart! A macabre gift).

ACT II. The Rosary. Although swarms of Enzo's sailors guard his ship, which is moored beside an island in the Fusina lagoon, they do not question Barnaba when, disguised as a fisherman, he brings Isepo to spy upon the captain (**Barnaba:** *Pescator, affonda l'esca* [Barcarolle]—Fisherman, sink the bait) and then departs. Enzo appears, gives sailing orders, and, passionately awaiting Laura, extols the beauty of sky and sea (**Enzo:** *Cielo e mar!*—Sky and sea). Laura is ferried to her lover's side by Barnaba, who withdraws mockingly as the two fall into each other's arms (**Enzo, Laura:** *Deh! non turbare*—Wait! Do not disturb with tragic fears). While Enzo makes final preparations for the voyage, Laura prays (**Laura:** *Stella del marinar*—Star of the mariner). Gioconda emerges from the hiding place where she has been waiting for vengeance. Goaded by Laura's passion for Enzo (**Laura, Gioconda:** *L'amo come il fulgor*—I love him like the splendor of creation), she is about to stab her rival when she catches sight of the rosary, her mother's gift. Filial devotion prevails. Gioconda warns Laura that Alvise is in hot pursuit and offers her skiff; Laura escapes just in time, as Barnaba leads in the furious Alvise. Rather than yield to the vengeful husband, Enza puts his vessel to the torch.

ACT III. The House of Gold. To the sound of distant dance music, Alvise vows to poison his erring wife (**Alvise:** *Si! morir ella de'!*—Yes, to die is her doom). When Laura enters his study, dressed to receive his guests, he tells her that she is to die for having loved another. Then he leaves her to drink a glass of poison which he says will kill her before the song she hears is ended (**Chorus:** *La gaia canzon*—The gay song). Unknown to Alvise, however, Gioconda has slipped in and, as soon as he has departed, substitutes a sleeping potion for the poison, telling Laura she will save her.

In a magnificent hall of the Cà d'Oro, Alvise greets the nobility of Venice and offers for their entertainment the "Dance of the Hours" (**Ballet**). Suddenly Barnaba drags in La Cieca, whom he has caught praying beside Laura. Enzo, believing Laura dead, unmasks and bitterly addresses her memory (**Enzo:** *Già ti veggo immota e smorta*—I already see you immobile and deadly pale). But Gioconda, knowing that Laura lies on her bier asleep, whispers to Barnaba that she will yield to him if he can save Enzo and bring Laura's body to the Giudecca. He agrees but seizes La Cieca as hostage, while Alvise, tearing aside a curtain, reveals the motionless Laura to his horrified guests.

ACT IV. The Orfano Canal. Two street singers bear the sleeping Laura to the ruined palace where Gioconda awaits her rival. With nothing to live for the unfortunate woman resolves on suicide (**Gioconda:** *Suicidio!*). When Enzo arrives to find that Gioconda has had Laura removed from the vault, he tries to stab her, but his hand is stayed by the voice of the awakening Laura. Overcome with gratitude for the woman who has saved both him and his beloved, Enzo leads Laura to the waiting skiff; they bid Gioconda farewell (**Enzo, Laura:** *Sulle tue mani l'anima*—Our souls upon your hands). When Barnaba comes to claim his reward (**Barnaba, Gioconda** [Finale]: *Ebbrezza! delirio! Mio sognc supremo!*—Delirious ecstasy! My supreme dream), Gioconda stabs herself, leaving him to scream vainly that he has murdered her mother.

PONCHIELLI, for the prelude to *Gioconda*, has drunk at the Verdian sources. His orchestral introduction is based largely on a melody sung in the first act of the opera by Gioconda's blind mother, La Cieca, during the aria, *Voce di donna*. This phrase occurs at the point when La Cieca, thanking the noble Laura for having saved her life, gives her a rosary with the words, *A te questo rosario, che la preghiere aduna, io te le porgo—accettalo!* ("I offer you these beads which have been told in prayer—accept them!"). Since the rosary plays a cardinal part in the development of the plot, its appearance as a musical theme in the prelude is most appropriate. Pitted against it is the dark, rhythmical motif of the villain, Barnaba, who at the end of the opera is to murder the blind woman. Although Ponchielli does not play his motifs so masterfully one against the other as does Verdi in the similar *Aïda* prelude, the effect is at once dignified and dramatic.

When the curtain has risen, we are in the hands of Boïto, who has called for a grand opening chorus of Venetians bound for the regatta. This Ponchielli carries off with *éclat*. But the basic musical weakness of *Gioconda* is revealed when the villain, Barnaba, appears. This character's lines are often sung in *recitative* (dramatic musical accents approaching the range of human speech in their inflection), and this is the composer's great weakness. When Ponchielli can sing, his melodies carry conviction and often beauty. But when he speaks, his recitative is dry and brittle, the musical line lacks vitality.

There follow in short order the entrance of Gioconda and her mother, the big ensemble in which Barnaba inflames the populace of Venice against La Cieca, the entrance of the tenor, Enzo, and finally the intercession of the haughty Alvise Badoero and his lady, Laura, when they spare the life of the blind woman. Since choral song and full-blown action are called for here, Ponchielli is in his element, offering a scene of dramatic movement and intensity not unlike the best moments of *Mefistofele* and the later *Otello*. The appearance of Alvise and his consort, accompanied by an armed guard, as they descend the Staircase of the Giants to the courtyard of the Doge's palace, carries a magnificent visual impression and the music supports the moment well. La Cieca's aria of thanks to Laura, *Voce di Donna*, is one of the staples of the contralto repertory, smooth and grateful to sing. But it is in the climax of this episode that Ponchielli shows his real theatrical genius. As the crowd disperses, Laura and her husband enter the Church of St. Mark, quiet comes over the courtyard, and Gioconda—with her mother—bids farewell to her lover, Enzo. *Come t'amo!* she exclaims. ("How I adore you!") At this point, as the motif of the rosary rises serenely from the orchestra in an E-flat major harmony, the voice of Gioconda soars on the phrase *t'amo* to a soft, sustained high B-flat, which the soprano holds as she crosses the stage toward the church. It is this moment, cutting like a shaft of light across the score, for which the true *Gioconda* devotee waits. By it he judges the vocal and dramatic worth of the artist who is singing the title role. . . .

The other numbers in this act are a conventional duet between Barnaba and Enzo followed by a soliloquy for the villain. Barnaba's monologue, *O monumento*, is perhaps the greatest disappointment of the score, for while the words are evocative and exciting, conjuring up the grandeur and cruelty of seventeenth-century Venice, the music is cast in the pedestrian type of recitative which Ponchielli seemed rarely able to avoid when writing in this form. The finale of the act, however, brings ample compensation. Here, for complete theatrical effect, Boïto and Ponchielli introduce first a chorus and ballet, then an offstage church organ and ensemble which prepare the way for a religious choral mood on stage, and finally the most beautiful melody in the opera: Gioconda's despairing *O Dio! Cuore! dono funesto!* ("O God! Heart! A macabre gift"), which—sung above the chorus —is used from this point on throughout the opera as the motif of the heroine's fruitless love for Enzo. It is on a note of nostalgia that the first-act curtain falls.

The second act, which takes place on an island in the Fusina Lagoon, concerns itself with sky and sea (*Cielo e mar*), as we are soon told in Enzo's famous aria. There come in rapid succession the opening chorus of sailors and children, Barnaba's fisherman ballad, and then the sentimental *Cielo e mar* itself. All of this is only background, setting the stage for the arrival of Laura, for it is about the mezzo-soprano that the second act revolves. First we hear her ecstatic duet with Enzo. Later, when the hero, for no apparent reason, goes below deck, Laura is left alone and sings the aria, *Stella del marinar!* ("Star of the mariner"). This prayer to the Virgin, like Barnaba's *O monumento* of the first act, is unfortunately musical rhetoric. It does not take wing. But a moment later, with the appearance of Gioconda, the opera is galvanized into full life and yields one of its richest moments: the duet of the two rivals for Enzo's love, *L'amo come il fulgor del creato!* ("I love him like the splendor of creation!"). This is, in its exuberance, no tune for musical purists—nor, for that matter, does its execution usually bring joy to the proponents of equalized vocal scales. Both of the women must sing from the marrow, bringing to the smoldering music all the passion its earthly sentiment demands. By way of contrast, the rest of the act is a bit pallid. Despite all the outward excitement of a naval pursuit and a burning boat, the score remains somewhat conventional; and, indeed, the music sung by the despairing sailors to the lines *Ah! più speranza, no, no, non v'è!* ("No hope is left us!") is not too dissimilar in melodic outline and rhythmical accent to the jubilant regatta chorus with which the opera opens, *Feste e pane!* ("Sport and feasting!").

In the third act *Gioconda* reaches at once its nadir and its zenith. The first of the two scenes, although well-drawn dramatically, is musically thin. Set in a private chamber of the *Cà d'Oro,* it begins with an aria allotted to Alvise, *Si, morir, ella de'!* ("Yes, to die is her doom!"), in which the proud nobleman decides that he will eliminate his wife, Laura, who has deceived him. Here, as in the preceding arias of Barnaba and Laura (note how, in the construction of Boïto's libretto, a solo air has been apportioned to every leading character), the music is impoverished and rhetorical. There follows a short duet for Laura and her husband in the course of which an offstage chorus sings a lilting barcarolle, one of the best melodies in the opera. Alvise informs Laura that, by the time this chorus has ceased, she is to drink a vial of poison. For some reason known only to the librettist, he leaves the room; Gioconda slips in during the offstage song, gives Laura a sleeping potion in place of Alvise's poison, which she secretes on her own person, and then laments the fate that makes her the instrument of Laura's passion for Enzo. As Laura collapses under the spell of the potion, the theme of Gioconda's hopeless love, *Ah! o cuore, dono funesto,* returns in the orchestra, to be taken up at length vocally by the unhappy heroine.

The second tableau of the act finds Ponchielli at his most resourceful in the technique of stage movement. This is luxurious grand opera and, artistically, the scene reaches a high degree of merit. The guests of Alvise assemble in the sumptuous great hall of the *Cà d'Oro.* To entertain them, the nobleman has arranged a splendid ballet in which the dancers impersonate the hours of the day and night. Despite many strictures over a course of years since *Gioconda* was first produced, the *Dance of the Hours* remains a milestone in choreographic music for the theater. It is well constructed, danceable, deftly orchestrated, and, above all, lends a strong glow and linear support to the scenario of the ballet itself.

At this point in the opera Ponchielli, instead of allowing the music to lag, as it might well have done after the brilliant ending of the *Dance of the Hours,* takes second wind and leads us into a finale that can rank with the noblest choral climaxes in the repertory. Of interest is the fact that this finale belongs to the second version of *Gioconda,* produced at Genoa three years after the opera's première at La Scala. In its ultimate form the episode can be compared favorably with similar places in the stage works of Gluck, Beethoven, Bellini, and Verdi. Based on a melody sung by Enzo when he learns of the supposed death of Laura, *Già ti veggo immota e smorta* ("I already see you immobile and deadly pale"), the music reaches a climax of shattering force as Alvise proclaims himself the murderer. Choral forces and solo voices are interlocked with the orchestra in a surging pattern; the great doors at the rear of the hall are thrown open, and Laura is seen upon her bier. Suddenly the orchestra sings alone the melody of *Già ti veggo,* reinforced by an amazing sonority and power that must thrill even the least responsive member of the audience. This scene is pure theater in its massing of colors and of action, its manipulation of chorus, ballet, and principals; and never once does the music let it down. The third-act curtain of *Gioconda* must be accounted, without reserve, as one of the glories of Italian opera.

For the conclusion of the work Ponchielli and his librettist have dispensed with all thought of external stage effect or of musical pomp. The drama has gone inward and the music, too, has taken on a nobler and more somber cast. After a brief orchestral introduction to the last act based on the O *cuore, dono funesto!* motif, we are led almost directly to the great aria of Gioconda, *Suicidio!,* as she sits alone in her hiding place on the island of Giudecca, filled with thoughts of approaching death. Only a heroic soprano can do justice to this solo which, with its top notes of steel and lower tones of molten lead, demands from a singer the utmost in vocal line, power, and nuance.

In the episode which follows, Enzo arrives seeking the body of Laura. The character of the tenor, already well defined with his third-act *Già ti veggo,* is here further expanded by a fine duet with Gioconda. And then the voice of Laura is heard. The noblewoman, safe in the den of Gioconda, has revived from her sleep and prepares to flee from Venice with Enzo. Two affecting musical reminiscences mark the couple's preparation for flight: the offstage *barcarolle,* sung once again by an invisible chorus, and a *reprise* of the rosary motif, associated with the memory of Gioconda's mother, whose life had once been saved by Laura. It is in debt for this kindness that Gioconda has renounced Enzo and helped Laura to escape. As she bids the lovers farewell, the three characters sing an extended trio which, for expressive value, is one of the most commanding features of the opera. But here in the fourth act all of the music maintains a consistently noble value which the three preceding acts, with their unevenness of quality, could not have led the listener to imagine.

As the trio ends and the lovers depart, the orchestra soars in a bold flash and then recedes into the murky pattern of the Barnaba motif as the villain appears to claim Gioconda. From this point to the end, inspiration rules in music and drama. The poetic lines are clipped and terse, their tonal treatment grimly powerful. As Gioconda puts off her would-be lover by adorning herself with gems, she sings the melodies in which she is heard at the great palaces of Venice—for Gioconda is a professional singer of songs. Here Ponchielli has made the dramatic soprano voice encompass passages of coloratura difficulty which rise ever higher in intensity until finally, just before Gioconda yields to Barnaba, she stabs herself. The opera ends unconventionally as Barnaba, kneeling beside the dead girl, shouts in her ear that he has killed her mother. There is no sustained musical climax for the baritone at this point, no intention of vocal display. His cry of rage, as he rushes away, is muffled by the final surge of the orchestra.

ROBERT LAWRENCE

RICHARD WAGNER (1813–1883)

Lohengrin

Libretto by the composer. First performance in Weimar, August 28, 1850.

Characters

The King's Herald	Baritone
King Henry the Fowler	Bass
Frederick of Telramund	Baritone
Ortrud	Mezzo-soprano
Elsa of Brabant	Soprano
Lohengrin	Tenor

The Story

ACT I. King Henry the Fowler, visiting tenth-century Antwerp to raise an army, holds court under an oak tree on the banks of the river Scheldt. He calls on the regent, Frederick of Telramund, to explain the local disorders. Telramund accuses his ward, Elsa, sister to the heir of Brabant, of murdering her brother. Elsa is summoned and describes the vision in which she beholds a knight in shining armor who will champion her cause (**Elsa:** *Einsam in trüben Tagen*—Lonely, in troubled days). Thrice summoned by the herald, Lohengrin appears, drawn up the river in a boat by a swan, to which he bids farewell (**Lohengrin:** *Nun sei bedankt, mein lieber Schwan*—Now be thanked, my beloved Swan). He betroths himself to Elsa on condition that she shall never ask his name, rank, or birthplace. If she does so, he must leave. On her assent, the king invokes divine guidance (**King Henry:** *Mein Herr und Gott*—My Lord and God), and the knight proceeds to defeat Telramund in a duel, thereby establishing Elsa's innocence.

ACT II. Huddling before dawn in the palace courtyard, Telramund's ambitious consort, Ortrud, spurs him on to assail Lohengrin's power. No sooner has Elsa, appearing on the balcony, voiced her serenity (**Elsa:** *Euch Lüften*—You breezes) than Ortrud appeals to her pagan gods for help (**Ortrud:** *Entweihte Götter*—Profane gods) and attempts to sow distrust in the mind of the bride. In a duet Elsa proffers friendship which Ortrud threatens to turn to her own use (**Elsa, Ortrud:** *Kehr' bei mir ein*—Come enter here). As day dawns, the nobles assemble, four traitors siding with Telramund against Lohengrin, whom the herald proclaims Guardian of Brabant. The courtiers welcome Elsa in her wedding procession (**Chorus:** *Gesegnet soll sie schreiten*—May blessings shower upon you). At the steps of the minster, first Ortrud and then Telramund attempt to break up the wedding, accusing Lohengrin of secrecy; but as the curtains fall, the king leads the couple into the church.

ACT III. Elsa's maidens escort her to the bridal chamber in the well-known chorus (**Chorus:** *Treulich geführt*—Guided by us). The rapturous duet of Elsa and Lohengrin (**Elsa, Lohengrin:** *Das süsse Lied verhallt*—The sweet song has died away) gives way to growing anxiety on the part of the bride, who at length questions the knight. Telramund and the four treacherous nobles interrupt the scene, but Lohengrin strikes his enemy lifeless and declares that he will make fitting answer before the king.

Again on the banks of the Scheldt, King Henry holds his assembly. Lohengrin reveals that he has slain Telramund in self-defense and explains his parentage (**Lohengrin:** *In fernem Land*—On distant shores): Parsifal was his father, the temple of the Holy Grail at Monsalvat is his home, and Lohengrin his name. As he departs in his boat, drawn by a swan, the bird vanishes and Elsa's brother Godfrey takes his place. A dove descends to draw Lohengrin's boat away as Elsa dies in Godfrey's arms.

LIKE almost everything that Wagner wrote, *Lohengrin* had deep connections with his life. From the heights of the loneliness to which as man and artist he had soared, Wagner longed for the same companionship with a woman which Lohengrin sought as he descended from Monsalvat, a woman who could believe in him even if she did not know whence he came. This wish of his is linked with an ancient myth which forbids the question as to ultimate knowledge and which took a new form in *Lohengrin*. Not altogether unjustifiably has Lohengrin's mysterious origin been connected with Wagner's birth and its problematic character.

Lohengrin seeks release and wishes to bring it about. But Elsa's release is not complete after Lohengrin rescues her from the dark power of Ortrud and Telramund. She seeks further release through that fateful question which destroys her happiness. Lohengrin, who came to free and to be freed, must himself give up the happiness of this earth and woman's love. The opera is full of unsolved mysteries, of the romantic world of the irrational, which enchants as it baffles the imagination of the spectator.

. . . . .

Deliberately Wagner turned from the old overture form and created in the prelude a free symphonic piece with a poetic basis. He explained that it symbolizes the miracle of the Holy Grail. Celestial brilliance enchants the ear in the sound of the eight-fold divided violins whose prolonged tones suggest the infinite spaces of heaven. The closer the Holy Grail comes, the more intense grows the desire and pain in the breast of the observer, until the holy vessel is unveiled to the gaze of the favored beholders. Slowly the legion of angels disappears again in the heights. Trumpets and trombones sound the climax after fifty-six bars of ever more intensified harmonies. The prelude plays through seventy-six bars and relates nothing of the tragic end of the opera, but closes with that quotation of the choral passage in the last act, in which King Henry and the people of Brabant join after they have heard Lohengrin's story:

Hör ich so seine höchste Art bewähren
Entbrennt mein Aug' in heiligen Wonnezähren.

Again Wagner seems to refer to that understanding which he longed for from his era, a thought now expressed with religious ecstasy.

Heroic music with trumpets, chorus, and ensemble statements reminds us that this romantic work has been called, with some justification, a choral opera. It is beside the point that the men of Brabant sometimes fall into that ominous *Liedertafel* style, which, since Mendelssohn, has ruled German singing societies —even here in America.

The chorus here fills a function similar to that enjoyed by the Greek tragedians. Wagner wished to express the characteristics of the German people. When the knights accompany the procession to the church in a double chorus, with a verse to express good wishes, that melody serves for an orchestral base, which resounded for the first time when Elsa at night mounted to the balcony to give free vent to her feeling of happiness. The famous bridal chorus is also composed in popular style. . . .

It has often been pointed out that the unity of all elements of the opera, the perfect balance of word, music, singing, declamation, orchestra, and choir, has brought about the unparalleled effect of this opera. Thus the orchestra in *Lohengrin* has not yet been assigned the prominent role which Wagner gave it later. It still lacks exclusive melodic leadership, nor do the vocal parts offer the declamation which we find in *Tristan* and *Die Meistersinger*. . . .

In *Lohengrin* Wagner [nevertheless] augmented the classical orchestra for purposes of color. Of all the various instruments there are three of each variety demanded: three flutes, three oboes (two oboes and one English horn), three clarinets (two clarinets and one bass clarinet), three bassoons, three trombones (two tenor trombones and one bass), one bass tuba, three trumpets, four horns, drums, and cymbals. Through the dividing of the wind instruments into three, every chord of the instrument section may be colored brightly or darkly. . . .

Wagner instrumentalizes according to psychological rather than exclusively musical principles. For specific persons or moods a specific instrumentation is demanded. Elsa is almost entirely characterized with soft wood-wind instrumentation, as at her first entry, the balcony scene, and the bridal procession. King Henry is always accompanied by trombones and trumpets.

Notice also the tonal contrasts between the king's speech and the entrance of Elsa, or the different coloring of the duet of Telramund and Ortrud, as compared with the following balcony scene. For the martial music in the bridge passage from the second to the third scene in the third act, eight trumpets in different keys are used, which symbolize the noise and bustle of the horses. Just as we observe a unity of instrumentation, so can we also speak of a unity of harmonic characterization. In spite of the changing modulations in the different scenes one main key prevails, as, for instance, in the first scene of the second act, between Ortrud and Telramund, F-sharp minor; in the second scene in the bridal procession, B-flat major; in the speech of the king in the first scene of the first act, C major, etc.

The principle of Wagner's classical leading motif is not yet carried out in *Lohengrin*. Thematic changes, in comparison with those of Wagner's later operas, are still very limited. There is a change of color rather than an inner change, but we can see how the themes are fitted to the changing scenes. The Lohengrin motif in the finale of the third act, when the swan appears and Lohengrin takes his leave, starts in major instead of minor. Other motifs are shortened, expanded, or divided.

Of the greatest poetic significance is the technique with which the same motifs are used in different places. This is true of the motif of Lohengrin as knight (first act, third scene) and the motif of the forbidden question. The knight motif is chiefly voiced with horns and trumpets, at Elsa's words, *Wie ich ihn sah, war er mir nah,* by three trumpets *pianissimo,* before that by three oboes and three flutes with the accompaniment of clarinets, harp, trumpets, and strings—in the latter case, in A-flat major, in the former in A major. The essential motif of the forbidden question appears for the most part as an admonition or threat. Its final invocation occurs when Elsa in the third act approaches the King's throne. The Grail motif resounds when Lohengrin proclaims Elsa's purity, but achieves its fullest realization only when the knight of the swan returns to the realm of the Holy Grail. It is woven into the entire story.

From the melodic point of view *Lohengrin* assumes a special position. While *Tannhäuser* is still sprinkled with arias such as the song of Venus which is in the tradition of older grand opera, the melodic line of *Lohengrin* develops from the word and spirit of the text. The melody does not yet depend completely on the spoken accent of the words as in the case of the later operas of Wagner. Though the language is treated as of equal importance with the music, *Lohengrin's* melody still sings. For his procedure in this opera Wagner used the designation "dramatic melody"; the harmony between note and word which in the later works of the poet-composer was so strongly emphasized, is here in complete balance. *Lohengrin* lacks the archaistic expressions which are often so awkward in the *Ring* and *Tristan.* Wagner's union of word and note is most complete in the scene between Ortrud and Telramund. Here the vocal part follows only the accents of passion. But even here the principal form is not abandoned, inasmuch as the two singers unite at the close of the scene for an oath of vengeance, declaiming in unison.

The musical form of the finale approaches the form of a Mozart *coda.* Such uniformity even as to rhythm and meter was never again reached by Wagner. . . .

From these characteristics it becomes evident that *Lohengrin* serves both to close an outworn development and to begin a new. In the year 1858 Liszt wrote: "With *Lohengrin* the old world of opera comes to an end. The spirit hovers over the waters and there is light."

PAUL NETTL

GAETANO DONIZETTI (1797–1848)

Lucia di Lammermoor

Libretto by Salvatore Cammarano, based upon Sir Walter Scott's *The Bride of Lammermoor*. First performance at Naples, September 26, 1835.

Characters

Normanno, follower of Lord Ashton .... Tenor
Lord Enrico Ashton .... Baritone
Raimondo, Lucia's tutor .... Bass
Lucia Ashton .... Soprano
Alisa, Lucia's companion .... Soprano
Edgardo .... Tenor
Lord Arturo Bucklaw, Lucia's prospective husband
Tenor

The Story

ACT I. Enrico Ashton, Lord of Lammermoor, Scotland, in 1669, laments his declining fortunes, which only his sister Lucia can save, by marrying Lord Arturo Bucklaw. Raimondo, Lucia's tutor, reminds him that Lucia is still mourning her mother's death; but Normanno, a follower of Enrico, reveals that Lucia has daily been meeting a lover whom he believes to be Edgardo of Ravenswood, Enrico's mortal enemy. Enrico is enraged (**Enrico:** *Cruda, funesta smania*—Raw, deadly passion) and, when hunters confirm Normanno's suspicions as to the identity of the lover (**Chorus:** *Come vinti da stanchezza*—As conquered by fatigue), vows vengeance (**Enrico:** *La pietade in suo favore*—My sorrow for him).

At a moonlit fountain near Ravenswood, Lucia, accompanied by her duenna, Alisa, comes for her tryst with Edgardo. She is frightened by the fountain where a Ravenswood once cast his murdered ladylove (**Lucia:** *Regnava nel silenzio*—The night reigns in silence) but dismisses her fears in the thought of Edgardo's love (**Lucia:** *Quando rapita in estasi*—When raptured in ecstasy). Edgardo arrives and tells Lucia that on the morrow he must leave for France. He wants before leaving to ask Enrico for her hand, but she dissuades him because of the still bitter feud between their families. (Enrico killed Edgardo's father and wrongfully seized Edgardo's lands.) They therefore plight their troth before God and bid each other a tender farewell (**Lucia, Ed-**

gardo: *Verranno a te sull' aure*—My ardent sighs will come to you on the wind).

ACT II. Normanno and Enrico, who have intercepted the letters Edgardo has sent Lucia, now plot to force her into marriage with Lord Arturo by preparing a forged letter which indicates that Edgardo is unfaithful to her. Lucia berates her brother for refusing to allow her to marry Edgardo (**Lucia:** *Il pallor funesto*—The deadly pallor); his answer is the forged letter. Lucia reads it and is in despair (**Lucia, Enrico:** *Soffriva nel pianto*—She was suffering in tears). Enrico again orders Lucia to marry Arturo; she protests that she would prefer to die, but Raimondo counsels her to do her brother's bidding.

The wedding festivities proceed (**Chorus:** *Per te d'immenso giubilo*—For you immense joy), but no sooner is the wedding contract signed than Edgardo returns to claim his bride. All present join in expressing their mingled emotions (**Sextet:** *Chi mi frena in tal momento?*—Who can restrain me at this moment?).

ACT III.* At Lammermoor the wedding guests are still enjoying themselves when Raimondo enters to announce that Lucia has murdered Arturo and has lost her mind (**Raimondo:** *Dalle stanze, ove Lucia*—From the chambers where Lucia went with her husband). Lucia now appears and, in a trance, greets Edgardo, whom she imagines she is marrying (**Lucia:** *Il dolce suono mi colpì di sua voce*—The sweet sound of his voice struck me; *Oh! gioia che si sente e non si dice!*—O joy which is felt but not spoken). As Enrico, Raimondo, and the guests watch in horror, Lucia now relives the scene following the signing of the marriage contract, begs Edgardo to have mercy on her (**Lucia:** *Spargi d'amaro pianto*—Cover my earthly veil with bitter tears), and falls near death.

Edgardo wanders amongst the tombs of his ancestors and muses on his anticipated death in the forthcoming duel with Enrico (**Edgardo:** *Fra poco a me ricoverò*—In a while a grave will shelter me). People coming from Lammermoor tell Edgardo that Lucia has lost her mind and now lies dying (**Chorus:** *Fur le nozze a lei funeste*—Her marriage was fatal to her). A bell signals her death; Edgardo mourns her fate, vows to join her (**Edgardo:** *Tu che a Dio spiegasti l'ali*—You who opened your wings to God), then plunges a dagger into his heart.

* A scene in which Enrico challenges Edgardo to a duel is customarily omitted at the beginning of this act.

LUCIA belongs to the category of horror opera. But it is a different kind of horror piece than, for instance, Puccini's *Tosca* or Strauss' *Elektra*, where the composer in each case has done his utmost to reflect the sanguine and nerve-racking quality of the plot in his music. If anything, Donizetti's music softens rather than enhances the gloomy character of the action. But in spite of the sentimental nature of much of the score *Lucia* is a true child of the romantic period in which it was born.

. . . . .

Lucia is, as a whole, such easy listening that it may seem gratuitous to call attention to this or that number. It is, however, possible for some hearers to concentrate to such a degree on the most famous numbers of the work, such as the Sextet and the Mad Scene, that they may overlook other pages in which the genius of Donizetti reveals itself at its most characteristic. The first two choruses of the opening scene, *Percorrete le spiagge vicine* and a little later the lilting *Come vinti da stanchezza*, are typical of their composer. They have, however, a slightly definable touch which some have declared to be Scotch. . . .

More important is Enrico Ashton's vigorous expression of his intention to avenge his wrongs upon Edgardo Ravenswood, regardless of the pain it may cause his sister, Lucia (*La pietade in suo favore*), which concludes in a spirited chorus of his retainers. Attention should be paid to the instrumental introduction to the second scene, the principal feature of which is a beautiful harp solo.

Thereafter Lucia's entrance air (*Regnava nel silenzio*) is heard followed by its livelier and more brilliant section (*Quando rapita in estasi*), unquestionably one of the finest moments of the opera. The hearer is scarcely likely to remain indifferent to the duet of Lucia and Edgardo (with Lucia's lovely phrase, *Deh! ti placa*) and the closing song of farewell (*Verranno a te sull' aure*) with its waltzlike lilt.

On the entrance of Lucia in the second act notice should be taken of the graceful and long-spun melody in the violins accompanying the soprano's words (*Ti rimprovero tacendo il mio strazio*) and a little later of Enrico's energetic melody (*Se tradirmi*) then developed into a duet between brother and sister.

The ensuing scene with the marriage contract begins with a straightforward festive chorus (*Per te d'immenso giubilo*). But the climax of the scene which arrives in a very brief time and which no listener can miss, is, of course, the great Sextet (*Chi mi frena*). The music from this point to the close of the act, with Edgardo's maledictions and vows of vengeance, is among the great episodes of Italian opera. We have been assured that Donizetti has written similar things in other operas (in *Anna Bolena,* for one), but as these works have vanished from the stage, the close of the second act of *Lucia di Lammermoor* may be conceded its unique eminence.

A scene of defiance between Edgardo and Enrico Ashton is usually omitted from the Metropolitan production, so that the third act is largely a matter of Lucia's Mad Scene and the death of Edgardo by suicide by the tombs of his ancestors. But the listener should be advised not to overlook Raimondo's narration of Lucia's sudden access of madness (*Dalle stanze, ove Lucia*) or the beautiful choral passage interrupting it (*Oh! qual funesto avvenimento*). The Mad Scene itself, though usually considered a brilliant florid showpiece, is in reality a good deal more. It recalls dramatically the melody of the love duet in the first act, and the orchestra has one particularly tender passage accompanying the mad woman's *Ah l'inno suona di nozze.*

Ordinarily Lucia's *Spargi d'amaro pianto* concludes the first half of the act. There is, however, a brief episode between Enrico and Raimondo . . . in which the preacher reproaches Lord Ashton for causing his sister's misfortune. The cemetery scene is ushered in by a fateful orchestral introduction. Then, after Edgardo's somber monologue, the chorus enters to apprise him, in a simple and charming melody, rather out of keeping with the sorrowful character of the words (*Fur le nozze a lei funeste*), of the death of his beloved. Edgardo sings out his life in the celebrated air (*Tu che a Dio spiegasti l'ali*) which countless repetitions have not robbed of its moving quality.

HERBERT F. PEYSER

GIACOMO PUCCINI (1858–1924)

Madama Butterfly

Libretto by Giuseppe Giacosa and Luigi Illica, based on the play by David Belasco and John Luther Long. First performance in Milan, February 17, 1904.

Characters

Benjamin Franklin Pinkerton, Lt. U.S. Navy .. Tenor
Goro, a marriage broker .... Tenor
Suzuki, Cio-Cio-San's servant .... Mezzo-soprano
Sharpless, U.S. Consul at Nagasaki .... Baritone
Cio-Cio-San (Madama Butterfly) .... Soprano
The Imperial Commissioner .... Baritone
The Bonze, Cio-Cio-San's uncle .... Bass
Yamadori, a wealthy suitor .... Baritone
Kate Pinkerton .... Soprano

The Story

ACT I. From a flowering terrace U.S. Navy Lieutenant B. F. Pinkerton inspects the house he has leased on a hill above the harbor of Nagasaki from the Japanese broker Goro. This officious little person has also procured him a Japanese wife—Cio-Cio-San, who is known as Madame Butterfly—and three servants, one of whom is Suzuki. Pinkerton confesses to the American consul, Sharpless, his fancy for the prospective bride (**Pinkerton:** *Amore o grillo*—Love or fancy) but admits that he does not regard the contract as permanent. The older man warns him that the Japanese girl may take her marriage seriously. Surrounded by her friends, Butterfly joyously arrives for the wedding (**Butterfly:** *Ancora un passo or via*—Just one more step). She explains to Sharpless and Pinkerton that she was forced to work as a geisha to support her family. Her relatives crowd around the marriage feast but desert Butterfly at the curse of her priestly uncle, the Bonze, who has learned that she has espoused Christianity for the sake of her future husband. Pinkerton orders all the relatives to leave; Butterfly changes from her wedding dress to a robe of white, and the act closes with a passionate love scene (**Butterfly, Pinkerton:** *Dolce notte*—Night of rapture).

ACT II. Three years later the deserted Butterfly sits in the living room of her house, asking Suzuki how many pennies are left them. Full of faith that Pinkerton will return, Butterfly tries to convince her maid (**Butterfly:** *Un bel dì*—One fine day). She is visited by Goro and Sharpless, who try vainly to persuade her to accept a wealthy suitor, Prince Yamadori. Goro and Yamadori leave. The Consul starts to read her a letter from Pinkerton (**Sharpless:** *Incominciate*—Begin, I beg you). When she tells him that she has borne Pinkerton a child (**Butterfly:** *Che tua madre dovrà prenderti*—Your mother will have to take you), he cannot bear to tell her that Pinkerton has married again and leaves. Suzuki drags in Goro who has been lurking outside; Butterfly threatens to kill him for saying her child is illegitimate, then throws him out. Cannon in the harbor announce the return of Pinkerton's ship, and Butterfly and Suzuki adorn the house with flowers (**Butterfly, Suzuki:** *Gettiamo a mani piene*—In handfuls let us scatter), preparing to watch at the window for the lieutenant's coming. Distant muted voices hum the melody of Pinkerton's letter.

ACT III. The sun rises on the same scene, where Butterfly is sleeplessly awaiting Pinkerton. She takes the child away to rest (**Butterfly:** *Dormi, amor mio*—Sleep, love of mine). The fickle lieutenant arrives with his American wife, Kate, and Sharpless to take the child. Pinkerton and Sharpless try to enlist Suzuki's aid in breaking the news to Butterfly; Pinkerton is full of remorse at Butterfly's faithfulness (**Pinkerton:** *Addio, fiorito asil*—Farewell, flowered shelter of joy and love). He leaves, unable to face his Japanese wife. When Kate, Suzuki, and Sharpless tell her the news, Butterfly promises that Pinkerton can have his son if he will call for him in half an hour. When all have left, Butterfly prepares to die. She then bids her child farewell (**Butterfly:** *Tu, piccolo iddio*—Beloved idol), places an American flag and a doll in his hands, and mortally wounds herself with her father's dagger. She dies just as Sharpless and Pinkerton return for the child.

IF OPERAGOERS had been as familiar with Debussy and, specifically, with *Pelléas et Mélisande* when they first heard *Butterfly* in 1904 as they have since become, it is hardly likely that Puccini's tragedy would have sounded as strange to them as it first did. What struck its early hearers most forcibly was the distinctive atmosphere it evoked and maintained. The Italianism of the music is scarcely ever in question; the Puccini *clichés* are strewn through the score. But it is particularly the harmony, inspired in such abundance by procedures domesticated by Debussy, which gives so many pages of *Butterfly* a mood of its own. These augmented intervals, these curiously altered harmonies, these parallel fifths and octaves, these secondary chords with strange suspensions and dissonances unexpectedly resolved or not resolved at all—these and much more emanate from Debussy's workshop, though without the sensitiveness, subtlety, and fluid movement that French master brought to them. It is by these essentially harmonic means, rather than by exotic rhythms, melodic formations, and special instrumental effects (abundant though they are) that Puccini creates with more or less verisimilitude an operatic Japan. He cannot rid his system of Wagner . . . though he is less barefaced in his citations than time and again in *Tosca.* He uses brief recurrent themes, figures, and *ostinati* as well as broad arches of melody, songful, swelling, and basically very much alive in its component parts.

Let us glance at a few of the high points of the score: the opera opens with an introduction which for a moment or two gives fugal treatment to a lively subject. . . . Before the end of the introduction a second, more rhythmic theme appears. Scraps of the fugal subject punctuate the talk of Pinkerton and Goro, whose chatter is also labelled with a little reiterated one-bar phrase made up of two chords over a staccato figure. The *scherzando* quality of the music continues, with reiterations of early material. A light, piquant melody *"of the chopstick order"* (Ernest Newman) at Goro's words *Qui verran: L'Ufficiale del registro* can scarcely escape the hearer. But not till the entrance of the Consul, Sharpless, and his dialogue with Pinkerton, does the music take on an outright lyrical character. As the naval officer motions Sharpless to a seat, the orchestra sounds the first measures of the *Star-Spangled Banner.* Out of this the composer proceeds to develop one of the principal melodies of the opera, *Dovunque al mondo.* The lyric current sweeps on. The passages based on the phrase accompanying *Salvo a poscioglierni ogni mese* are one of the high points of the first act, and there is a recurrence of the *Star-Spangled Banner* quotation as Pinkerton sings the words "America forever!" Another typical Puccinian tune, *Amore o grillo,* begins shortly afterwards and expands in sweeping cantilena.

The arrival of Cio-Cio-San and her relatives, whose voices are heard backstage before they actually come into view, brings us the music which will be associated with the fragile charm and the sweetness of Butterfly. It is in two parts, the first a *largo* phrase culminating in a chord characterized by an augmented fifth and blending with the voices of the bride's girl companions with entrancing effect. The second part, a 6–4 melody in which Butterfly's whole devotion and tenderness seem concentrated, broadens and reaches its climax as Cio-Cio-San concludes her entrance air (incidentally, one of the most difficult entrances in opera) on a soaring high D-flat.

The ensuing scene, in which Butterfly and her relatives as well as Pinkerton, Sharpless, Goro, and Suzuki take part, belongs to the finest portions of the work. Here Puccini has achieved charming effects of characterization with uncommon skill. The orchestral writing abounds in delightful conceits. As a painter of delicate musical miniatures the composer here accomplished things he never equalled elsewhere. Two themes which detach themselves from the canvas we shall do well to notice—one in E-flat minor at Sharpless' "Miss Butterfly"; the other, a sternly expressive one heard as Cio-Cio-San contemplates reverently the sheath of the dagger with which, at the close of the opera, she brings about her own death.

Before we reach the great love duet which concludes the act, we hear another striking episode, the dread curse launched by the Bonze because Butterfly has flown in the face of tradition by marrying a foreigner. Appalled by the Bonze's raging imprecations, the friends and relatives withdraw muttering maledictions from the distance. Pinkerton comforts and reassures his trembling bride, and their duet opens with a sweetly caressing phrase in A major as the groom sings the words, *Viene la sera.* The scene which follows and develops at length, but with great theatrical cunning and cumulative melodic effect, is one of Puccini's happiest inspirations. It reaches its peak in the fullest expansion of the love theme heard on Cio-Cio-San's first entrance and dies away in a melting *decrescendo* as the curtains close. No thought here of Far Easterners in exotic settings! An Italian soprano and tenor are singing out their hearts with never a thought of anything but the conventional operatic stage and the palpitating audience out front!

An exotic introduction opens the second act. Suzuki prays to an orchestral accompaniment with soft, strange harmonies. To call the attention of the gods Suzuki softly strikes a little bell. A strong descending theme in the orchestra asserts itself and pervades not a little of the early part of the scene. It is a derivative from the vigorous phrase to which attention was called in the first act during the gathering of the wedding guests. But the outstanding number of the act and, peradventure, of the entire opera is the aria, *Un bel dì,* in which Cio-Cio-San envisions the return of her husband. Here again, on a very simple and even obvious melodic formula, Puccini builds up a number unfailing in its emotional punch. It is unfortunately impossible to call attention to the many striking features of this act. Two of them, however, cling stubbornly to the memory. The first is the mellifluous duet sung by Butterfly and Suzuki, when they scatter the blossoms of the cherry trees in honor of Pinkerton's expected return. Here again Puccini is Italian first and Japanese a poor second. The next is the pathetic scene of the fruitless vigil, with the child and the faithful Suzuki dropping off to sleep and Butterfly, unshakable in her trust, watching for her beloved the whole night through. It is a singular piece of music, with a background of softly humming voices and a long-breathed melody given out under an accompaniment of detached, staccato chords. A long-drawn passage, monotonous, if you will, but providing just the drowsy atmosphere for a scene of heart-searching poignance in its very monotony.

An extended and elaborate interlude, cunningly employing a whole series of short, cutting themes and longspun lyric melodies, heard for the most part in preceding scenes, divides the second from the third act. It does not in the least give the impression of being an afterthought, as one might gather considering that it belongs to the revised version of the opera. Once more we hear singing backstage—this time the voices of sailors in the harbor. When the curtain rises, we see the unhappy Butterfly still at watch. Dawn has come, and the gradual animation that fills the music depicts with psychological veracity the break of day. A series of ninth chords, progressing now chromatically, now in whole tones, reminds the hearer of Puccini's debt to Debussy. . . .

As Cio-Cio-San, at Suzuki's behest, retires to her chamber to rest, she sings to her still sleeping baby a touching and simple lullaby, *Dormi, amor mio,* quite un-Puccinian in character and of narrow melodic compass like a northern folk song. Between the two short strophes of the tune Suzuki interjects, in the manner of a *ritornelle,* the little phrase *Povera Butterfly!*

The tragedy now hastens to its close; Pinkerton arrives in company with Sharpless, leaving his American wife outside. A somber, heavy theme is heard, not wholly unlike the fateful phrase which, in *Tosca,* accompanies Cavaradossi to his death. Pinkerton, at last aware of the misery he has brought about, breaks out in lamentations; not, indeed, like an American naval officer, but in the most tearful manner of an Italian tenor! His

D-flat air, *Addio fiorito asil,* is a hypersentimental melody in which the orchestra mercilessly doubles the vocal part. The song is undeniably effective, but the lachrymose hypocrisy of the air offends. There is far truer pathos in the farewell of Butterfly to Suzuki and in the passionate grief of the mother's leave-taking from her child. The *andante sostenuto: O a me, sceso dal trono,* has an exaltation that is incredibly moving. The last bars of the opera are remarkable. The orchestra with its fullest power gives out in bare octaves a savage tune which simulates a harsh, Japanese character. The opera ends in a wild shriek, an unresolved dissonance which sounds far more biting than it looks on paper. "This, Puccini seems to be saying at the finish, was the poor thing's dream; and *this* is the reality!" Thus does Ernest Newman explain the bitter catastrophe.

HERBERT F. PEYSER

JULES MASSENET (1842–1912)

Manon

Libretto by Henri Meilhac and Philippe Gille, based upon Abbé Prévost's *L'Histoire de Manon Lescaut.* First performance in Paris, January 19, 1884.

Characters

Guillot, Minister of France .... Tenor
De Brétigny, a rich nobleman .... Baritone
Poussette, Javotte, Rosette
Soprano and two Mezzo-sopranos
Innkeeper .... Bass
Lescaut of the Royal Guards .... Baritone
Manon, Lescaut's cousin .... Soprano
Le Chevalier des Grieux .... Tenor
Le Comte des Grieux, the Chevalier's father .... Bass

The Story

ACT I. In the courtyard of an inn at Amiens, in 1731, an elderly roué, Guillot, has ordered dinner with his friend de Brétigny for three gay actresses, Poussette, Javotte, and Rosette. While they dine, the swaggering officer Lescaut comes to wait for his young cousin Manon, who is expected by the coach on her way to a convent. To the animated comment of village onlookers (**Chorus:** *Entendez-vous la cloche?*—Do you hear the clock?), the travelers arrive, Manon among them. Greeted by her cousin, she describes the excitement of her journey (**Manon:** *Je suis encore tout étourdie*—I am still so giddy). While Lescaut goes off to look after the luggage, Guillot makes advances to the girl and then offers his carriage but is repulsed. Lescaut returns, warns Manon to protect her virtue (**Lescaut:** *Ne bronchez pas, soyez gentille*—Don't stumble, be good), and then goes to the barracks to gamble. Manon reflects wistfully on the gay life of Guillot's companions (**Manon:** *Voyons, Manon, plus de chimères*—Come, Manon, no more dreaming). When the handsome young Chevalier des Grieux arrives, she is ready to yield to his rapturous love-making and go off to Paris with him in old Guillot's coach (**Des Grieux, Manon:** *Nous irons à Paris*—We shall go to Paris).

ACT II. Manon and des Grieux are living happily in their Paris apartment, although the girl already conceals the fact that an unknown suitor is sending her flowers. Lescaut and de Brétigny arrive, the former to demand that des Grieux marry Manon, the latter to warn her that the young Chevalier is about to be kidnapped by his father and she had better turn instead to him. Manon lets des Grieux go off to post a letter asking his father's permission to marry her. Sadly she bids farewell to the little table where they have so often dined (**Manon:** *Adieu, notre petite table*—Good-by, little table). Des Grieux returns, dreaming of an idyllic life with his beloved (**Des Grieux:** *En fermant lex yeux* [*Le Rêve*]—Closing my eyes). A knock disturbs the couple. Answering it, the Chevalier is seized by his father's emissaries and is dragged away.

ACT III. The holiday crowd makes merry on the *Cours la Reine*, where the young actresses seek to evade their protector Guillot while Lescaut sentimentally addresses them (**Lescaut:** *O Rosalinde*). Preceded by a crowd of wealthy courtiers, Manon is ushered from her sedan chair by her new lover, de Brétigny. She preens herself on her dazzling beauty and luxury (**Manon:** *Je marche sur tous les chemins*—I travel all roads), then sings a gay gavotte in praise of youth and pleasure (**Manon:** *Obéissons quand leur voix appelle*—Let us obey when the voice calls). She is piqued by the news which she overhears from a new arrival, the elderly Count des Grieux, that his son is about to enter holy orders. Learning that the Chevalier has grown cold to her charms, Manon pauses only to watch a divertissement (**Ballet**) before she orders her cousin to direct her to Saint Sulpice, where young des Grieux is preaching.

In the dim sacristy of the ancient church, the faithful recount the eloquence of the new abbé. Unimpressed by his son's virtue, the Count tries to persuade the young man to renounce his vocation and marry some suitable girl (**Count:** *Épouse quelque brave fille*—Marry some virtuous girl). Spurning his father's advice, des Grieux falls on his knees to pray for strength to resist his memories of Manon (**Des Grieux:** *Ah! fuyez, douce image*—Flee, sweet image). The girl arrives almost immediately and is still too fascinating for him (**Manon:** *N'est-ce plus ta main*—Isn't it your hand); again the lovers flee in each other's arms.

ACT IV. The Hôtel de Transylvanie, a famous gambling house, is crowded by pleasure seekers, among them Guillot and his three young companions. Manon and des Grieux arrive, seeking to improve their fortunes. While the Chevalier settles down to a game with Guillot, Manon and the three girls celebrate their philosophy of living for the moment (**Manon:** *A nous les amours et* *les roses!*—To us love and roses). Losing every hand, Guillot accuses des Grieux of cheating and goes off to call the police. They arrive with the Count, arresting the young man and threatening his beautiful mistress with deportation.

ACT V. On the road to Havre, where Manon is to be deported to Louisiana, the Chevalier attempts with Lescaut's help to intercept the convoy of unfortunate women and rescue his beloved from exile (**Guards:** *Capitaine, ô gué, es-tu fatigué*—Captain, there, are you tired?). Des Grieux succeeds with a bribe, and Manon falls exhausted into his arms. She sinks to her knees and asks for pardon, murmuring that now she can die in peace (**Manon, des Grieux:** *Ah! je sens une pure flamme*—Ah, I feel a pure flame). Her lover tries to rouse her, but, dreaming of their happiness together, Manon expires.

MANON is an *opéra comique*—that is to say, it contains quantities of spoken dialogue. But the composer and his admirable librettists, Henri Meilhac and Philippe Gille, have handled this feature somewhat differently from the manner in which it is treated in *Carmen* and scores of other works. Here the spoken lines are not permitted to interrupt the flow of the music. Instead, they are uttered against an orchestral background which is light but which enhances rather than covers them. They are, moreover, so charming in themselves that one feels they would be thoroughly marred by a delivery in recitative or in a broader *arioso.**

Massenet was confronted with a problem when he composed *Manon.* Was it not obvious that a story so impregnated with the feeling of the eighteenth century, of the elegances, formalisms, and artificialities of the epoch, should be treated in music which should precisely mirror these qualities? He had, on the other hand, a deeply human tale to deal with, a tale demanding a warmly human and sensuous musical style to interpret and communicate it. Massenet was artist and skilled technician enough to find a balance between what might ordinarily have resulted in contradictions of style. He contrived to evoke and sustain the atmosphere of eighteenth-century France. And at the same time

* Unfortunately the spoken dialogue is frequently omitted from American productions of this work. It is a pity, for *Manon,* as well as other *opéras comiques,* "play" better when the dialogue is included.—C. A. L.

he managed to bring to his music what it needed in the way of warmth, charm, voluptuousness, passion, and even poignant melancholy.

It is easy to isolate themes, phrases, melodies, and full-sized musical numbers in *Manon.* The brief prelude acquaints us with at least three melodies which we encounter at various stages of the opera. There is the jubilant, festive music associated with the merrymaking throng in the *Cours-la-Reine* scene, followed ironically enough by a brief, folklike phrase sung by the cruelly indifferent archers who, in the last act, accompany the wretched Manon and her unfortunate fellow-deportees on the dreary road to Havre and subsequent exile. Hard upon this and at its full length we hear that fluent, impassioned melody of love with which des Grieux addresses Manon in the gambling house, where he stakes all for the sake of her favor. It was perhaps phrases such as this which caused the composer to be hailed as a diminutive Wagner; for the passage begins strikingly like the theme of flight in *Die Walküre,* though it broadens out immediately afterwards into what we have long come to recognize as a true Massenet melody.

The ensemble, which at the rise of the curtain depicts the arrival of a coachful of travellers, is full of bustling animation and punctuated in the orchestra by the sound of the driver's whip. With the appearance of Manon we have at once her musical picture drawn in the round, first from the orchestra, then from her own lips. The delicious, syncopated melody, *Je suis encore tout étourdie,* characterizes for us at once the shy, confused, but inquisitive girl on her first trip, filled with wonder at the big world, a little hysterical yet quickly ready to accept such attentions as anyone elects to pay her. Lescaut, Manon's cousin, the self-appointed guardian of the family honor, has a motif of his own, a kind of short, martial, swaggering cadence. And Massenet gets further under the skin of this bragging, roistering fellow in the delectable song of admonition he addresses to the inexperienced girl, *Ne bronchez pas, soyez gentille.* Des Grieux is preceded by a melodic label which clings to him for a long time in the opera—a 'cello cantilena, suave and tender, against a pulsing accompaniment. Melodies then tread on each other's heels like the duet, *Nous irons à Paris tous les deux* and the touching one to which des Grieux sings the words *Une retraite inconnue et profonde,* which will follow the lovers through the opera to the tragic outcome on the road to Havre.

The second act begins with des Grieux' 'cello melody, supplemented this time with a light and charming little cadential coda of staccato notes, which belongs unmistakably to Manon and her coquetry. The arrival of Lescaut and de Brétigny brings more music picturing Manon's soldier cousin. And notice should be taken of a theme, one of the finest in the whole work, that asserts itself when Manon hears from de Brétigny of the plan to abduct her lover, and expands in a thrilling dramatic outburst at the fall of the curtain, when the kidnapping has occurred. Before this, however, come two of the most celebrated airs in the opera and, for that matter, in all Massenet—Manon's nostalgic farewell to her little table, with its simple accompaniment of chords of a somewhat archaic character; and des Grieux' moving and tender narrative of his dream and of the emptiness of his life without his beloved.

The bustling festival scene at the *Cours-la-Reine*, sometimes most injudiciously omitted, is introduced with an exquisitely sculptured little prelude in the form of a minuet, which is one of the jewels of the score. Passing over the delectable song of Lescaut, we come to one of the outstanding episodes of the work—the colloquy of the elder des Grieux with de Brétigny and then with Manon herself, in which the spoken words, lightly accompanied, assume almost the quality of music itself. Yet the climax of the scene is Manon's brilliantly florid aria, *Je marche sur tous les chemins*, whose text is one of the masterpieces of French operatic poetry. A kind of flashing, scintillant fanfare in the orchestra punctuates the utterances of Manon, in the glittering splendor of a *grande cocotte*. And, as she expresses her wish to die in a burst of laughter when die she must, her voice soars in a shining cadenza to a radiant high D.

Solemn organ harmonies usher in the scene in the Saint-Sulpice Seminary. Massenet's technical learning has here enabled him to paint a really atmospheric little tone picture of monastic severity and to write at this point a striking little *fugato* followed by a captivating *scherzo*, in which the chattering and elegant ladies who have heard des Grieux' first sermon express their admiration of his eloquence. The ensuing meeting of des Grieux with his father, carried on largely in dialogue, shows the older man in the role of a somewhat cruel ironist. However, there is no irony in the lovely and persuasive phrase in which he urges his son, if he needs must marry, to choose a girl worthy of him and of his family. Left to his own thoughts des Grieux breaks out into another of the most celebrated pages of the opera, the yearning and impassioned *Ah! Fuyez*, with its vigorous and dramatic middle part against distant sounds of a religious canticle; Manon contrives in short order to weaken the rivets of her lover's moral armor. The means she adopts is the irresistibly caressing and seductive melody, *N'est-ce plus ta main.* With inexpressible poignancy this same melody sounds in the orchestra when, in the last act, the exhausted Manon expires in des Grieux' arms.

There are striking things in the gambling scene of the *Hôtel Transylvanie.* A mysterious, impersonal rhythmic motif, which supports much of the conversation, allows us to hear the clinking of coins and the suppressed excitement of the gamesters. Then there is Manon's gracious air, urging her companions to make the most of their years. The betrayal of the lovers by the treacherous Guillot is built upon to a broad and sonorous finale, the music of which reminds one of similar pages in various operas of Verdi, Meyerbeer, Gounod, and even Massenet himself.

The touching final act is brief. Most of its themes and melodies are recalls from earlier scenes, but they are invested now with a pathos they have acquired from the changed dramatic circumstances. One detail should be noted—the dying Manon's touching and childlike joy at the sight of the evening star, which she apostrophizes as a "beautiful diamond," adding a touching little word of self-reproach: "You see, I am still a coquette." This, as well as certain further melodic evocations and sorrowful twilight touches in the closing pages, indicates that, among other things, Massenet was a true dramatic psychologist.

HERBERT F. PEYSER

RICHARD WAGNER (1813–1883)

Die Meistersinger von Nürnberg

Libretto by the composer. First performance in Munich, June 21, 1868.

Characters

Walther von Stolzing	Tenor
Eva, daughter of Veit Pogner	Soprano
Magdalene, Eva's companion	Mezzo-soprano
David, apprentice to Hans Sachs	Tenor
Veit Pogner, goldsmith	Bass
Sixtus Beckmesser, town clerk	Bass
Hans Sachs, shoemaker and poet	Baritone
Fritz Kothner, head of Mastersingers	Baritone
Eight other Mastersingers	Four Tenors, two Baritones, two Basses
Night watchman	Bass

The Story

ACT I. The knight Walther von Stolzing tries to attract the attention of young Eva Pogner as she sits at her devotions with her nurse, Magdalene, in St. Katherine's Church in sixteenth-century Nuremberg (**Chorus:** *Da zu dir der Heiland kam*—When to thee our Saviour came). After the services the women are joined by Magdalene's admirer, the apprentice David. They explain to the ardent Walther that Eva is to be betrothed the next day to the winner of a song contest conducted by the Mastersingers' Guild. Eva begs Walther to compete, and Magdalene promises David many rewards if he can help Walther be made a Mastersinger. The women then retire as other apprentices arrive to prepare for a preliminary trial. David explains to Walther the requirements of a Mastersinger and describes how he studies poetry and singing as well as shoemaking with Hans Sachs (**David:** *Mein Herr! der Singer Meister-Schlag*—Dear sir, the singer's master-crown is not won in one day).* Piqued by the apprentices' teasing, David points to Walther and says there'll be

* Portions of the scene between David and Walther are frequently cut in actual performance.

another laughingstock today, that Walther intends to stand trial without any previous training (**David:** *Ja, lacht nur zu!*—Yes, go ahead and laugh. Today I'm not "it"). Then he joins the other apprentices in wishing good luck to the new applicant (**David, Apprentices:** *Das Blumenkränzlein*—The wreath of flowers). The entering Mastersingers are led by Eva's father, the goldsmith Veit Pogner, who promises to sponsor Walther for guild membership. After roll call, Pogner describes the song contest for Eva's hand (**Pogner:** *Nun hört, und versteht mich recht!*—Now listen and understand me correctly). After animated discussion of the contest, Walther is introduced and tells of his background and training (**Walther:** *Am stillen Herd*—By the silent hearth). The town clerk Beckmesser, also a suitor for Eva's hand, is chosen to act as "marker" or judge of Walther's attempt at a song that will satisfy the requirements of the guild. Before hiding in his curtained marker's booth, he tells Walther he'll be allowed only seven mistakes, each to be recorded by a chalk mark. Kothner, president of the guild, reads Walther the rules for composing a master song (**Kothner:** *Was euch zum Liede Richt'* [Tabulatur]—What belongs to correct song); then Walther is told to begin. The knight's unconventional improvisation (**Walther:** *Fanget an* [Trial Song]—Now begin) fails to please the jurymen but delights the apprentices. Beckmesser leaves the marker's booth before the song is completed, his slate completely covered with chalk marks. Only Hans Sachs appreciates the new talent and begs for a more thoughtful judgment. While Beckmesser and the other Mastersingers excitedly find fault with Walther's song, Sachs and the apprentices listen to its conclusion. The verdict of the guild: "Rejected and outsung."

ACT II. As Midsummer Night falls on a Nuremberg street corner, Magdalene learns that Walther has failed his test and angrily refuses David (whom she partly blames for Walther's failure) any of her goodies. Other apprentices, who have eavesdropped on their conversation, tease David. As he begins to scuffle with them, Sachs appears and orders him to bed. Eva and her father return from a walk; they talk of the morrow's contest, and Pogner first suspects that Eva is in love with Walther. Learning of the knight's failure from Magdalene, Eva in despair decides to call upon Sachs for help. Returning to his workbench now set up by his door, Sachs is intoxicated by the lilac's fragrance and reflects on Walther's provocative song (**Sachs:** *Wie duftet doch der Flieder*—How sweet the lilac smells). His monologue is interrupted by Eva, who hints that she would like him to compete for her hand since she can marry none other than a Mastersinger. Angered by his statement that he's too old and that she would be a child as well as wife to him, Eva inadvertently discloses that she really loves Walther. Magdalene calls to Eva to come home to bed; during the women's animated conversation Sachs' suspicions are aroused, so he secretes himself behind his partly closed door where he can overhear what is going on. Eva tells Magdalene to sit in her window that evening and pretend to listen to Beckmesser's promised serenade of the song by which he hopes to win Eva's hand. Then before Magdalene can drag Eva into the house, Walther appears, and the girl rushes to her lover's arms. He recounts the morning's sad experiences, and they plan to elope (**Eva:** *Geliebter, spare den Zorn*—Beloved, save your anger). As the night watchman makes his rounds, Eva goes in to get a traveling cloak. Sachs acts to prevent the elopement by brightly illuminating their road to escape. While they are pondering what to do, Beckmesser comes down the street to sing his serenade. As if struck by a new idea, Sachs opens his door and places his workbench just outside it. Then as Beckmesser starts to sing, Sachs begins hammering on his last and singing a lusty cobbling song (**Sachs:** *Jerum! Jerum! Halla halla he*). Beckmesser protests, but Sachs insists he must complete Beckmesser's shoes in time for the contest and continues his work and singing. Beckmesser again implores Sachs to stop, this time by flattering him: he'd like his opinion of the song by which he hopes to win Eva. Sachs finally agrees to act as "marker," to use his hammer if Beckmesser breaks a rule. The clerk commences (**Beckmesser:** *Den Tag seh' ich erscheinen*—I see the day appearing); Sachs finds many false accents to hammer to; the infuriated Beckmesser turns on him, but Sachs insists "good songs must scan." Beckmesser sings still louder to drown out Sachs, and soon the whole neighborhood is aroused. David, who thinks Beckmesser has been serenading Magdalene, beats the clerk unmercifully. Men and women appear in their night clothes and variously observe and participate in the tumultuous scene. Sachs makes his way to Eva and Walther, pushes Eva into her father's arms, and drags Walther and David, whom he has pulled off Beckmesser, into his shop, barring the door behind him. As peace returns, Beckmesser painfully makes his way home, and the night watchman once more makes his round.

ACT III. Deeply engrossed in a book as he sits in his study, Sachs hardly hears the apologies of David for his unruly conduct (**David:** *Ach, Meister, wollt' ihr mir verzeih'n*—Ah, master, won't you forgive me?). At length the Master bids the youth recite his verses for St. John's Day, which is dawning outside (**David:** *Am Jordan Sankt Johannes stand*—St. John stood on the Jordan strand). Left alone, Sachs muses on the madness of mankind and his own confused feelings for Eva (**Sachs:** *Wahn! Wahn! Überall Wahn!*—Madness, madness! Madness everywhere). Walther enters and tells of a wondrous dream. Recognizing a Mastersong in the making, Sachs takes the words down and instructs the knight how to perfect its musical form (**Walther:** *Morgenlich leuchtend*—Morning was gleaming). When they have gone to dress, Beckmesser hobbles in, lame from his beating and ridiculous in his finery. He spies the song and pockets it, thinking it to be a work of Sachs. When Sachs returns, Beckmesser accuses him of plotting to win Eva for himself (**Beckmesser:** *O Schuster, voll von Ränken*—O cobbler, full of tricks). The cobbler catches the clerk in the theft of the poem, but tells Beckmesser that he may keep the paper. Beckmesser is overjoyed at Sachs' generosity, but insists that the cobbler never disclose that the poem is by him. Eva next enters on the pretext that her shoe hurts. When Walther sees her, she utters a cry of delight, and he is inspired to finish the last verse of his festival song. Sachs tells Eva that she has just heard a Mastersong, and she falls weeping on his shoulder. Finally he composes himself, yielding her over to Walther. She turns to Sachs and in impassioned song tells him she owes all she is to him, that were her choice free that day she'd choose him to be her husband (**Eva:** *O Sachs, mein Freund!*—Oh Sachs, my friend!). Sachs tells her he knows the story of Tristan and Isolde and that it was time the right man did appear or he might have been as sorry as King Marke. Magdalene and David now enter, and the cobbler invites them to witness the christening of a new creation—the Mastersong just completed by Walther (**Sachs:** *Ein Kind war hier geboren*—A child was born here). So that David can be a bona fide witness, Sachs promotes him to journeyman. Led by Eva, the five then rejoice at the dawning of new hope and love and depart for the festival (**Quintet:** *Selig wie die Sonne*—Blessed as the sun).

The guilds assemble on the banks of the Pegnitz, waving their banners as they march in. The apprentices dance with their sweethearts (**Dance of the Apprentices**), but are interrupted by the arrival of the Mastersingers, who take their places on a platform at the left of the stage. When Sachs appears, the populace bursts into a spontaneous chorus of acclaim and affection (**Chorus:** *Wach' auf! es nahet gen den Tag*—Awake, daybreak nears). Sachs, deeply moved, expresses his gratitude (**Sachs:** *Euch macht ihr's leicht*—What you do lightly). Beckmesser is then ushered to his place and nervously sings the stolen song, distorting it ludicrously (**Beckmesser:** *Morgen ich leuchte*—Morning I shine). When the crowd laughs him to a halt, he turns furiously on Sachs, who disclaims authorship and calls upon the true author. Walther appears, delivers the song (**Walther:** *Morgenlich leuchtend* [Prize Song]—Morning is gleaming), and wins both the Mastersinger's laurel and Eva's hand. He at first refuses the Master's medal at the hands of Pogner, but is persuaded by Sachs to recognize the honor (**Sachs:** *Verachtet mir die Meister nicht*—Don't disparage the Masters).* Eva takes the wreath from Walther's head and crowns the cobbler-poet, while the crowd shouts approval.

"I CANNOT get it out of my mind. I feel it, and cannot understand it. I cannot remember it, nor can I forget it. Even when I grasp the whole of it, I still cannot measure it. It sounded so old, and yet it was so new, like the songs of birds in lovely May."

This is Hans Sachs' first response to Walther's trial song, and it is also our first response to *Die Meistersinger*. From the beginning we succumb to its irresistible charm, its bright, vibrant rhythm, its easy, uninhibited joyousness. We find ourselves haunted afterward by the memory of Hans Sachs, of a few exquisite isolated sounds, and by a feeling of musical bounty as boundless as the sea. Yet, simultaneously, we run into the paradox that puzzled Hans Sachs: *Meistersinger* itself is both old and new; it corresponds completely to our idea of Wagner one minute, and refutes it as completely the next. Where and how is this opera old, where is it new? The question becomes imperative, but tantalizingly elusive.

We recognize at once that the central ideas of *Meistersinger*, renunciation and convention, are old. We have seen Wotan, in the *Ring*, renounce his own power and existence in an effort to save his world. In *Meistersinger*, we find Hans Sachs refraining from winning Eva for himself to achieve her happiness with Walther.

The problem of convention, of the individual and his rela-

* Most of Sachs' apostrophe to German art is invariably cut in all but complete, "festival" performances.

tion to society, is also familiar. In *Tannhäuser*, *Walküre*, and *Tristan*, it is symbolized by loves which society will not sanction; in *Lohengrin*, by the great man whom society cannot know or comprehend. In *Meistersinger*, it is represented by Walther's unconventional music which the conventional Masters refuse to admit. As Sachs remarks, "He who is born a Master is in the very worst position of all among the other Masters."

We soon discover, too, that this opera, unlike the *Ring* and *Tristan*, does not presuppose any knowledge of mythology or philosophy, and that the action consequently speaks for itself.

When the dispute between Walther and the Masters breaks out, we cannot help wondering whether it is autobiographical. This is precisely the case. And therefore, contrary to general belief, it is Sachs' interpretation of the nature of musical rules—since Sachs is speaking for Wagner—and the comments of the Masters and people that are important to us, rather than the peculiar details of the *Tabulatur*.

To Walther—the composer—Sachs explains the origin and necessity for rules. "Many people," he says, "impelled by the first love of their youth, succeed in making a beautiful song. The spring sang for you. But after the summer, autumn, and winter of life, and all its struggles, have passed, then it is those who can still sing beautiful songs who are known as Masters. . . . The rules of the Masters help to preserve later on what love and spring have given you unawares . . . that is why they were made." And when Walther asks him how he is to begin his song according to the rules, Sachs replies, "You set them yourself, and then follow them."

To Beckmesser and the Masters—the critics—the shoemaker declares that he thinks it wise, "once a year to put the rules themselves to the test, to prevent their losing vigor and validity through the sluggish routine of habit." Then, when these critics still find it impossible to make head or tail of Walther's song according to their own lights, Sachs suggests that "if you want to measure something that does not fit into your rules, look for its own rules first."

The Masters' comments on Walther's song: "obscure meaning," "no trace of melody," "no coloratura," "sheer torture to the ears," ring only too true. We have heard them ourselves. A particularly cutting bit of satire is Kothner's virtuously indignant: "He even jumped up from the chair!" Like much music criticism, it has nothing to do with the point.

Wagner himself gives further prooof of the autobiographical element in his own prose writings. He says, speaking of Beckmesser, "This Marker is well known (or perhaps, is *not* well known to our critics) . . ." And he emphasizes the fact that his works frequently failed because they were distorted in performance, and that the failure was blamed on the work rather than on the production. We see exactly that happen in the last act of *Meistersinger*. Beckmesser makes a hopeless mess of Walther's song, and the Masters and people refuse to believe it good until the knight sings it correctly. Then they exclaim, with delightful *naïveté*, "This is something else! Who would have thought that the right words and way of performance could make such a difference!"

The music, however, presents a much more subtle and difficult problem. Our first reaction to the overture is that it is utterly new and completely different. The music really seems to have suffered a C-change. This feeling continues through the first act, which opens with the chorale in C major and closes in the same key. But in the second act, we begin to have our doubts, and in the third, we are confronted by a prelude which is *echt* Wagner in the *Tristan* style. Then we find the opera ending with the Prize song and final chorus again in C major.

. . . . .

Wagner constructs the music according to his customary *leitmotif* system, using themes that express with extraordinary felicity the essential character or mood of a person or situation—themes which are therefore particularly hard to label precisely with words. One of the most beautiful of these is the progression of the three triads of E—A-flat—E-flat in the woodwinds and brass, which refers to Walther's dream. When it first appears, as Walther tells Sachs, "*Ich hatt' einen wunderschönen Traum*," it is preceded by triads on C and G that heighten its own unearthly, miraculous quality. It is repeated about five times more in that scene, once in the next when Sachs christens the melody, and once in the last, when the pupils say: "*Alles gespannt, 's gibt kein Gesumm', da rufen wir auch nicht Silentium!*" just before Walther sings his Prize song.

We cannot help being struck by the brilliantly graphic reflection of the stage action in the music—a reflection which shows the interior as well as the surface of its object. *Meistersinger* has more physical action than any of the other music-dramas, but it is just possible that, because the action appears so tangibly in the music, the work loses less than its predecessors when it is only heard and not seen. This pictorial quality reaches its heights in the two great pantomime scenes in Acts I [the opening scene in the church] and III [Beckmesser's actions and thought processes as he limps around Sachs' empty study, finds the song, and steals it].

As in the *Ring* and *Tristan*, we find Wagner repeating large sections of music to point up similar dramatic situations. For instance, the recitative sections of the passage in which Kothner reads out the rules of the *Tabulatur* are repeated note for note, in the same key of C, when Sachs declares that—also according to the *Tabulatur*—the new melody by Walther must be christened. The melodic phrases between the recitative passages in the latter case, however, become quotations and developments of the opening chorale—which also dealt with christening—instead of themes concerning the Masters.

In the Night Watchman's song and horn call Wagner combines old and new methods. The use of a genuine night watchman's song of the middle sixteenth century is new, while the horn sounding G-flat is old. We have already seen Wagner use this G-flat out of the key with the rest of the horn call in both *Götterdämmerung* and *Tristan*.

But it is in the fourth scene of the third act that we reach the dramatic climax. Until now—except for the prelude to the act and the *Wahn* monologue—events have been moving along easily and humorously. Here, suddenly, unexpectedly, the action becomes compressed, the music intensified, and the relationship between Sachs and Eva is laid bare before our eyes.

As the scene opens, Eva, richly dressed in gleaming white, but pale and sad, slowly enters Sachs' workshop. She and Sachs have a conversation purportedly about her new shoes, actually about the question of Eva's marriage. As Sachs is investigating the shoe problem, Walther, in shining knightly apparel, enters from the chamber. Eva and Walther, transfixed at the sight of each other, remain motionless. Sachs, pretending not to notice, remarks casually that he heard a beautiful song today, and wishes someone would sing him the third verse. Walther, still gazing at Eva, sings it. Sachs comments to her, "Listen, child, that is a Mastersong." Then he brings her shoe back from the bench and puts it on her foot. "Try it," he urges, "Stand up. Does it still hurt?"

And Eva, who has been watching and listening spellbound, suddenly bursts out crying bitterly, sinks on Sachs' breast, and clasps him to her, sobbing. Walther comes over to them, and presses Sachs' hand passionately. Sachs finally masters himself and tears himself away with an appearance of ill-humor, so that he leaves Eva involuntarily leaning on Walther's shoulder.

This final, decisive moment of Sachs' renunciation of Eva is expressed, not by words, but by an overwhelming *fortissimo* outburst of the full orchestra in the theme of Sachs' *renunciation,* with all the chromatic and rhythmic potency of which Wagner is capable. The treatment of this situation is so wonderful because it is so psychologically true—because we know from our own experience that, in such a situation, everyone feels the issue intuitively, and no one need say anything.

Sachs quickly changes the subject, and the music resolves imperceptibly into his Shoemaking song. But Eva draws him to her again. What would she be without him and his love? He has made her everything that she is. And if she had the choice, she would marry him. Only—she no longer has that choice, now that she has fallen in love. Sachs replies quietly, "My child, I know the sad story of Tristan and Isolde. But Hans Sachs is a wise man, and wants no part of King Marke's fate."

This, certainly for the first time we hear it, is the most astounding experience for us in the whole of *Meistersinger.* For here, accompanying Sachs' words—and in their original tone color—are two themes from *Tristan* (the first theme of the prelude, and the second King Marke theme from Act II). The effect is electrifying and totally unbelievable. Composers have quoted themselves before. Mozart uses a theme from *Figaro* as a dance tune in *Don Giovanni.* But there it is no more than a quotation; it has no dramatic significance, entails no stylistic difference. Here, in spite of the passionate music that has preceded it, this *Tristan* music is so utterly out of style and color that it brings us up short. There is no excuse for such a violation of the musical artistic unity except on dramatic grounds. This passage, more than any other in all the music-dramas, proves that Wagner's music makes sense only from the dramatic point of view, and at the same time justifies the use of music in drama. For not a thousand words could show so absolutely the incompatibility of Marke's action with Sachs' ways of thinking, as these ten measures which are in themselves incompatible with the rest of the music.

After this, Sachs continues more lightly, "Still, it was high time I found the right person for you, or I might have given in after all!" The tension lessens, Sachs calls for the christening of Walther's melody (in C major), and the scene ends with the meltingly beautiful quintet.

Finally, in the last scene, we hear the Prize song in its finished form. And for once, in such a situation, we are not disappointed. There are many books, plays, movies in which the hero is praised to the skies as a great painter, musician, or poet; yet his art, when we finally see or hear it, lets us down. . . . But Walther's Prize song, which Sachs extols so highly, actually comes up to expectations. For Wagner had the intelligence to choose for his hero the artistic field in which he himself was at home and in which he himself excelled.

But when all is said and done, the real difference between *Meistersinger*, and the *Ring* and *Tristan*, lies not in its outward grand-opera trappings of arias, choruses, dances, processions, but in the personality of Hans Sachs. Sachs alone, of all Wagner's characters, is well adjusted to his environment and integrated within himself. All the others are at war either with themselves or their surroundings. Sachs is not neurotic like Wotan; he is relaxed and sure of himself. He extends towards others a wise, tolerant sympathy and understanding, yet remains at the same time detached enough to see the humor of a situation which they, being deeply involved in it, fail to notice. He has a thoughtful, philosophic turn of mind, a great, generous capacity for loving. Now and then he lets slip a hint of loneliness or melancholy; but under even that there lies a profound serenity. It is this serenity, coupled with Walther's eager young fire, that gives *Meistersinger* its unique color and atmosphere.

LILIAN E. FOERSTER

VINCENZO BELLINI (1801–1835)

Norma

Libretto by Giuseppe Felice Romani, based upon a story by Alexander Soumet and Louis Belmontet. First performance in Milan, December 26, 1831.

Characters

Oroveso, the Archdruid	Bass
Pollione, Roman proconsul	Tenor
Flavio, a centurion	Tenor
Norma, High Priestess of the Druids	Soprano
Adalgisa, a virgin of the Temple	Mezzo-soprano
Clotilde	Soprano

The Story

ACT I. Deep in their sacred forest the Druids and warriors of ancient Gaul, led by their priest Oroveso, gather at the altar of Irminsul to pray for revenge against the invading Romans (**Oroveso and Chorus:** *Ite sul colle, o Druidi*—Go to the mountain top, Druids). As they retire, the Roman proconsul Pollione tells his friend Flavio that he no longer loves Norma, who has borne him two children, and has instead transferred his affections to the young priestess Adalgisa (**Pollione:** *Me protegge*—A higher power than they protects and defends me). Pollione and Flavio retreat as Norma's entrance is heralded by the chorus (**Chorus:** *Norma viene*—Norma comes). The priestess prays for peace (**Norma:** *Casta diva*—Chaste goddess). She is especially loath to punish Pollione, whom she loves deeply (**Norma:** *Ah! bello a me ritorna*—Ah, handsome one, return to me). As the Druids withdraw, Adalgisa arrives to pray for strength to resist her Roman lover (**Adalgisa:** *Deh, proteggimi*—Protect me). Pollione begs her to flee with him (**Pollione:** *Vieni in Roma*—Come to Rome), and she promises fidelity.*

ACT II. In the rude dwelling where she has concealed her children, Norma tells her confidante Clotilde of her fears for Pollione's departure. Clotilde hides the children as Adalgisa timorously enters to confess that she has met her lover in the temple (**Adalgisa:** *Sola, furtiva*—Alone, furtively I was awaiting him).

* *Norma* was originally presented in two acts, Acts I and II, III and IV being combined.

Norma gently releases Adalgisa from her vows, but her kindness turns to fury as Pollione enters and she learns that he is the girl's lover. She accuses the Romans of treachery (**Norma:** *O di qual sei tu vittima*—Of whom are you a victim?) as Adalgisa vows to perish rather than take him from Norma's side. Pollione desperately pleads with Adalgisa to flee with him while there's time, but she stoutly refuses. A distant signal sounds defiance to the Romans.

ACT III. Dagger in hand, Norma tries to bring herself to murder the children, who lie sleeping in her cave dwelling. Failing, she resolves on death for herself and asks Adalgisa to take the children and care for them and marry Pollione. Adalgisa pleads with her to look at the children and find new will to live (**Adalgisa:** *Mira, o Norma*—See, Norma), and the two women vow eternal friendship (**Adalgisa, Norma:** *Sì fino all' ore*—Yes, to the last moments).

ACT IV. The Gallic warriors assemble at their altars, where Oroveso announces that Pollione is being replaced by a more cruel commander and counsels submission for the present, leading to ultimate revolt (**Oroveso:** *Ah! del Tebro*—I, too, strain at the yoke of the Roman).

Believing that Adalgisa will send back her lover, Norma joyously awaits the girl, but is horrified to learn from Clotilde that her friend's supplications have been in vain. Norma summons the populace to the temple to call for warfare. Clotilde rushes back to report that a Roman intruder has profaned the sanctuary, and soldiers drag in Pollione. Norma dismisses the throng to vaunt her power over the Roman (**Norma:** *In mia mano*—In my hands). She promises him his life if he will renounce Adalgisa and return to her; he refuses and in fury she threatens to punish him by destroying Adalgisa (**Norma:** *Già mi pasco*—I am already enjoying your anguished glances). When the warrior begs for mercy, Norma again summons the assemblage and heroically admits her own guilt; stunned by Norma's sacrifice, Pollione suddenly realizes too late that she is his true love (**Norma:** *Qual cor tradisti*—What heart you betrayed). The unhappy woman begs Oroveso to care for her children (**Norma:** *Deh! non volerli vittime*—I do not want them victims of my fatal mistake) and then leads Pollione with her to the funeral pyre.

WHATEVER the reasons for the seeming failure of *Norma* at the start of its career, the reason for its continuing success can be explained by Bellini's music. The overture to *Norma* still seems effective in the theater, but it no longer turns up on symphonic programs as it used to do. The simplicity of Bellini's purely orchestral writing may seem naive today, and we do not find the apposite instrumentation and spontaneous verve that Rossini achieves in his finest overtures. At the curtain's rise, however, Bellini contrives one of the most effective opening scenes to be found in any opera. This is the real musico-dramatic overture to *Norma*. The episode begins in the simplest possible way: in the basses we hear the repeated tonic of G major; then he adds the bare dominant. From this rudimentary establishment of tonality evolves a succession of melodious phrases which create an extraordinary mood of nobility and spaciousness. Oroveso, the leader of the Druids and Norma's father, enters accompanied by his priestly flock. He plangently announces, *Ite sul colle*, "Go to the hill," for Norma will soon appear in the sacred grove to crop the holy mistletoe. This central rite of the Druids is described in Pliny's *Natural History* (XVI, 249). In the succeeding unison chorus, *Dell' aura tua profetica*, a mood of sober dedication and controlled intensity is strikingly projected.

In strong contrast to the opening scene is that which follows it. Where before all was solemn dedication, we now find an agitated recitative in which Pollione, a Roman proconsul, defines his dilemma to his aide-de-camp, Flavio. Tired of his proscribed marriage with Norma, he has become entranced by the charms of a younger priestess, Adalgisa. He is obsessed with her and describes his dream of living in Rome with his newest conquest, *Meco all' altar di Venere*. The finely proportioned phrases of his aria, the appropriate accentuation, are testimony to the beneficent influence of Rubini upon the composer. . . . The ardent impetuosity of Pollione's character is further revealed in the *cabaletta*, an *allegro* pendant to the *cavatina*. . . .

Pollione's exit is followed by the reappearance of the Druid priests and priestesses, headed by Norma. From the first note of Norma's first recitative, she is obviously no ordinary woman, but is commanding, wilful, deeply emotional. The energetic immediacy of Bellini's recitatives and their truth of accent form a worthy vehicle for her wide-ranging moods. After an extended introduction in which the solo flute announces the principal theme, Norma launches into the great *Casta diva*. The long phrases of this intricately articulated melody are so spaciously set out, so gracefully balanced, that the entranced listener is apt to lose sight of the significant dramatic function of this scene. The figure of Norma is merged with that of her ancient prototype, the poetess-priestess wrapped in her singing robes, evoking the primordial White Goddess in one of her lovelier aspects, the moon. Each sinuous contour of her melody is pure incantation. The poetry and majesty of this moment dissolve the conventions of stylized opera and we find ourselves face to face with primitive ritual.

The conclusion of Norma's *scena* is on only a slightly lower plane. An accompanied recitative, *Fine al rito,* a magnificently energetic pronouncement, leads directly into the florid *cabaletta, Ah! bello a me ritorna,* which is an extended aside for Norma. She speaks of her love for Pollione and her desire for his return to her side. These measures with their impetuous figurations and chromatic scales vividly express the grandeur of Norma's nature. The march that accompanies the exit of the chorus at the conclusion of this scene is an operatic excerpt that was once as familiar and possessed as exact connotations as the *Lohengrin* wedding march does today: it was the call to supper at any evening party with formal pretensions.

A solitary figure appears on the now empty stage to a beautiful orchestral interlude; Adalgisa enters the sacred grove. The younger priestess is cast in a less heroic mould than Norma. Her temperament is gentle; her sense of duty, strong. She confesses she is not immune to Pollione's protestations. She kneels and sings a short prayer, *Deh! proteggimi, o Dio!* one of Bellini's most persuasive inventions. This brief passage illustrates clearly one of Bellini's most characteristic melodic devices, the use of the triplet on either the second or fourth beat.

Adalgisa is interrupted at her devotions by the impetuous Pollione and, doubting her powers of resistance, she begs him to leave her in peace. A double duet ensues, *Va crudele,* followed by *Vieni in Roma.* These duets, Bellini admits in a letter to his uncle, are not a high point in the score. This judgment seems rather severe. Undeniably their rhythmic and harmonic similarity, plus the conventional device, twice repeated, of giving the full melody first to the tenor and then *in toto* to the mezzo-soprano, produces a certain feeling of stasis; yet this is not to deny that the melodies themselves possess charm and conviction.

The orchestral introduction to the second scene graphically presents the alternating agitation and tenderness struggling in Norma's breast. In a dynamic recitative she expresses her doubts about Pollione's intentions toward her and their children. She is interrupted by Adalgisa, who proceeds to unburden her conscience. A duet of classical simplicity and dignity, *Sola, furtiva al tempio,* evolves out of the preceding recitative. As Adalgisa describes the circumstances and symptoms of her love, Norma is filled with sympathetic recollections of her own wooing by Pollione. The principal melody is Adalgisa's; its long phrases, closely related musically, but subtly differentiating each idea of the text, are effectively complemented by Norma's asides. Here with simplest means Bellini gives the impression of writing more than notes, so immediately and persuasively is the emotional content of each phrase communicated to the listener. This passage typifies the classic spirit that pervades much of *Norma.* The duet is rounded out by a *cabaletta, Si fa core e abbracciami,* embellished with much coloratura and a rapturous cadenza in thirds. Here the formal conventions are exactly appropriate to this moment of rapport between the two priestesses. Sympathetic understanding is soon shattered, however, by Norma's request for further information. Norma is beset by suspicions when Adalgisa shyly admits her lover is a Roman. The tension is effectively maintained by an insistent figured accompaniment, marked *pianissimo;* but when Norma learns the identity of Adalgisa's beloved and beholds Pollione, her wrath explodes in a burst of vehement coloratura. This passage, *Ah non tremare,* with its flashing scales, its large intervals, its repeated attacks upon top C, when executed with sufficient vigor and accent can produce a breath-taking effect. Surely Lilli Lehmann had these measures in mind when she delivered her famous dictum that Norma is more demanding than the three Brünnhildes.

In striking contrast to this outburst is the succeeding trio, *Oh! di qual sei tu vittima,* with those long, mellifluous phrases that Bellini manipulates so cannily. The conflicting emotions of Norma, the stricken Adalgisa, and the embarrassed Pollione, are skillfully interwoven to form a genuinely moving ensemble. . . .

The second act opens with a prelude whose chief melody, later sung by Norma to the words, *Teneri, teneri figli,* is ample proof of Chopin's debt to Bellini. The opening scene, conducted wholly to a recitative which achieves great force with maximum economy, is one of the most shattering in all opera. We see Norma wrung with anguish, goaded to a point where she even considers murdering her children because they are Pollione's sons. (Shades of Medea!) The extraordinary effect produced by a simple figure for the strings over a *tremolando* accompaniment between the moment Norma raises the dagger and her realization that she is incapable of the deed is eloquent testimony to Bellini's ability to make a few notes seem more expressive than a thousand.

The rest of this scene, the second between Norma and Adalgisa, consists of a duet in three sections. The first, *Deh, con te, con te li prendi,* in straightforward 4–4 time, is Norma's plea that Adalgisa take the children to Rome with their father. The second episode, the famous *Mira, o Norma,* for all its celebrity, for all its delicious opportunities for vocal nuance, has always seemed, to this writer at least, on a slightly lower level of inspiration than the duet, *Sola, furtiva al tempio,* in the preceding scene. Here the exact correlation of the parts seems less deeply persuasive than the informal balance of the earlier duet. The concluding movement of this *scena a due, Sì fino all' ore,* expresses in a cascade of thirds and sixths the reconciliation of the two priestesses.

The final scene represents the summit of Bellini's achievement. Every measure contributes to the propulsive action; each subtly contrasted episode builds steadily to an overwhelming climax. The reintroduction of Oroveso and the Druid priests at the beginning of this scene stresses the essential balance and unity of the score by suggesting the opening of the opera. The action has been interior, private, in the middle two scenes of the work; now it returns to the open and the frame of public events. The priests are still champing at the bit to rise against the tyranny of Rome. In a broad, sweeping aria, *Ah! del Tebro,* Oroveso exhorts his followers to remember their duty of wrath. Norma enters to a beguiling woodwind passage. She is radiant, believing that Pollione will now return to her, that everything will be as it was in the first days of their love. Learning that the unrepentant Pollione plans to abduct Adalgisa by force, her ardor turns to fury and in a coruscating bit of coloratura she vows that Roman blood shall flow in torrents. Norma then summons the Druids and sanctions the long-delayed rebellion; to the insistent rhythms of *Guerra, guerra,* Bellini paints a mood of barbaric ferocity. When Pollione, captured in his attempt to carry off Adalgisa, is dragged in as the human sacrifice, which, in Druid thought, the dedication of such an enterprise requires, Norma, symbolically, is again incapable of violence. Just as she could not murder her children, so she can not drive home the blade into Pollione's heart. To cover her agitation, she dismisses the multitude and in the great duet, *In mia mano alfin tu sei,* Norma and Pollione plead and argue. Here in the interest of dramatic truth the formal duet patterns break down. Over a persistent figure the melody, tense with the smoldering emotions of hatred and love, advances now in abrupt interjection, now in a broad pleading phrase. This is musical declamation of the most moving sort, and flames into passionate utterance in the concluding *allegro*. Norma summons the throng and now names herself the sacrificial victim. The simplicity of her announcement—just two words, *son io*—is a masterpiece of understatement. The hush of horrified dismay at her words is depicted in a series of softly thudding chords. At this moment Norma stands revealed in all her tragic stature. From this moment to the end of the opera, the mood of tragic exaltation never falters. Pollione is stunned, humbled by Norma's act, and his love for her is reawakened. The detached phrases of *Ah! troppo tardi* convincingly convey how deeply he is stirred. This profoundly moving passage is capped by that which follows it. In the dignified key of E minor, over a simple, brooding figure, Norma sings the anguished arioso, *Deh! non volerli vittime*. Nowhere else in this opera, so filled with beautiful passionate melodies, does Bellini touch such heights of emotional intensity. This leads directly into the E major section of the finale which twice surges to a stirring climax. A brief *allegro*, as Norma and Pollione together mount the funeral pyre, brings the opera to a close.

William Ashbrook

WOLFGANG AMADEUS MOZART (1756–1791)

Le Nozze di Figaro

Libretto by Lorenzo da Ponte, based upon Beaumarchais' play. First performance in Vienna, May 1, 1786.

Characters

Figaro, servant of the Count . . . . Bass
Susanna, maid of the Countess, engaged to Figaro
Soprano
Dr. Bartolo . . . . Bass
Marcellina, Bartolo's elderly helpmate . . . . . Contralto
Cherubino, a page . . . . Mezzo-soprano
Count Almaviva . . . . Baritone
Basilio, an elderly music teacher . . . . Tenor
Countess Almaviva (Rosina) . . . . Soprano
Antonio, the gardener . . . . Bass
Don Curzio . . . . Tenor
Barbarina, the gardener's daughter . . . . Soprano
Two peasant girls . . . . . . Soprano and Mezzo-soprano

*The Story**

ACT I. Figaro, former barber of Seville, now in the employ of Count Almaviva and planning to marry the Countess' maid Susanna, is busy measuring the room the Count plans to give the young couple. He thinks it conveniently located should either the master or mistress ring during the night; Susanna objects that it is too near the Count, who has designs on her (**Figaro, Susanna:** *Se a caso, madama*—If by chance your lady should call you during the night). When Susanna has left, Figaro threatens revenge on the Count (**Figaro:** *Se vuol ballare*—If you would dance). Crafty Dr. Bartolo, former guardian of the Countess, persuades his housekeeper Marcellina to sue Figaro for breach of promise, as a means of avenging himself on the man who made him lose his ward and sweetheart (**Bartolo:** *La vendetta*—Glorious vengeance). Susanna returns and exchanges insults with Marcellina, who finally leaves. The page Cherubino now comes to ask Susanna's protection from the Count, who found him alone with Barbarina. He loves all women, the boy says (**Cheru-**

* Originally written in two acts, *The Marriage of Figaro* is almost never produced that way today. The four-act version here given is the one commonly presented in the world's opera houses.

bino: *Non so più cosa son, cosa faccio*—I do not know what I am or what I do), and then hides as his master arrives to flirt with the maid. Basilio, the music teacher, comes in to spread gossip as the Count also hides. The Count, infuriated by Basilio's insinuations about Cherubino's love for the Countess, finally reveals himself; Susanna pretends to faint. Relating how he surprised Cherubino with Barbarina, the Count discovers the page's hiding place in Susanna's room and is horrified to learn that Cherubino has heard all his conversation with Susanna. Mollified by compliments of the peasantry, the Count offers Cherubino a commission. Figaro taunts the page with the rigors of army life that lie ahead (**Figaro:** *Non più andrai farfallone amoroso*—No longer will you go philandering night and day).

ACT II. In her luxurious boudoir the Countess bemoans the fading of Almaviva's love (**Countess:** *Porgi amor*—Lend, o love, something in exchange for my sorrow). To trick the Count into approving his marriage with Susanna, Figaro plots with her to compromise their master. Cherubino, who comes to woo the Countess before departing (**Cherubino:** *Voi che sapete*—What do you know about love?), is to participate in the plot dressed as a girl. Thus he will play "Susanna" in a rendezvous with the Count. Susanna fits him in a headdress (**Susanna:** *Venite, inginocchiatevi*—Come here and kneel). The women hear the Count approach and, fearing his wrath if he finds the page with his wife, hide Cherubino in a closet. The page upsets a chair in the closet and arouses the Count's suspicions. The Countess replies that it is merely Susanna. Almaviva orders "Susanna" to come out, but the Countess forbids her to come forth as a "point of honor." The Count therefore orders his wife to accompany him while he gets a crowbar to break the door down. Susanna, who has meanwhile slipped back into the room, aids Cherubino to escape through the window; then she shuts herself in the closet. When the Count returns to force the door, it is Susanna who emerges. The Count is contrite and almost gives in to the returning Figaro's request that he sign his and Susanna's wedding contract. However, the gardener Antonio enters to report that a man has jumped into his flower bed from the Countess' window. Figaro takes the blame but is almost caught in the lie when Antonio produces papers that the escaping man dropped. He is finally able to answer the Count's queries as to what the papers are—Cherubino's commission—by adroit prompting from the Countess and Susanna. Marcellina enters, with Basilio and Bartolo, to press charges that Figaro is pledged to marry her.

ACT III. In his audience room Susanna promises the Count a rendezvous (**Count, Susanna:** *Crudel! perchè finora*—Cruel one! Why have you made me suffer so up to now?); but as she leaves, he overhears a remark which makes him suspect a ruse. He is furious and vows he will not be vanquished by his own servants (**Count:** *Vedrò mentr'io sospiro*—Do I have to see my servant happy while I sigh?). Marcellina arrives, accompanied by Bartolo and the lawyer Don Curzio. Figaro must either marry her or pay her an indemnity. But before the marriage takes place, Marcellina discovers that Figaro is her long-lost son; the father is none other than Bartolo! Susanna hurriedly enters with a bag of money which she presents to the Count; the money will free Figaro to marry her. On seeing Figaro and Marcellina embracing one another, however, she imagines herself jilted and soundly boxes Figaro before he and the others can explain the true situation. The Count leaves in a huff while the rest go off to spread the happy tidings. The Countess, awaiting Susanna to hear news of their latest scheme to trick the Count, again mourns her husband's indifference (**Countess:** *Dove sono i bei momenti*—Where are the beautiful moments?). Antonio tells the Count he is sure Cherubino has returned and is somewhere disguised as a girl. The Countess dictates to Susanna a note from Susanna to the Count, confirming the rendezvous (**Countess, Susanna:** *Che soave zefiretto*—What gentle zephyrs will swell tonight); they seal the note with a needle, to be returned. The peasantry arrives for the wedding procession, which includes Cherubino, whose disguise is revealed by the Count. During the festivities, enlivened by a gay fandango, Susanna, at last a bride, slips the invitation to the Count, who pricks his finger on the needle.

ACT IV. Barbarina, armed with a lantern, looks in the garden for the needle which the Count has given her for Susanna and which she has lost. After she inadvertently tells Figaro of the assignation, the disillusioned man launches a complaint against womankind (**Figaro:** *Aprite un po' quegl' occhi*—Open your eyes a little). When Susanna arrives and pours out her love for Figaro (**Susanna:** *Deh vieni, non tardar*—Come, do not delay), her bridegroom thinks she is referring to the Count. Susanna hides, and the Countess appears, disguised as her maid. She is wooed by Cherubino—to the great anger of the Count and Figaro. Figaro emerges to punish Cherubino and in the scuffle is cuffed by the Count, who leads the Countess away, still thinking her to be Susanna. Figaro now makes love to Susanna in her disguise as the Countess, which he has penetrated. He regrets his mistrust of Susanna. When the Count returns, however, Figaro is caught in the act of making love to the supposed Countess. Calling forth all the others to bear witness, the Count openly accuses Figaro of treachery, but is convinced of his mistake as soon as the Countess appears and the truth comes to light. He repents of his philandering, begs the Countess' pardon (**Count:** *Contessa, perdono!*—Countess, forgive me), and accepts the fact that Susanna is now Figaro's wife. The opera ends in rejoicing as each of the couples is happily reunited.

IF *The Marriage of Figaro* can be said to have one predominant quality, a trait characteristic of both the play and the operatic setting, it is perpetual motion. Nothing stands still; the moments of poise are rare and come as an unexpected relief in a plot of constant and highly concentrated action. An entire evening's entertainment could be made of the events of the finale of the second act alone! Confusion piles upon confusion; half a dozen miniature plots arise, come to a climax, are resolved, or left at a moment of crisis.

Yet in all the confusion and mercurial speed of dramatic complications, there is order. Music is, inevitably, highly organized; order in sound is its essence. Mozart's own comment was that although in certain dramatic situations the music might appear to forget itself and overstep formal bounds, it must never cease to be music. Form and text work hand in hand. So, in *Figaro*, even while sustaining the perpetual motion, adding to the excitement of the countless crises, portraying mood and character, and covering a great deal of action, the music remains music, clear and satisfying from the formal point of view.

Everything is functional in *Figaro*. Pity the poor director who finds it necessary to shorten the show! The omission of any ensemble is dramatically impossible, for each one is necessary to the continuity of the story. The arias, so often points of rest and commentary in the eighteenth century, are vital to our knowledge of the characters. We would never completely know Figaro without the dancing satire of *Se vuol ballare*, the buoyant horseplay of *Non più andrai*, and the bitterness of *Aprite un po' quegl'occhi*. Each shows a different vein in his personality, and without any one he would be far less human. The Countess, far too well-bred to open her heart in company, shows us its full tenderness and complexity in her two soliloquies, musical portraits of a mature and infinitely interesting personality. Cherubino's youthful effusions are musically youthful, too; comparison of his rhythmically naive melodies with the more varied ones of the Countess will give the clue to character immediately. Susanna, after three acts of musical bouncing—the patter-like staccato line which is her favorite form of speech—reveals an entirely different side of her nature in *Deh vieni, non tardar*.

At one point in the opera, an aria performs the function of an ensemble. This is Susanna's song in Act II, which calls for a great deal of action and is dramatically a duet with Cherubino. Performing this aria in a solo concert would make no more sense than performing the violin part of a trio alone! The point of the piece is its action, the working out of Cherubino's disguise, and Cherubino must do the greater share of the acting. Experienced in stage timing, Mozart allowed just enough time for Susanna to complete the disguise easily before directing Cherubino to walk around the room. Less repetition of text or shorter orchestral interludes would have rushed the actors; more would have created static moments. . . .

For the most part, the pace and continuity of *Figaro* depend on the ensembles. Of the action-filled finales, much has been said; certainly they are unique in their time as examples of continuous musical and dramatic texture. It is in the shorter ensembles, however—the duets and trios, and the remarkable sextet—that Mozart gives some of his surest strokes of characterization and musical humor.

. . . . .

The opening duet between Figaro and Susanna tells us musically something about Figaro (that once he has an idea, it is hard to change his mind), something about Susanna (that her nature is cheerful, playful but persuasive), and something about the action on stage (that it involves starting from a fixed point and reaching farther and farther—in this case, measuring the room).

Another revelation, and the most important here, is the relationship between Figaro and Susanna. We find them in disagreement, melodically as well as dramatically, over which is the more important, the arrangement of the furniture or Susanna's new hat. These two ideas will never mix, throughout their married life; if Mozart had believed so, he would have designed the two melodies as counterpoints to each other.

The disagreement is only a minor one, however. Both themes are in the same key, and there is no violent clash of character.

It takes a little persistence, but Susanna eventually wins Figaro over to her idea and her melody.

All is well. The bridal couple is singing in parallel thirds and sixths; they love each other and their agreement is perfect—and it is important to the story that we know this. It is the sureness and naturalness of their love which makes the rift between the Count and Countess all the more poignant, assures the success of the plots against the Count, and gives credibility and humor to the fury of each of the lovers when the other is supposedly unfaithful.

In contrast, the second duet shows Figaro and Susanna in a disagreement more serious. "Doubts and suspicions chill me," he says, while she protests, "Your suspicions wrong me." The musical lines disagree as well, first in rhythm and then by moving in opposite directions.

The portrayal of character is the main concern of the trio in Act I. The ensemble is set off by a moment of crisis: Basilio, hinting to Susanna that Cherubino's infatuation for the Countess is becoming obvious, is suddenly confronted by the Count—while Cherubino himself listens, concealed in the armchair. This is the Count's first musical appearance, and we are aware of his personality immediately—commanding, accustomed to being obeyed without question, forceful to the point of abruptness.

Basilio, on the other hand, speaks with legato suavity over appropriately shifty harmonies, the perfect courtier and the perfect spy.

Susanna's playful patter has now become more nervous, with good reason. The discovery of two men in her room, especially by a habitual scandalmonger, would unsettle any girl.

Strategically, Susanna faints—to a descending scale in the orchestra—but she recovers with surprising vigor as the two men try to place her in the very chair where Cherubino is hiding. A syncopated motif in the violins, to be heard again later in the trio, is a witty comment on the situation.

Basilio, oily as before, assures the Count that what he has said about Cherubino was only rumor. After his calm phrase, Susanna's *forte* outburst is proof enough that at least a part of his story is true; as Gluck commented, the violas never lie!

It is significant that the Count, in telling how he caught Cherubino once before, adopts Basilio's melody, for he has also used Basilio's tactics, spying rather than commanding. Here Mozart uses an amusing touch of instrumental color. The strings move downward with the inevitability of the Count's move toward the chair; the woodwinds are saved for the moment when he lifts the cover and finds Cherubino; the strings quietly move upward again. Everyone, including the orchestra, is speechless with surprise. This is perhaps the funniest single moment of the first act, and Mozart plays it with the musical equivalent of a poker face. Like Susanna's appearance from the closet in Act II, it is deftly understated.

Basilio cannot conceal his delight at this little scandal, and gives a melodic giggle. Next, pouring his own oil on the fire, he repeats his assurance that it was only a rumor. This bit of satire is Mozart's own idea, quite unplanned by the librettist but devastating in its effect on both Susanna and the Count. (Perhaps one reason for the success of the Mozart-da Ponte combination was that the texts allowed for some imagination on the part of the composer.)

Of the ensembles with musical emphasis on action, the most obvious is the "letter duet" in Act III. Again Mozart's sense for stage timing comes to the singer's aid. Susanna is not expected to take shorthand; she has just enough time between phrases to write in a ladylike script what the Countess dictates. And what a human touch: she misses one phrase, and must ask her employer to repeat it!

Mozart rarely repeats a text without dramatic justification, and the progress of the drama usually requires some musical change in the repetition. Here the restatement of text is the most natural event possible: the secretary reads back what she has written. This time, however, no time for writing is necessary, so the phrases overlap one another closely.

A musical repetition may come about without a repetition of text, but some element of similarity in situation must be present if the form is really to illuminate the drama. In the trio of the second act, the composer has used a well-established pattern, the sonatina, which fits the dramatic pattern admirably: the exposition, or statement of two points of view, an abbreviated development preparing for the return of the first theme, and the return itself, with new consequences.

The situation is this: someone is in the Countess' closet. The Countess insists that it is Susanna; the Count, justifiably suspicious, demands in his usual imperious tone that she come out.

Susanna, in hiding, wonders what this is all about, while the Countess—searching for a plausible answer, over a rather uncertain chromatic accompaniment—explains that Susanna is trying on her wedding dress. This is the second theme of the sonata, the second point of view.

The preparation for the return, musically the traditional

build-up of the dominant chord, brings a quick exchange of conflicting commands, the Count again ordering Susanna to come out and the Countess forbidding it. Now we arrive at the musical restatement, but with a dramatic change. The Count gives a new command: if she will not appear, she must at least speak. The Countess' reaction is uncontrolled panic.

She calls to "Susanna" to be silent. The Count, his suspicions even stronger now, ominously warns her to take care, while Susanna comments aside that only a scandal can result.

The brilliance of Susanna's part in this ensemble is curious, considering the dramatic situation. A young lady in hiding can hardly hope to remain undiscovered while running repeatedly up to high C. Mozart never intended to put her in such danger; originally the two soprano parts were reversed through most of the trio, with Susanna appropriately singing the inner voice and the Countess taking the excited runs. Some editions are still printed this way, but tradition has since assigned the lower part to the Countess' heavier voice. The composer would have been disturbed, no doubt, but Susanna retains her high C's.

The following duet, between Susanna and Cherubino, again concentrates on action. As a variety of melody was appropriate for the variety of ideas in the trio, the single purpose—escape—here calls for a single musical idea. The composer builds the entire duet on one little motif.

There is no development of the theme in a symphonic sense, but it whirls in the mind, now in one key, now in another, as the two run from door to door, find all locked, wonder what to do, and discover the convenient window. It rises in agitation as Susanna protests; it goes briefly into the minor key with charming mock-tragedy as Cherubino bids her farewell, and it ends in the air—as he jumps.

Music can give a clear indication of psychological state, even without special aid from the text. An excellent example is the name-calling duet between Marcellina and Susanna. (I can be nicer to you than you can be to me, you hussy.) Poor Susanna, less experienced in courtly battle tactics, is on the defensive from the start. Marcellina leads; Susanna can only follow suit, repeating her melody.

Marcellina offers her double-edged compliments calmly, over a soft accompaniment; Susanna bursts out with her own in an agitated *forte*. Not until Susanna finds her weak spot—her age—does the older woman explode. Now the process begins again. The entire text is repeated, but here the two situations are reversed: Susanna is sure of herself now, Marcellina on the defensive. She attempts to change the subject, pulling away from the key of her defeat, but Susanna immediately returns to it. She offers her compliments, but Susanna is much quicker with her answers—she needs no time for thought now! Delighted with her success, she teases like a child—"Your age, your age, your age"—until her rival gives up the battle and departs, infuriated.

Again in the duet between Susanna and the Count (Act III) we hear two emotional states in contrast. The Count is lovesick, beyond any doubt. The uncertainty of A minor, a definite tension in the harmony, and a suggestion of palpitations of the heart betray him.

Susanna answers much more calmly, in the brighter C major, but obligingly modulates to the Count's key as she promises to meet him in the garden. Now the Count can relax. An expansive phrase in A major (a happy compromise of tonality) shows his confidence.

Meanwhile Susanna, in her characteristic staccato line, begs our pardon for her lie. She is nearly caught in the lie, as Mozart again turns a text repetition to dramatic advantage: she carelessly says "no" when she means to say "yes." A sudden dissonance shows us that the Count is suspicious of the slip, but the dissonance smooths out as Susanna hastily corrects herself.

The joke is worth repeating, but the second time Mozart gives her a mistaken "yes" for variety. The Count's questions are coming so fast, by now, that even an honest witness might become confused! Susanna is a clever enough actress, however, to appear to agree with him by the end of the duet. They sing in the most convincing of parallel thirds, although their ideas are directly opposed.

It is hard to single out one predominant idea in the sextet of Act III; everything said so far applies to it in some measure. In a deliciously funny situation, the recognition of Figaro as the long-lost child of Marcellina and Bartolo, we are shown musical characterization (the two parents seen in a new and sympathetic light), relationship (the three happy characters balanced against the two disturbed ones), action (Susanna's misunderstanding and its explanation, linking her musically with first the unhappy group, then the happy one), and a most delightful instance of repetition of text for comic effect, the succession of "*Sua madre?*" and "*Suo padre?*" as Susanna incredulously questions one person after another.

Emotional state is skillfully drawn. The calmness of legato lines and harmonies firmly rooted in long pedal points for Figaro, Marcellina, and Bartolo contrasts with the abrupt phrases and angry dotted rhythms of the Count and Curzio. Susanna, seeing Figaro embrace her old rival, takes fire musically, in an agitated phrase which might be serious.

Marcellina explains everything, in a phrase that—curiously—bears a resemblance to her exaggerated compliments of the first act. She is still the same person, though the orchestra shows her a calmer one now.

Formally, this is the return of the opening theme, another example of the dramatic use of the sonata form. The first statement brought the son into the family; the second brings in the daughter-in-law as well. Now the reunited family's happiness contrasts with the dissatisfaction of the Count and Curzio, who break into the blissful ensemble with forceful threats and sharp changes of key.

Effective in its formal design, rich in detail, always a source of added life for the drama—sometimes far beyond the actual demands of the text—the music of *Figaro* is perpetually amazing to its closest students, a delight to opera-goers, and a boon to actors. No more can be said of any dramatic music. It is both beautiful and functional; it does its work excellently, and it never ceases to be music.

KATHERINE GRIFFITH McDONALD

CHRISTOPH WILLIBALD VON GLUCK (1714–1787)

Orfeo ed Euridice

Libretto by Raniero de' Calzabigi. First performance in Vienna, October 5, 1762.

Characters

Orfeo	Contralto
Amor	Soprano
A Happy Shade	Soprano
Euridice	Soprano

The Story

ACT I. Before the tomb of his beloved wife Euridice in the Greece of mythical antiquity, the poet and singer Orfeo sits dejectedly while his friends lay wreaths on her grave and lament her sudden death (**Chorus:** *Ah! se intorno*—Ah, if around this fatal urn). Bidding them leave him, Orfeo gives vent to his despair and loneliness, eventually resolving to find Euridice in the underworld and bring her back (**Orfeo:** *Chiamo il mio ben cosi* —This way I call my love). Suddenly Amor, god of love, appears and announces to Orfeo that the gods, moved by his sorrow, will allow him to descend to Hades and bring back Euridice on condition that he avoid gazing upon her until they return to the world of men (**Amor:** *Dalla cetra tua dolci tuoni*—From your lyre produce sweet sounds). Alone once more, Orfeo overcomes his doubts and fears and, overjoyed at the thought of again seeing his beloved, sets out for the infernal regions (**Orfeo:** *Addio, o miei sospiri*—Good-by, o my sighs).

As Orfeo approaches the entrance to the underworld,* a crowd of Furies angrily demand who it is that dares to invade their realm, guarded by the monster Cerberus (**Chorus:** *Chi mai dell' Erebo*—Who is the mortal nearing this region?). Advancing into their seething midst, ignoring smoke and hell-fire, the poet strikes his lyre and begs the Furies to take pity on one tormented like themselves (**Orfeo:** *Deh placatevi con me*—Make peace with me). Touched by the gentle sounds, the horde demands to know why he is there (**Chorus:** *Misero giovane, che vuoi?*—Poor young man, what do you wish?). Moved at length by his strange plight and eloquent music, the Furies allow him

* Usually the beginning of Act II.

to pass through the gates of Hades, after which they break once more into frenzied writhing (**Dance of the Furies**).

ACT II. In the Elysian fields, the blessed spirits move peacefully against a landscape of space and light (**Dance of the Blessed Spirits**); a Happy Shade sings blissfully of the absence of earthly care (**Happy Shade:** *E quest'asilo*—This pleasant shelter is welcome). Orfeo enters in search of Euridice, pausing to exclaim at the pure air, the bright sky (**Orfeo:** *Che puro ciel!*—What a clear sky!). But only the sight of his beloved can ease his sorrow, he informs the Shades, who almost at once lead in the veiled Euridice. Remembering not to look back at her, Orfeo grasps his wife by the hand and starts with her on the long journey to the outer world, while the blessed spirits wish them well (**Chorus:** *Torna, o bella*—Return, beautiful one, to your spouse).

ACT III. Still leading Euridice by the hand, Orfeo reluctantly pauses to listen to her anxious entreaties. Is it really he? Is she to live again? Does he love her no more? Why does he not look at her? Averting his face with difficulty, Orfeo urges her to hasten with him and trust in his love (**Orfeo, Euridice:** *Su, è con me vieni*—Come, come with me). But the disconsolate Euridice refuses to advance, lamenting the fact that she has been liberated from death only to face a still colder fate: her love is no longer returned (**Euridice:** *Che fiero momento*—What a proud moment). Unable to endure his anguish, Orfeo turns in desperation to embrace his wife, who at once breathes a farewell and dies. Beside himself with grief and remorse, the poet declares that he cannot live without Euridice (**Orfeo:** *Che farò senza Euridice?*—What will I do without Euridice?). Drawing his dagger, he is about to stab himself when Amor appears and stays his hand. Declaring that Orfeo has passed the test of faith and constancy, the god restores Euridice to life and bids them resume their journey (**Euridice, Orfeo, Amor:** *Gaudio son al core*—A pleasure to the heart are these pains of love).

Led by Amor to the altar of the Temple of Love, the happy couple are joined by the multitude in celebrating love's triumph with dance and song (**Ballet**).

SINCE the earliest dawn of opera, composers have tried to link music to drama in a meaningful way, carrying out Monteverdi's principle: "The words should be the master of music, not the servant." In his own century, Gluck became the champion of this cause, giving a long-neglected dramatic impact to *Orfeo.*

It is possible, in most works of the eighteenth century, to discuss arias, ensembles, recitative, chorus, and orchestra separately. With *Orfeo,* this is out of the question. The interaction is too close, too organic, for any separation. Aria and recitative are mingled, and the line between the two is faint. Traditional forms are abandoned entirely or used with great freedom. . . .

Throughout the opera the aria *is* the action, not an abstract commentary on the action. There are few soliloquies—most of the singing is done in company—and the soliloquy itself has become freer and wider in scope. Orfeo's first solo scene, the long compound structure in Act I, is an example. The form is the same as that of *Che farò,* somewhat expanded: a brief air, a passage in recitative, a repetition of the air with different text, another recitative, and a third stanza of the air.

The melody is a gracious one, gently curving. Orfeo calls to his beloved, but receives no answer except the echo—an offstage orchestra of oboe and strings which repeats delicately the last few notes of his phrase. The idea is not new; Gluck is following an old tradition of echo effects, always striking in music. . . . Here the emotional effect is greater than mere trickery, however. The plaintive oboe emphasizes Orfeo's own loneliness, the sense of hopelessness growing with every repetition.

Gluck varies the instrumental color slightly with each repetition of the air, finding a slightly darker sound for each successive stanza. Beginning with a string orchestra and two flutes, he replaces the flutes with the French horn as Orfeo muses upon the sadness of the woods where Euridice once roamed. Even the brook murmurs sorrowfully—and the orchestral texture becomes more complex, the gently whispering violins colored by the bassoon and English horn. The echo orchestra, meanwhile, remains the same and is active even in the recitatives, which are nearly as melodic as the airs. There are no dry recitatives in *Orfeo;* both voice and orchestra are musically expressive. The melody is measured, more regular in pulse than the French accompanied recitative, and often supported by the loveliest of harmonies. Listen for a phrase of deeply affecting simplicity as Orfeo, having lingered over her name—carved upon the trees, echoed by the hills—cries, "Euridice is no more—and I still live!"

. . . . .

. . . After the optimistic conclusion of the first act, the stern opening measures of Act II have the effect of the sudden tightening of a string: the tension is present immediately; the pitch of the drama is raised. Musically as well as dramatically, we have left the gentler world of the surface; we face the gates of hell.

Orfeo's harp is heard at a distance, and in somber unison the chorus of Furies demands to know who dares come among them. Their music, which returns again and again to unify the scene, is well calculated to terrify the intruder: angular in melody, bizarre in spirit, perilous with dissonance and sudden modulation. Sharp accents in the strings and the acid tone of the oboe, no longer wailing quietly offstage, give an added biting quality to their outbursts.

Orfeo's answer is the greatest possible contrast. Softly, mildly, to the warm accompaniment of the harp, he leads them from their ferocious C minor to the calmer E-flat major. His phrases, in the most ingratiating Italian style, remain smooth and melodious even when the Furies shout their abrupt "No!" in a conflicting key. He cannot hope to overpower them; it is only by winning their pity he can approach his goal.

As he closes his first plea, there is an instant of silence. The Furies—touched enough, at least, to pay attention to this mortal —ask softly, "Unhappy youth, what do you want?" Then, resolute again, they return to their *fortissimo* raging. Let him beware, they say; the horrors of condemned souls surround him here.

Orfeo has discovered their hearts, however, and he pursues his advantage. He, too, is a soul in torment, he tells them, for he carries his hell within him. His melody becomes less lyrical, his phrases shorter, and delicate dissonances appear in the harmony.

Perhaps it is the dissonance which works the charm, the Furies' realization that Orfeo's misery is somehow linked to their own. Hushed now, the Furies ask in amazement how their anger could have been calmed so suddenly. Orfeo continues with a passage which would melt an iceberg on contact. The short phrases are almost sobs now, and the harmony is the most affecting so far. Can these creatures not imagine what it is to love, he asks? A chord highly charged with emotion, the Neapolitan sixth, underlines his plea, and the violins echo his sighs.

It is an excellently planned work of persuasion, progressing from the formally beautiful to the intensely personal, and the Furies make no more attempt to resist. The forbidding gates open slowly. Needless to say, Gluck remembers to close the gates again after Orfeo has passed through safely, and the Furies disappear little by little. . . . Here is a scene of musical continuity unparalleled in its time. . . .

A wild dance of Furies, reflecting the French tradition of inserting a ballet wherever possible, is the pivoting point of the act. Beginning with ominous string tremolos, it grows to a climax of frenetic brilliance, emphasized by sharp syncopated rhythms—still in the fearful realm of the underworld—then suddenly subsides, preparing us for the Elysian fields we are about to enter. The familiar ballet of the happy spirits and the exquisite air shared by the Shade and her companions are doubly beautiful in this context, coming like mild sunlight after the musical storms that preceded them.

Into this serene world Orfeo wanders, and he exclaims in amazement at its beauty. Here Gluck makes his most effective use of the accompanied recitative. The orchestra leads the way, sets the mood, and sings the principal melody. The murmuring of the river and the twittering of songbirds are skillfully suggested by the instruments long before Orfeo mentions their presence. . . .

The shadow of a minor key falls upon the music, again anticipating Orfeo's words. Even here he finds no happiness; without Euridice, there can be no loveliness. The oboe's melody, so serene in the major, takes a poignant coloring now.

It is only the remembrance of his beloved—her eyes, her voice, her smile—that brings back the major key. The tranquillity of the Elysian fields has vanished from the music, however. More complex harmonies, rapidly changing, show Orfeo's restlessness, and the passage ends rather bleakly in A minor. Beauty and sorrow have competed, and sorrow has been victorious; here we see tone-painting and character depiction combined, the mood of the scene contrasted with the mood of the person, all done with the simplest musical means.

In its general form, Act III approaches the Italian tradition of alternative recitative and aria more closely than either of the previous acts. Again, the French opera shows some influence in detail. The recitative is still accompanied, and generally melodic rather than declamatory in character; the duets are more free in form than the Italian models. Gluck's ability to accentuate the emotional content of his text brings the long dialogue to life. Within the framework of the classic story, Orfeo and Euridice are an intensely human husband and wife, suffering in a situation which neither wholly understands.

Orfeo has foreseen the difficulty of his promise. His first reaction to the gods' requirements was one of foreboding: "Unhappy wife! What will she say, what will she think? My heart trembles at the thought." Now, the situation realized at last, the restless F-minor introduction to Act III tells us that he is uneasy once more. Trying to ignore his fears, Orfeo begins the recitative confidently in the major key, but soon the minor coloring appears again—a hint of the tension to come.

Euridice seems to awaken gradually. Her phrases, broken and hesitant at first, grow more coherent and confident as she becomes conscious that she is alive again, and that her husband is with her. Gluck indicates a sudden *pianissimo* as, for the first time since their separation, she calls him "*mio caro*"; her happiness finds expression in the most intimate of undertones.

Here Orfeo makes an unforgivable mistake. She speaks of love, and he abruptly changes the subject, urging her to hurry. This is far from his normal behavior, and Euridice is naturally puzzled. Almost playfully she scolds him: why is he suddenly so cold? Has she perhaps lost her former beauty? A gentle motif in the violins, repeated a tone higher after each phrase, lends winsomeness to her questioning. Though the harmonic progression ascends—usually an indication of rising emotion—Euridice's calm vocal line, with its logically repeated phrases, shows that she is neither frightened nor angry. At this point, she is merely feminine, gently teasing her lover for a compliment.

Upset by this turn of events, Orfeo can only go around and around in his own vocal line. Euridice's plea is simple: one look will be enough. An abrupt stab from the orchestra warns us that one look will mean disaster.

Bewildered and hurt by his refusal, Euridice finally loses her temper, and the calm, controlled line gives way to wider leaps and angry accents. We expect an aria of fury at such a moment, but Orfeo has another resource. His music charmed the fiends of the underworld; can he not charm his wife as well? Lovingly he tries to persuade her to come with him.

Euridice interrupts his phrase with a more agitated one; she will stay in the realms of the dead rather than suffer such torment. The duet shows little of the melody-centered concept. Each phrase, each new turn of thought brings a new musical expression, so that there is a minimum of melodic repetition in the course of the ensemble. The uncertainty of syncopated rhythm, the emotional tension of the harmonic progressions, and the introspective quality of sudden shifts to a slower tempo—all reflect the state of mind of two confused and miserable people. . . .

Feeling more alone than ever, Euridice confesses her terror in a brief recitative, the orchestra becoming progressively more agitated beneath her short, sobbing phrases.

The aria which follows shows Euridice at the height of her

despair. How cruel, after the sweet forgetfulness of death, to return to life and be rejected! The opening melody . . . is interrupted by a slower phrase, the change of tempo again reflecting her own uncertainty. As she recalls the serenity of the Elysian fields, we hear a quieter, more lyrical melody, this time in the relative major key. Even here, however, the warm atmosphere is a little clouded with syncopations, throbbing alternations of loud and soft phrases, and a slight darkening of the harmony.

Now the aria becomes a duet, as Orfeo voices his own despair in a few broken phrases. The effect is that of one actor speaking "aside" while another plays the principal scene. A return to the present situation brings back the C-minor agitation, and the struggle goes on.

Euridice feels her strength failing; her vocal line, so vigorous a moment ago, becomes more and more restricted until it is little more than a single note. Subtly changing harmonies under a repeated note can be deeply moving, as we see: heartbroken, she bids him farewell in a phrase so simple—yet so Italian—that Puccini would have been proud of it. "Good-by. Remember me always!"

Who could resist this appeal? Not Orfeo, certainly. He defies the gods, he turns to her—and she dies immediately, abruptly, without even a traditional set of cadence-chords. . . . The emptiness of the following silence is more expressive than any orchestral climax could be.

Suddenly frantic, Orfeo realizes what he has done. In vain he tries to call her back, while the orchestra echoes his panic. The aria occurring here is no mere showpiece for the contralto's *legato* line but an outburst of the cruelest desperation and self-reproach. Gluck indicates the tempo as *Andante con moto* (not *Adagio*, as it is often performed) and pierces the melody with sharp *sforzando* impulses. He tries again to win her back, and realizes that there is no hope; the question "*Che farò*" becomes an obsession, returning again and again. "What shall I do without her? Where shall I go?" This is repetition not for the sake of musical logic alone, but for the greatest intensity of dramatic impact.

Orfeo is surely a unique creation, the product of two operatic cultures, the child of French drama and Italian melody. Fulfilling Monteverdi's motto, the words *are* master of the music; yet the music is a servant of such nobility and grace that it may (like Barrie's Crichton) serve as the master on occasion.

KATHERINE GRIFFITH MCDONALD

GIUSEPPE VERDI (1813–1901)

Otello

Libretto by Arrigo Boïto, based on Shakespeare's *Othello.* First performance in Milan, February 5, 1887.

Characters

Montano, former Governor of Cyprus ...... Baritone
Cassio, captain under Otello .... Tenor
Iago, ensign under Otello .... Baritone
Roderigo, a Venetian gentleman .... Tenor
Otello, Moor of Venice, Governor of Cyprus .. Tenor
Desdemona, Otello's wife .... Soprano
Emilia, Desdemona's companion and Iago's wife Mezzo-soprano
Lodovico, Venetian Ambassador .... Bass
A herald .... Baritone

The Story

ACT I. A roaring tempest besieges the harbor of Cyprus as Otello, a Moorish general in the Venetian army at the end of the fifteenth century, and governor of the city, returns, exulting in victory over the Turks (**Otello:** *Esultate!*—Exult! The proud Moslem is buried in the sea). His comrade Iago, jealous of Otello's preferment of Cassio over himself as the general's captain, confides his discontent to Roderigo, then plots the dismissal of his rival by plying him with drink and urging him to extol the virtues of Desdemona, the general's wife, who Iago knows is secretly loved by the youthful Roderigo (**Iago, Chorus:** *Inaffia l'ugola!* [Brindisi]—Quench your thirst). The drunken Cassio is provoked by Roderigo into a duel, which is halted only by the reappearance of Otello from his castle. When Iago feigns astonishment over the duel, Otello angrily demotes the befuddled Cassio and bids the others leave. Attracted by the uproar, Desdemona appears as the storm yields to moonlight and joins Otello in a rapturous love duet (**Otello, Desdemona:** *Già nella notte densa*—Already in the dark night all noises begin to subside).

ACT II. Iago calls Cassio to a room in the castle and suggests that he await Desdemona in the adjacent garden to plead for her intercession with Otello on his behalf. When the erstwhile captain has left, Iago cynically declaims his own creed of cruelty and evil (**Iago:** *Credo in un Dio crudel*—I believe in a cruel God). Suiting the action to the word, he next plants in Otello's mind a seed of suspicion of Desdemona, who is first glimpsed strolling with Cassio in the garden. She then returns alone to greet a delegation of women, children, and sailors bearing gifts and flowers (**Chorus:** *Dove guardi splendono raggi*—Wheresoe'er you look are rays of splendor). Otello softens at her beauty, but the next instant his suspicions are confirmed when, as Iago has suggested, she pleads with her husband for Cassio's reinstatement. Fearing that Otello is ill, Desdemona seeks to soothe him with a handkerchief he once gave her and is shocked to see him throw it angrily to the ground, whence it is retrieved by her companion, Iago's wife Emilia. While Desdemona reaffirms her love for the unhappy Moor, Iago forces the unsuspecting Emilia to give him the handkerchief, which he conceals (**Desdemona** [**Quartet**]: *Se inconscia, contro te*—If I have ever unconsciously offended you, husband). The women leave. Accusing Iago of banishing forever his peace of mind and hopes of success, Otello falls upon him in a rage (**Otello:** *Ora e per sempre*—Farewell forever, saintly memories). Iago replies with "proof"—one night he heard Cassio in his sleep murmuring of Desdemona's love (**Iago:** *Era la notte*—It was night; Cassio was sleeping). Furthermore, he says, he has seen in Cassio's hands one of Desdemona's handkerchiefs. Crazed with jealousy, Otello vows revenge, to which the hypocritical Iago pledges his aid (**Otello, Iago:** *Sì pel ciel*—Yes, by the marble sky I swear).

ACT III. In the great hall of the castle Iago shows Otello where to secrete himself so that he may eavesdrop on a forthcoming conversation between him and Cassio, which will prove beyond doubt Cassio's and Desdemona's treachery. Otello hints his suspicions to Desdemona, who pleads her innocence (**Desdemona:** *Dio ti giocondi*—God make you happy). Though he asks her to fetch the handkerchief, she insists on pleading once again for Cassio. Otello accuses his wife of perfidy, whereupon she falls on her knees and, in tears, swears she has nothing to conceal (**Desdemona:** *Esterrefatta fisso lo sguardo*—Frightened, I gaze at your fearful mien). Otello leads her from the room, then reflects on his sorrow (**Otello:** *Dio mi potevi*—Had it pleased heaven to try me with affliction). Iago enters to say that Cassio has arrived, so Otello takes his place behind the column. Then Iago, who has planted the handkerchief in his doublet, manipulates the man's innocent conversation so as to convince Otello of Desdemona's guilt (**Iago** [**Trio**]: *Quest' è una ragna*—This is a spider's web). The Moor prepares to murder his wife. He promotes Iago to captain and then, joined by the others with the exception of Cassio, welcomes Lodovico, the Venetian ambassador. A document announces the recall of Otello to Venice and the appointment of Cassio as governor of Cyprus. The disappointment is too much for Otello, who hurls Desdemona to the ground before the company and refuses to listen to her anguished lament for his lost love (**Desdemona:** *A terra! Sì, nel livido fango*—Yes, prostrate here, I lie in the dust). Aside, Iago tells Roderigo to murder Cassio during the night so Otello will remain as governor. Violently the Moor dismisses everyone but Iago, who sees his general swoon with rage and then gloats at his own triumph.

ACT IV. In her bedroom, Desdemona sits at her dressing table and sings the sad Willow Song (**Desdemona:** *O Salce! salce!*—O Willow, willow) to Emilia, who, at her request, adorns the bed with her wedding veil. Giving Emilia a ring, she bids her a touching good night. No sooner has Desdemona said her prayers (**Desdemona:** *Ave Maria*) and retired than Otello enters stealthily, blows out the candle, and kisses his sleeping wife. She awakens and begs forgiveness but is strangled by the Moor. Emilia rushes in with word that Cassio has killed Roderigo; discovering Desdemona, she cries for help. Iago, Lodovico, and Cassio appear, but Iago escapes when his wife discloses his perfidy. The agonized Otello kills himself (**Otello:** *Niun mi tema*—No one fears me even if I'm armed).

CRITICS are in the habit of bracketing *Otello* and *Falstaff* as the inestimable fruits of Verdi's old age. Insofar as the two are extraordinary products of senescence they are right. Yet there are vital differences between them. In *Falstaff*, despite lovely details and endearing if isolated blooms, the composer's melodic fecundity is largely exhausted. In *Otello* it still flows in abundance and amplitude, enhanced by a subtly transfiguring harmonic foundation and permeated with a sense of dramatic psychology very different from the theatrical artifice of even so fine a work as *Aïda*. Where in *Falstaff* we have fragmentation, we still have in *Otello* the grand, unbroken line.

To be sure, this line shapes itself into flowing melodic contours or characterizing shapes and formulas only gradually. The score opens with a tremendous, cyclonic outburst for full orchestra, reinforced by organ tones and thunderous noises. A terrific chord of the eleventh leads off into a storm painting that has few rivals in opera. Wild *arpeggios*, disheveled chromatics, dissonances, syncopations, sharp lightning figures, shuddering *tremolos*, ringing fanfares, combine in a tempestuous fresco. A series of prickly staccato triplet figures disengages itself momentarily. Only with the choral outcry, *Dio, fulgor della bufera* do we hear a more sustained and swelling phrase. The short interjections of Iago, Cassio, Montano, and Roderigo flash by our ears, like chips in the turbulent maelstrom of sound. Not till the entrance of Otello does the music begin, in a manner of speaking, to organize itself. This entrance, though a passage of only twelve bars, sets the key of high nobility which never deserts the score, whatever the torments and villainies it may become its office to communicate. It is, also, perhaps the most taxing entrance phrase an operatic character was ever called upon to sing. *Esultate*—"Exult"—calls the victorious chieftain in clarion tones. The music is magnificent in its breadth and elevation. But it makes a terrific demand on the upper register of a tenor, half of it sustained above the staff and even touching a high B-natural.

Shrewd man of the theater that he was, Verdi took care not to permit the treacheries of Iago to follow on the very heels of this heroic summons. To be sure, Iago in a few passages of recitative and *arioso* voices his hatred for the Moor. But he is still subtly ironic rather than vengeful, as his unharmonized phrase indicates: "Cassio is his lieutenant and I, God save the mark, his Moorship's ancient." The jubilant Cypriots, meanwhile, celebrate the destruction of the Turkish fleet by lighting a bonfire and singing a fire chorus—a sparkling *scherzando* and a wholly operatic episode, if you will, which has nothing to do with Shakespeare. But it provides a pleasant *intermezzo* that functions both as a background and a transition.

The way is now clear for Iago's proposal of what amounts to a drinking bout. A curious, almost childish figure of three staccato notes, first bald, then harmonized, leads Iago to insist on a toast to the Moor and Desdemona. At the mention of the gentle lady Cassio sings a brief but exquisite phrase, *Essa infiora questo lido,* of a simple but entrancing melodic style peculiar to this opera. Presently comes Iago's drinking song proper, *Inaffia l'ugola,* a fine, rollicking tune, with nevertheless a certain sinister undercurrent. Two things in it should be noted: the use in the introductory bars of a sharply defined grace note which is a characterizing trait of much of Iago's music in subsequent scenes; and the heady, descending chromatic scale on the word *beva* ("drink").

The development of this carousing air into a full-fledged ensemble and this, in turn, into the quarrel scene, the fight, and Otello's wrathy intercession are adroitly built up, but less significant than the rapturous love scene of Otello and Desdemona which fills the remainder of the act. The dispersal of the throng to a series of simple harmonies over an *ostinato* figure could scarcely be less pretentious or showy. In the most effortless manner imaginable Verdi establishes the dreamy mood of the duet which, for sheer, rapturous beauty, stands above anything he ever wrote. It is marked by a marvelously tender rise and fall of feeling and, though actually a succession of melodies flowing effortlessly into one another, will repay closer scrutiny than it is possible to give here. Observe, as you listen to this masterpiece of construction, the expressive major and minor ninth chords which introduce Otello's phrase *Già nella notte densa;* the soaring passage, *Ingentilia di lacrime;* Desdemona's lovely *Disperda il ciel gli affani;* Otello's swooning *Ah! la gioia m'inonda* which culminates in the ecstatic melody of the kiss theme—a phrase which recurs with indescribable poignancy in the last scene of the opera. And after the two voices briefly join above silvery instrumental *arpeggios* the curtains close on an exquisitely emotional postlude for divided strings.

The second act begins with a suave orchestral introduction. It sets before us a picture of Iago in all his insinuating smoothness and it is distinguished especially by an assertive triplet, which we shall meet repeatedly in the music associated with the archvillain. The short colloquy of Iago and Cassio is built almost exclusively on the former's only phrase and especially on his four-note characterizing figure. Then, when Cassio leaves, Iago drops the mask and intones his awesome *Credo.* This great page, perhaps the most celebrated of those monologues Verdi wrote in his maturest period, begins with a stark and powerfully accented theme in bare octaves followed by a long and sardonic woodwind *tremolo.* Actually, the monologue is built up with great economy of material. Its chief ingredients are the gigantic octave phrase, the four-note Iago figure with its emphatic triplet and several modifications of it, in addition to sinister *tremolos* and *staccati.* A softer, harmonized version of the demonic octave theme appears several times before the number ends in a shriek of devilish laughter.

From now on Iago distils his poison by the most insinuating means. Never was Verdi so subtle in his portrayal of evil as in this act. In a serpentine passage, *E un idra, fosca, livida,* he provides an inimitable musical equivalent of "the green-eyed monster which doth mock the meat it feeds on." The passage is the more uncanny for its absence of harmonization.

As if unwilling to maintain the terrible mood too long, the composer at this point introduces another operatic ensemble, the *mandolinata,* a gentle chorus of homage by the islanders to Desdemona, charming with its rhythmic lilt and its touch of Italian folk melody. Its lovely, fluent accompaniment in arpeggiated sixteenth notes supplies a facile bridge to the resumption of real dramatic business.

We must mention in this act four episodes in particular—the handkerchief quartet—a collective picture of dramatic states, as remarkable in its way as the far more famous quartet in *Rigoletto* and based on Desdemona's beautiful phrase, *Dammi la dolce e lieta parole;* Otello's farewell to war, ending with the heartbroken cry, "Otello's occupation's gone" (a number of magnificent vigor and breadth of phrase, with its sonorous trumpet flashes and, for the singer, its brilliant high B-flat); Iago's dream story, with its insidious suggestions and that half-spoken *Desdemona soave! Il nostro amor s'asconda* calculated to drive Otello into a madness of jealousy; and the fierce oath and duet of vengeance. This last brings us back into the fierce melodic phraseology of the early Verdi. But woe to the conductor who attempts to refine its supposed vulgarity; he will succeed only in ruining the number, whose strength is in its undissembled theatricality!

The third act contains some of the noblest pages of the opera. It opens with a dark recall in the lower strings of the phrase about "the green-eyed monster," under a staccato rustle of violas, and then develops somewhat like the working-out section of a symphonic movement. The entrance of Desdemona, following Iago's whispered hint to the Moor to "remember the handkerchief," brings us a dialogue between the Moor and his lady which, beginning in an almost courtly tone, progresses into tragedy of the most lacerating kind. And it does so largely by means that are fundamentally melodic. Here and there Verdi reaches back into the past for suggestive effects—not at all inappropriately, Otello's threats about what may befall his wife if she loses the handkerchief which his mother "had of an Egyptian" recalls a savage passage of Amonasro's in the Nile scene of *Aïda.* The passionate *cantabile* of Desdemona's *Io prego il cielo* stands in its poignance and simplicity above everything else Verdi had written up to that point. The more terrible is that volcanic outburst in which the maddened Otello blasts his gentle spouse with insults and drives her from his presence.

It is not excessive to claim that Verdi's setting of Shakespeare's

"Had it pleased Heaven to try me with affliction" stands on a level of pathetic grandeur with the poet's lines. The numbness of agony past words sounds from those triplets and unchanging syncopated weavings above a seemingly changeless organ point on A-flat; and like a sudden shaft of moonlight on a bank of thunderclouds is that *pianissimo* harmony of the ninth which envelops the end of Otello's phrase, *E rassegnato al volere del ciel.* Such unnatural quiet gives place once more to an explosion of violence. This, in turn, to blitheness and an affectation of pleasant humor. Iago jests lightly with Cassio about his *amour* with a certain Bianca. Otello, hiding behind a pillar, half hearing and wholly misunderstanding, thinks he notes from Cassio's lips scurrilous allusions to Desdemona. His tormented cries, *L'empio m'irride,* contrast with the limpid and charming *scherzo* which develops out of the merry badinage.

The great finale is true opera. . . . Certainly, the thing is masterly in construction, dramatic force, characterization, and melodic substance. Nor does it close the act in the traditional manner. The throng leaves the stage, Otello (as in Shakespeare) falls in a trance, and Iago, to a derisive orchestral *tremolo,* places his foot on the fallen lion. The closing bars rank with the most terrific in opera.

If *Otello* is the greatest creation of Verdi, its fourth act is the greatest part of *Otello.* It has a mood, a color, a phraseology absolutely its own, never yet rivalled, never even remotely imitated. It is Italian, yet in part, at least, it is also strangely un-Italian. It opens with an extraordinary phrase in the English horn—the first notes of Desdemona's Willow Song. The singularity of it springs from a modal touch that marks the falling intervallic succession C-sharp, B-sharp, G-sharp. . . .

The Willow Song (in strophic form, its successive repetitions seasoned with subtle variations of accompaniment and harmony) is but one of the priceless jewels which stud this act. Nothing in the work is more absolutely devastating than Desdemona's sudden wildly passionate outburst of farewell to Emilia, when her companion leaves her for what, something tells her, will be the last time. The passage is only five bars long—yet five more soul-shattering bars have never been written.

An unearthly calm descends on the hapless woman and fills her prayer which she addresses to the Virgin. The *cantabile, Prega per chi adorando,* is the most spiritualized page in Italian operatic literature. The sinister entrance of Otello, intent on the execution of his bloody plan, is so original and extraordinary a thing that the Italian critics present at the first performance of the opera could not say enough in praise of it. It is an awful succession of somber leaden phrases in the lower strings, punctuated by nervous staccato sixteenths, which are presently reiterated with a cumulative effect of terror and which accompany the strangling. . . . Directly on the heels of this we hear the theme of the kiss, which has not been employed since the opening act.

The scene of the murder, though it goes to no unnecessary lengths of physical horror, has never been surpassed in awfulness by any composers of the so-called Veristic school. And for all its pity and terror the concluding act of *Otello* ends with music which draws tears from the listener. The entire literature of opera contains nothing more noble and yet so indescribably moving as the Moor's apostrophe, *Niun mi tema.* The last measures recall [an] echo . . . of *Parsifal;* and the Moor takes his own life, as in Shakespeare, "killing myself to die upon a kiss," whose plangent theme is sounded with psychological felicity as the curtain falls.

HERBERT F. PEYSER

RUGGIERO LEONCAVALLO (1858–1919)

Pagliacci

Libretto by the composer. First performance in Milan, May 21, 1892.

Characters

Tonio, a strolling player	Baritone
Canio, master of the troupe	Tenor
Nedda, Canio's wife	Soprano
Beppe, a player	Tenor
Silvio, a villager	Baritone

The Story

PROLOGUE: Tonio, one of a troupe of strolling players, announces that this drama is no make-believe, but a slice of reality (**Tonio:** *Si può*—A word).

ACT I. The troupe of actors arrives. Their leader, Canio, jealously helps his wife Nedda from the cart and announces to the villagers that the performance will take place at seven in the evening. He warns them that he will tolerate no flirting with his wife (**Canio:** *Un tal gioco*—Such a game). The vesper bells call the peasants to church; and Nedda is left alone to listen to the birds (**Nedda:** *Stridono lassù*—Freely flying up there, they shriek). The deformed clown, Tonio, makes violent love to her but is repulsed with a whip. He is followed by the villager Silvio, who woos her with better success (**Nedda:** *Non mi tentar*—Do not tempt me). The lovers are seen by Tonio, who summons Canio out of revenge for his dismissal by Nedda. Silvio escapes, and Nedda refuses to tell Canio his name. Another player, the kindly Beppe, protects Nedda from her husband's knife. Left alone, Canio confesses how he must play his role and act a clown, though his heart is broken (**Canio:** *Vesti la giubba*—Put on your costume).

ACT II. The townspeople assemble to witness the play. In the absence of her husband Pagliaccio (Canio), Columbine (Nedda) is serenaded by Harlequin (Beppe) (**Beppe:** *O Colombina*—O Columbine), who drives the innocent buffoon Taddeo (Tonio) from her chamber. Taddeo insists he loves Columbine but gives her up gracefuly when he sees that she and Harlequin love each other. Pagliaccio returns unexpectedly, Harlequin escaping just in time. When Pagliaccio questions Columbine, Taddeo supports her statement that she is innocent. Canio, obsessed by jealousy, forgets his part in the play (**Canio:** *No, Pagliaccio non son*—No, Pagliaccio, no more) and stabs Nedda. Dying, she calls Silvio from the audience, and Canio stabs him also.

THE INTRODUCTION to *Pagliacci* is shaped much along the lines of the *Cavalleria* prelude. An energetic figure, terminating in an upward flourish that has been likened to the crack of a whip, opens it and is many times repeated. This animated beginning is followed by a sharp change of mood, as a solo horn dolorously gives out a phrase that later forms the culmination of Canio's lament, and is, together with the prologue, the most celebrated number in the opera. The mood changes, and now we are given one of the principal phrases of the love music of Nedda and Silvio, a passionate melody. A return of the bustling opening, after an energetic development, breaks off and makes place for Tonio and his prologue. This prologue is partly declamatory and partly flowing melody. The most famous portion is the tune, *E voi piutosto,* which is used later as an orchestral interlude between the two acts. It is worth remarking that the high F so often sung by Tonio was not written by Leoncavallo at all. The score contents itself with a D-natural. A brief repetition of the opening *vivace* theme rounds out the introduction.

Trumpet fanfares off-stage, drums and cymbals behind the scenes begin the first act. Amidst the tumult and the acclaim of the peasantry for the arriving comedians several lively tunes and figures stand out—things like *Viva Pagliaccio, Evviva il principe* and the rhythmic *Ognun applaude.* A pleasant little ensemble is built on the melody of the phrase, *Venite, onorateci, signori e signore, a ventitre ore.* The action proper starts up quicker than it does in *Cavalleria.* Canio's banter with some of the villagers has more earnestness than jest in it. His *cantabile, Un tal gioco,* owes something to Wagner, though it is no direct derivation.

This short scene done, the composer gives us a bagpipe and a bell chorus. Doubtless the idea came from *Cavalleria* and the function of these ensembles is the same—to fill up space and to consume time. The sound of chimes is paired with a bass of empty fifths, the chorus imitating the "ding, dong" of bells. Two things should be noticed in this episode ensemble—the use of the melodic triplet, somewhat as in *Cavalleria;* and the resemblance of the melody at *Ah già tutto irradiasi* to one of the principal tunes in Chabrier's rhapsody *España*. The voices of the chorus fade away in descending chromatics.

When the crowd leaves, Nedda appears, perturbed at the menacing glances of her husband. But presently, over a shimmering orchestra, she apostrophizes the flocks of birds soaring above her and then embarks upon her *Ballatella*, a lighthearted air, with a swaying chief melody, *Stridono lassù*, over pretty instrumentation, but in itself filling no dramatic purpose whatever. Then Tonio enters accompanied by some of the better known tunes of the opera—the D-flat *cantabile, So ben che difforme* and Nedda's *scherzando, Hai tempo a ridirmilo*, upon which a number of pages are built up. As he leaves in a cold fury, the orchestra gives out a sharply accented theme in octaves which Leoncavallo unquestionably drew from the scene of Ortrud and Telramund in *Lohengrin*.

The love scene with Silvio is introduced by allusions to that sentimental phrase heard in the prelude. It is heard contrasted with the somber Wagnerian motif. But the passionate scene quickly broadens to tender lyrical expanses in music that floods the scene and robs the lovers of all idea of caution. Tonio leading Canio and heralded by his sinister jealousy theme surprises them. The clown's brief pursuit of his rival is carried out to music of hectic violence. His rage, his attempt to kill his wife, and the quick intercession of Beppe are mirrored with obvious fidelity in the orchestra. Then, when Canio is left alone to meditate on his woes, he breaks into the most famous number of the opera, the sob song. It begins with a piece of declamation, *Recitar*, above both sustained and detached chords. After an outburst of grim laughter comes the *arioso, Vesti la giubba*, with the culminating *Ridi Pagliaccio!* and violent sobbings. Often it is the intensity of these sobs rather than the quality of the singing which stirs the listeners to the greatest paroxysms of applause. The orchestra repeats and somewhat varies the song, as Canio stumbles from the stage. . . .

It is the chief melody from the prologue which forms the backbone of [the interlude before the second act]. The act proper begins with one of those festive ensembles not very dissimilar to that which opened the first. The play within the play offers some new inspirations—a graceful minuet, punctuated with flashing scale passages, the off-stage serenade of Harlequin, and the pretty *gavotte*, which quickly acquires a tragic significance as Nedda struggles to remain "in character," despite the terribly realistic threats of her husband.

The murder is consummated to the screams of the townsfolk. And as Canio, dropping his bloody knife, utters the words, *La commedia è finità* the orchestra shrieks the phrase, *Ridi Pagliaccio!* and a tumult of falling octaves, not unlike the conclusion of *Cavalleria,* brings the curtain down.

HERBERT F. PEYSER

CLAUDE DEBUSSY (1862–1918)

Pelléas et Mélisande

Libretto by Maurice Maeterlinck. First performance in Paris, April 30, 1902.

Characters

Golaud, grandson of King Arkel . . . . Baritone
Mélisande . . . . Soprano
Geneviève, mother of Golaud and Pelléas . . Contralto
Arkel, King of Allemonde . . . . Bass
Pelléas, half-brother of Golaud
Tenor or High Baritone
Yniold, son of Golaud . . . . Soprano
A physician . . . . Bass

The Story

ACT I. Prince Golaud, a lonely widower and grandson of King Arkel of Allemonde, wanders through a wood where he has become lost while hunting. By a fountain he finds Mélisande, who crouches in fear at his approach. She, too, is lost, but at first she refuses to accompany Golaud, who urges her to come away with him. She finally consents, on the condition that he will not touch her.

In a somber room in the castle, King Arkel listens to his daughter-in-law Geneviève read a letter which her son Pelléas has received from his half-brother Golaud (**Geneviève:** *Voici ce qu'il a écrit*—This is what he has written). Golaud has married Mélisande, although Arkel had wished him to marry a princess of his choice, and begs permission to bring her home. Arkel agrees to receive Mélisande at the castle and persuades Pelléas to give up a journey so that he may be near his sick father and so that he, too, may welcome the bride.

From a terrace of the castle Geneviève shows Mélisande the dark vistas around them, entrusting her to the care of Pelléas when she leaves.

ACT II. Pelléas takes Mélisande to a cool fountain in the park (**Pelléas:** *Vous ne savez pas*—You do not know), where she permits her long hair to fall into the water. Wilfully tossing the ring which Golaud gave her, Mélisande lets it fall into the fountain, where it is lost in the bottomless pool. They return to the castle, agreeing to tell Golaud the truth if he should ask the whereabouts of the ring.

In his apartment in Arkel's castle, Golaud tells Mélisande that his horse bolted into a tree, injuring him slightly (**Golaud:** *Ah! Ah! tout va bien*—Ah! Ah! all goes well). Mélisande begins to cry, saying that she can no longer remain in the castle. As Golaud takes her hands to comfort her, he notices that her ring is missing and frightens her into lying. When she tells him that she left it in a grotto near the shore, he insists that she and Pelléas go look for it, although it is night and she is afraid.

At the grotto's entrance, Pelléas and Mélisande grope through the darkness so that she will be able to describe to Golaud the place where she has said she lost the ring (**Pelléas:** *Oui, c'est ici*—Yes, it is here). Seeing three old men, asleep, Mélisande becomes frightened and urges Pelléas to take her away.

ACT III. Mélisande sits at her tower window, combing her hair (**Mélisande:** *Mes longs cheveux*—My long hair). Pelléas approaches and seizes her long tresses, tenderly declaring his love for her. Golaud breaks in upon the scene and, laughing nervously, reprimands Pelléas and Mélisande for acting like children.

In the stagnant vaults beneath the castle, Golaud points out to Pelléas the odor of death which pervades the place.

As they emerge from the vaults, the older man warns his younger half-brother to avoid the company of Mélisande, who is expecting a child and cannot be disturbed (**Golaud:** *Oui, elles se sont refugiées*—Yes, they have taken refuge).

Near a window at the front of the castle, Golaud questions his son Yniold as to Pelléas' attention to Mélisande (**Golaud:** *Viens, nous allons nous asseoir ici, Yniold*—Come, we will seat ourselves here, Yniold). He holds Yniold up to Mélisande's window, but learns nothing to indicate her guilt, although Pelléas is with her.

ACT IV. Pelléas meets Mélisande in a corridor in the palace to tell her that he is leaving Allemonde (**Pelléas:** *Je sors de la chambre de mon père*—I am just leaving my father's room). Arkel enters to console Mélisande (**Arkel:** *Maintenant que le père de Pelléas*—Now that the father of Pelléas). He is horrified when Golaud enters in a rage and throws Mélisande to the floor, accusing her by inference of infidelity. Golaud rushes away as Mélisande sobs that he no longer loves her, and Arkel observes sadly that if he were God he would have pity on the hearts of men.*

* The scene following this is usually cut in performances, but is happily included in recorded versions of the opera. It shows Yniold at play and watching a shepherd drive sheep to the slaughterhouse and is a valuable

Pelléas awaits Mélisande for a last tryst at the fountain in the park (**Pelléas:** *C'est le dernier soir*—This is the last evening). Mélisande finally arrives. The lovers' passionate avowal of love is interrupted by Golaud, who kills Pelléas with one blow from his sword.

ACT V. Old King Arkel has summoned a physician to the castle, where Mélisande lies dying, having given birth to a child. Eagerly, but in vain, Golaud tries to discover whether her love for Pelléas was innocent. The servants of the castle enter the death chamber as Mélisande, finding only sadness in her newborn daughter's face, slips away into the tranquility of death. Arkel leads Golaud from the room in silence as the curtain falls.

PROVIDENCE almost appears to have created Maeterlinck for Debussy even as it created Debussy for Maeterlinck; and there seems a kind of symbolical propriety in the circumstances that the two men were born within no more than a week of each other. Mutually they provided the solution of their peculiar artistic problem.

"Young Debussy had been reaching out towards a new musical language to the mastery of which he could at least feel that he had attained at the very time when the Belgian dramatist's play was published," declared Ernest Newman. "The composer's dilemma was that of the playwright reversed: he felt that with his new musical idiom he could create a new type of opera, yet he did not know where to look for a libretto which would match the fluidity and the finesse of that idiom."

Today, as we consider *Pelléas et Mélisande,* it seems almost incredible that the work should have been the product of two minds rather than of one. That the composer asked for certain curtailments and minor alterations in the text does not affect the issue in the slightest. The poet was aware from the first that the usual symmetries of musical construction would be inappropriate to the shadowy theme of the action and the kind of diction in which it was conveyed. Debussy's musical slant was strangely analogous. He found that, in opera, people "sang too much"—that lyric drama, in short, contained too much music for its own

---

contrast between the darkness of the scene before and the great passion of the scene following.—C. A. L.

sake. The drama should "lead" and music, duly submissive, should "follow." . . .

Debussy's repudiation of vocal melody in favor of a declamatory style has an indisputable esthetic soundness. It is based on a fundamental appreciation of the rhythms and the inflections of the French language. Over a century earlier Jean Jacques Rousseau had spoken of a type of recitative "appropriate to the simplicity and clarity of our tongue" which some day a French musician would realize. And he declared that the voice should move in narrow intervals, neither rising nor sinking too much. The best recitative, he added, "is that in which one sings least." Beyond question he would have found in *Pelléas* the truest example of the system he advocated.

. . . . .

. . . *Pelléas* is a monument of stylistic unity. Its hallmarks, harmonic, melodic, and otherwise, have long been as much the common property of music makers as the idiom of Wagner. It is a curious paradox that some of us obtain our earliest instruction in *Pelléas* by way of Puccini. *Madama Butterfly,* for instance, is an entire repository of Debussyan formulas; even more so is the less familiar *Girl of the Golden West.* In his noble *Amore dei tre re* Montemezzi has known how to utilize features of the *Pelléas* score with poignant effect.

One cannot avoid references to thematic labels or, if you must have it so, its "leading motifs." We know that Debussy scornfully dismissed the motifs of Wagner as "visiting cards," thereby displaying a singular misapprehension of them. His own themes, associated with this or that character, object, or dramatic contingency, are utilized in a manner different from Wagner's and to other psychological and constructive ends. Yet lists of "guiding themes" have been repeatedly made in the case of *Pelléas,* just as they have been of *Der Ring des Nibelungen* or of *Meistersinger.*

One hears the first of these with the very opening measure of the short orchestral introduction. It is that brooding phrase of four bars associated with the forest in which Golaud, having lost his way, comes upon the tremulous and sobbing Mélisande. Its mystery and other-worldly strangeness proceed from the Dorian mode (substantially the key of D minor without accidentals) on which it is based. Three other themes (as well as a repetition of the forest motif) follow—one of fate, another of Mélisande, a third, closely allied to it, typifying her *naïveté.* Recalls of these materials and still another more ardent phrase, symbolizing Golaud's love, constitute, in various permutations and changes, the melodic substance of the first scene.

It may be as well to call attention at this point to some of those features of which the lovely fabric of *Pelléas* is woven—the harmonies of the ninth, the secondary sevenths with all manner of altered tones, the profuse employment of the raised fifth, and the innumerable chords proceeding in parallel motion irrespective of the consecutive fifths forbidden by the schoolmen. Notice should be taken, too, of those *ostinati*, with which the pages of the work are full, and which Debussy plainly derived in large part from Russian sources.

The opera had already been completed when Debussy found himself obliged to extend and elaborate those instrumental *entr'actes* between the successive scenes in order to allow more time for the changes of sets. Yet these passages include some of the most interesting of the score. The first of these possesses a particular interest since in the last eleven bars Debussy was haunted by the "phantom of old Klingsor," which he dreaded. These measures, with only slight modification, come directly out of the transformation music in the first act of *Parsifal*, a work which at one period exerted a mighty spell on the French composer.

One of the simplest, yet most noteworthy pages of the opening act greets us with the beginning of the second scene—the letter of Golaud which is read to the venerable Arkel by Geneviève. The phrase *allume une lampe au sommet de la tour qui regarde la mer* is utterly magical in the inexplicable sense of foreboding which fills it. And yet it is nothing more than a short passage of recitative over detached chords leading to an expressive citation of the short Mélisande phrase. Then for a moment we seem to catch from afar the voice of Mussorgsky. The entrance of Pelléas is announced by a three-bar phrase which will be heard over and again through the work. The ensuing garden scene and the short colloquy of Pelléas and Mélisande about the departing ship and the threatening night offers us another of those moments in which the composer has captured that sense of nameless dread and fatality that constantly recurs through the play.

In the second act we meet the clear, enchanting music of the fountain as well as a phrase which may, for better or worse, be termed the theme of awakening desire. Later, from the mouth of the irritated Golaud, we have a saturnine motif in trombones and tuba associated with his sinister wish for vengeance. In the scene of the cavern, where the blind beggars have taken refuge, the hearer should be careful not to miss that momentary musical representation of the sudden shaft of moonlight, with its scintillant flood of harp *glissandi,* woodwind, tremulous strings, and cymbals softly sounded.

The succeeding act is rich in exquisite and characteristic beauties. Mélisande's tower song, which opens it, is without accompaniment and suggests in its modal formation and peculiar melodic phraseology an ancient folk tune. An enchanting night theme, with other themes commingling, leads to the episode in which the blond hair of Mélisande falls about the shoulders of Pelléas, to three giddy bars of swiftly descending chords. . . . The dark menace of Golaud's words and actions as he shows Pelléas the fetid subterranean vaults of the castle has its oppressive counterpart in the music. How wondrously fresh, luminous, and fragrant by contrast is that sparkling transmutation into tone of the sunshine and dewy freshness of flowers which Pelléas jubilantly greets on emerging into the upper air!

We cannot, unfortunately, tarry at befitting length over the wondrous fourth act. The best the listener can do is to concentrate with the utmost attentiveness on every measure. The maltreatment of Mélisande by the senselessly jealous Golaud is one of the most emotionally devastating scenes in all opera. It terminates in that phrase of heart-shaking compassion uttered by Arkel to seven bars of orchestral music which are absolutely without parallel in music: "If I were God I should have pity on the hearts of men!" And Debussy has here shown a positively Wagnerian power of creating, on the very heels of such an episode, the greatest climax of the whole work in the interlude which follows, where the music of fate bursts and shatters with the dread force of a tidal wave.

Mélisande's avowal of her love for Pelléas ("Since when have you loved me?" "Always!") is marked by an effect unlike any other in opera. Instead of unloosing an instrumental torrent Debussy has gone so far in understatement as to ask us to supply our own reaction. This he does by leaving everything to the listener's proper imaginative response with exactly two blank bars for the orchestra!

Mussorgsky must have stood godfather to the opening of the laceratingly poignant fifth act. It begins with phrases portraying pity (a moving figure in major and minor thirds) which bear an impress of the composer of *Boris.* There are no cries, tears, or screams in this act—nothing but a pathos that wrings the heart the more surely for its subduing gentleness. The entrance of the silent women servants, who arrive, like harbingers of death, to foreboding, agitated staccato octaves, is a last instance of Debussy's power to express nameless dread by the simplest musical means. The soundless demise of Mélisande, "mysterious, even as are all of us," more almost than any other such scene in opera, brings the illusion of an actual passing. The postlude on which the curtain descends does not attempt, even for a consolatory moment, to lighten the dark enigma of finality.

Herbert F. Peyser

GIUSEPPE VERDI (1813–1901)

Rigoletto

Libretto by Francesco Maria Piave, based upon Victor Hugo's *Le Roi s'amuse*. First performance in Venice, March 11, 1851.

Characters

The Duke of Mantua	Tenor
Borsa, a courtier	Tenor
Count and Countess Ceprano	Baritone and Soprano
Rigoletto, court jester	Baritone
Marullo, a courtier	Tenor
Monterone	Bass
Sparafucile	Bass
Gilda, Rigoletto's daughter	Soprano
Giovanna, Gilda's nurse	Soprano
A page	Soprano
Guard	Baritone
Maddalena, Sparafucile's sister	Mezzo-soprano

The Story

ACT I. Strolling among the courtiers who throng the ballroom of his palace, the Duke of Mantua boasts of his many conquests (**Duke:** *Questa o quella*—This or that one). His hunchback jester Rigoletto suggests that his master win the Countess Ceprano by imprisoning her husband. Ceprano, furious, vows to abduct a young girl whom he believes to be Rigoletto's mistress. Another elderly noble, Monterone, whose daughter has been seduced by the Duke, forces his way in and curses Rigoletto for his cynical mockery. The jester broods over the curse.

ACT II. Late at night Rigoletto hurries to the secluded house where he has hidden his daughter, Gilda. Before opening his gate, he is addressed by the professional assassin Sparafucile, but dismisses him, reflecting that his tongue works as much harm as the other's dagger (**Rigoletto:** *Pari siamo*—We are equal). Rigoletto softens as he greets Gilda (**Rigoletto:** *Deh non parlare*—Ah! Do not remind this wretched soul). Summoning her nurse Giovanna, he warns the two of possible enemies (**Rigoletto, Gilda:** *Veglia, o donna*—Safely guard, madam, this flower). As Rigoletto leaves, the Duke himself slips into the garden and makes passionate love to the girl, telling her that he is a poor student, Walter Maldé (**Duke:** *E il sol dell' anima*—Life is love, the sun of the soul). After he leaves, the girl dwells tenderly on his name (**Gilda:** *Caro nome*—Dearest name) and then retires. Meanwhile, the cynical courtiers intercept Rigoletto in the street, blindfold him, and bid him to help them abduct Ceprano's wife. In his confusion he places a ladder against his own wall. The courtiers laugh at this chance to outwit Rigoletto (**Chorus:** *Zitti, zitti*—Quickly, quickly), break into his house, and carry off his daughter. Rigoletto tears off his mask, finds Gilda's scarf. The curse has fallen.

ACT III. The Duke paces a room in his palace, fearing that his courtiers have robbed him of Gilda (**Duke:** *Parmi veder le lagrime*—I seem to see tears). Soon they return to tell him that she is in an adjacent chamber (**Chorus:** *Scorrendo uniti*—As we ran united down the remote road). He rushes away to join her. Rigoletto now comes in search of his daughter, frantically begging the courtiers to help him find her (**Rigoletto:** *Cortigiani*—Oh, you courtiers). At last the girl runs to her father and, as the company withdraws, confesses the long courtship and treachery of the Duke (**Gilda:** *Tutte le feste*—Every holiday in the church). Monterone is led by a guard through the room to prison, and the broken-hearted Rigoletto now promises to redress his wrongs (**Rigoletto:** *Si, vendetta*—Yes, vengeance), but Gilda tries to stop him because she loves the Duke.

ACT IV. On a dark night Rigoletto and his daughter wait outside the lonely inn where Sparafucile and his sister Maddalena dispatch their victims. The jester forces Gilda to watch the Duke, who has come to flirt with Maddalena, laughing meanwhile at the inconstancy of women (**Duke:** *La donna è mobile*—Women are fickle). As Maddalena leads on the noble victim whom Rigoletto has hired Sparafucile to murder, Rigoletto comforts Gilda (**Duke, Maddalena, Gilda, Rigoletto:** *Bella figlia dell'amore*—Pretty maiden, child of love). The jester tells Gilda to go dress herself as a boy and meet him in Verona; he then pays Sparafucile and departs. Meanwhile Maddalena urges her brother to spare the Duke and kill Rigoletto instead. Sparafucile refuses, but promises her that he will find some other victim. The next arrival is Gilda, who overhears the plot and gladly sacrifices herself to save the Duke. When Rigoletto returns, he is given a sack by Sparafucile. On hearing the voice of the Duke, trolling his familiar song, he frantically cuts open the sack and finds, instead of the Duke, the body of his own daughter (**Rigoletto, Gilda:** *Lassù in cielo*—In heaven above). The curse is fulfilled.

THE SHORT introductory orchestral page with which *Rigoletto* begins is not musically or poetically on a level with the lovely prelude to *Traviata*. On the other hand it stands above the meaningless instrumental preface to *Trovatore* in that it prepares the mind of the listener for the tragedy to follow. With a few sharp strokes: dotted rhythms hurled out by the trumpets and trombones, menacing diminished seventh chords, and briefly sobbing syncopations, it establishes a mood along the lines laid down by so sound an esthetician as Gluck. As in *Traviata* the curtain rises on festivity and dances. These are neither much better nor much worse than most of Verdi's dance music, which, except in *Aïda*, has always something of the village band about it. One number, a minuet, rises briefly to the level of a much-watered Mozart reminiscence. The music of this opening scene first skims over lively dialogue, broken by a pleasantly animated chorus flavored with chromatic passing notes. Drama sets in with the arrival of Monterone and the fateful curse he launches against the reckless jester. This imprecation crystallizes into a powerful musical formula, of essentially harmonic nature, which returns to lend dramatic point to certain crucial episodes of the piece.

The thought of the dread curse dominates the opening of the following scene. The wonderful colloquy which ensues between Rigoletto and the formidable Sparafucile ranks beyond question among the greatest things Verdi had accomplished up to this period. The somber, portentous dialogue is carried forward over a trailing, heavy-footed melody uttered *pianissimo* by muted 'cellos and basses to a sinister, throbbing accompaniment. The color of the scene is wholly extraordinary. Hard upon it follows one of those great Verdian monologues, Rigoletto's *Pari siamo*, which is like a foretaste of things to come in *Otello* and *Falstaff*. At the root of this music lies the unmistakable menace of the thematic motto of the opera—Monterone's curse.

Gilda comes before us to tender woodwind accents. Her duets with Rigoletto bloom like fragrant melodic flowers, particularly the girl's recollections of her dead mother. Musically this portion of the act is superior to the love duo with the disguised Duke, which closes rather tritely in a D-flat *vivacissimo*, *Addio, addio, speranza ed anima*. The *Caro nome* aria forms a bridge to the kidnapping scene. Perhaps we should mention at this point the conspirators' chorus, the whispered *Zitti, zitti,* growing from sibilant murmurs to strongly accented shouts. It is exactly the same type of ensemble Verdi had already written a few years earlier in *Macbeth*, for the scene of Banquo's murder, the sort of thing Gilbert and Sullivan were to burlesque so pricelessly in *Pinafore* and the *Pirates of Penzance*.

The following act opens rather conventionally with the Duke's air, *Parmi veder le lagrime*, which is hardly one of the most memorable pages in the score. The robust choral account of the successful seduction, *Scorrendo uniti remota via*, is better. The rest of the act belongs to Rigoletto, who grows in tragic stature from minute to minute. Note the heartbreaking pathos in his poor efforts at merriment while searching for a trace of his stolen daughter, the power and grandeur in his *scena, Cortigiani, vil razza dannata*, which presently dissolves into the jester's tearful appeal to the unfeeling courtiers (note too the plangent 'cello melody which supports his plea). The emotional curve of the music rises steadily. How affecting, yet how simple, the confession of Gilda of her love for her seducer! As if to kindle Rigoletto in his fierce resolve for vengeance, Monterone passes briefly over the stage. Then comes one of the most singular strokes in all Verdi. An impetuous tune, *Si vendetta*, whose fierce cheerfulness seems to belie the furious sentiments behind it, gathers speed, power, momentum. Can this really be an utterance of avenging fury? Long after *Rigoletto* was written, the great baritone Victor Maurel found the answer to the apparent discrepancy between music and text, by singing the passage in raving, stentorian accents. Verdi caught the point at once. "You have done something psychological, Maurel," he told the artist, and then added: "Yet when *Rigoletto* was composed, singers were not concerned with psychology!"

The closing act possesses a quality of drama, an atmosphere, a force of contrast, and a quality of imagination which even Verdi rarely achieved in such a balance and unity. Taken by itself *La donna è mobile* is a cheap tune, a vulgar tune. Yet it is one of the best loved tunes in the whole world. Its popularity, however, is not the measure of its genius, which is rather to be judged by the role the song plays in the drama. Trivial or not in itself it is absolutely the right melody in the right place. A consummate stroke of characterization, it places the irresponsible gaiety of the philandering Duke in proper perspective. More, it throws a shaft of light athwart a fundamentally somber scene and provides in its setting and context an effect of contrast (particularly when the Duke trolls it out to its full length after Gilda's murder) whose piercing dramatic irony even the most insensitive opera-goer can hardly resist. Indeed, it is rare that audiences are not awed by the pity and terror implicit in this masterly *coup de théâtre.*

. . . At once the most celebrated [number] in the score and a great inspiration, if ever there was such [is] the quartet, *Bella figlia dell' amore,* which might be said to form the center of gravity in the last act. The wonder of this incomparable page will be fully apparent only to him who takes the trouble of breaking it up, so to speak, into its component parts. That is to say, the average *passive* ear will perceive in the quartet primarily a smooth, cunningly built, and wholly beautiful piece of music. But whoever reduces it to its elements will perceive that each of the four voices, perfectly as they adjust themselves to one another, constitutes by itself a miraculous piece of independent character portrayal. At one and the same time Verdi gives us the romantic frivolity of the Duke, the mockery of Maddalena, the poignant grief of the betrayed Gilda, and the boding threats of the misshapen father. It is perhaps the supreme example in operatic music of dynamic emotional opposites fused to form a purely musical synthesis of the utmost beauty.

There is still the storm—at once theatrical realism and symbolism of a superior order. Verdi assuredly learned from Beethoven's *Pastoral Symphony* and from Rossini's *William Tell.* Yet his tempest in *Rigoletto* is different, though in its way as unique. Not its least remarkable feature is the chorus humming backstage in chromatic thirds, like the moaning of winds. Verdi used those chromatic thirds in the first scene of *Trovatore,* as well, though in a different connection. But here we have an effect of color, utilized much later by Debussy and other moderns. Yet who shall say that they applied the device with a potency comparable to that achieved by Verdi about a half century before them?

HERBERT F. PEYSER

RICHARD WAGNER (1813–1883)

Der Ring des Nibelungen—

A Trilogy with Prologue

Librettos for the entire *Ring* by the composer.

Das Rheingold

First performance in Munich, September 22, 1869.

Characters

Rhinemaidens:

Woglinde	Soprano
Wellgunde	Soprano
Flosshilde	Mezzo-soprano
Alberich, a Nibelung or gnome	Bass
Fricka, queen of the gods	Mezzo-soprano
Wotan, king of the gods	Bass-baritone
Freia, goddess of youth and beauty	Soprano
Fasolt, a giant	Bass
Fafner, a giant, later a dragon	Bass
Froh, god of the fields	Tenor
Donner, god of thunder	Baritone
Loge, god of fire	Tenor
Mime, a Nibelung, brother of Alberich	Tenor
Erda, goddess of the earth	Mezzo-soprano

The Story

Scene I. In the greenish depths of the Rhine three mermaids—Woglinde, Wellgunde, and Flosshilde—play gaily about the precious Rhinegold, which they have been assigned to guard by Wotan, father of gods and men. Approached by the Nibelung dwarf Alberich, they tempt and taunt him. Hailing the Rhinegold, which now shines through the water, they awaken Alberich's greed (**Rhinemaidens:** *Heiajaheia! Rheingold! Leuchtende Lust!*—Heiayaheia! Rhinegold! Radiant delight!) In fury he renounces them and forswears love in order to win the power of the gold (**Alberich:** *So verfluch' ich*—Love curse I now). Snatching their magic treasure he disappears, leaving them in darkness.

Scene II. Near their newly built castle Valhalla, Wotan and his spouse Fricka awaken. They fear to lose Freia, goddess of youth, whom the brother giants Fafner and Fasolt have demanded as payment for their labor in building the fortress. Pursued by the giants, Freia hurries in, calling for help (**Freia:** *Wo harren meine Brüder*—Where are my brothers waiting?). Wotan stalls for time and hurriedly consults Loge, crafty god of fire. Loge tells the assembled deities that no substitute for Freia has been found; but in his search he did hear of some gold which Alberich had stolen from the Rhinemaidens and which he had been able, because he had forsworn love, to fashion into a ring that gave him power to rule the world. It was the Rhinemaidens who told Loge about the gold—with a request that he ask Wotan to get it and give it back to them (**Loge:** *Immer ist Undank*—Ingratitude is ever Loge's reward). Hearing of the dwarf's priceless treasure and the power it has brought him, the giants agree to accept the Rhinegold instead of Freia. They leave, carrying Freia off as hostage.

The gods now begin to grow old. Realizing that immortality will be forfeit without the goddess of youth, Wotan determines to wrest the gold from Alberich. He disappears with Loge into a sulphurous cavern which will lead him to the land of the Nibelungs.

Scene III. Deep in his cavern, Alberich gloats over his riches and his power over the Nibelungs, whom he has enslaved. Tormenting his brother Mime, Alberich demonstrates the magic of the Tarnhelm, a helmet which makes the wearer invisible (**Alberich:** *Schau', du Schelm!*—See, you scamp), and disappears. Mime describes to Wotan and Loge the sources of Alberich's power. Suddenly Alberich returns, driving a group of Nibelungs before him with his whip. Loge tells Alberich that he and Wotan have come to see a demonstration of his powers. When Alberich turns himself into a toad to show the Tarnhelm's magic, Wotan instantly puts his foot on the tiny creature and snatches the helmet from its head. Reappearing in his own shape, Alberich writhes under the heel of the gods, who bind him and carry him off as a prisoner.

Scene IV. Wotan and Loge return to the earth's surface, dragging the cursing Alberich with them. When Wotan exacts all the gold, the Ring which the dwarf has fashioned, and the Tarnhelm in exchange for Alberich's freedom, the dwarf calls his curse down upon all who shall possess the Ring of the Nibelung (**Alberich:** *Bin ich nun frei?*—Am I then free?).

Erda, the earth goddess, now rises out of the ground and prophesies that the Ring will bring doom to the gods if it remains in their hands (**Erda:** *Weiche, Wotan, weiche!*—Wisely, Wotan, wisely!). Wotan is then compelled to surrender the entire treasure to Fafner and Fasolt. Freia returns to the gods. Fasolt and Fafner quarrel over dividing their riches. Fafner kills his brother and hurries away with the gold, while Wotan muses solemnly on the first manifestation of Alberich's curse (**Wotan:** *Furchtbar nun*—Fearsome now). After a moment of storm the skies clear and a shimmering rainbow bridge appears, leading to Valhalla. Wotan hails his magnificent palace (**Wotan:** *Abendlich strahlt*—See how the sun). From the valley the Rhinemaidens are heard lamenting their lost treasure, and Wotan, turning, bids Loge to silence them. Their cry persists, however, as the gods proceed toward Valhalla.

RICHARD Wagner's *Der Ring des Nibelungen* stands today as the most monumental musical achievement to weather the test of time. The immensity, audacity, and magnificence of its structure still remain unrivalled. Think of it! Over twelve hours of music. And this was the product of almost a century ago, an era when technical devices were in their infancy. But even at that time Wagner dared to cope with the underwater swimming of the Rhinemaidens, the scene transformations which take place before the eyes of the audience, the Ride of the Valkyries, the Magic Fire around Brünnhilde's rock, and the final complicated tableau in *Götterdämmerung*. Even today many of the master's stage directions cannot be fully realized.

No less startling is the music which mirrors human emotion and dramatic action. We see, so to speak, with our ears the sweep of the flowing Rhine, the splendor of Valhalla, the crackling fire, Erda's mysterious prophecy, the unbridled jubilation of the Valkyrie cry, the malevolent spite of Alberich. . . .

The *Ring* has its inconsistencies, inevitable when we remember that Wagner drafted the poem for this epic in reverse order. Originally he had planned to deal with but one portion of the legend—*Siegfried's Tod* (the death of Siegfried), but after completing this poem, he felt that the life of the young Siegfried should be included, and for further clarification, the poems of *Die Walküre* and *Das Rheingold* were prepared. And in *Das Rheingold,* we see that few events occurring before the rise of the curtain bear import to the drama that will follow. We need only know of Wotan's pact with the giants to trade Freia in return for their building of his cloud-castle, Valhalla, and Loge's mission to find a suitable substitute to ransom Freia. We also learn of Wotan's infidelities to his wife Fricka, while the Rhinemaidens inform us that the gold which they guard can enable its owner to master the universe if he is willing to forswear the delights of love.

Musically the *Ring,* composed during a period of over twenty years, betrays a natural but definite discrepancy in style. Actually, however, this is in complete harmony with the ideas and events that take place throughout the long period of time covered in the four dramas. How apt are the generally lucid orchestrations and simpler harmonies of 1853 for the description of the more innocent *Rheingold* drama, as compared to the more obscure harmonies and dark, heavier orchestrations of 1874, which fittingly describe the treachery and deceit that result in the final overthrow of the gods and their adversaries in *Götterdämmerung.*

The opera *Rheingold* commences with a lengthly *prelude,* introduced by the single tonic major note of E-flat. In the 5th bar, a similarly sustained dominant note joins the first one, and shortly thereafter the music gains rhythmic momentum as G alternating with the other two notes completes the E-flat major triad. Thus up to the 48th bar, the music has only outlined the frame of the *Rhine* motif, but finally as F and A are added, we hear the ripple-like flow of the river which has evolved from the basic E-flat triad.

The rhythm continues to accelerate as the swelling tonal pattern sweeps through many of the orchestral instruments. Even with the parting of the curtains, and the song of the *Rhinemaidens,* the key of E-flat is maintained.

But the disturbance of the placid atmosphere established through the tonic mood of the prelude occurs with the more forbidding key of G minor announcing, by its introduction of darker harmonies and somber instrumentation, the arrival of the crafty Nibelung, the dwarf, Alberich.

After the lovesick wretch fails in his attempt to win any of the taunting maidens, we hear an accentuated *appoggiatura*-like motif characterizing the dwarf's *frustration.*

Slowly the early morning sunlight penetrates the waters. First the music rhythmically hints at the gold which begins to shine in its rock bed. Then, as the light broadens, the *gold* motif is solemnly uttered by the horns in the key of G, and when the treasure glistens in the blinding beams of the sun's rays, its brilliance is described by the piercing trumpet in the key of C.

The Rhinemaidens' account of the potential power of the gold introduces a new motif. This soon develops into that of the important *ring* which can be fashioned from the metal.

Only by sacrificing the pleasures of love can the treasure ever be won, cries Woglinde. The importance of this new theme, *the forswearing of love,* is accentuated in its introduction by the voice, for as we will later discover, comparatively few of the *Ring* themes are ever sung.

Alberich, mindful of the failure of his amorous quests, has little difficulty in deciding to make the sacrifice and steals the gold from the rock. A descending scale figure in the strings swells to a forte in a rising sequence and then slowly subsides before melting into a somewhat similar, but more relaxed phrase in the harp. This music represents the scenic change from the bottom of the river bed to a misty mountaintop.

As dawn breaks, we are reminded of the *ring.* Then as the mists and clouds disperse, and a view of the completed castle emerges in the distance, this diminished theme changes into the majestic D-flat major music of *Valhalla.*

The similarity between these two themes comes as no surprise when we consider that the drama of the *Ring* cycle concerns the struggle for power between Alberich and Wotan. It is therefore quite natural that their symbolic counterparts, the ring and the castle, should possess a common musical heritage. Wotan's triumphant greeting to the new fortress is anticipated by the suggestion of the *spear* motif, heard a few moments later in the same scene, to epitomize the power by which he rules.

The domestic argument between Fricka and Wotan is in the main set forth through chordlike recitative music, liberally punctuated by a variety of themes including a lovely new one depicting the goddess' hope that her *feminine charms* will bind the restless Wotan to the hearth of their new home. Again the music is sung by the voice. Note the inviting quality of the rich contralto coloration against an unobtrusive tremolo in the orchestra.

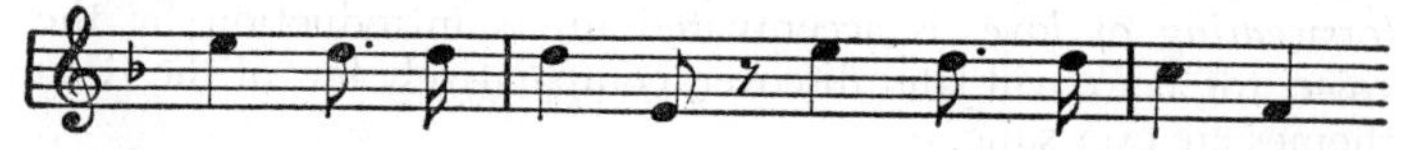

Freia's first appearance as she flees from the approaching giants is heralded by an abbreviated minor version of her own chromatically scaled theme. (Later, when it symbolizes *womanhood,* we will hear it in major, and in a more leisurely and seductive manner.) Freia's theme is immediately joined by the music of her *flight.*

Her pursuers, *the giants,* Fafner and Fasolt, come upon the scene accompanied by a rhythmic theme, emphasized in the tympani and associated with their heavy cumbersome step.

Earlier we heard a hint of this same theme when Fricka reminded Wotan of the bargain he had previously concluded with the giants for the building of Valhalla.

Immediately the subject of the agreement arises, and the *compact* is suggested by a three-note ascending triad based on the rhythm of the giants which prefixes itself to the descending scale of the *spear.*

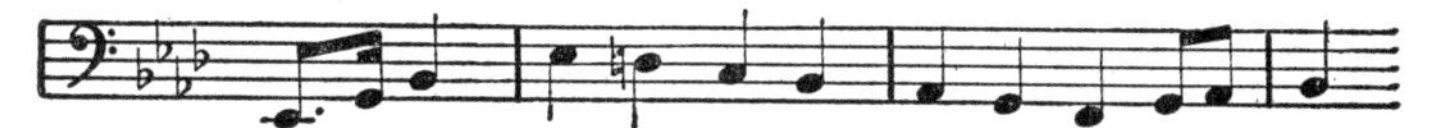

Fafner assures Fasolt that if they can wrest Freia away, the gods will soon become old and weak and fade away from the lack of her *golden apples.*

Finally Loge, the demigod of *fire,* arrives. The music represents his crafty nature, as well as the crackling of his flames.

Loge tells how he has found only one, Alberich, who would forsake the charms of *womanhood.*

When the giants seize Freia as hostage, Wotan agrees to seek the desired ransom, and descends with Loge to Nibelheim, while the scene shifts to the bowels of the earth. During the interlude accompanying this transformation we hear the restless music of *flight,* similar in treatment to a portion of the better known second-act prelude of *Die Walküre.* This grows into an orchestral fabric of almost unleashed savagery climaxed by the blasting of the *gold* accompanied by the forge of the *Nibelungs.*

Further emphasis is given to this typical example of a rhythmic theme when we hear its unaccompanied pounding beats on the backstage anvils describing the slavish toil of the Nibelungs at their forges in bondage to Alberich. Note too the similarity in its rhythmic structure to the motif of the *giants.*

Later, another *appoggiatura* theme stemming from Alberich's *frustration* appears. This is *bondage,* which describes Alberich's menacing desire for power over the universe.

Alberich greets his guests and immediately assures Wotan that the gods, like the Nibelungs, will soon serve his own will. As he outlines his plan for the destruction of the deities, we hear *Valhalla,* a squeezed perversion of *Freia's* music, and finally as an accompaniment to the conclusion of this terrifying prophecy, the savage motif of *bondage.*

The dwarf's vanity is no match for Loge's cunning, and Alberich is soon captured and carried off by his guests, who return to the scene at the top of the mountain. The interlude representing *ascent,* like the earlier music of the *descent,* displays some of the most abandoned scoring heard in the entire opera, featuring a review of several themes heard in the previous scenes.

Just as Alberich received the gold with a curse, so he passes it on to its future holders with a fierce imprecation that will bring death to all who possess the treasure. Here we are introduced to two new motifs. First we hear another of the rhythmic sort, whose gnawing quality represents the *Nibelung's work of destruction.* Then comes the music of the *curse* itself, which, like three of the earlier mentioned motifs, assumes a more pronounced emphasis through its initial introduction in the voice.

During the balance of the *Ring,* this motif is generally assumed by the tuba, as, for instance, in the passage immediately following the murder of Fasolt.

Wotan yields his newly won treasure only when he is admonished by Erda, the all-wise goddess of the earth, of the validity of Alberich's curse and the inevitable downfall of the gods. Erda's emergence from the earth is depicted by a theme denoting her mysterious authority. Actually it is the *Rhine,* in a minor key.

Finally when she prophesies the *twilight of the gods,* a new theme, actually *Erda* in a descending pattern, appears.

The gods prepare for their entrance into Valhalla: Donner calls together the storm clouds as his new arpeggio-triad theme appears.

This is followed by another arpeggio-triad phrase representing the *rainbow* over which the celestial host will proceed into its new home.

Wotan broods over Erda's grim prediction. A new idea, as yet unexplained to the audience, occurs to him, while the orchestra proclaims the gleaming triad-arpeggio motif of the *sword.*

Only in *Walküre* do we learn that this represents the concept of a new race, the Wälsungs, who Wotan hopes will protect the gods from destruction.

Once more the motif of the *rainbow* is sounded, and as the gods proudly move toward the mighty structure of Valhalla, the curtain slowly falls.

PAUL JARETZKI

Die Walküre

First performance in Munich, June 26, 1870.

Characters

Siegmund .... Tenor
Sieglinde, Siegmund's twin sister .... Soprano
Hunding, Sieglinde's husband .... Bass
Wotan .... Bass-baritone
Brünnhilde, Wotan's daughter .... Soprano
Fricka .... Contralto
Eight Valkyries . Four Sopranos, four Mezzo-sopranos

The Story

ACT I. Siegmund the Wälsung, or son of Wälse, by which name alone he knows his divine father, Wotan, seeks shelter from a storm in the hut of Hunding and his wife, Sieglinde. Sieglinde comforts her guest and asks him to stay a while. Hunding arrives presently from a hunt. At dinner Siegmund describes his birth and childhood (**Siegmund:** *Friedmund darf ich nicht heissen*—"Peaceful" may no one name me; *Ein starkes Jagen auf uns stellten die Neidinge an*—Our foes pressed hard on our heels) and the recent fight in which he lost his weapons (**Siegmund:** *Ein trauriges Kind*—A forlorn maid). During the latter recital, Hunding recognizes Siegmund as a mortal enemy, but the laws of hospitality require him to allow the guest safety for a night's rest. Sieglinde, deeply attracted by the stranger, gives Hunding a strong sleeping potion, and the two retire. Alone, Siegmund reflects on his father's promise that he would find a sword in his hour of need (**Siegmund:** *Ein Schwert verhiess mir der Vater*—A sword, my father promised me). Sieglinde returns and tells him that she has been married by force and that a stranger at her wedding drove a sword into a tree from which he said it would one day be taken by a man strong enough to remove it (**Sieglinde:** *Der Männer Sippe*—The host of kinsmen). Unaware that he is her twin brother, Siegmund woos Sieglinde (**Siegmund:** *Dich, selige Frau*—You, blessed bride), and they sing ecstatically (**Siegmund:** *Winterstürme wichen dem Wonnemond*—Winter's storms are stilled by lovelit May; **Sieglinde:** *Du bist der Lenz*—You are the spring). Siegmund wrests his father's sword from the ash tree where it has been thrust by Wotan (**Siegmund:** *Nothung, Nothung!*—Needful, Needful!), and the two flee into the dawn.

ACT II. In a rocky mountain pass, Wotan instructs Brünnhilde, leader of the warrior daughters, or Valkyries, whom he has begotten by Erda, to protect Siegmund in his forthcoming fight with Hunding. Brünnhilde joyously greets her father (**Brünnhilde:** *Hojotoho! Hojotoho!*), then warns him that Fricka is approaching and that she seems to be highly incensed about something. Fricka appears, demanding that Wotan uphold the marriage vows of Hunding and Sieglinde and refuse his protection to his son Siegmund (**Fricka:** *So ist es denn aus*—To this has it come; later, *Du schuf'st ihm die Noth*—You made the need). Wotan reluctantly yields and after explaining to Brünnhilde the history of the ring, the Wälsungs, and the Valkyries (**Wotan:** *Als junger Liebe*—As young love's delight faded),* now orders her to protect the pursuing Hunding against Siegmund. Brünnhilde protests, and Wotan furiously commands her to do his bidding. The escaping lovers, Siegmund and Sieglinde, enter. Sieglinde throws her arms about Siegmund, then pushes him

* Much of Wotan's recital of past events is cut in current repertory performances.

away, bemoaning her loss of honor (**Sieglinde:** *Hinweg! Hinweg!*—Away, away!). Hearing Hunding's horns in the distance, she becomes delirious, then faints. Brünnhilde approaches to warn Siegmund of his approaching death (**Brünnhilde:** *Siegmund, sieh' auf mich!*—Siegmund, look at me!). The Wälsung's devotion to Sieglinde so moves the Valkyrie, however, that she promises the lovers her protection in spite of Wotan's order. As Siegmund aims a deadly blow at Hunding, Wotan extends his spear to shatter Siegmund's sword, and Hunding thrusts his blade into Siegmund's breast. Brünnhilde, who has recoiled in terror at the sight of Wotan, snatches the pregnant Sieglinde and carries her to safety. Wotan kills Hunding with a contemptuous gesture of his hand, then vows vengeance on Brünnhilde.

ACT III. After a prelude known as "The Ride of the Valkyries," her warlike sisters greet Brünnhilde, who has brought Sieglinde with her. She sends the sorrowing widow alone to a forest hiding place near where Fafner guards the Rhinegold, first giving her the shattered sword of Siegmund for their future son, Siegfried (**Brünnhilde:** *Fort denn, eile*—From here, hasten). Brünnhilde remains behind to face the pursuing Wotan. For her disobedience in protecting Siegmund, she will be put to sleep on the Valkyries' rock, a prey to the first man who shall awaken her. Brünnhilde asks whether her "crime" merits such punishment (**Brünnhilde:** *War es so schmählich*—Was it so shameful?). Wotan replies "yes" and despite Brünnhilde's passionate attempts to justify her actions, he remains adamant. At her final supplication he makes a single amendment to her sentence: a magic fire will protect her from any man but a fearless hero. Wotan leads Brünnhilde to the rock where she will sleep and bids her farewell (**Wotan:** *Leb' wohl du kühnes, herrliches Kind*—Farewell, you most audacious, splendid child!); then he summons the magic flames.

WHEN the curtain fell on the close of *Das Rheingold,* we saw the happy spectacle of the gods, led by their chieftain, Wotan, as they moved over the rainbow bridge toward the new celestial mansion, Valhalla. What plot then, we may question, as we approach the second of the *Ring* series, *Die Walküre,* might possibly emerge from the seemingly happy *Rheingold* drama in which the gods achieved their goal, the Valhalla fortress and the ransom of Freia?

But as we review the *Rheingold* events, a number of unsolved problems present themselves. The Nibelung dwarf, Alberich, forswore the most priceless of man's blessings, the gift of love, in order that he might utilize the power of the ring which he stole from the Rhinemaidens. Alberich then fell prey to a cunning plot whereby Wotan and Loge succeeded in wresting the treasure from him. But just as Alberich obtained the ring by means of a curse (the sacrifice of love), so he relinquishes the ring only after uttering a more fearful oath foretelling death and destruction to all who shall possess the fatal ring.

Anyone inclined to doubt the potency of this imprecation need only recall the quarrel between the two giants, in which Fafner slew his brother, Fasolt, for possession of the ring.

A second unsolved problem has been introduced in *Das Rheingold:* Wotan's own attempt to cope with his difficulties by consulting Erda. She it was who warned him that the destruction of the gods would follow his possession of the ring. In her counsel lies his only hope. At this point, near the close of *Das Rheingold,* Wotan's plans are still shrouded in mystery, their only clue, though unexplained in the text, being suggested in the orchestral motif, the *sword.*

We must also remember that Fricka, Wotan's wife, was by no means resigned to the philanderings of her husband, and she can undoubtedly be expected to seize the first opportunity to counter any attempt on his part to alter or bypass the sanctity of the matrimonial laws which it is his duty to uphold.

Thus, as we enter the *Walküre* drama, we naturally seek the answer to these unsolved enigmas. But surprisingly enough, even by the end of this opera's lengthy first act, we have found only hints to the partial solution of one of these queries, Wotan's mysterious plan. Indeed, during this first act we do not even meet a single *Rheingold* character, but instead find three new ones. In fact in the entire *Walküre* we recognize only Fricka and Wotan from their previous introduction in *Das Rheingold.*

Die Walküre opens with a short prelude suggesting a relentless storm.

As the tempest reaches its climax, we hear the *thunder* motif of *Rheingold* followed by a diminished sequence, which serves later to characterize the stormy atmosphere near the close of *Walküre's* second act.

The storm subsides, and the curtain rises, revealing the crude interior of Hunding's wooden hut, built about a huge ash tree.

Accompanied by the motif of *fatigue* (somewhat reminiscent of the downward scale theme representing Wotan's *spear*) the wearied Siegmund enters and falls exhausted by the hearth.

Hunding's wife, Sieglinde, appears and tending the needs of the stranger, offers him refreshment. He drinks, and their eyes meet. At this moment a new motif, that of *love*, preceded by a broad version of *flight*, symbolizes the awakening of their mutual feelings.

The use of *flight* here suggests the hapless fate of the fugitive pair, who are seemingly the constant victims of a cruel destiny. Finally this episode concludes with the introduction of a new motif, the *Race of the Wälsungs.*

Since we know nothing at this point of the Wälsungs, this music can merely serve here to characterize the unknown bond which exists between Siegmund and Sieglinde.

They are startled out of their trance by noises from the stable, announcing the homecoming of Hunding. As he appears at the doorway of the dwelling, the blast of the *Hunding* motif in the brasses portrays his barbarian nature.

. . . . .

The first act continues as Hunding suspiciously regards Siegmund and Sieglinde, remarking on the similarity of their features, while the orchestra sounds the motif of Wotan's *spear:* the first intimation of their affiliation with the chief of the gods.

An additional clue is offered when Siegmund describes how he became separated from his father, while the *Valhalla* motif informs us of the existing affinity between father and castle.

As Siegmund concludes his narrative of the Wälsungs' woes, we hear a new motif, the *heroism of the Wälsungs,* a stately phrase which divides itself into two equal parts.

Hunding, having found that Siegmund is the enemy he has been pursuing all day, challenges him to battle on the following morning but promises safe shelter for the night according to the traditions of hospitality.

Left alone, Siegmund calls for the weapon which his father had promised him would appear in time of need. Suddenly the embers of the fire fall together, as the flames surge up, and the reflection reveals a shining sword hilt stuck in the side of the ash tree. The orchestra now proclaims the glorious *sword* motif in its original key of C, suggesting the meaning of Wotan's mysterious plan at the end of *Rheingold.*

Sieglinde soon returns and relates how at her wedding to Hunding, a stranger thrust the sword into the tree. During this detailed account, we again hear *Valhalla,* thus linking the stranger with Siegmund's father who but a short time ago was characterized in the same manner.

Suddenly the doors burst open, and the moonlit spring air pervades the room. The couple sing on the couch and express their love for each other. First Siegmund sings his famous aria, *Winterstürme.*

Win - ter - stürme wich - en dem Won - ne - mond,

Then Sieglinde, in her *Du bist der Lenz,* introduces a new motif of love.

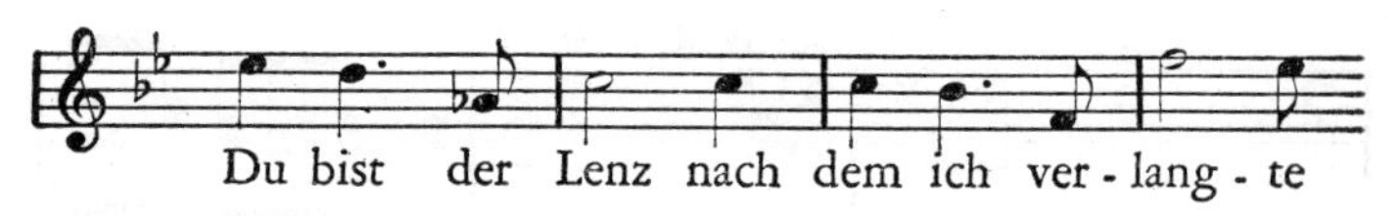
Du bist der Lenz nach dem ich ver - lang - te

The latter part of the duet is frequently punctuated by *womanhood,* the phrase previously descriptive of Freia, goddess of youth and beauty.

Finally, as the pair discover that they are twin brother and sister, *Valhalla* returns again to intimate their relationship to Wotan.

The act closes as Siegmund draws the sword from the tree, claims his sister as bride, and flees with her into the night while the music of the *sword, flight,* and *bondage* brings the orchestral postlude to its climax.

Seemingly then, the first act of *Walküre,* occurring a number of years after *Rheingold,* is actually the final exposition of the *Ring's* prologue which must be understood before we can proceed with the tremendous dramatic conflict for world power. The apparently unrelated love-drama of Siegmund and Sieglinde suddenly begins to emerge (through the interplay of old and new motifs) as part of the mysterious plan which Wotan has conceived at the end of *Das Rheingold.* And it is this lawless love of Siegmund and Sieglinde which ignites the spark leading to the inevitable destruction of the gods.

When the second-act curtain rises, we find Wotan confident of the success of his plans. His woes, however, soon begin as Fricka appears to gain satisfaction for Hunding's complaint. If there were moments of winsomeness in the personification of the *Rheingold* Fricka, all such traces are now absent, as the outraged goddess tempestuously approaches her husband in the rocky mountain pass. With relentless fury she pleads Hunding's cause and forces her spouse to agree to the death of his own illegitimate son, Siegmund, to uphold the moral code of her marriage laws, to which Wotan himself is pledged.

After Fricka has departed, Wotan confides to his favorite Valkyrie daughter, Brünnhilde, how he had created the warrior maidens and the twin-born Wälsungs as a bulwark against attack. Here, then, we learn directly of the full purpose of the Wälsung offspring—Wotan's mysterious plan.

Other questions are answered here. Fafner, fearful of losing the Nibelung hoard, has transformed himself into a dragon and without enjoying the pleasures and power which could easily be his, avidly guards his treasure in a forest cave. Wotan realizes that as long as the gold is held by the dragon, his own dynasty remains secure. But he is mindful of Erda's warning that should Alberich regain the ring, then the twilight of the gods would quickly follow. And Wotan's unrest is well founded, for he knows that just as he created the Wälsungs and Valkyries to secure him empire, so too has Alberich prepared for his own vengeance against the gods. The dwarf, bereft of love's power, has forced a woman to bear him a child of spite, Hagen. Wotan must face Alberich's threat with the realization that the Wälsungs, his cherished hope for the gods' salvation, must be abandoned and furthermore Brünnhilde, who had disobeyed his command, and protected Siegmund, must likewise be cast off from the gods as an example to others who would rebel against the god's authority. Wotan still hopes to evade eventual disaster by surrounding Brünnhilde with a magic fire so that only the strongest of heroes (Siegfried, the unborn son of Siegmund and Sieglinde) may awaken her. Together they can fulfill the Wälsung's mission.

At the same time, though never present during *Walküre,* we have felt the terrible impact of Alberich's drive to regain the ring.

In *Rheingold* we saw that the Rhinemaidens' golden treasure could be utilized only at a tremendous premium. Wotan, to pay off a bad debt, the mortgage on Valhalla, acquired the ring through theft, without paying its price. It would have been a different matter had Wotan's theft been for the benevolent purpose of restoring the gold to the Rhine, for not only would the rights of justice have been proclaimed, but Alberich's chances for world domination would have been immediately nullified. But since

Wotan's selfish motives prompted him to do otherwise, it is natural that justice must eventually prevail against him. Alberich, like Wotan, has accomplished a theft, but unlike the god, in forswearing love, he has acknowledged the price of the ring. For this reason, until the treasure is returned to the Rhine, it is Alberich alone who has the right to enjoy the advantages offered by the gold's magic power.

As the curtain falls on the second *Ring* drama, the motif of *fate*, heard against the music of the fire, warns that Wotan is no longer his own master, but the slave to the destiny that awaits him.

PAUL JARETZKI

Siegfried

First performance in Bayreuth, August 16, 1876.

Characters

Mime	Tenor
Siegfried	Tenor
The Wanderer (Wotan)	Bass-baritone
Alberich	Bass
Fafner, transformed into a dragon	Bass
Forest Bird	Soprano
Erda	Mezzo-soprano
Brünnhilde	Soprano

The Story

ACT I. Deep in the forest near the cave where the giant Fafner, transformed into a dragon, guards the Rhinegold, the Nibelung dwarf Mime works at his forge, attempting to make a sword too strong for young Siegfried to break in his hands. It is here that he has reared Siegfried, following the death of his mother Sieglinde, in the hope that the youth may slay the dragon and seize the gold for him (**Mime:** *Zwangvolle Plage*—Wretched duty).

Siegfried bounds in, teasing Mime with a young bear he has caught. He soon shatters the sword which the dwarf has made and turns on him in anger. The dwarf whines at Siegfried's abuse of him; the youth replies that he cannot endure Mime and forces him to reveal the story of his birth. Siegfried then orders Mime to forge the sword or he will beat him and then forge it himself. When Mime asks Siegfried what he will do when he has the sword, the youth replies he will leave Mime and be free (**Siegfried:** *Aus dem Wald fort*—Out of the forest). The boy then runs off. Wotan, disguised as a Wanderer, enters, challenging Mime to a battle of wits. Mime is terrified by the Wanderer's prophecy that he will die by Siegfried's hand. The youth returns and forges the fragments of his father's sword which Mime took from the dying Sieglinde and has carefully preserved (**Siegfried:** *Nothung, Nothung, neidliches Schwert*—Nothung, wonderful sword!). Mime meanwhile prepares a poisoned drink to get rid of the hero, after the boy has killed the dragon with the new sword.

ACT II. Mime's brother, Alberich, keeps vigil at the entrance to Fafner's cave. The Wanderer warns Alberich that Mime is bringing Siegfried to slay the dragon. As dawn breaks, Mime leads Siegfried to the cave but is soon driven away by the youth, who lies down under a tree to listen to the birds. He cuts himself a pipe to imitate their song, then takes up his horn. Its tones wake the sleeping dragon, whom Siegfried promptly kills. Licking the blood from his fingers, he is able to understand a bird's message (**Forest Bird:** *Hei! Siegfried gehört nun der Nibelungen Hort*—Siegfried now holds the Nibelung hoard). As he goes off into the cave to look for the hoard, Mime and Alberich reappear, quarreling over the gold. When Siegfried returns with the Tarnhelm and Ring, Mime offers him the poisoned drink. The hero slays the dwarf, then turns to listen again to the bird. Excited by its story of the sleeping Brünnhilde, waiting for him on her fire-encircled rock, Siegfried hastens to follow the bird out of the wood.

ACT III. In a wild region at the foot of a mountain, the Wanderer summons Erda to learn the fate of the gods. Even the goddess of the earth cannot save them. She is dismissed. Siegfried enters, on his way to Brünnhilde, and defies the power of Wotan. The Wanderer's spear, symbol of his power, is shattered by the impatient young hero, who is angered by Wotan's attempts to keep him from approaching Brünnhilde. Then Siegfried hurries away.

Siegfried reaches the mountaintop where Brünnhilde lies sleeping. Bravely breaking through the flames, he awakens the warrior maiden with a kiss. She greets the sunshine (**Brünnhilde:** *Heil dir, Sonne*—Hail to you, sunshine); he woos her passionately. At first she hesitates to yield her godhead (**Brünnhilde:** *Ewig war ich*—Immortal was I), but at last the lovers fall into each other's arms, unmindful of the fate that pursues the ring.

THE MOMENT that Wotan sealed his bargain with the giants to build the Valhalla citadel in exchange for Freia, goddess of youth, the chieftain doomed the gods to certain destruction. His fulfilment of the pact would betoken the loss of Freia's golden apples, whose magic secret gave the gods eternal youth. To redeem the goddess called for a ransom far beyond the gods' own realm and therefore to be attained only by means of a felony. Since honesty is the basis of divine law, its dethronement by a divine ruler takes from its usurper his right to master destiny. Thus Wotan, former ruler of gods and men, must become the slave of fate.

In futile attempts to avert the inevitable, Wotan sought frequent counsel, but the advice on which he acted led him only closer to the unavoidable twilight of the gods. Wotan's first counsellor, Loge, reported on the Rhinegold, the only substitute acceptable to the giants in exchange for Freia. It was Loge, too, who instructed Wotan how to outwit Alberich and take from him the all-powerful ring. Alberich's curse on the ring in turn necessitated Wotan's visit to Erda, who in *Das Rheingold* prophesied the gods' downfall and later opened her mind to him. It was she who bore him the Valkyrie maidens as protection against threatened attack. But in *Die Walküre,* Wotan is forced by Fricka to abandon his plan for the Wälsungs. And when Brünnhilde disobeys the god's command to fight against the Wälsung, Siegmund, the Valkyrie is cast off by her divine father. It is Brünnhilde who suggests to Wotan that the Wälsung Siegfried be allowed to fulfill the mission of the gods. And in this third drama of the *Ring, Siegfried,* we witness how this advice leads to the shattering of Wotan's spear by Siegfried, who now becomes the active force in the destruction of the god's power.

When we meet Wotan in the first act of *Siegfried,* we find the god filled with renewed confidence. The time has come when his Wälsung grandson, Siegfried, is ready to commit the murder of Fafner and the rape of the ring. Therefore, disguised as a Wanderer, the chief of the gods descends to the surface of the earth to observe these important events.

Wotan knew, of course, that the young hero, Siegfried, had been reared by the Nibelung dwarf, Mime, brother of Alberich, in the hope that he, Mime, might through Siegfried win the treasure for himself. To learn of Siegfried's progress, and to vitiate the threat of Mime in the fight for the hoard, Wotan, the Wanderer, makes his first visit to the cave of the dwarf. (This scene, as is often the case in the *Ring* operas, also serves as a general review of the events of the preceding operas.)

The *Wanderer's* motif, in two parts, conveys the stately grandeur which Wotan attributes to himself.

In the first chord of each of its four meaures, this music is reminiscent of the chromatic *Walküre* motif of *eternal sleep*, which served to describe the moment when Wotan kissed Brünnhilde into her magic slumber.

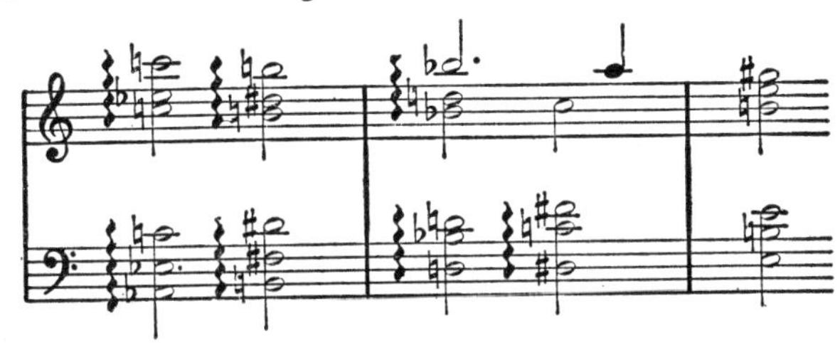

Mime is far from cordial to his uninvited guest, who he suspects is a spy come to interfere with his own plan to win himself the ring. But the power of Wotan's spear still suffices to bind the dwarf (we hear the *spear* motif throughout this scene), and Mime is forced to agree to a test of wits wherein Wotan promises to forfeit his head if he cannot answer three queries posed by the Nibelung.

As Mime propounds his course, we hear the motif of *reflection*.

The dwarf first interrogates the Wanderer about the Nibelungs, and as the events of *Rheingold* are reviewed, we hear the motifs of the *forge,* the *ring,* and *bondage.*

To the second question concerning the race of the giants, the music follows the themes of the *giants* and the *ring* with the *dragon:*

And finally when Mime asks about the race which dwells among the clouds, the Wanderer proudly replies to the lofty music of *Valhalla,* gloriously expounded in the original key of D-flat. This is followed by the *Rhine* (or *nature* to which it now extends) and *Erda.* Then, when Wotan describes the spear by which he rules the world, we hear first the downward scale of the *spear,* followed immediately by an ascending scale (almost an inversion) representing Wotan's *divine power.*

The magnificence of the orchestral texture accompanying the Wanderer's description of Wotan's power (a power which we know is in truth greatly diminished and nearing its end) is a subtle device to convey the god's delusions of grandeur concerning the state of his own authority.

The Wanderer has solved Mime's three enigmas; he chides the dwarf for not asking a riddle whose solution would serve Mime's own purpose. (He means, of course, the very question by which Wotan shortly traps his adversary.) Mime orders the Wanderer to leave, but the god insists that according to the traditions of such contests, Mime must now offer his head in forfeit if he cannot answer the questions of the Wanderer. The weight and urgency of the music which accompanies Wotan's insistence gives us the first clue of the serious intent behind his visit to this cave. As Mime answers the questions concerning the Wälsungs, Siegfried, and the sword, we hear their respective motifs. The motif of *Siegfried* was first heard in *Walküre* when Brünnhilde named Sieglinde's unborn son.

But when the Wanderer asks his opponent the very question which Mime himself should have asked him—namely, who shall forge anew the shattered splinters of the sword, Nothung? —the dwarf fails the test. Wotan assures him that he has no use for his head, and leaves it to one who knows nothing of fear—of course, Siegfried.

The next visit of the Wanderer takes place at the opening of the second act when he comes to the mouth of Fafner's cave. Here, for the first time since the terrible moment of the *Rheingold* curse, we meet Alberich, who patiently awaits the coming of the dragon's slayer, the liberator of the hoard.

The music of the prelude portrays both the grim horrors of the forest and the Nibelung's tireless efforts for revenge, featuring a review of the motifs depicting the *giants*, the *dragon*, *reflection* (heard in a dramatic descending sequence), the *Nibelung's work for destruction*, the *curse*, climaxed by *bondage*.

The restless motif of the *distress of the gods*, first heard in Wotan's *Walküre* narrative, heralds the Wanderer's arrival.

Alberich quickly recognizes his enemy, who assures him that he has come to observe events, not to create them. The Nibelung dwarf taunts Wotan with the knowledge that the god, having paid the gold to the giants in return for Freia (we hear the *treaty*), can never attack Fafner to regain the ring, since the very spear on which the runes of his treaties are etched would crumble to dust as a result of such dishonor. (This Wotan has already acknowledged in the *Walküre* narrative.) Alberich further reminds his adversary that Fafner is doomed by the curse and should the dwarf regain the gold, the gods can expect a speedy ending.

When Wotan counters that the gold will belong to him who slays the dragon, the Nibelung admits that he is fully aware of the Wälsungs, who were created by Wotan to perpetrate the deed, Fafner's death, which the god himself dares not attempt.

Wotan warns Alberich that he must contend with his brother,

Mime, since it is he who reared the hero to win him the ring; Wotan insists that Siegfried, untutored by the gods, will stand or fall by his own strength, and finally, tongue in cheek, awakens Fafner to recommend that the dragon relinquish the hoard to Alberich and avert the coming conflict.

Fafner, of course, possessed by his greed, refuses the suggestion.

Wotan departs. All things must go their accustomed way—and so too will the coming strife for the ring. Such is his comment.

Both Wotan and Alberich concede Siegfried's inevitable victory over Fafner. However, the god is also aware that a definite choice of events will have to follow. Siegfried, though ignorant of the power of the ring, may take the treasure (as the Forest Bird will advise), as a token of his victory over the dragon. However, if perchance he should ignore the hoard, Alberich and Mime will surely fight one another for it. Against this possibility Wotan has already taken the precautions he deems necessary. He calculates that Mime alone can probably not withstand his brother in strife. But with the protection of Siegfried, Mime will prevent the hoard from returning to Alberich. Thus of the two Nibelungs, Mime alone portends danger. And as we saw in the first act, Wotan is satisfied that *he* has disposed of the menace of Mime by winning his head in a test of wits and willing it to Siegfried.

The second-act meeting between the principal contestants—Wotan and Alberich—for the domination of the ring, demonstrates a stalemate. Wotan knows Siegfried will defeat Fafner, but does not concede that the downfall of the gods is still inevitable. Although Alberich is correct in his prediction of Wotan's destruction, the Nibelung does not regain the treasure for himself.

The magnificent raging prelude of the third act presages the arrival of Wotan and the impending downfall of the gods. We hear the *distress of the gods*, the *spear*, the frequent alternations between the ascending *Rhine-nature* and the descending *downfall of the gods*, the *Wanderer*, all climaxed again by *bondage* and followed shortly thereafter by the rise of the curtain on *fate*.

Wotan summons Erda from her slumber. During this invocation, we find a new form of *flight*.

Erda rises from the bowels of the earth to the music of *eternal sleep*.

Wotan informs her that as a world wanderer he seeks her counsel. (The fact that the supposedly all-wise earth mother does not recognize Wotan suggests the extent of the gods' loss of power.)

The Wala advises, while we hear a portion of her *Rheingold* warning, that he go to the Norns. Wotan counters that they cannot change or alter events, that he must learn how a rolling wheel can be stayed (how his downfall may be averted). Erda's confusion is characterized by the same music which in *Götterdämmerung* describes the First Norn's realization of her waning power.

When the earth mother advises the Wanderer to question Brünnhilde, he describes how the Valkyrie was punished for her defiance of her father's command. Erda cannot fathom the weird events which have taken place during the period of her slumber. To the same music which appears during a portion of Brünnhilde's *Immolation Scene* in *Götterdämmerung*, she scoffs at the god who urges defiance, yet punishes it, who guards right and discards it, ruling only through falsehood.

Wotan's ire is aroused. To the music of the *Wanderer*, he discloses the true purpose of his visit, asking how a god can conquer his own fear. Erda now recognizes the intruder's identity and begs to be released from his spell. Wotan answers that he no longer fears the inevitable downfall; indeed it has become his foremost desire. And as he announces his final plan, we hear a new motif, the *heritage of the world*.

Wotan declares that the Wälsung, Siegfried, untainted by greed and motivated by love, is exempt from the curse of the ring. The hero will awaken Brünnhilde. Knowing the full portent of the ring's threat, she will return it to the Rhine and deliver the world from Alberich's dreadful curse.

To the music of *eternal sleep*, Erda sinks down again into the earth.

Siegfried now appears on the scene, led by the Forest Bird. Wotan interrogates the hero, who relates how he forged the sword, slew the dragon and, later, Mime. The youth becomes impatient with the interference of the old man. The god asks for patience and respect, but this Siegfried refuses, citing his hatred for Mime and threatening a similar end to his present antagonist. Siegfried sarcastically remarks that the Wanderer's loss of one eye was surely due to a similar interference on his part.

In the face of Siegfried's defiance of authority, the very characteristic which Wotan instilled into the Wälsungs, the god soon loses his composure and attempts to dominate the situation.

Wotan warns the hero not to incur his anger, which could only be fatal to them both. *Frustration*, first heard in the scene with Fricka in *Die Walküre*, possesses him once more.

Siegfried insists that if the "old man" will not point out the way to Brünnhilde's rock, he must find the path himself. Faced by this defiance from the offspring of his own creation, Wotan is finally aroused to take a stand against his grandson. With *frustration* raging furiously in the orchestra, the god attempts in vain to instil fear into the youth. As Siegfried joyously approaches the threatening sea of flames which spring up around the mountain, Wotan extends his spear to destroy the steel, which he had previously caused to be broken in the hand of Siegmund. Siegfried meets the challenge, and with one stroke of his sword shatters the spear. As Wotan takes his leave, the motif of *Erda*, followed by the *downfall of the gods*, reminds us once more of the Wala's *Rheingold* prophecy.

We have seen that even before the start of *Das Rheingold*, Wotan's dishonor fated him to ultimate destruction. In the first three *Ring* dramas, the forces of destiny have continuously worked to compel Wotan to alter the plans which he believed might save the gods. Near the peak of his reign Wotan was able to tap the wisdom of Erda. Now his spear can barely muster enough power to coerce the earth mother from her deep sleep, let alone fulfil his need for counsel.

In *Siegfried* we witness the ironic workings of fate whereby Wotan, who forged obstacles to check the flood of impending doom, actually created the instrument, Siegfried, who renders the god completely powerless.

As long as the idle Fafner possessed the gold, the ring could not be used against the gods. Only Wotan's offspring, Siegfried, could free the hoard, and place it where the power of Alberich could bring about the final tragedy of *Götterdämmerung*.

Fate once more intervenes in the tragic conclusion to Wotan's encounter with Siegfried. At the close of *Walküre*, Wotan had decreed that only a hero, unafraid of his spear point, might break through the fire surrounding Brünnhilde's rock. Such was the monarch's decree to preserve his daughter for the man who was to inherit his own mantle. Now it is the audacity of this very hero, Siegfried, which defies not only a barrier of Wotan's making, but the god himself.

The stage is now set for the final tragic chapter in the struggle between Wotan and Alberich. However, in the last of the *Ring* operas, *Götterdämmerung*, it is their respective offspring, Siegfried and Hagen, who perpetuate the strife. Hagen destroys Siegfried and is himself annihilated. The forces of both Wotan and Alberich are swept away by fire and water, the Rhinemaidens retrieve their gold, and so the way is prepared for a new and better era.

PAUL JARETZKI

Götterdämmerung

First performance in Bayreuth, August 17, 1876.

Characters

The Three Norns	Contralto, Mezzo-soprano, Soprano
Brünnhilde	Soprano
Siegfried	Tenor
Gunther, a Gibichung	Baritone
Hagen, Gunther's half-brother, son of Alberich	Bass
Gutrune, Gunther's sister	Soprano
Waltraute, a Valkyrie	Mezzo-soprano
Alberich	Bass
The Rhinemaidens:	
Woglinde	Soprano
Wellgunde	Soprano
Flosshilde	Mezzo-soprano

The Story

PROLOGUE. Crouching near the Valkyries' rock, the three Norns spin the rope of destiny. It breaks, foreshadowing the end of the gods' supremacy. They disappear. As day dawns, Siegfried and his bride, Brünnhilde, emerge from their cave (**Brünnhilde:** *Zu neuen Thaten*—To new deeds). Innocently placing the fatal ring on Brünnhilde's finger, Siegfried accepts her horse, Grane, which he rides away to further adventure, leaving his bride to await him.

ACT I. The Gibichungs, Gunther and his sister Gutrune, sit in their dwelling by the Rhine, asking counsel of their half-brother, the evil Hagen, son of the Nibelung dwarf, Alberich. Hagen, plotting to secure the power of the ring, suggests that Gutrune marry the hero, Siegfried, and Gunther take Brünnhilde for wife. On Siegfried's arrival Gutrune gives him a potion, prepared by Hagen. Instantly the hero forgets Brünnhilde and awakens to the beauty of Gutrune. He even promises to help Gunther win the hand of the warrior maiden. Gunther and Siegfried pledge blood-brotherhood (**Gunther, Siegfried:** *Blühenden Lebens*—Blossoming life). The two men depart to fetch Brünnhilde, leaving Hagen gloating over his plans (**Hagen:** *Hier sitz' ich zur Wacht*—Here I sit on watch).

Musing alone on her rock, Brünnhilde is visited by her sister Waltraute, who brings a message from Wotan: The gods face destruction; only the return of the ring will save them (**Waltraute:** *Höre mit Sinn was ich sage!*—Let your soul hear what I am saying). Brünnhilde refuses to yield it. Siegfried, disguised in his magic helmet to resemble Gunther, approaches, wrests the ring from Brünnhilde, and woos her on behalf of the Gibichung.

ACT II. Hagen, still keeping watch at Gunther's dwelling, is haunted by his father, Alberich, and promises to obtain the ring from Siegfried. The hero arrives and asks for Gutrune. Hagen summons the vassals to the double wedding. Gunther appears with the horrified Brünnhilde, who swears that Siegfried is her husband. Siegfried swears on spear point that her tale is untrue (**Siegfried:** *Helle Wehr, heilige Waffe*—Bright and holy weapon). Brünnhilde makes a similar oath; then, deeply wounded by Siegfried's apparent desertion, yields to Hagen's suggestion and discloses the hero's vulnerable spot: a blow in the back will kill him. These two, with Gunther, join the wedding procession of Siegfried and Gutrune.

ACT III. The three Rhinemaidens are disporting themselves in the Rhine, bewailing the loss of their gold. Siegfried approaches, having wandered away from his hunting party. In vain they plead with him to restore the ring. The hunters arrive. Hagen offers

Siegfried another potion to restore his memory. The hero describes his youth (**Siegfried:** *Mime hiess ein mürrischer Zwerg*—Mime was the name of a grim dwarf). As he tells of his love for Brünnhilde, Hagen stabs him in the back. Siegfried dies with Brünnhilde's name on his lips.

In the hall of the Gibichungs, Gutrune awaits the return of the hunting party. Hagen brutally announces Siegfried's death. Gunther insists that the ring belongs to him. The half-brothers fight over its possession. Gunther is slain. Hagen vainly tries to snatch it from the dead Siegfried, whose arm rises in protest. Brünnhilde then draws the ring from her husband's finger and orders a mighty pyre for his funeral (**Brünnhilde:** *Starke Scheite*—Mighty planks). She calls for her steed Grane and herself rides into the flames. The Rhine overflows its banks, and the Rhinemaidens regain their gold. In the sky is seen the heavenly castle of Valhalla, consumed by flames. Flood and fire have purified the earth.

EVERYTHING about the final drama of the tetralogy is superlative, and most of all the music. There is about *Götterdämmerung* a spaciousness, a prevailing immensity exceeding anything of the sort in Wagner's other creations. And this immensity, this heroic dimension, is an element that fills the work from the first to the last measure and of which the hearer becomes instantly aware. . . .

Fortunately it is no longer deemed necessary to omit the introductory scene of the Norns, as used to be the practice at the Metropolitan. . . . The scene used to be called long and dull. It is definitely not long and most assuredly not dull. Apart from its moody grandeur and mystery, these pages are *absolutely essential* to the proportions of the prologue as a whole. The 17 bars which precede the rise of the curtain have a breadth and an elevation which set them apart from the beginnings of any of the preceding *Ring* dramas. The opening chords, now in E-flat minor and in 6–4, recall Brünnhilde's awakening in *Siegfried.* But how different they have suddenly become, especially when, as here, they are succeeded by the theme of the *Rhine* and its component *arpeggios!* . . . As the curtains open, the *awakening* chords yield to the harmonies of the *fate* theme, which from this point will rarely leave us. Then a *pianissimo* chord of the minor ninth, for woodwind, tubas, bass trumpet, and muted strings, introduces a new and boding theme—that of the *Norns* winding their fateful rope, likewise a series of steadily modulating *arpeggios*, similar to the *Rhine* motif, yet subtly different in its shape and implications.

The Norn scene actually takes the form of a twice recurrent three strophe ballad. . . . Its refrain is the questioning phrase "*Weisst du, wie das wird?*" In various successions and permutations, the scene brings us motifs we have heard more or less frequently in the course of the tetralogy—the motifs of *fate*, the *death song*, *Valhalla*, the *fall of the gods*, *eternal sleep*, Loge and the diverse aspects of his *fire*, *divine power*, *Alberich's curse*, the *gold*, the *Rhine*, the *ring*, Siegfried's *horn call*, the *sword*—but varied, elaborated, and treated with fresh subtilizations of harmony as well as new distributions and contrasts, which confer on them new dramatic implications. The actual interchanges of the Norns take the form of epic narrative. In an *external* sense the first half of the *Götterdämmerung* Prologue, which takes the place of the conventional prelude, is without action in the ordinary theatrical meaning of the term until the breaking of the rope. Action in the truest Wagnerian significance is confined to the music, the stage picture being a visualization of "deeds of music" in the composer's own phrase.

It is only when the Norns have descended to their mother, Erda, that *visible* action takes the upper hand and continues with scarcely more than two interruptions till the close of the second act. The second half of the Prologue—the love scene and the joyous parting of Siegfried and Brünnhilde—is reached by way of a transitional daybreak episode. This sunrise is a decorative effect of dramatic symbolism, and has a parallel in the daybreak of the second act which leads from the nocturnal Alberich-Hagen colloquy to the violent happenings shortly to ensue. In the Prologue the change from night to full sunlight is achieved without the slightest sense of haste in the space of 45 bars, and yet the change of mood is astounding. It also acquaints us with two of the most superb themes in *Götterdämmerung*—the first, a mutation of Siegfried's *horn call*, broadened into a virile 4-4 that pictures the now mature hero.

Directly after it we hear the incomparably tender motif of *Brünnhilde the woman*, one of Wagner's priceless inspirations. . . .

As the pair emerge from their cave, the music is of an almost blinding radiance in its surge and ecstasy. The phrases of *Siegfried the Hero* and of the exultant Brünnhilde bring the latter's first words, sung to her own caressing motif, "*Zu neuen Thaten, theurer Helde.*" Upon these outpourings there soon follows another lovely new theme, *Heroic Love.*

At Brünnhilde's words "*der Held, dem ich nun mich neige*" the glowing music recalls in the oboe that tender phrase to which, in the last act of *Siegfried,* the fearless youth had uttered the preponderating melody of the duet "*O Heil der Mutter die mich gebar!*"

The various themes, notably those of *Brünnhilde,* the mature *Siegfried, Heroic Love,* expand, entwine, take on new pace and impetus, and are joined by the motifs we have heard in portions of the preceding two dramas. We recognize without difficulty the motifs of the *Valkyries* and their *Ride,* the familiar *horn call, Siegfried* himself, the *ring* and, as Brünnhilde embraces the hero after the words "*Brünnhilde brennt dann ewig heilig dir in der Brust,*" the grandly expansive melody of the *world's heritage.* The theme of the *dragon* recurs, briefly combined with a form of Siegfried's *horn call,* when the hero momentarily alludes to his combat with Fafner; and when the erstwhile Valkyr asks him to greet her steed, Grane, in her name, we hear for a moment the theme of love which we remember from *Die Walküre,* where it had to do chiefly with the fated Siegmund and Sieglinde. And as we reach Brünnhilde's rapturous "*O heilige Götter,*" the motif of Siegfried's yearning for freedom, which we first heard in the opening act of *Siegfried,* contributes to the refulgence of the gleaming textures. Swellingly harmonized, it accompanies the departure of Siegfried allied to the themes of the *Ride, Brünnhilde,* and, naturally, the *horn call* as the hero sounds it from below; and as she smilingly waves to him in a gesture of farewell, the orchestra brings that strongly accented phrase from *Siegfried,* "*Er ist mir ewig, ist mir immer.*"

With the closing of the curtains on the prologue begins *Siegfried's Rhine Journey,* a favorite of years' standing on symphonic programs but never so effective in the concert hall as in the opera house, where the hero's fateful course, from complete joy to the tortuous involvement into which he is straying unawares is clearly demonstrated. . . . . . .

Gradually the sunlight of the tone picture is clouded by shadow. The melody of the Rhinedaughters gives way to the themes of the *ring* and the *renunciation of love*, with increasingly somber harmonies set against murmurings of 'cellos and violas; the fanfare of the *gold*, first by horns, then in the bass trumpet, followed by the sinister chords of *bondage* and the malign *power of the ring*—(a derivative from the *Rhinemaidens'* song). Thereupon, the musical stage having been set with the full subtlety of the Wagnerian "art of transition," there enters, *marcato e pesante*, a heralding phrase of the *Gibichungs*, and the curtain rises on the first act proper.

. . . . .

The early pages of the first act take on a very different musical character: a new chapter has opened. We have entered a world of deception and, with one exception, of "masks"—to borrow a penetrating word of Paul Bekker. That one exception is Hagen. He is the reverse side of the medal stamped on the other with the features of Brünnhilde and, together with her, the only *active* agent in a mimic world otherwise peopled with marionettes. Hagen's musical symbol, a figure of two notes, represents one of Wagner's greatest characterizing and structural triumphs. It is essentially a harmonic device woven by the composer with overpowering and suggestive effect into the texture of the score. Formed by the descending step of a tritone—the augmented fourth—it has a savage element in common with the motif of Fafner, the dragon. In the three acts of *Götterdämmerung* it asserts itself again and again with the most sinister and pervading menace.

. . . The musical phrase of the Gibichungs is distinguished by its dotted rhythm [and a marchlike character].

It underlies the first pages of [the first act] and is preceded by the symbol of Hagen, which at first wears a comparatively smooth, almost gallant character. As the scene progresses, the *Gibichung* theme, associated with other motifs well known to the listener, recurs with growing significance. The interchanges among Hagen, Gunther, and Gutrune occur over an incessantly changing play of motifs, in themselves familiar, but in new formations like bits of colored glass in a kaleidoscope.

It is at this stage that we begin to experience some of those trenchant phases of the *Götterdämmerung* music which place it in a different and a subtler sphere than the preceding *Ring* dramas. Let me offer a case in point: Just before Hagen's words "*Brächte Siegfried die Braut dir heim,*" the wood wind gives out in mysterious *piano* a suggestion of the *Tarnhelm* theme, in a form more eerie than before, through new chromatic devices. . . .

From this Wagner presently derives a new, insidious motif suggesting treachery by magic, properly followed by Hagen's theme and likewise by the symbol of the Gibichungs. For her part the simple and credulous, yet amiable Gutrune has uttered her words "*Du Spötter, böser Hagen*" to an enticing new theme:

A few bars later this expands into the lovely, twining phrase "*der Erde holdeste Frauen friedeten längst ihm schon.*"

The arrival of Siegfried and his horse on a little boat is one of the great episodes of the act. It is built up and brought to a dramatic and musical climax with consummate effect. Siegfried's horn call which has pervaded the tissue of the score for several preceding pages is associated with the Rhinemaidens' song as Hagen describes the hero's approach on the river. As he hails him, the orchestra accompanies his words with a theme containing Hagen's characteristic interval and whose evil significance will be properly appreciated only in the second act when it appears in the tremendous chorus of the Gibichung vassals. At this point, however, the quickening tempo adds to the growing excitement of the hero's arrival. The *Gibichung* motif in an animated *staccato* form precedes the appearance of hero and horse. The arrival is significantly accompanied by Alberich's crashing *curse*. Gutrune's first delighted glance at the handsome newcomer is pictured by a timid yet bewitching oboe phrase, whose sweetness asserts itself above the tumult of the orchestra. Then, just before Siegfried inquires which man is Gibich's son, there is a lordly proclamation of the *Gibichung* theme . . .

In this limited space, the analyst can do little more than call attention to a few cloud-piercing heights of the matchless score.

The listener must be left to draw upon his recollections of the previous dramas of the cycle, concentrating as best he can on the myriad changes which Wagner's imaginative and technical resources have worked upon them. The tender phrase of Gutrune's *greeting* must be cited, as she hands Siegfried the cup containing the drink which is soon to rob him of his memory.

The equally important theme of her *welcome* will later acquire a bitterly poignant sense.

The serpentine motif of *forgetfulness,* heard as Siegfried puts the drinking horn to his lips, tells better than any words how completely, in the twinkling of an eye, the hero is in the grip of a spell. From this point (at which, as Jean de Reszke was in the habit of saying, "Siegfried's soul died") the fated Wälsung becomes a puppet, the obliging instrument of Hagen's dominating will.

In a particularly pathetic moment he hears from the mouth of Gunther those words which, long ago, he had heard when the Forest Bird had promised him Brünnhilde on her fire-girt rock. For a moment he struggles to recall words he seems to have heard before. But the weird harmony of *forgetfulness by magic* quickly makes clear how wholly Siegfried is now a mere helpless pawn. The music of the Blood Brotherhood oath, while it begins with the fine, chivalrous phrase "*Blühenden Lebens labendes Blut,*" tells its own bitter story.

The phrase to which Gunther sings the words "*Bricht ein Bruder den Bund*" becomes a sardonic symbol as the tragedy advances.

Siegfried's inquiry why Hagen has taken no part in the Blood Brotherhood oath brings the latter's reply that his cold, sluggish blood, which will not even redden his cheeks, would suit but ill to "bonds of fire." And Wagner has made clear the tragedy of Hagen, the loveless and prematurely aged, by citing ironically at this point the theme of Freia's *golden apples.* Gunther and Siegfried now prepare to leave for their journey to Brünnhilde's rock, the orchestra turbulently seething with combinations of Loge's chromatic *trickery, Hagen's* motif, the *Ride of the Valkyries,* Siegfried's *horn call,* and Wotan's *spear.* Hagen is asked to keep watch before the hall. His monologue, *"Hier sitz' ich zur Wacht,"* forms the basis of the dark interlude between the two scenes of the first act. This interlude is, in its fashion, a counterpart of Siegfried's *Rhine Journey.* Its function is to connect two scenes of dissimilar character and to supply by means of its thematic, harmonic, and coloristic components a transitional panorama. Once again we experience Wagner's "art of transition" in full magnificence. But the color scale is here based on aspects of darkness, rather than on a transition from gleaming sunlight to a somber mood.

It begins almost identically with Hagen's *Watch Song,* and the opening bars bring us Hagen's potent theme, forming the bass of the syncopated chords of the Nibelung's *hatred.*

We hear a darkened form of Siegfried's *horn call,* the theme of *Siegfried,* of Wotan's *spear,* and the expressive phrase from Hagen's monologue *"Ihr freien Söhne frohe Gesellen,"* which from now on takes the importance of a leading motif. The theme of the *Rhinemaidens* appears in a dissonant, harmonically sable vesture. Gradually these measures merge into several that show a momentary but almost uncanny likeness to *Parsifal.*

Gradually, through the themes of the *ring* and *Brünnhilde* we find ourselves back on the Valkyrie *Rock*. The scene presently to follow—the visit of Waltraute and her plea to her sister to rescue the doomed gods by restoring the ring to the Rhine—reminds us of the Ride of the Valkyries. . . .

Waltraute's narrative presages Brünnhilde's great lament in the last scene. We hear in it reminders of the Wotan narrative in the second act of *Die Walküre*. . . . The passage "*Des Stammes Scheite hiess er sie schichten zu ragendem Hauf*" is, indeed, a foretaste of Brünnhilde's "*Starke Scheite schichtet mir dort.*" But still more memorable, as showing Wagner's incredible ability to think himself back into the very feelings and colors of a work he had completed years earlier, is that melting passage from Wotan's Farewell at Waltraute's words: "*da brach sich sein Blick, er gedachte, Brünnhilde, dein!*"

The listener should give particular attention to Waltraute's futile appeal, "*Hör' mich, hör' meine Angst,*" with its agonized dissonances, and then to Brünnhilde's exalted phrases, which sweep aloft on the theme of the *world's heritage*: "*Denn selig aus ihm leuchtet mir Siegfrieds Liebe.*"

Musically speaking the subjugation of Brünnhilde by the disguised Siegfried is as poignant as anything in the work. A new motif, the symbol of *murder*, almost suggests the thrust of a knife. The themes of the *curse* and the *Valkyr* writhe together for mastery in the struggle with Siegfried; the pitiful conquest of Brünnhilde and her half-swooning collapse in the hero's arms is set to the moving phrase of the once protecting Siegfried. When Siegfried draws the sword he plans to lay symbolically between the conquered Valkyr and himself—stark octaves of the theme of the *sword-barrier* and the motifs of the *sword*, Nothung, the Wotan *spear*, and *Hagen* combine in an overwhelming example of tragic counterpoint. And it is phenomenal in what effortless manner the music suddenly clarifies itself when Siegfried, discarding his feigned, roughened voice, utters in natural tones the phrase "*Nun, Nothung, zeuge du dass ich in Züchten warb.*"

The second act is intense in its music no less than in its drama, from the first bars of its portentous prelude. This page is made up of themes already familiar to us, but even the most familiar motifs and phrases appear to take on a new and expanded grimness and dimension. The syncopated harmonies of the Nibelung's *hatred* seem here to have grown gigantically and acquired a wholly new menace. Beneath these black chords the deeper orchestral voices trace in implacable octaves a descending melodic progression closely related to the mood of Hagen's *Watch Song.* This, with occasional interjections of the motif of *bondage* and the formula of *Hagen* bring, as the curtains part, a soft, meaningful allusion in the third trumpet to the measures "*Ihr freien Söhne frohe Gesellen*"; then, as a shaft of moonlight strikes the crouching figure of Alberich, the themes of *bondage* and the *ring* merge. This material reappears in the course of the nightmare dialogue that ensues, together with music now well known to us though, by the alchemy of the Wagnerian genius, always exhibiting baffling new facets.

Again Wagner changes from night to sunlit day in a short space, yet with the utmost spontaneity. Musically, the fascinating passage merits close attention. This daybreak, less than 50 bars long, is built on a supple figure, treated in canon over a pedal on B-flat. Various new themes soon populate the lively scene. One of these, which is soon to assume a large importance, and which accompanies Gutrune as she comes from the Gibichung hall to welcome the hero, is the jubilant *call to the marriage.*

This is soon to be followed by the lovely theme of Gutrune's *greeting,* heard in its most enamoring form at Gutrune's words: "*Lasset uns sie hold empfangen.*"

We have reached the threshold of one of the most powerful passages of the act—Hagen's rough summons to the Gibichung vassals. The gathering of the clans is accompanied by the rude sounds of cowhorns and a number of important themes, outstanding among which is the strongly accented one depicting *Hagen's wicked glee.* The episode is further colored by that augmented fourth which is Hagen's particular label. To the tremendous expansion of the virile ensemble, numbers of other great themes and melodies now contribute, and the chorus reaches a massive climax in a stupendous yet genuinely simple march tune.

This tune supports the first words of Gunther's greeting, as he returns with the pale and downcast Brünnhilde. The depressing transformation of a phrase of the *Ride of the Valkyries* instantly mirrors the state of the captive's spirit. The *Call to the Marriage,* clothed in rich chromatic harmony, sustains his ensuing greetings. The *sword* motif culminates in a crashing dissonance as Brünnhilde, looking up for the moment, catches sight of Siegfried. From this point the music discourages description, in its self-explanatory frenzy and wild beauty. Not even Isolde's cries of pain during her sea voyage quite equal the anguish of Brünnhilde's "*Betrug, schändlichster Betrug*"

or her "*Heisset Brünnhild, ihr Herz zu zerbrechen.*" The awesome scene reaches its peak in her oath on the spear, "*Helle Wehr, heilige Waffe!*"

with the *murder* theme as its foundation. The ensuing pages paint delirium unbridled. Not till the throng, headed by Siegfried and Gutrune, leaves the stage, is there a period of relative calm and even then the tragic mood is too savage for true respite.

The musical delirium is alleviated by passages of a musical loveliness which even Wagner has rarely matched. With pathos he recalls the motif of Siegfried's *treasure of the world* in Brünnhilde's bitterly ironic words to Hagen, "*Ein einz'ger Blick seines blitzenden Auges,*" as she mocks his idea of taking vengeance on her betrayer; and the incomparably expressive transformation of the theme of *love's rapture* from Siegfried at "*Nicht eine Kunst war mir bekannt.*"

. . . . .

Götterdämmerung's final "superlative" is its last act, fashioned with the utmost cunning. The first scene is a shrewd psychological achievement. After the fearful preceding tension the hearer feels the need of emotional contrast and musical relief. The first pages supply these elements. . . . Then, however, we are led back to the moods of *Das Rheingold,* with an evocation of the river in its earliest musical formula. The song of the water maidens is heard and the bright fanfare of the *gold.* Then, however, appear two new themes associated with the Rhinemaidens, strikingly different from their simple melodies in the prologue of the tetralogy but, if possible, even more enamoring.

The trio of the river daughters, in limpid, undulant phrases, is buoyed up by sinuous *arpeggio* figures of sixteenth notes that lend it an enchantment different from anything we have encountered in the cycle up to this point, and new chromatic vocal figures on the syllables "*heia la la lei la la*" enrapture us with a new element of grace.

The loveliness of the maidens' song is further enhanced when Siegfried appears and engages in banter with the nixies. Soon the music becomes charged with portent. Its texture is clouded. Motifs and harmonic colors from the past scenes trouble the melodic surfaces and tinge the sweet chromatic contours with sadness. And after reminding the hero that he once possessed "a glorious gift" (appropriately sung to the theme of Brünnhilde) which he irresponsibly discarded, they swim away, their liquid tones echoing from the distance.

In old-style opera the scene which follows would undoubtedly have been introduced by a hunting chorus. Here, however, the orchestra supplies the action. And so, after incredibly ingenious thematic combinations, we arrive at Siegfried's tale of his youthful adventures. It is essentially the old narrative, such as has formed a stock in trade of opera through generations of the lyric stage. Musically, Wagner animates and revitalizes it by the symphonic background he has fashioned, with absolute logic, out of the pertinent themes from *Siegfried.*

. . . . .

After the fatal blow the stricken hero continues the ecstatic narrative of his bride's first awakening. The music inevitably parallels the *Siegfried* episode. Then, on the three-note formula of *fate,* he murmurs his last words. There is no break, however, in the continuity of the ensuing music. Directly upon Siegfried's death there follows the great threnody. Kettledrum beats precede a scale figure of sixteenth notes which soon, associated with four mighty chords, forms the solemn, crushing *death* motif, whose majestic recurrence binds, like a refrain, the whole shattering death march.

A review of the dead man's life [through motific evocation] is seen from the perspective of his bier. . . . Toward the close, as the stage mists begin to disperse, we hear, twice over, the tender phrase of *Brünnhilde's womanhood,* leading to the gloomy chords of *bondage* and the *power of the ring,* as well as a recall in funereal minor of a phrase of *Siegfried the hero.* At this point the scene reopens on the deserted Gibichung hall. We hear the themes of the nerve-racked *Gutrune,* tormented by premonitions of disaster. Alarming thoughts of the wild Brünnhilde obsess her, echoed in eerie chromatic sounds of the *Valkyr* themes, while she imagines herself to hear broken, staggering tones of Siegfried's horn. The entrance of Hagen, soon followed by the body of his victim, the grieving Gunther, and the throng of Gibichung vassals, brings the prevailing agitation to a climax.

In a fierce but momentary episode Hagen fells his half-brother while the theme of the *sword* causes the murderer to shrink back in terror as he seeks to grasp the ring from the murdered hero's finger. Brünnhilde advances majestically from the background. Then, after replying calmly to the recriminations of the distraught Gutrune, she begins the sublime immolation scene, of which we have had a foretaste in Waltraute's narrative. The themes of *divine power,* of *fire,* and of *Siegfried* combine polyphonically in an imposing march movement. Gradually, as she contemplates the countenance of the dead Siegfried, the music assumes a tender character. To the motif of fate she utters the essential philosophy of the *Ring*: "*Alles, alles weiss ich, alles wird mir nun frei;*" and at the phrase, "*Ruhe, ruhe, du Gott!*" a lovely iteration of the *Valhalla* theme establishes its mood of consolation. The words "*Grane, mein Ross! Sei mir gegrüsst!*" open in ecstatic succession the *fire* motifs, the themes of the *Valkyries* and their *ride, Siegfried* and the radiant phrase of *redemption by love*, momentarily glimpsed during the third act of *Die Walküre* but reserved for this last, crowning application.

The last pages, after Brünnhilde's final utterances, form a gigantic epilogue and summation of the musical and spiritual sense of the tetralogy. After the wreck of the Gibichung hall, the score seems suddenly clarified. We return to the song of the *Rhinemaidens* in its first unsullied purity, then to its luminous combination with *redemption by love*. Once more this miraculous counterpoint is heard, followed by the pealing music of *Valhalla*, expanded like a mighty chorale, the theme of *divine power* set against it like a heroic figuration. A final exposition of Siegfried's motif, encompassed by *Loge's* flickering flames; then amid a sonorous murk of cymbals, the descending theme of the *fall of the gods*. Finally, like a last transfigured *benison*, there soars over the smoking ruins of this primeval world, the lucent melody of *redemption by love!*

HERBERT F. PEYSER

RICHARD STRAUSS (1864–1949)

Der Rosenkavalier

Libretto by Hugo von Hofmannsthal. First performance in Dresden, January 26, 1911.

Characters

Octavian, Count Rofrano	Mezzo-soprano
The Marschallin, Princess von Werdenberg	Soprano
Baron Ochs von Lerchenau	Bass
Notary	Bass
Milliner	Soprano
Animal vendor	Tenor
Valzacchi, an intriguer	Tenor
Annina, his companion	Contralto
Three orphans	Two Sopranos and Mezzo-soprano
A singer	Tenor
Leopold, Blackamoor, and Hairdresser	Mimes
Von Faninal, a wealthy parvenu	Baritone
Marianne	Soprano
Major domos	Tenors
Sophie, Faninal's daughter	Soprano
Innkeeper	Tenor
Commissioner of Police	Bass

The Story

ACT I. In her great baroque boudoir in eighteenth-century Vienna the Princess of Werdenberg (the Marschallin) is wooed by her young lover Octavian (**Octavian:** *Engel! Nein! Selig bin ich*—Angel! No! Blessed am I). When they are interrupted by the visit of the Marschallin's cousin, the huge bloated Baron Ochs, Octavian disguises himself as his mistress' maid Mariandel, with whom the baron promptly attempts to flirt. Ochs has decided to marry Sophie, the young daughter of the wealthy Herr Faninal, and now looks for a young cavalier to court his fiancée in the prescribed manner by presenting her with a silver rose. The Marschallin suggests Octavian for the mission. Her boudoir is soon crowded by a procession of cooks, hairdressers, milliners, petitioners, and a singer who offers a sentimental aria (**Tenor:** *Di rigori armato*—With my heart steeled against love). A pair of Italian intriguers, Valzacchi and Annina, offer their help as spies to the Baron and are told to keep an eye on Mariandel. When the room is cleared, the Marschallin muses on her lost youth (**Marschallin:** *Da geht er hin*—Now go your ways) and remains in a wistful mood when Octavian returns (**Marschallin:** *Ach, sei er gut*—Command yourself). Impatient at her apparent remoteness, Octavian rushes off without a kiss. The Marschallin sends the silver rose to follow him by messenger.

ACT II. The excited parvenu Faninal waits for the emissary of his future son-in-law in his garish salon, where his young daughter stands transfixed with fervor at her approaching happiness; her duenna Marianne watches the arriving coaches through the window. A swarm of lackeys heralds the arrival of Octavian, who presents the rose and then joins Sophie in a rapturous duet (**Octavian, Sophie:** *Wo war ich*—Where was I). After a brief moment alone with Marianne, they are joined by Faninal and the Baron; the Baron proceeds to disgust Sophie with his coarse attentions and sentimental reminiscences (**Baron Ochs:** *Mit mir* —With me). When the two men go off to discuss the dowry, Marianne is called away to quiet the tumult aroused by the Baron's retinue, and the young people are left alone. Octavian finally persuades Sophie to turn to him for support (**Octavian:** *Mit Ihren Augen voller Tränen*—With your tear-filled eyes; **Sophie:** *Ich möchte mich bei Ihm verestecken*—I wish I could hide with you), and they are in each other's arms when the Baron's spies, Annina and Valzacchi, seize them and summon the Baron and his suite. Octavian thereupon defends Sophie's honor with his sword and wounds the Baron in the wrist. Sophie swears she will never marry the Baron, but her father insists she will marry whom he says—i.e., the Baron—or spend the rest of her days in a convent. Annina gives the Baron a note ostensibly from Mariandel, appointing a rendezvous (**Annina:** *Herr Kavalier*—Worshipful sir), but is so outraged at his niggardliness in rewarding her that she decides to double-cross him.

ACT III. Valzacchi and Annina are preparing a dingy room in a questionable tavern to receive the Baron and Mariandel, who come in and start supper (**Octavian:** [Mariandel]: *Nein, nein, ich trink kein Wein*—No, no, I drink no wine). A series of heads appears at every door and window, as arranged by Valzacchi, to terrify the Baron.

Annina rushes in, dressed as a widow, and claims the Baron as the father of her children. The police arrive and summon Faninal, who calls in Sophie to prove that Mariandel is not his daughter, as the Baron has suggested to save face with the police. Octavian retires to remove his girlish clothes, and the Baron is struggling furiously to avoid his accusers from all sides when the Marschallin makes a superb entrance. After Sophie tells Ochs that she and her father are "done with him," the Marschallin dismisses the Baron, forcing him to give up Sophie, then brings the young couple together, musing on their future happiness as they express their bewilderment and joy (**Marschallin, Sophie, Octavian:** *Hab' mir's gelobt*—I made a vow). As the great lady goes off to comfort Faninal, the lovers are left alone to sing of the miracle that has united them (**Sophie, Octavian:** *Ist ein Traum*—'Tis a dream).

STRAUSS' sentimentalism came most truly into focus in *Der Rosenkavalier*. The cause, no doubt, was to be found in the nature of Hofmannsthal's dramatic fiction. Its chief motif—the graying Marschallin with her nostalgia for youth and philosophy in accepting the flight of time—fairly exudes sentimentality, albeit a dignified, not a mawkish one. Yet we have to thank this sentimental slant for the finest music in the opera—the last pages of the first act, the grandiose trio in the third.

The Marschallin is, incidentally, one of the great figures of operatic portraiture and her place is not far beneath two other related personages of lyric drama—Mozart's Countess Almaviva and Wagner's Hans Sachs. But there are other memorable characters, both full drawn and small scale, crowding this richly populated canvas. If the Marschallin is a female counterpart of Sachs, the Baron Ochs is a cousin under the skin to Sir John Falstaff. As for Octavian, what is he but a sophisticated variant of Cherubino?

Many hairs have been split as to why Strauss assigned this role [Octavian] to a trousered soprano rather than to a man. The answer is so absurdly simple that the far-fetched and even psychopathical explanations repeatedly put forward are almost unbelievable. Quite aside from the fact that opera is peopled with innumerable women in men's garb (often on purely vocal grounds) Octavian *has* to be a woman for the simple reason that he is obliged twice to assume female disguise in the opera, and it is preposterous to imagine a man, in female garments, singing in a man's voice and yet preserving an illusion of reality. In just what kind of voice do the advocates of a male Octavian suggest that the Mariandel of the third act should carry out "her" scene with the Baron long enough to deceive that experienced and Rabelaisian dupe?

Hofmannsthal's text deserves to be digested for its own fine sake and for its evocation of a place and of a period. But our present concern is music. *Der Rosenkavalier* is immensely full of music, good, better, and less good. It is not a "number" opera in the conventional sense; yet it contains numbers just like the works of Wagner's maturest period. It has innumerable themes, too, leading motifs if you will, though they often differ in character and in function from Wagner's. The vocal treatment, the handling of text, the balance between voices and orchestra are sometimes better contrived than in Strauss' preceding operas. Occasionally the words of Hofmannsthal are submerged in the orchestral torrent; at other moments they are conveyed effortlessly to the ear. The waltzes constitute a chapter by themselves, though, contrary to a very current idea, they are by no means the best things in the score.

Unlike *Salome* and *Elektra, Der Rosenkavalier* opens with a prelude which is less a preparation for what is to follow than an essential part of the action itself. It is well, perhaps, that music cannot make its meanings more concrete than it does. Speaking once of his *Till Eulenspiegel* Strauss flatly refused to interpret for a questioner the literal significance of a particular passage, alleging that "it might give offense." This brisk introduction to the scene in the Marschallin's boudoir might do no less. In any case, the listener who has ears to hear and some knowledge of the facts of life may be trusted to paint his own picture.

The exuberant, aggressive, upward-leaping theme which the horns give at the outset will be heard many times in the course of the opera and has reference to the adolescent impetuosity of Octavian. The music gathers pace and momentum, and at one point a direction in the score prescribes that "from here on the entire *crescendo* should be carried out parodistically." There is no need of laboring the point, however. The orchestra—notably the horns—work themselves up to a paroxysm which then yields to a tranquil and satiated mood as the curtain rises. The music grows sentimental and is punctuated with birdlike chirpings. One hears impassioned *cantabile* phrases, now fast, now slow, now agitated, now calm. The hectic impression yields for a moment with the words of the Marschallin, *Du bist mein Bub*, which always sounds a little like a travestied take-off of Sieglinde's *Du bist der Lenz* in *Die Walküre*. Then a passionate phrase paints the embraces of the lovers. The music continues on its highly variable and nervous course, the line of melody never long sustained. With the little breakfast scene we come to the first of the waltzes, a pretty clarinet melody . . . Like other waltzes in this opera it is short-breathed, and comes to no very definite close.

The scene proceeds in the same excited vein, the self-control of the Marschallin contrasting with the perturbations and ecstasies of her youthful admirer. The rhythmic movement of the music is, consequently, choppy, the pageant of themes vivid but dishevelled. The characterization, none the less, is masterfully sustained; the composer can paint in a couple of bars a picture of the Marschallin with no more than the phrase *Ach sei er gut.* The confusion preceding the arrival of the Baron Ochs brings us still another waltz phrase, *Fahr er schnell in seine Kleider.* . . .

It is impossible to consider here the myriad welter of details which accompany the Baron's arrival or the Marschallin's levee, a true evocation of the artifices of the rococo period—which deserves a close study for its own sake. The lyric kernel of this animated and tumultuous scene is two-fold—the trio of the three noble orphans (first in minor and then, when they have received the Marschallin's gratuity, repeated in a luminous major), and the flowing air of the Italian tenor. The latter melody is purest Strauss *cantabile* and not an attempt to imitate the Italian lyricism of the period. Yet the composer, without attempting any feat of archaism, achieves his suggestive purpose most admirably.

With the departure of the motley throng we reach, in the scene between Octavian and the Marschallin, one of the high points of the opera and of Strauss' inspiration generally. The scene is of melting lyrical beauty and tenderness throughout, from the monologue, *Kann mich auch an ein Mädel erinnern,* with its exquisite introduction, transparent as chamber music, through the sweetly sorrowful page, *Die Zeit, die ist ein sonderbar Ding* (notice those tiny strokes of the clock of which the Marschallin speaks). And if Strauss had written nothing but that exquisite passage *Zum Grafen Octavian gib's ab* (with the ethereal phrase, *da drinn ist die silberne Rose*) and the transfigured orchestral postlude, he would have had to be set down among the divinities of music.

The second act, with its bustling introduction, is no less varied than the first, though different in character. We meet here the amazing theme of the silver rose—an enchanting series of apparently unrelated chords instrumented in a fashion that causes it to glisten like the silver rose itself. The bittersweet harmonic confusion it brings into the suave melodies with which it is drastically associated lends a delectable seasoning to the musical texture. Grandiose is the climax which Strauss builds up for the arrival of Octavian and the presentation of the rose. The clash of radiant timbre has almost the effect of a blinding sunburst. The duet of Octavian and Sophie, which follows, soars dizzyingly into a kind of melodic empyrean. Then, with some new waltz measures, Strauss brings the listener back to earth and to the more animated, if less lyrical, traffic of the act.

This act is as musically diversified as it is closely packed with incident. The duet of the two young people, suddenly grown conscious of their feelings for one another, without reaching the height of the earlier one, has a grace all its own. Then come the intrigues of the Italian schemers. The noisy irruption of the Baron's lecherous retinue, and at last the preposterous duel of Ochs and Octavian, the thunderous discomfiture of the former, and finally, the letter scene tricking the Baron into an assignation with the imaginary Mariandel in a vulgar pothouse. And here the music dissolves into heady waltz melodies.

These and other waltzes form a large part of the background for the third act. This act opens with a rustling, scurrying, dissonant introduction which is, in reality, a six-voiced *fugato*, leading to a pantomimic scene at the rise of the curtain. Waltzes played by an off-stage orchestra lend realism to the picture of sordid pleasure. The "supper" of the Baron and the disguised Octavian offers much in the way of coarse tomfoolery to a good deal of waltz music.

The plot engineered against Ochs by the intriguing Italian pair and their own confederates, the appearance of the police, the shrieks of a horde of children—all these things resolve themselves into an orgy of noise. The scene is unquestionably longspun, but with the arrival of Faninal, Sophie, and, at last, the Marschallin herself, music of a finer grain once more gains the upper hand.

By a well-developed transition, both musical and emotional, the mood is gradually set for the supreme moment of the opera —the great Trio, in which the Marschallin voices her resolve to renounce her young lover—, her dignified withdrawal, and, finally, the duet in which Sophie and Octavian fall into each other's arms. The Trio, as noble a piece of ensemble music as opera contains and ranking with such lyric monuments as the *Rigoletto* Quartet, the *Meistersinger* Quintet, and *Lucia* Sextet, grows, incredibly enough, out of one of the tawdriest waltz tunes of the supper scene. If ever a cheap melody was ennobled and sublimated it is here, and it is scarcely possible to hear this music without tears. No less a feat did Strauss accomplish in writing a duet to follow this grandiose inspiration that should not seem a flagrant anticlimax. Yet the intoxicating duo of Sophie and Octavian, *Ist ein Traum, kann nicht wirklich sein*—twice repeated and separated by a superb orchestral passage with thrilling modulatory effects, appears actually to intensify the effect of the Trio. Melodically it seems an outgrowth of the duet "*Möchte jeder brave Mann,*" of Papageno and Pamina in *The Magic Flute*, as well as of Schubert's song, *Heidenröslein*. But derivative or not, it sets a priceless crown on the whole opera. And at its repetition the glittering sounds of the silver rose theme chime through it.

But Strauss does not bring down the curtain on this swelling burst of emotion. The final touch is like a detail out of a *commedia dell' arte*. The little Negro page appears and, by candlelight, seeks a lost handkerchief in the deserted and darkening room, scene of both so much fooling and tenderness. He finds it, waves a good-bye to the audience, and the little *scherzando* epilogue ends bravely and brilliantly on a good, old-fashioned dominant-tonic cadence.

HERBERT F. PEYSER

RICHARD STRAUSS (1864–1949)

Salome

Libretto by Hedwig Lachmann, based upon Oscar Wilde's play. First performance in Dresden, December 9, 1905.

Characters

Narraboth, a young Syrian, captain of the guard	Tenor
Page	Mezzo-soprano
Two soldiers	Basses
Cappadocian	Baritone
Salome, daughter of Herodias	Soprano
Slave	Soprano
Jokanaan, a prophet	Baritone
Herod Antipas, Tetrarch of Judea	Tenor
Herodias, his wife	Mezzo-soprano
Five Jews	Four Tenors and Bass
Two Nazarenes	Tenor and Bass

The Story

On the moonlit terrace of a Judean palace, Narraboth, captain of Herod's guards, watches the beautiful Salome with infatuated eyes, as the young princess sits within the banqueting hall. His soldiers comment on the prophet Jokanaan, whom they are guarding imprisoned in a cistern on the terrace. Salome emerges, weary of the admiration of her lascivious stepfather, Herod. She is fascinated by the voice of the prophet (**Jokanaan:** *Jauchze nicht*—Rejoice not) and prevails on Narraboth to release Jokanaan, who steps forth and denounces Herod and his wife Herodias. Salome voluptuously addresses the prophet (**Salome:** *Ich bin verliebt in deinen Leib*—I am in love with your body), who retreats, scandalized, into the cistern. The despairing Narraboth stabs himself. Herod and Herodias come forth with their attendants, tempting Salome to return to the feast. Herodias is incensed at the insults directed at her by Jokanaan, but she cannot bring Herod to harm the holy man. Five Jews discuss the nature of God and debate the validity of the prophet (**Quintet:** *Das kann nicht sein*—That cannot be). Two Nazarenes appear, reporting the miracles of Jesus and confirming the prophecies of Jokanaan, whose voice interrupts their talk. Herod begs Salome to dance for him (**Herod:** *Tanz für mich, Salome*—Dance for me, Salome), offering in return to grant any request she may make. Over the protests of Herodias, Salome performs the **Dance of the Seven Veils.** Falling at Herod's feet, she demands that she be brought, on a silver charger, the head of Jokanaan. Herod is alarmed; Herodias approves. Vainly Herod suggests alternative rewards, but finally he agrees to fulfill his promise. The executioner goes down into the cistern and after a deathly silence reappears with the prophet's head. Salome seizes it and addresses it passionately (**Salome:** *Du wolltest mich nicht deinen Mund küssen lassen*—You wouldn't let me kiss your mouth). Even Herod is shocked, and, as ominous clouds darken the scene, he rises to go inside the palace. A stray moonbeam falls upon Salome, who has kissed the mouth of Jokanaan. Gazing with horror and disgust, Herod orders the soldiers to kill the princess.

THE POSITION which Richard Strauss' opera *Salome* occupies in the realm of the lyric theater is unique. Despite the fact that the score lacks two indispensable and basic elements of music, namely the mystery of true spiritual content and the warmth of genuine human feeling, it is nevertheless unmatched in its dramatic power and immediacy of effect.

The strange contradiction of its undeniable forcefulness, despite its equally undeniable deficiencies, is further sharpened by the fact that although a religious atmosphere is frequently required by Oscar Wilde's poem, there is not one passage of a truly religious mood in the entire score.

Strauss, a free-thinker, generally preferred to steer clear of religious plots. While at work on the composition of his pantomime *The Legend of Joseph* he complained to his friend and librettist Hugo von Hofmannsthal of the difficulties he experienced in composing music for religious subjects. He was more at home in the world of urbane wit or the atmosphere of depravity and evil, which play such a prominent part in his earlier operas.

Salome was Strauss' first operatic success. He was forty-one when he wrote it—an age at which many composers show that they have reached that point in life where fascination with the world of men begins to fade in favor of the world of the spirit. Strauss never experienced this inner reorientation.

There is no doubt that he never again reached the peak of expressive intensity that is so characteristic of *Salome*. . . .

. . . In this work perhaps more than in any other, Strauss

wrote with compelling conviction. This is not to say that at other times he was a "commercial" composer, willing to subordinate his inventive genius to the real or imagined demands of the box-office. He was doubtless sincere in his approach to music. Yet his preoccupation with success and financial reward was, as Gustav Mahler put it, "an integral part of his inspiration": he could never quite resist striking the pose of the Virtuoso Composer. Consciously, Strauss' attitude towards music was one of honesty and integrity. Unconsciously, however, he lacked that straightforwardness and simplicity which are the earmarks of artists of the highest stature.

This lack, far from handicapping his creative abilities, turned out to be the primary factor responsible for his tremendous skill in presenting his material.

. . . . .

The libretto of *Salome* was an almost ideal match for the personality structure of Strauss. Although the religious element, as personified by Jokanaan, lies in the foreground, the opera deals primarily with Salome's attempts at conquering not the prophet but the man. It is essentially a story of the clash between the world of physical pleasures and the world of the spirit. It is the story of the momentary triumph and ultimate self-destruction of a purely materialistic attitude. . . .

Great operatic masterpieces can come into being only when the libretto is intimately related to the very essence of a composer's personality. . . .

In *Salome* Strauss could be completely himself. . . . The atmosphere of sensuality, the corrupt lustfulness that permeate Wilde's poem, were grist for his mill. The passages expressive of the world of Jokanaan and the Nazarenes, on the other hand, are for the most part curiously banal and lack real religious fervor.

Let us consider, for instance, the motif of Jokanaan's prophecy: the strong, if artificial, steps of successive fourths suddenly give way to a weak and rather sentimental progression of chromatic half steps. It is not until three bars before the end of the theme that a decidedly mysterious mood reappears.

. . . . .

. . . And how stereotyped the music of the Nazarenes sounds! This passage, an orchestral restatement of a melody sung earlier by Jokanaan, serves as background to their account of the miracles worked by Jesus. How unctuous it seems in its two-part setting!

Oddly enough, this banality is not detrimental to the dramatic effect of the opera. Granted that the moments of religious connotation are not so convincing musically as the rest of the score. Yet, placed amidst the agitated outcries of Salome and Herod, their very paleness becomes almost an artistic virtue.

In *Salome* Strauss had a story that gave him a chance to conceal many of his weaknesses, at the same time permitting him to make the most of his strong point—his ability to portray the passions and the viciousness of man—without the need to ascend to the realm of human spirituality.

That is why *Salome* is, after all, a masterpiece: the story offers a perfect setting for the particular gifts of the composer. Little necessity arises for an expression of deeply felt emotion; no occasion for restraint and simplicity; no room for the sweeping gesture of profound tragedy.

It is remarkable that a work should be able to sustain interest for ninety minutes without these elements, usually indispensable to the lyric stage and great music. But, then, *Salome* is like an ingeniously designed and perfectly built mechanism. It makes its effect with machine-like precision. It works like a clock.

Like Salome herself, however, it suggests a body without a soul.

ERNEST GOLD

RICHARD WAGNER (1813–1883)

Tannhäuser

Libretto by the composer. First performance in Dresden, October 19, 1845.

Characters

Venus . . . . Mezzo-soprano
Tannhäuser . . . . Tenor
A shepherd . . . . Soprano
Hermann, Landgrave of Thuringia . . . . Bass
Four minstrels . . . . Two Tenors, Baritone, Bass
Wolfram von Eschenbach . . . . Baritone
Elisabeth, the Landgrave's niece . . . . Soprano

The Story

ACT I. The minstrel Tannhäuser has grown weary of the enchantments of Venus, with whom he has spent a year and who tempts him to remain in her magic caverns beneath the Wartburg, near Eisenach in Germany (**Venus:** *Geliebter, sag'*—Beloved, tell me). Fauns and bacchantes riot through the cave; the sirens' call echoes from the grottoes (**Chorus:** *Naht euch dem Strande!* [Bacchanale]—Approach these shores). Although willing to sing the praises of his mistress, the knight is tired of her charms (**Tannhäuser:** *Dir töne Lob!*—All praise to you). Her promise of revels and delights only makes him long all the more for the simple pleasure and pain of earthly life. When the angry goddess heaps scorn upon Tannhäuser's hopes for salvation, he exclaims that his hope rests with the Virgin Mary (**Tannhäuser:** *Mein Heil ruht in Maria!*—My hope rests in Mary). The magic cave at once fades away.*

Tannhäuser finds himself in a sunny valley near the castle of the Wartburg; a shepherd is singing of spring (**Shepherd:** *Frau Holda kam*—Dame Holda came). As a procession of pilgrims passes on its way to Rome, the knight falls penitently to his knees. Distant church bells are drowned out by the song of hunting horns as the Landgrave and his minstrels return from the chase and greet Tannhäuser, their long-lost friend, begging him to journey back to the castle with them. Wolfram von Eschenbach reminds him that in the past his singing has won the love

* This is the Dresden version of this scene, currently presented at the Metropolitan Opera. See footnote, page 240.

of the Landgrave's niece, Elisabeth (**Wolfram:** *Als du in kühnem Sange uns bestrittest*—When we were contesting in song). Hearing Elisabeth's name, the minstrel promises to resume his courtly life.

ACT II. Elisabeth joyously enters the Hall of Song in the Wartburg, where she first heard Tannhäuser's voice (**Elisabeth:** *Dich, teure Halle*—Dearest Hall of Song, I greet you again). Ecstatically she welcomes the knight and reveals how much she has suffered from his absence. The Landgrave and his niece receive their guests in a stately procession (**Fest March and Chorus:** *Freudig begrüssen*—Joyously we greet) after which the Landgrave decrees a contest of song in praise of love (**Landgrave:** *Gar viel und schön*—Very often and beautifully). The winner is to receive from Elisabeth whatever he may ask. Pious Wolfram, the first to sing, delivers an idealized tribute to Elisabeth, whom he too has loved (**Wolfram:** *Blick' ich umher*—Glancing around this fair gathering). He is followed by Tannhäuser, who, his soul still possessed by Venus, affronts the company by his description of delights of a profaner kind (**Tannhäuser:** *Dir, Göttin der Liebe*—You, goddess of love). The ladies rush from the hall in dismay. The horrified knights draw their swords against the sinner, but Elisabeth, who has remained, intervenes and pleads for his redemption (**Elisabeth:** *Zurück von ihm!*—Away from him). The Landgrave promises Tannhäuser forgiveness on condition that he join the band of pilgrims bound for Rome. Falling at Elisabeth's feet, the remorseful knight kisses the hem of her robe and then rushes from the hall.

ACT III. Wolfram comes upon Elisabeth at prayer before a shrine in the Wartburg Valley, now dark with the shadows of an autumn evening. The song of the returning pilgrims is heard (**Chorus:** *Beglückt darf nun dich*—Once more with joy), but Elisabeth looks in vain for Tannhäuser among them. Broken with grief, she prays to the Virgin to receive her soul in heaven (**Elisabeth:** *Allmächt'ge Jungfrau*—Almighty Virgin). Wolfram, gazing after her as she departs, takes up his harp and conjures the evening star to guide her way (**Wolfram:** *O du mein holder Abendstern*—Oh you, my lovely evening star). When night falls, Tannhäuser returns, ragged and weary. He tells Wolfram of his pilgrimage to Rome in abject penitence; of his joy at seeing so many others granted pardon; of his despair when told by the Pope that he can no more be forgiven for his dalliance with Venus than the papal staff can break into flower (**Tannhäuser:** *Inbrunst im Herzen*—Fervent in heart). Obdurate in his loyalty to the goddess, he summons her enchantments once again (**Tannhäuser:** *Ach, lass mich nicht*—Ah, let me not seek in vain). As Venus appears on her couch, Wolfram begs the knight not to renounce his hope of redemption, finally invoking the name "Elisabeth." Tannhäuser stands as if transfixed, and at this moment Elisabeth's funeral procession winds down the valley (**Chorus:** *Der Seele Heil*—Receive the soul). With a cry, Venus disappears into the darkness. With Wolfram's help Tannhäuser staggers to the coffin, implores Elisabeth to pray for him in heaven, and dies. Dawn breaks upon the scene as a chorus of pilgrims appears over the hill, singing of a miracle that has taken place: the Pope's staff, which they bring forward, has blossomed with green.

TANNHÄUSER represents Wagner's intention to create a new kind of stage work, based on conventional operatic structure but greatly improved, in his opinion, so as to benefit both drama and music. To achieve this, he modified form and content to advance the action as a continuous development. . . .

The Overture to *Tannhäuser* follows but greatly expands the pattern set by Weber in his operatic overtures. . . . It elaborates symphonically on the opera's story, the struggle between piety and sensualism. This was hardly a revolutionary musical idea at the time, but it was adventurous for a young composer to presume to introduce so much orchestral exposition into a form of entertainment generally considered the absolute kingdom of the voice. The chorale theme of the *Pilgrims' Chorus,* which opens the Overture, starts out quite conventionally but soon projects a mood of restless longing through chromatic harmonies. . . .

The middle section of the Overture, depicting the revels of the Venusberg, is even more advanced in the sensuous urgency and lush textures of both its chromatic harmonic style and its rich orchestration. Less molten in character is the smouldering, languid motif of Venus' handmaidens, luring sinners to the cloying sweetness of perfumed bowers.

. . . A study of the characters of Venus and Kundry [in *Parsifal*] will reveal the unfolding of Wagner's ideas about the embodiment of lustful sin in the person of a woman, but it is curious to note that in each instance he turned to creatures out of pagan mythology and supernatural superstition. In his attempt to create a super-woman who could personify all the qualities he wished to suggest, Wagner actually lessened the theatrical realism of worldliness and hearkened back to the witches, ghosts, furies, and *dei ex machina* of earlier *opera seria*. In Venus, the juxtaposition of a romanticized classical goddess against a rather syrupy, sentimental, two-dimensional stereotype of Victorian Christianity seems odd indeed, and must be counted another of *Tannhäuser's* transitional traits. . . . In the Dresden version of *Tannhäuser* currently in use at the Metropolitan,* the presentation of Venus and her court is far less effulgent and overblown than in the deliriously Teutonic Paris version, and it is possible to detect a shadow of the classical simplicity with which Gluck (whom Wagner greatly admired) treated mythical immortals. The tenets of the romantic movement decreed, however, that the senses be set free from classical bondage; so Wagner developed a more imaginative and subjective musical vocabulary. Thus the abandoned climaxes and surging, probing harmonies of even the Dresden edition, suggest every possible intensification of the senses.

But if Wagner, like other romantics, had little use for the power of understatement, he was not yet ready to abandon traditional operatic forms such as the aria, duet, ensemble, and chorus; indeed he never did abandon these, but objected to them only when they interfered with the drama instead of furthering it. His aim was to force these recalcitrant entities into submissive partnership in a continuous whole. . . .

A good example of straightforward vocal style is Tannhäuser's *Hymn to Venus*, whose simple harp-chord accompaniment at first suggests a recitative. Broken chord figures, used merely for harmonic fill-in, are found just as frequently in the accompaniment parts of the entire opera as are symphonically developed passages heralding Wagner's more advanced talents. *Tannhäuser* contains several *leitmotifs*, but they do not extend to the whole drama—the *Hymn to Venus*, for example, is not one of them—

* Season of 1954–55. Earlier the Paris version (generally presented in the world's opera houses) had been given at the Metropolitan. The Dresden version was written first; Wagner prepared the second, Paris, version on the occasion of the opera's première in the French capital to satisfy the Parisians' demand that every opera contain a ballet. In revising the scene for the Paris production, Wagner added not only the ballet but also additional music for Venus and Tannhäuser. Many American critics and much of the public seemed to prefer the more familiar Paris version, but all were grateful for the opportunity to hear the Dresden version, generally considered the more consistent stylistically.—C. A. L.

nor had Wagner yet discovered their full possibilities as material for dramatically relevant elaboration in purely orchestral terms.

The transition from the Venusberg to the valley near the Wartburg is accented by the loneliness of the Shepherd's song with English-horn *obbligato*, presaging the use of similar devices in both the first and third acts of *Tristan*. Just as Venus is a transplanted classical goddess, so the Shepherd is a romanticized remnant of the stylized pastoral idylls later to be recaptured in the opening part of Giordano's *Andrea Chénier*. At the first entrance of the Pilgrims we are given a taste of the choral style which characterizes *Tannhäuser;* often monolithic, yet harmonically plastic and supple, it reflects Wagner's nationalistic loyalty to the church-chorale tradition of Luther, Bach, Crüger, Vulpius, and many other German masters. In many sections, particularly the ensembles, Wagner breaks into the texture with imitative voice entrances, but seldom does he give us any thoroughly linear counterpoint as in *Meistersinger*. Religious passages gain an austere intensity and noble solemnity of dedication through the use of unison melodies sung by all the voices, as in parts of *Parsifal*.

The energetic Prelude to Act II turns out to be no prelude at all but a concerted exposition section of Elisabeth's entrance aria, *Dich, teure Halle. . . .* Wagner assigns to the orchestra some ebullient lines, giving them the same Weber-like curvature and resiliency that graces a similar piece, the Prelude to Act III of *Lohengrin*. Elisabeth's aria is unmistakably allied to the old style in its exciting progression toward an applauseworthy high B-natural, but in Wagner's treatment of this standard form he evolved a certainly individual novelty. The voice part is sustained in character rather than designed to display vocal technique with rapid phrases like those played by the orchestra. Elisabeth's melodic lines are not evenly metered, following the text in a clever compromise between declamation and conventional stanza singing. The orchestra obligingly subsides into a few supporting chords when Elisabeth first enters, but, though this sounds like an opening recitative, it is actually a substitute for the usual slower middle section of the aria; the first section has already been played without any voice at all. Thus, by compressing the form of the aria and by contrasting Elisabeth's sustained line against the animation of the orchestra, Wagner has produced an abbreviated number whose impact on the audience is due as much to novelty as to tradition.

The ensuing duet of Tannhäuser and Elisabeth, too, is of readily identifiable origin, with canonic voice entrances and intervals of thirds and sixths between the voices. Nine bars by

Wolfram make it unexpectedly, however, a momentary trio. The melodies are garnished with a number of turns, an Italian and Weberian form of embellishment of which Wagner remained fond all his life, but which in later works he transferred almost entirely to the orchestral parts. The entrance of the guests into the Wartburg is pure, old-fashioned grand opera; like Verdi in *Aïda,* Wagner apparently felt that there is a time and a place for a rousing, orthodox march. . . .

Wolfram's *Blick' ich umher* begins with a few chords in the strings of an obviously and conventionally prefatory character, and the voice line, which attempts to set speech into a natural rhythm without resorting to mere recitative, seems labored. The harp accompaniment is a mere series of broken chords, a far cry from Beckmesser's serenade in *Meistersinger,* where modality and inexpert execution are pungently and adroitly lampooned. At least one biographer has attributed the stodginess of this piece to Wagner's lack of personal sympathy with Wolfram's prudish, cut-and-dried point of view as contrasted with that of Tannhäuser, whose impassioned apostrophe to Venus is, in fact, Wagner's own plea for greater freedom and genuine feeling. . . .

In the ensemble which closes the act, Elisabeth sets forth a *leitmotif* associated with Tannhäuser's prayer for divine pardon. . . . Another important musical idea is the march theme of the Pilgrims' journey to Rome, heard during the Landgrave's reproach to Tannhäuser. Treble chords suggest the sustained faith which guides the Pilgrims' footsteps, while a walking figure in the bass suggests the footsteps themselves as they progress up and down across the countryside. . . .

Act III shows the most progressive Wagner at work. The Prelude is a symphonic paraphrase of Tannhäuser's experiences between the second and third acts. . . . First the Pilgrims' march theme is heard, then the plea for mercy first voiced by Elisabeth, then a new motif suggesting Tannhäuser's remorse, anguish and despair. This leads into the chromatic, yearning strain of the *Pilgrims' Chorus.* . . . After a return of the march theme, a rushing figure in the violins is heard for the first time since the Overture, where it appeared only as an *obbligato* to the main *Pilgrims' Chorus* theme. This leads to a forceful statement by the brass choir of a theme signifying redemption. . . . The rushing figure and Redemption theme are now alternated most effectively, suggesting Tannhäuser's despair at being unable to gain pardon; the prayerful mood returns to close the piece quietly, telling us that the resigned Elisabeth is still praying for Tannhäuser. In *Elisabeth's Prayer,* which follows after the curtain's rise, simplicity of chords and line indicate an utmost economy of means. Somehow this section seems rather stilted and static, as though Wagner were content at this period in his career to rely on the stock, sterilized, prayerful attitude of countless traditionally virtuous operatic heroines; for it was sensuousness which aroused his imagination, and he had not yet found how to give three-dimensional credibility to a character whose existence seemed to him so abstract. Not so Wolfram, who is here transformed from a figurehead with a mouthpiece into a dignified and compassionate human being. In a lengthy postlude to the *Prayer* scene, too, Wagner has adventurously tried to further the drama through orchestral means alone, as Elisabeth takes leave of Wolfram without addressing him but explaining, through gestures and facial expression, that she appreciates his solicitude but does not wish him to accompany her. Wolfram's solo, the *Song to the Evening Star*, is definitely a musical retrogression to conventional forms, but its position in the scene makes it credible and affecting. It leads, after an orchestral repetition, directly into Tannhäuser's entrance, which is announced by a searing, chromatic bass theme signifying damnation.

Tannhäuser's *Rome Narrative* is generally considered the finest vocal number in the score. Not only does it weave together various motifs in a technically and emotionally well-organized pattern, but it combines them with the voice part in a way that clearly indicates Wagner's growing awareness of the new medium implied by his ideas. The motifs of anguish and of redemption . . . figure prominently in the orchestral progression which keeps pace with Tannhäuser's story. The climactic moment is accented with admirable simplicity as Tannhäuser recites the Pope's verdict while the orchestra repeats the motif of damnation. The remainder of the opera is devoted to recalling the Venusberg scene in a flickering fantasy which owes its origins to both Mendelssohn and Weber, then to a choral finale in which the nucleus of *Parsifal* is apparent. The *Pilgrims' Chorus* is repeated in unison to form a musically very simple but sweeping and compelling conclusion.

The idea of concluding on such a note, with an aurally and emotionally overpowering majesty, characterizes all of Wagner's works and can be traced to the existence of grand opera, traditionally, as a spectacle. In Wagner's hands, however, this device, like many others, became imbued with a new character; he wrote not an ensemble finale but a musical peroration of the drama which, as he gained in skill and artistic stature, came to mean a full resolution of the various musical themes which had conflicted and contrasted throughout the work. If in *Tannhäuser* this summation has not yet attained the architectural complexity which Wagner later achieved, it lacks nothing of the appropriate grandiosity of feeling called for by his new musical and dramatic ideas.

JOHN W. FREEMAN

GIACOMO PUCCINI (1858–1924)

Tosca

Libretto by Giuseppe Giacosa and Luigi Illica, based upon Victorien Sardou's *La Tosca.* First performance in Rome, January 14, 1900.

Characters

Cesare Angelotti, escaped political prisoner	Bass
Sacristan	Bass
Mario Cavaradossi, a painter	Tenor
Floria Tosca, a singer	Soprano
Baron Scarpia, Chief of Police in Rome	Baritone
Spoletta	Tenor
Sciarrone	Baritone
Shepherd boy	Soprano
Jailer	Baritone

The Story

ACT I. Cesare Angelotti, former consul of the Roman Republic, freshly escaped from the Castle of Sant' Angelo, where he has been held as a political prisoner, seeks refuge in the Attavanti Chapel of the majestic baroque church of Sant' Andrea della Valle. Hardly has he concealed himself when the ancient Sacristan of the church shuffles in, followed by the painter Mario Cavaradossi, who admits that his portrait of the Madonna on the wall was inspired not only by the Lady Attavanti but also by his beloved Floria Tosca, a famous singer of Rome (**Mario:** *Recondita armonia*—Hidden harmonies of various beauties). When the Sacristan leaves, Angelotti ventures out, but his friend Cavaradossi, thrusting a lunch basket into his hands, hurries him away as Tosca makes her entrance and pleads with the painter for a rendezvous in the country (**Tosca:** *Non la sospiri*—Are you not longing for our little house?). After a jealous moment when she sees some features of the Attavanti in Mario's painting, Tosca is reassured by Cavaradossi's protestations of love (**Mario:** *Qual'occhio al mondo*—What eyes in the world can match the ardor of your black eyes?). When she departs, Cavaradossi summons his friend and takes him off to hide at his villa. Meanwhile the Sacristan returns with a crowd of choirboys whose frolickings are interrupted by the majestic entrance of Baron Scarpia, head of the Roman police, in search of Angelotti. When Tosca returns to meet her lover, she finds instead the cynical but amorous Scarpia, who plays upon Tosca's jealous weakness by insinuating that Mario is having an affair with the Attavanti. As Tosca tearfully leaves, a Te Deum commences. Unmoved by the religious procession and rite which follow, Scarpia resolves that he will send her lover to the scaffold and possess Tosca himself (**Scarpia:** *Va, Tosca*—Go, Tosca).

ACT II. In his magnificent apartment in the Farnese Palace, Scarpia muses over his situation (**Scarpia:** *Ella verrà*—She will come). He then discusses his prospects with his agents, Sciarrone and Spoletta, who, with other attendants, bring in Cavaradossi, now in custody for protecting Angelotti. The painter refuses to give any information about his friend and is led away to the adjacent torture chamber just as Tosca arrives, dressed in her gala robes for the concert in Queen Caroline's apartment below, where she has been singing. While the groans of Cavaradossi echo from the next room, Scarpia questions Tosca and finally succeeds in prying from her the name of Angelotti's hiding place. Cavaradossi is at once released and is led in, bleeding. When he discovers that Tosca betrayed Angelotti, he curses her and cries defiance at the tyranny of Scarpia (**Mario:** *L'alba vindice*—The revenging dawn breaks). Furiously Scarpia orders his minions to remove the painter. Alone with the Baron, who reveals his desires (**Scarpia:** *Già, mi dicon venal*—They already call me venal), Tosca vainly pleads for mercy (**Tosca:** *Vissi d'arte*—I live for art and love). Finally she promises to yield to his advances as the price of her lover's freedom. Scarpia then summons Spoletta and orders a mock execution for Cavaradossi, after which he will be free. No sooner has he written out a passport for Tosca and her lover than the singer stabs him. After placing a crucifix on his breast and candles at his head and feet, she slips away.

ACT III. On the battlements of the Castle of Sant' Angelo, the voice of a shepherd is heard at dawn. Soon Cavaradossi is led to a waiting jailer; with a bribe he obtains permission to write a last letter to Tosca (**Mario:** *E lucevan le stelle*—And the stars were shining). Soon Tosca herself hurries in and tells him of Scarpia's murder and of the simulated execution. He can hardly believe the news (**Mario:** *O dolci mani*—O gentle hands). The lovers ecstatically plan for the future (**Mario, Tosca:** *Trionfal di nova speme*—Triumphant with new hope). Tosca retires as the firing party advances and draws. When their work is accomplished, she hurries to Cavaradossi's side, horrified to find that the man is dead: Scarpia has betrayed his promise. Distant shouts announce that the Baron's murder is discovered, but Tosca is too quick for her pursuers: she leaps over the battlement to her death.

IT IS not easy to describe the peculiar individuality of Puccini's score or to judge by what means it achieves it. Sometimes it seems as if its brutality is heightened by the employment of strongly accented, reiterated notes in the formation of phrases, themes, melodies. It has the true Puccini profile; yet you could never mistake half a dozen bars of *Tosca* for something in *Manon Lescaut,* in *Bohème,* in *Butterfly*. It is utterly and inescapably itself, and limited as Puccini's musical vocabulary undoubtedly was, he never repeated what he said in this opera.

Tosca utilizes numerous characterizing themes and melodies, now brief and cutting and violent, now sensuous and longspun. The method is not the symphonic treatment of Wagner, though to Wagner the Puccini of *Tosca* is profoundly indebted. . . . The texture of the score is rarely polyphonic. The vocal writing alternates between forceful declamatory utterance and sweeping cantilena buoyed up by the orchestra. The harmony is marked by the undisguised use of fifths and by chords progressing in parallel motion.

Tosca dispenses with a prelude. The curtain rises after three violent chords given out full force by the orchestra. These chords form the motif of Scarpia and seem to concentrate in their narrow compass all his fiendish brutality. They are immediately followed by a series of panting, syncopated harmonies like terrified footsteps, the music characterizing the fugitive Angelotti. Several repetitions of this material, supplemented by some quieter though nervous bars, bring us to a tripping 6–8, *allegretto grazioso,* a fussy little tune associated with the Sacristan. The latter talks querulously for a few moments, to himself, till bell sounds are heard, and he intones a short *Angelus Domini.*

Soon Cavaradossi, entering to work on a picture representing Mary Magdalen, interrupts the old fellow's devotions. The orchestra gives out, *andante moderato,* a broad, melodic theme, marked by four descending notes—one of Puccini's typical *Tosca* phrases, followed by a series of chords marked by successions of consecutive fourths. Then, as Cavaradossi begins to paint, he sings the first of the famous solo numbers of the opera, the aria *Recondita armonia,* prefaced by an instrumental introduction built over a pedal and harmonized with plentiful fourths and fifths. It is a broad, flowing, sentimental tune, the accompaniment for the most part doubling the voice. A breathless exchange follows between the painter and the terrified Angelotti, whose trembling alarm is painted anew in syncopated chords.

The arrival of Floria Tosca puts an end to the scene between the two men. At first she is heard, calling the name of Mario in irritated tones from outside. The entrance of the sumptuous but jealous and somewhat irascible beauty is accompanied by an expressive lyrical melody, which will recur frequently—in increasing expansiveness. It is followed presently by another famous phrase, *Non la sospiri la nostra casetta,* an *allegro moderato,* with effective retards, out of which develops a typical impassioned Puccinian duet. Shortly thereafter follows a second voluptuous duo, in the course of which we hear what is perhaps the most famous and the tenderest love theme of the opera, an *andante moderato* in E major to which are set Tosca's words *Si, lo sento ti tormento senza posa.*

The lovers abandon themselves to the intoxication of their feelings. Only when Tosca has left does the painter remember the plight of Angelotti. Cavaradossi gives forcible vent to his feelings about the villainous Scarpia, who, with his agents, is hot on Angelotti's trail. Presently, however, there is a great commotion. A false report of Bonaparte's defeat occasions wild jubilation of a rout of choirboys, headed by the Sacristan. Their excitement culminates in a spirited 6–8 melody, *E questa sera gran fiaccolata,* which Puccini indisputably obtained from Wagner. It is an unabashed adaptation, rhythmically and otherwise, of the ensemble of David and the Apprentices in the first act of *Die Meistersinger.* Suddenly, upon these festive tones, break the dread sounds of Scarpia's three chords as the police chief, breathing fire and fury, breaks in upon the merrymakers, in company with some of his cringing and serpentine agents. He gives orders to prepare for a Te Deum of victory but soon turns to more unpleasant business. He is after Cavaradossi and, through him, Angelotti, the escaped prisoner.

The scene is constructed with consummate theatrical cunning. Part of the musical vertebra of the big *crescendo,* which builds up to the close of the act, is a bell figure of four notes. . . . The characters are differentiated in masterly fashion throughout the weighty ensemble. Against the priestly canticles and the murmured prayers and responses of the faithful are outlined Tosca's recriminations and the triumphant gloatings of Scarpia at his success in rousing her jealousy. And after a grandiose *Te aeter-*

num Patrem omnis terra veneratur it is the awesome theme of the police chief which brings down the curtain in a crash of sound.

The second act opens with a descending phrase in octaves obviously derived from the nervous, syncopated motif of Angelotti in the early part of the opera. Scarpia is at his supper. Through the open window float sounds of music. An orchestra is heard playing a gavotte on a floor below, where Queen Caroline is supposed to be entertaining General Melas. It is a pretty and graceful tune, said to have been composed by Puccini's father. The interlude is of short duration, however, for Scarpia has stern, inquisitorial business on hand which the orchestra mirrors with sinister threats. The nerve-racking atmosphere is enhanced by the sultry lower tones of the flute. A striking and dramatic effect of contrast is briefly obtained as the sounds of the cantata, performed at the queen's reception, mingle with the sparse, moody accents of the orchestra. Abruptly Scarpia slams the window shut, violently cutting off the soaring notes of Tosca's voice, as they rise above the invisible chorus.

From here on the brutal, bloody business of the act rises steadily, underscored with a kind of sadistic frenzy by music which sears like acid or burns like a white hot iron—music that raves and struggles in spasms—and yet, every now and then, bursts into lyrical passages that distill a pitiless torment of their own. It is amazing what emotional variety the composer achieves with means that are portentous and yet fundamentally simple. Even the hard, cynical courtesy of Scarpia in the first stage of his dealings with the still defiant Tosca has its faithful equivalent in the tones of the music.

The pendulum swings momentarily the other way as Cavaradossi, incensed at Tosca for betraying the secret of Angelotti's hiding place, bursts into a fierce shout of triumph when news comes that Bonaparte has defeated the forces of Melas. A brief but exuberant march melody is uttered by the painter, *L'alba vindice appar*, which concludes in a short, fiery trio. It ends as Cavaradossi is dragged away struggling, the orchestra giving out a phrase of great power.

Tosca, now maddened, asks her tormentor to name his price. A mordant phrase of four slow, descending notes underlines his sardonic reply: "To fair ladies I do not sell myself for paltry sums of money!" There follows more orchestral hysteria, with shuddering tremolos and short, sharp thrusts. The broken beat of drums is heard, "leading the escort of men about to die on the scaffold." Upon the uncanny quiet of the moment Tosca now breaks in with the most celebrated lyrical effusion of the entire opera, the aria, *Vissi d'arte.*

Much has been written against this number and with reason. It does preposterously delay the dramatic action. Moreover, it is unquestionably a show-piece and leaves the impersonator of Scarpia in the embarrassing quandary of not knowing for some minutes what to do with himself. But Puccini's instincts were in the last analysis sounder than those of his detractors. He realized that the act needed a broad, sentimental, lyrical center of gravity and Tosca's prayer, which is emotionally justified, supplies it. . . . The . . . aria is flowing and effusive, a showman's trick, a prima donna's holiday. But not all the monkeyshines of hundreds of singers have diminished its effectiveness.

The rest of the act speaks for itself. One passage must be cited, another of those *Tosca* themes, so narrow in its compass yet so telling in its use of broadly emphasized notes, that *andante sostenuto* in F-sharp minor, which precedes the stabbing, then accompanies a part of Tosca's pantomime with the dead body. The last measures of the scene are equally macabre, especially that terrifying accented chord, enhanced by a roll of distant drums, as Tosca drops the crucifix on the rigid and bleeding form of her late persecutor. And we hear, draped as it were in funereal black, the one violent and prodigious theme of the man before whom all Rome had trembled.

The final act opens with a long and elaborately pictorial introduction. At first, horns give out, unharmonized, a decisive phrase, of sharp rhythmic contours, that later forms the melody of the duet which the lovers sing, unaccompanied and in octaves, to the words *Trionfal di nova speme l'anima freme.* At the rise of the curtain deep, muffled basses form a long pedal over which a variety of modulatory effects are heard. There is a series of primitive—and indeed archaic—triads in descending motion.

Over these an invisible shepherd sings a simple melody, *Io de sospiri.* The tune itself is an authentic Tuscan folk song, whose origin Puccini himself freely acknowledges. Dawn breaks over Rome, and the chimes of matin bells are heard . . .

. . . The dawn music of *Tosca* is unquestionably one of the big things of the score. When Cavaradossi is brought on under military guard, the orchestra gives out the first phrases of the yearning and lachrymose air, *E lucevan le stelle,* perhaps the most famous number in the opera after *Vissi d'arte.* The painter, overcome by memories of the past, tries to write, while from the orchestra there rises in its most luscious harmonies the principal love melody of the opera.

The tearful aria of Cavaradossi, a luxuriant outpouring of grief, intended to be delivered with great sentiment, is sung for the greater part in unison with the orchestra which sustains the panting melody, in unadorned octaves. An excited instrumental passage accompanies the arrival of Tosca with Scarpia's safe-conduct. The ensuing scene of the lovers loses itself in soft and harmonious melodic growths and exfoliations and culminates in the proud, triumphant tune which we heard at the opening of the act.

The tragic business now hastens to its close. Here, too, no less than in the second act, the music creates its astonishingly oppressive atmosphere. A new theme is heard, *largo con gravità*, which has something solemn, poignant, and terrifying about it, in spite of its penetrating simplicity. It is this theme which marches along with the ill-starred couple to their doom.

Not even with the shooting of Cavaradossi does the tenseness of the score relax. The rush and agitation of the music which paints the discovery of Scarpia's murder and the mad pursuit and appalling death leap of Tosca fairly rend the listener's nerves. And as she springs into the void, the orchestra, as if in bitterest irony, shrieks out Cavaradossi's lovelorn phrase, *Oh! dolci baci, o languide carezze.*

HERBERT F. PEYSER

GIUSEPPE VERDI (1813–1901)

La Traviata

Libretto by Francesco Maria Piave, based upon Alexandre Dumas *fils' La Dame aux camélias*. First performance in Venice, March 6, 1853.

Characters

Violetta (La Traviata)	Soprano
Flora Bervoix	Soprano
Marquis d'Obigny	Bass
Baron Douphol	Baritone
Dr. Grenvil	Baritone
Gastone	Tenor
Alfredo	Tenor
Annina, Violetta's maid	Soprano
Giorgio Germont, Alfredo's father	Baritone

The Story

ACT I. In her luxurious drawing room in the Paris of the 1850's the frail courtesan Violetta Valéry holds a brilliant party. One of her titled friends introduces a young stranger, Alfredo Germont, who has loved her from afar and now toasts her in a spirited drinking song (**Alfredo, Chorus:** *Libiamo, libiamo* [Brindisi]—Let us drink). As the company withdraws to an adjoining room to dance, Violetta suffers an attack of faintness. Alfredo solicitously remains behind and confesses that he has adored her since the day he first saw her, a year before (**Alfredo:** *Un dì felice*—One happy day). Violetta hesitantly dismisses him (after promising to see him the next day) and bids her other guests good night. Left alone, she wonders if this can be the hero of her dreams, a man who would truly love her (**Violetta:** *Ah, fors' è lui*—Ah, perhaps it is he). But then she shakes off this weakness and, resigned to a lonely and frivolous lot, abandons herself to the giddy pursuit of freedom and pleasure (**Violetta:** *Sempre libera*—Always free).

ACT II. Alfredo, who has induced Violetta to share with him an idyllic life in a villa at Auteuil, rejoices in his happiness (**Alfredo:** *De' miei bollenti spiriti*—My fiery spirits). He is shocked to discover that she has been secretly disposing of her possessions to defray expenses and rushes off to Paris to arrange his affairs.

As Violetta is reading an invitation from her old friend Flora to a ball that evening, Alfredo's father, the elder Germont, is shown in. He begs her to renounce Alfredo in order to provide a more conventional background for the impending marriage of the young man's sister (**Germont:** *Pura siccome un angelo*—Pure as an angel). Crushed, Violetta at first refuses, but she gives in when Germont speaks again of his daughter and predicts that in time Alfredo will tire of her anyway (**Violetta:** *Dite alla giovine* —Tell the young girl). The father thanks her and then retires as the unhappy girl writes Flora her acceptance and begins a farewell note to Alfredo, who returns suddenly. Puzzled by her tears and her haste in leaving, Alfredo sits down to await the expected arrival of his father. Germont reappears just as his son is handed a note from Violetta announcing that she has left him forever. Alfredo jealously misinterprets her motive, refuses to be comforted by the sunny picture Germont paints of their native soil in Provence (**Germont:** *Di Provenza il mar, il suol*—The sea and soil of Provence), and vengefully rushes away to follow Violetta.

ACT III. Flora Bervoix has ordered a band of gypsies to entertain the guests who have gathered on her terrace (**Ballet**). Alfredo strides in and recklessly starts to play cards. Shortly Violetta enters on the arm of an old admirer, who challenges Alfredo to a game. When the others go in to supper, Violetta cautions Alfredo not to provoke a duel. Thinking she fears for her admirer, he calls the guests back to the terrace and, flinging his winnings at the feet of Violetta, asks them to witness that now he owes her nothing. Half-fainting under the insult, she still protests her love (**Violetta:** *Alfredo, di questo core*—Alfredo, you cannot understand all the love in this heart), while the entire company, now including the elder Germont, heaps reproaches on Alfredo.

ACT IV. Violetta lies dying in the bedroom of her now modest Paris apartment. Her doctor tries to cheer her, but to the maid he admits that her mistress has only a few hours to live. When they have gone, Violetta rereads a letter from Germont advising her that both he and Alfredo will soon come to see her and bidding her get well. It is too late, she sighs, remembering past joys and praying for forgiveness, for she knows the end is near (**Violetta:** *Addio del passato*—Farewell to the past). After a brief interlude in which a street carnival echoes gaily through the window, Alfredo rushes in. Informed by his relenting father of Violetta's sacrifice, he begs her to leave Paris with him forever (**Alfredo, Violetta:** *Parigi, o cara*—We shall leave Paris, dear). Exhausted by emotion, she attempts to rise but falls back in a fit of coughing. The alarmed Alfredo sends for the doctor as Violetta appeals to God not to let her die now that happiness seems so near (**Violetta:** *Gran Dio! morir sì giovine*—Great God! to die so young). Germont, contrite, enters with the doctor and blesses Violetta, who gives Alfredo a locket for the innocent young girl he will some day wed (**Violetta:** *Se una pudica vergine*—If a modest maiden). Animated by a strange joy, she cries that she feels life returning and expires in the arms of her lover.

THE MOST outstanding element in Verdi's score of *La Traviata* is his use of the current forms and devices to obtain a greater dramatic truth. It had been the custom of Italian composers during the first half of the nineteenth century to write operas as vehicles for individual singers to display their special virtuosities. Verdi had constantly been drawing away from this empty concept of composition. It is true that more than once he had an individual singer in mind for a particular role, but this was chiefly when he was inspired by some dramatic potentiality. By 1853, when Verdi composed *Traviata,* he had so completely mastered the techniques of his day that he was able to employ them definitively. More than this, *Traviata* contains seeds that were to bear fruit in later operas.

In the first act Verdi uses familiar forms and devices with a previously unknown dramatic effectiveness. In the duet between Violetta and Alfredo, *Un dì felice,* wherein Alfredo makes his avowal of love, Violetta's rejoinders are coloratura phrases of the most brilliant kind. Her reply, *Ah se ciò è ver,* is thus couched in the *demimondaine* insincerity which was the conversational currency of Violetta and her class. The use of coloratura effects for their inherent and almost hypocritical fluency and sparkle is a masterly stroke of characterization.

This is additionally effective when it is contrasted with the straightforward, deeply felt phrases of Alfredo, which are especially significant since his protestation *Di quell' amor* is used again and again in the course of the opera as the theme representing the love of Violetta and Alfredo. The use of part of an aria as a theme was not novel with Verdi; he makes similar use of *La donna è mobile* and Azucena's *Stride la vampa.*

Verdi allies form and dramatic situation most closely in the *scena* which concludes the first act. The *scena* is a double-aria form, dating back to the early eighteenth century; it consists of a preliminary recitative, a first aria in slow tempo followed by a faster aria of contrasting mood. Many well-known arias are in this form: Norma's *Casta diva*, Lucia's Mad Scene, and the first aria of the Queen of the Night. Verdi achieves a wonderfully fluent approach to this form when he actually furthers the dramatic development of the plot and allows the prima donna ten gratifying minutes of uninterrupted song alone on the stage.

These famous arias, *Ah, fors' è lui* and *Sempre libera*, introduce us most realistically to the character of Violetta and her reactions to Alfredo. In the first air, to a charmingly introspective melody, she attempts to analyze her new emotion and then, perhaps for confirmation, she repeats Alfredo's *Di quell' amor*; then in a magnificently florid recitative she declares it folly for a woman of her kind to think of a serious attachment.

She launches into the great *Sempre libera*, proclaiming it is for her to live in the unreal vortex of the *demimonde* forever. In the melody he has provided for this aria Verdi has crowded all the brilliance and emptiness of her way of life. With great dramatic consistency, this expression is likewise made in terms of formidable coloratura. Most effectively, near the end of the aria, Alfredo, off-stage, reaffirms his plea by singing a variant of the *Di quell' amor* theme, while Violetta executes flashing, ascending scales and a breath-taking succession of high C's.

Another scene in which the listener is struck by Verdi's sensitive approach to this opera is the encounter of Violetta and Germont in the second act. The sequence of emotions experienced by these characters is well realized and intensified in the music. The meaningful lines of recitative that precede Germont's plea set the whole relationship between the two characters in a minimum of words. The baritone's suave description of his daughter, *Pura siccome un angelo*, is a melody full of opportunities for sustained *bel canto*. It is followed by an *agitato* passage for Violetta, *Non sapete*, in which the melodic line makes clear her unsettled emotions. Then Germont sings a melody, *Un dì quando le veneri*, envisioning that time when Violetta is no longer young, to a melody typical of Verdi at this period with its pattern of repeated thirty-second notes.

The high point of the duet is rightly focussed on Violetta's consent to give Alfredo up, *Dite alla giovine*. This episode is simplicity itself—a scale-wise melody in E-flat major. Germont's responses, *Piangi, piangi*, demonstrate, in a masterly way, by their contrary motion, the poignantly different positions of the characters. *Traviata* is full of these effective musical devices. The duet closes with another moving episode, *Conosca il sacrifizio,* in which the *rapprochement* between Violetta and Germont is achieved, concluding with a passage in protracted thirds.

Much effective music brightens the party scene at Flora's, known variously as Act III or Act II, scene 2. It begins with two bright choruses of Gypsies and Picadors. Certain rudimentary attempts at local color are made by the introduction of tambourines, but musically they bear the unmistakable stamp of early Verdi. The finest point in the scene is the relentless *idée fixe* for the scene of Alfredo's gambling with the Baron. Verdi reiterates a certain feverish figure, a device which Massenet adopted for his *Manon* in the *Hôtel Transylvanie* scene.

There are a brief *aria dell' ira* (an old-fashioned name for this type of operatically expressed wrath) for Alfredo, *Ogni suo aver tal femina,* and a pathetic aside which Violetta sings several times, ending *Pietà gran' Dio, pietà di me,* which deserves mention in this scene. But its most effective point is the concluding ensemble *concertante* . . . expressing simultaneously the differing emotions of his characters: . . . the forgiving Violetta, the outraged Alfredo, and the helpless Germont.

The last act, as is typical of the early Verdi, is the touchstone of the opera. The prelude begins with a passage for the violins *divisi* in their upper register, symbolizing the inherently introspective character of Violetta. This is followed by an overcharged melody of great beauty which rises to an almost unbearable climax on the A-flat in alt, and ends with a long trill.

After a short and excellently understated scene with the doctor, interspersed with snatches of the prelude, Violetta, speaking aloud, reads a letter, the melody of *Di quell' amor* faint in the strings. Then in a magnificently despairing aria, *Addio del passato,* she bids the world goodbye. This simple aria is the antithesis of her *Sempre libera,* and in it Verdi has caught the consistency of fever and pain. This is soon followed by an ecstatic reunion with Alfredo set to that wonderful, surging type of figure he was to employ later in the *Ballo in Maschera* love duo. *Parigi, o cara,* the succeeding duet for Violetta and Alfredo, contains tenderly beautiful melodies but is disappointingly formal in design, ending as it does in a long cadenza *à deux*. Surely if Verdi had written this scene later in his career, he would have given freer treatment to a moment of such devastating implication.

A passage of well-expressed despair is the *Gran Dio! morir si giovine,* which Violetta sings after her futile attempt to rise. Foreshadowing the accompaniment to Desdemona's *Esterrefatta fisso* are the ominous chords to Violetta's *Prendi, quest' è l'imagine*. This is followed by her touchingly ethereal *Se una pudica vergine*, punctuated by an implacable rhythm. And then to *Di quell' amor* she speaks of her illusion of returning strength; a climactic *Gioia*, and she dies.

There are many other excellent and well-known parts of *Traviata:* Germont's *Di Provenza* with its many opportunities for the baritone and Alfredo's engaging *De' miei bollenti* with its superlatively natural declamation. Important, too, is the familiar cello theme of the prelude to the opera which becomes Violetta's heartbreaking *Amami Alfredo . . .* [all in the second act]. *Traviata's* tight hold on the repertory is due to its essential nature: the enlightening work of a maturing genius with as great inducements for singers to undertake its roles as for audiences to listen to it again and again.

William Ashbrook

RICHARD WAGNER (1813–1883)

Tristan und Isolde

Libretto by the composer. First performance in Munich, June 10, 1865.

Characters

Sailor	Tenor
Isolde	Soprano
Brangäne, Isolde's companion	Mezzo-soprano
Kurvenal	Baritone
Tristan	Tenor
Melot	Tenor
King Marke	Bass
Shepherd	Tenor
Steersman	Baritone

The Story

ACT I. Against her will, the proud Irish princess Isolde is being conducted by the knight Tristan over the seas to the court of his uncle, King Marke of Cornwall, whom she is to marry. Taunted by the songs of a sailor (**Sailor:** *Frisch weht der Wind*—Fresh blows the wind), she rails at her captor (**Isolde:** *Tod geweihtes Haupt!*—Death-consecrated head) and, through her maid Brangäne, bids him come forward and face her wrath. After Tristan declines and his aid Kurvenal sends an insulting message, Isolde tells Brangäne how, long before, Tristan had fought with the Irish knight Morold, who had gone to Cornwall to collect the tribute due to Ireland and to whom Isolde had been affianced (**Isolde:** *Von einem Kahn* [Narration]—From a boat). Morold had been killed, Isolde continues, and Tristan injured, and she relates how she made the mistake of nursing the Cornish knight back to health instead of slaying him in vengeance. Recalling how Tristan repaid her tenderness by returning to claim her for his uncle, she concludes with a curse upon his head (**Isolde:** *Fluch dir, Verruchter!*—Curse you, villain). Brangäne attempts to comfort Isolde; but, overwhelmed by shame and bitterness, the princess decides to drink a death potion which she bids her maid prepare from a magic store bequeathed her by her mother. The shouts of sailors reveal that the ship is nearing land (**Chorus:** *Ho! he! ha! he!*). Kurvenal enters to bid the women prepare to land; Isolde refuses to leave the ship until Tristan has come to beg her pardon for past acts. Tristan soon appears. Calling on him to atone for the murder of Morold, Isolde refuses to put him to death by the sword, as he suggests, but bids him drink of the death potion with her. Meanwhile the horrified Brangäne has substituted a love philtre in the cup which Tristan and Isolde now raise to their lips. After a pause, they are overcome by the magic and yield to the passion that has hitherto been stifled (**Isolde, Tristan:** *Tristan! Isolde!*). Aghast at what she has done, Brangäne rushes to separate the lovers as the ship docks on the coast of Cornwall, where they are greeted by King Marke and his court.

ACT II. In the castle garden, Isolde hears the horns of the king's hunting party recede into the sunset and tells Brangäne to signal Tristan that it is safe for him to enter. The princess absolves the maid of responsibility for substituting the love potion (**Isolde:** *Dein Werk? O thor'ge Magd!*—Your act? O foolish girl), bidding her now to keep watch for Marke's return. Tristan rushes in; the lovers exchange passionate declarations* as they invoke the longed-for night to descend upon them (**Tristan, Isolde:** *O sink' hernieder, Nacht der Liebe*—O sink upon us, Night of Love). Lost in each other's embrace, they ignore Brangäne's repeated warnings that the hours are flying (**Brangäne:** *Einsam wachend in der Nacht*—Watching alone in the night) and so are surprised by the king, who appears with his party and halts in consternation. There is a long pause; day begins to dawn, At last Marke sorrowfully berates Tristan for his treachery, calling upon all to see how the truest of the true has proved false (**Marke:** *Sie ihn dort, den treu'sten*—See him there, the truest). Tristan, offering no defense, tenderly invites Isolde to share his dark future (**Tristan:** *Wohin nun Tristan scheidet*—Where Tristan is going now). When she agrees, he kisses her gently on the forehead. Marke's knight Melot draws his sword in fury and advances on Tristan, who drops his guard and allows himself to be wounded.

ACT III. Tristan awaits Isolde in his ruined castle of Kareol in Brittany, where a shepherd pipes mournfully to indicate that no ship can be seen. Lying on a couch, the knight wakes from a fevered sleep and turns to Kurvenal, the faithful servant who has brought him from Cornwall to recuperate from his wound (**Tristan:** *Dünkt dich das*—Do you think so?*). In his delirium Tris-

* *Tristan* is rarely presented uncut, and the majority of cuts occur in the Act II love duet and in the Act III *Dünkt dich das* and succeeding pages given to Tristan. The reasons generally given for the cuts are that

tan assures Kurvenal of Isolde's return (**Tristan:** *Isolde kommt!*—Isolde comes), painting a vivid picture of the ship that will bring her to him (**Tristan:** *Und drauf Isolde, wie sie winkt*—And there Isolde, how she waves!). Almost at once the shepherd's pipe is heard playing merrily. Beside himself with joy, the knight listens as his servant describes the actual ship's arrival, and when Isolde is sighted, he wildly tears the bandage from his wound (**Tristan:** *Mit blutender Wunde*—With bloody wound). Isolde rushes in, and Tristan dies in her arms. Marke and Melot, who have pursued Isolde, burst upon the scene and are engaged in battle by the grief-stricken Kurvenal, who slays Melot and is in turn mortally wounded by the king's defenders. The senseless Isolde is revived by Brangäne, who reveals that she has told Marke of the love potion and that he has come not to punish but to forgive. But the magnanimous king is too late. Isolde, gazing with rapture upon Tristan's face, breathes a final invocation (**Isolde:** *Mild und leise wie er lächelt* [Liebestod]—Gently, faintly, he is smiling), and then sinks, lifeless and transfigured, upon his body.

TRISTAN *und Isolde* casts over us the spell of a single great emotion. This spell never weakens or breaks, but from the first to the last, by focussing and sustaining our attention, envelops us in one mood of unparalleled intensity.

The secret of this magic lies in the formal structure. Although we respond to *Tristan* as if it were the most spontaneous and untrammelled expression of emotion, the music-drama itself is very far from being such an expression. It is, rather, a brilliantly planned and consummately executed work of art which gives us the *impression* of being true to life. If it were actually true to life, if Wagner, under the influence of his own passion, had made of *Tristan* a photograph of his romance with Mathilde Wesendonck, then his performance, like that of the actor who lives his part, or the singer who feels as he sings, would have failed. For art is not just a state of being; it is a process of communicating. Consequently, Wagner could not merely set forth his experience and philosophy; he had to make them understand-

(1) the opera would otherwise be too long and (2) there are almost no tenors strong enough to sing the entire role of Tristan. If you are following a libretto, don't be alarmed if you lose your place; just watch carefully for the first line when there is a change of singer.—C.A.L.

able. He had to present his ideas so clearly and convincingly that his audience would grasp the situation and believe in it.

In order to achieve this, he arranged his material through repetition and variation to highlight the inner logic of the drama. It is this formal structure which gives the music-drama its unity and drive, and sets before us, instead of the chaotic and irrational emotion of actual experience, a clear and highly poetic conception of the passion of Tristan and Isolde.

Let us consider first the structure of the art-work as a whole. Here Wagner has promoted movement and unity by two methods. In the first place, he has cut down the number of breaks in the presentation so that in the entire music-drama there are only the two divisions between the acts. The music of each prelude forms a continuous texture with that of the succeeding act, and the acts themselves are uninterrupted by any change of scenery. In the second place, Wagner has chosen to present the spiritual rather than the physical qualities of the Tristan legend and has treated the subject in such a way as to develop it naturally into a symmetrical form. A different type of subject, one centering on physical action, could not easily create such a form. Action is essentially progressive, and it cannot, like an idea or an emotion, occur twice. On the other hand, the very nature of symmetry demands a certain degree of repetition.

The three acts of *Tristan* form a set of three variations on the relationship between Tristan and Isolde. In the first act, we see this relationship from Isolde's point of view, in the second, from the lovers', and in the third, from Tristan's. The total form, however, is more complex than this, for two other patterns occur simultaneously: one, that of the continuously developing emotion, and the other, that of the particular similarity between the first and last acts. The second and third patterns enrich the first: the second, by providing variety, together with the momentum which carries the whole form through from start to finish, and the third, by emphasizing the unity of the entire music-drama.

In the first act, Isolde describes the past and present of her relationship with Tristan. She tells how, disguised, he came to her to heal his wound, how she discovered his identity as the slayer of her betrothed, Morold, how she allowed him to go free, and how he is now taking her to be the bride of his uncle, King Marke. Her reason for letting the knight escape she explains to Brangäne as pity, to Tristan, as the desire for a more complete revenge later on. This is the basic variation. The second pattern shows the drinking of the love potion, and the revelation of passion which results from it.

In the second act, this latter pattern becomes a part of the variation itself, so that the lovers describe not only the events which Isolde has related, but also the drinking of the love potion. This potion, however, has illuminated for them like a flash of lightning the true character of their relationship. Tristan and Isolde realize that they have betrayed each other by denying their love for the pomp and circumstance which surrounded them. They have been deceived by the splendor of their worldly positions into a blind adherence to the conventions of their society. Isolde had realized that for this situation the only solution was death and a union after death. Tristan, when she offered him the drink, had understood it also. And the two, expecting death, had revealed their love. In their conversation, the Day symbolizes the empty illusions of life, and the Night, the profound and completely lucid understanding of death. It is this death which they had sought from the love potion and which Tristan seeks again at Melot's hands. The second pattern in this act shows the development of the lovers' passion from their first rapture at being together again, to their desire for release and union in death.

The third act variation incorporates the second pattern of the previous act, so that the thoughts which seethe in Tristan's mind are not only those of his illness, and of the drink, but also of the longing for the Night of death. When he regains consciousness in Kareol, he has been wandering in the realms of the Night, but Isolde has not followed him there. In his terrible yearning to see her, he must tear himself away from the Night and seek her in the burning Day, that they may die together. Delirious, he imagines that the torch which kept them apart is still alight. Will it never go out? Kurvenal tells him that Isolde is coming. But the ship is not yet in sight, and presently, the shepherd's melody catches Tristan's attention. He remembers that he heard it in his youth; it always brought woeful tidings. To what fate was he born? To long to die, but not to die of longing. This deathless melody, which once sent him to Isolde to be healed, is now bringing her to him, that he may recover completely. But how can he recover, when the poison of the drink she gave him is beyond any power to cure? A little later, he sees a vision of Isolde as she comes over the water, smilingly bringing him consolation and final peace. At that moment, the ship comes into sight, and Kurvenal goes to welcome Isolde. Tristan, in the intoxication of his excitement, feels that he has raised himself from death, and in this Day in which he has finally found Isolde again, once more harks back to his first meeting with her: as then he fought Morold with bleeding wounds, so now will he greet her. At her call, he imagines it the torch which separated them. As the sound ends, he thinks the light has gone out, and staggers toward her.

This act is shot through with ideas and emotions which spring directly from those in the other two. The second pattern shows Tristan's emotional development from a state of quietness near to death, to the most unbearable tension. The third pattern, in which this act appears so similar to the first, stands out very clearly. Both acts take place in the atmosphere of the sea, one on board a ship which is about to land, the other, on the seacoast, waiting for a ship. In the first, Isolde is hoping for Tristan to come to her, that they may drink the death potion together. In the second, Tristan is longing for Isolde to come to him, also that they may die together. The first act culminates in the drinking of the potion which foils the lovers' wish for death. The last act grants their wish.

So far, we have considered the structure of the art-work as a whole, as that structure is defined by the text. Let us now analyze it as it is presented to us by the music. Wagner uses three definite techniques in *Tristan,* in order to assure a continuous movement and to strengthen the unity of the text. The first of these, the *leitmotif,* is the method by which the composer-dramatist adds definite meaning to his themes and emotional connotations to his text.

The second is the symmetrical use of off-stage voices and solo instruments: the sailor's voice in Act I, opening the two first scenes; Brangäne's voice in Act II, occurring in two similar sections of the love duet; the horn call beginning Act II; and the shepherd's piping, at the end of the prelude to Act III and recurring throughout the act.

The third method is the most striking of all. It consists in the repetition of a large section of music at a point in the music-drama quite distant from the original. The repetition may be a reproduction of the model, even to the exact key, or it may be a variation of it in the same or another tonality. The reason for the repetition may be either a reappearance of a verbal phrase, in which case the music sets the text at its face value, or it may be the recurrence of a particular mood, underlying a different text, in which case the music sets the unexpressed meaning of the words. Some of the sections originate in the preludes, others, in the more lyric vocal passages. The most important instances of this repetition follow:

From the prelude to Act I: the first 12 measures appear almost intact, both when Brangäne sings *Kennst du der Mutter Künste nicht?* and when Isolde repeats the words (I, 4); the first

21 measures are repeated, with the insertion of other phrases, as Tristan and Isolde drink the love potion (I, 5); the first 17 measures, with the addition of one supremely moving chord, accompany Tristan's *O König, dass kann ich dir nicht sagen* (II, 3); and finally, the first 20 measures augmented to cover 24 measures of 2–2 meter (instead of 6–8) are intoned as Tristan dies.

From Isolde's narrative *Von einem Kahn* (I, 3) a considerable amount, some of it in the original key, appears in her conversation with Tristan (I, 5) and it also accompanies the knight when he recalls Isolde's healing (III, 1).

From the prelude to Act II: the first 20 measures after the string tremolo appear identically during the interlude when Isolde awaits Tristan (II, 1); 7 measures of the opening tremolo, together with 14 from the end of the prelude accompany Tristan's *Ach Isolde, süsse Holde,* and 6 measures of the tremolo occur again at *Noch losch das Licht nicht aus* (III, 1).

Finally, from the duet (II, 2) *So starben wir,* and the conclusion of the duet beginning *Wie es fassen,* comes all but the last 19 measures of the *Liebestod* (III, 3). The first 11 measures of the *Liebestod* correspond to the opening of *So starben wir,* and they are joined imperceptibly to the following 38 measures, which repeat the duet *Wie es fassen* in diminished meter. In these repeated sections, the voice sometimes varies from the original, but the orchestra remains the same.

In conclusion, let us look at the pattern of the material within the individual acts. Wagner has done away with the old operatic technique of rigidly separating recitatives and aria, and replaced it by a continuous process of greater or lesser lyricism. He has not, however, rejected the principle of form itself. He has merely eliminated certain set forms which result from the application of the principle, forms which, when dutifully adhered to, resemble a nicely clipped box hedge, smooth and perfect in outline. But who would argue that the tree which has escaped the gardener's zeal lacks form, simply because it is not completely symmetrical? And who does not find it more rewarding to study the tree, noting all the fascinating little irregularities and counterbalances that give it its own unique and beautiful shape, than to gaze on the box hedge, where one glance will find everything? Wagner's musical form resembles the tree; following the form of the text, it grows freely, but not shapelessly, and the determining pattern is there, although it is sometimes hidden, as are the branches of a tree, under the leaves.

Let us take the so-called love duet (II, 2) as an example. It opens with the motif of Ecstasy (Ernest Newman*). Then comes a long section made up of two parts. The first of these deals with Day and Night and culminates in *O sink hernieder*. This leads into the second part, beginning with Brangäne's warning, and ending with the answer, *Lausch', Geliebter!* The next long section also consists of two parts. The first concerns Day and Death, and fulfils itself in *So starben wir*. Again, Brangäne's voice breaks in, opening the second part, and once more the lovers answer with *Lausch', Geliebter!* The final portion of the duet, *O ewige Nacht*, summarizes the foregoing material, like a coda, and ends with the same theme of Ecstasy which introduced the scene. The two large sections are not identical; the second is a variation of the first, shorter, but making up in intensity what it lacks in length.

There are other examples of form. For instance, after Marke's entrance (III, 3), each of Brangäne's pleas to Isolde begins with the *So starben wir* motif, a tone higher each time (C, D-flat, D), until Isolde begins the *Liebestod* on E-flat. In fact, all the other more lyric sections have definite forms: *O König* is in three-part song form, the last part being considerably varied, and Isolde's reply is a shortened variation of it. Tristan's *Muss ich dich so versteh'n* is a song of four stanzas, each beginning alike, and then varying increasingly.

But why do we, the audience, so seldom notice the formal structure and its smaller patterns? There are two reasons. In the first place, form constitutes for Wagner the means to an end, and not the end itself. Therefore, by varying the repetition and veiling the joinings of different sections, he makes it just inconspicuous enough so that, while we still receive the logical and unified impression which it creates, we do not consciously observe it. In the second place, the music-drama in performance is extensively cut. The music of which *O sink hernieder* is the result and climax practically disappears, while three of the four stanzas of *Muss ich dich so versteh'n* are completely eliminated.

With all its cuts, *Tristan und Isolde* nevertheless remains tremendously effective. And although we are not—and should not be—conscious of the form during the performance, we may still remember, at some time, that this same form is the method which makes possible our perception of the lovers' emotion.

LILIAN E. FOERSTER

* Foremost Wagner scholar.—C.A.L.

GIUSEPPE VERDI (1813–1901)

Il Trovatore

Libretto by Salvatore Cammarano, based upon a play by Antonio García Gutiérrez. First performance in Rome, January 19, 1853.

Characters

Ferrando, a captain of the guard	Bass
Leonora, a noble lady of Aragon	Soprano
Inez	Soprano
The Count di Luna	Baritone
Manrico, a troubadour	Tenor
A gypsy	Baritone
Azucena, a gypsy	Contralto
A messenger	Tenor
Ruiz	Tenor

The Story

ACT I. The Duel. In the guardroom of Count di Luna's castle in fifteenth-century Aragon, men are on watch to apprehend the wandering troubadour Manrico, who, as a rival to the Count himself, has been serenading the duchess Leonora. The captain, Ferrando, keeps his men awake by telling a story (**Ferrando:** *Abbietta zingara*—An abject gypsy): the tale of a gypsy who was burned to death for bewitching the Count's younger brother and of her daughter, Azucena, who avenged herself by abducting the child and was thought to have burned him at the same stake where her mother perished.

The lady Leonora tells her companion Inez of the troubadour's serenade (**Leonora:** *Tacea la notte*—The placid night was silent) and admits her love for him (**Leonora:** *Di tale amor*—Of love like this, what can be said?). Manrico's serenade echoes from the distance (**Manrico:** *Deserto sulla terra*—Abandoned on the earth), but the Count reaches the castle before him and, despite Leonora's efforts to thwart a conflict, engages his rival in combat.

ACT II. The Gypsy. Pounding at their anvils in the mountains of Biscay (**Anvil Chorus**), the gypsies gather about the crone Azucena as she calls for vengeance for her mother's murder (**Azucena:** *Stride la vampa*—The flames crackle). As the band disperses, Manrico, who has survived the duel with the Count, remains to ask Azucena of his parentage. She confesses that it was her own child whom she inadvertently burned at the stake (**Azucena:** *Condotta ell' era in ceppi*—She was led in chains) but tries to conceal that Manrico is in fact di Luna's brother. Manrico attempts to explain the mysterious force that once prevented him on the battlefield from killing di Luna (**Manrico:** *Mal reggendo*—Weakening at the furious encounter). Manrico's friend Ruiz calls him back to lead his men to rescue Leonora; Manrico leaves, over Azucena's protestations.

At the convent cloister where Leonora plans to retire, believing Manrico dead, the Count prepares to intercept her (**Count di Luna:** *Il balen del suo sorriso*—The light of her smile surpassed the ray of a star). At the last moment Manrico intervenes, escaping with his lady.

ACT III. THE GYPSY'S SON. The Count has pitched his camp near the castle of Castellor, where Manrico has taken Leonora. Here his soldiers capture Azucena and torture her into a hinted admission that Manrico is her son (**Azucena:** *Giorni poveri*—In my days of poverty I was still happy).

Within the castle Manrico and Leonora prepare for their wedding (**Manrico:** *Ah, sì, ben mio*—Ah, yes, my treasure), but their plans are rudely shattered by the news that Azucena has been captured. The horrified Manrico vows vengeance (**Manrico:** *Di quella pira*—The horrible fire of that pyre).

ACT IV. THE PUNISHMENT. Ruiz brings Leonora to the courtyard of the Aliferia Palace, in whose dungeon Manrico has been confined by the Count. She muses on her love for the troubadour (**Leonora:** *D'amor sull' ali rosee*—The languid sighs of love fly on rosy wings). With the solemn Miserere for the dead, the despairing Leonora hears the voice of her lover (**Manrico:** *Ah, che la morte*—O, that death is now late in coming). She decides to purchase his freedom by yielding to the Count, who now appears (**Leonora:** *Mira, di acerbe lagrime*—See my tears of agony) and rejoices at di Luna's acquiescence (**Leonora:** *Vivrà! contende il giubilo*—He shall live; my joy contrasts with what you tell me).

In their dismal cell, Manrico and Azucena talk of the happy freedom of the mountains (**Manrico, Azucena:** *Ai nostri monti*—Back to our mountains). Their dream is cut short by the entrance of Leonora, who announces her lover's freedom. Manrico refuses to leave without her; then, on realizing she must have bought his freedom by yielding to the Count, he berates her bitterly. The poison she has taken to escape the Count acts more quickly than she anticipated, and Leonora dies at Manrico's feet. When Count di Luna discovers her deceit, he orders Manrico to the stake and forces Azucena to watch his death. But the gypsy is avenged: as the curtain falls, she tells the Count that he has executed his own brother.

A DISCUSSION of *Il Trovatore* resolves itself into a chronicle of "song hits," spirited, impetuous, vehement, tender, dashing, elegiac, trashy. Many are built on trivial dance rhythms whose underlying cheerfulness is often ludicrously at variance with the sentiments of the text. But in a larger sense they do capture the unrestrained emotions of the piece. Many of these fierce *allegros*, darting *cabalettas*, and sweet airs are embellished with brilliant *cadenzas* and other ornamental fripperies which go to make a singer's holiday. Only when we hear a master like Arturo Toscanini conduct the work are we made aware that the instrumentation is not really so blatant and tawdry as it usually sounds and that the score does contain inspired fancies. We discover likewise to our amazement that certain of the opera's most rowdy tunes, like the trio at the end of the first act, are actually, for all their slapdash impetuosity, more vital than vulgar.

There is such a thing as a *Trovatore* melodic style. We meet it in the very first scene, to which operagoers do not ordinarily pay sufficient attention. The shortest, most unpretentious kind of orchestral introduction invokes a kettledrum roll, twice repeated, and followed by falling and rising arpeggiated triplets, sharply accented, with intervening fanfares. These primitive materials seem intended to call the audience to attention rather than to perform a dramatic function. A few measures of recitative and of choral response in the *Trovatore* manner bring the simple and somewhat lugubrious narration of di Luna's captain, Ferrando, about the tragedy of the old Count's children (*Di due figli*). The second part of the narrative, *Abbietta zingara*, changing from common time to 3–4 time, although marked "mysteriously," is one of those incorrigibly cheerful dance tunes, with detached notes and a figure in sixteenths, whose melodic nature hardly suggests the feeling of its words. Rather more in keeping with Ferrando's shuddersome story about the "gloomy midnight hag" is that soft *Lento*, for strings, whose unharmonized melodic line, with the step of the augmented fifth, seeks to establish an appropriately eerie atmosphere and directly afterwards gives place to those identical chromatic thirds which the composer had employed in the last act of *Rigoletto* to imitate the moaning of the wind. The subsequent chorus of superstitious soldiers and servants, *Sull'orlo dei tetti,* with its vigorous triplets, is really eloquent when delivered in the breathless threefold *pianissimo* Verdi prescribes. And the wild shout on the chords of E and of A as the midnight bell suddenly strikes may well have excited listeners in the early [eighteen-]fifties.

The second scene opens with Leonora's beautiful aria, *Tacea la notte placida,* and its preceding recitative which contains the eight lovely bars in A-flat, *Come d'aurato sogno*—the voice soaring in quietly ecstatic clarinets and a trill of violins. The aria itself is assuredly one of those *Trovatore* songs in which Henry Chorley, who loathed Verdi as violently as he did Wagner, detected, nevertheless, "a sweet, affectionate mournfulness which raises them high among examples of their class." The level, unfortunately, is not sustained, for the ensuing *allegro giusto, Di tale amor,* is not much more than a showpiece, with wide leaps, scales, and *staccati,* designed to be executed with brilliance and, as most sopranos deliver it, only secondarily an emotional outpouring.

The recitative with which the duties of the Count di Luna begin is not musically impressive nor is the sentimental *romanza,* sung backstage to harp chords, by any means one of Manrico's happiest assignments. Yet it contains four measures (*e sola speme un cor*) we shall do well to notice, for they play an important part in the famous Tower Song in the fourth act, while in later years Verdi was to return to them in one of the loveliest moments of the Nile scene of *Aïda*—the *romanza, O Patria mia.* Not much is to be said for the trio and the duel scene that bring the act to an end. The melody *Di geloso amor sprezzato,* particularly, is one of the commonest things the composer ever wrote and, except when there are artists who can breathe fire and fury into it, absurdly out of keeping with sentiment and situation.

The second act, which acquaints us with the most important and magnificently characterized figure of the whole work, Azucena, begins with the universally known Anvil Chorus. It is really in three parts—the orchestral introduction, with its grace notes and tinkling triangle, the octave sequences, *Vedi! le fosche notturne,* and finally the chief melody, *Chi del gitano,* with its punctuating anvil strokes both on the strong and weak beats of the measure.

Azucena's tale of horror and mania for revenge are then set before us in the *canzone Stride la vampa.* This E-minor tune virtually in waltz time (3–8) is indisputably one of Verdi's great inspirations despite what seems like an outward triviality. Here again the composer has provided a skeleton which it behooves the singer to infuse with living spirit. That the master realized how suggestive this melody could be is clearly indicated by its recall later in the scene and again in the concluding act of the opera with the dramatic purpose of a leading motif. The gypsies gone, Azucena's mind is once more busied, and in greater detail, with the savage story of her mother's death. Her entire scene with Manrico, for his part, tells of his duel with di Luna in a broad virile *cantabile* melody, *Mal reggendo,* to which Azucena brings an answering tune, hardly less fine and characterizing her with sureness of instinct, *Ma nell' alma del ingrato.* Another agitated song for Azucena, *Perigliarti ancor,* follows her scene with Manrico, who replies with a passage in frank dance measure, *Un momento puo involarmi*—a genuine *Trovatore* melody.

The scene before the cloister begins, after a short recitative, with one of the most familiar sentimental songs of the work—di Luna's *Il balen,* with its assortment of ornaments and cadenzas. Doubtless in certain out-of-the-way communities the song has become common property as "Tempest of the Heart" among persons who have never realized its operatic source. Almost on the heels of this love tune Verdi has favored di Luna with still another stirring air, though in rousing rather than melting vein, *Per me ora fatale,* with a brief but telling chorus of detached exclamations, *Ardir! Andiam,* which after a repetition of the Count's air is carried out at great length. A fluent ensemble of nuns' music, based on the simplest of harmonies, leads to the big finale, the rescue of Leonora before she has taken her irrevocable vows in the nunnery and then the great, expansive closing chorus, *E deggio e posso,* with its ecstatic, broken phrases for Leonora and more sustained melodies for the embattled parties of di Luna and Manrico.

The chorus of soldiers beginning the third act, *Or co' dadi, ma fra poco,* with its refrain of wholly popular character, *Squilli echeggi la tromba,* scarcely calls for more comment than the earlier Anvil Chorus or the Soldiers' Chorus in *Faust.* The best pages in the remainder of the scene belong to Azucena, with her *Giorni poveri vivea* and her energetic *Ah! deh! rallentate,* and the ensuing ensemble. Verdi reaches full stature, however, in the next scene, with Manrico's love song, *Ah sì, ben mio*—one of the choicest pages in *Trovatore,* and in all of Verdi. The passage *De mei destini* might almost have come out of Mozart. It ought to be delivered with the refinement of Mozartean *cantilena,* a fact which only too few singers, unhappily, appreciate. A duet for the fated pair, which follows, is frequently omitted in performance—

a regrettable contingency, although the music does not rise to the level of the previous love song. Straight on the heels of Manrico's tender avowals, however, we meet one of the great "hits" of the score, the *cabaletta, Di quella pira,* a vibrant brawling tune which Verdi originally sketched in 4–4 rather than in the later 3–4 time; and which, however it may be sung, never fails to set its hearers on fire like a battle cry. The custom of introducing a high C toward the close is the product of vocal vainglory—Verdi himself wrote nothing higher in it than an A-natural.

With the exception of a spirited trivial duet between Leonora and di Luna, the last act of *Trovatore* is one of the great masterpieces of opera. The very instrumentation of the first bars, with its triplets in low clarinets and bassoons, introduces a color all its own into the texture of the music. Leonora's recitative and aria *D'amor sull' ali* is one of the most tenderly elegiac pages in Verdi. Without break there follows the great central feature of the Tower scene—the solemn *Miserere* of the hidden chorus (at first unaccompanied, then a series of rhythmic chords, with prominent trombones), an effect Verdi was to use again in the last act of *La Traviata.* Over this is poised Leonora's despairing *Quel suon, quelle preci,* with its effects of broken sobs to which the composer reverted in voicing the despair of Amneris; and lastly, the song of the imprisoned Manrico, with its simple harp accompaniment, *Ah! che la morte ognora*—a tune done to death by generations of organ-grinders, yet absolutely unfailing in its effect. The episode is built up, repeated, and varied. One of the effects which the listener should not overlook derives from the passing notes heard as Leonora's melody moves to its closing cadences.

The scene of the Count and Leonora, if dramatic in its intention, is nevertheless a musical enfeeblement. Its outstanding pages are Leonora's appeal, *Mira, di acerbe lagrime,* and the later duet, *Vivrà! contende il giubilo,* both of them effective in their way if not equal in inspiration to what went before.

Soft brass chords, simple but telling, evoke the atmosphere of the dungeon, the last episode of the work. There is great tenderness in the dialogue of Manrico and Azucena, followed by a shudder of terror, and a dramatic recall of the *Stride la vampa* melody, as the gypsy momentarily quails at the thought of her impending doom. Verdi had good reason for warning his librettist not to make Azucena go mad. The reason is that matchless song— *Ai nostri monti*—"Home to Our Mountains"—a melody which it would scarcely be excessive to describe as one of the tenderest and best-loved heart songs of the human family. The closing pages, with the death of Leonora after futile entreaties to her beloved to save himself, acquire an added poignancy as the slumbering Azucena murmurs her nostalgic melody in her sleep. And when, after the last trio and the deaths of Leonora and the hapless troubadour, Azucena hurls at the Count the words "He was your brother! Mother, thou art avenged!" we are ready to agree with Verdi that the gypsy in this supreme moment "becomes stupendous."

HERBERT F. PEYSER

WOLFGANG AMADEUS MOZART (1756–1791)

Die Zauberflöte

Libretto by Emanuel Schikaneder. First performance in Vienna, September 30, 1791.

Characters

Tamino . . . . Tenor
Three ladies, attendants of the Queen of Night
Two Sopranos and Mezzo-soprano
Papageno . . . . Baritone
Queen of the Night . . . . Soprano
Three genii . . . . . . Two Sopranos and Mezzo-soprano
Monostatos, a Moor . . . . Tenor
Pamina, daughter of the Queen of the Night . Soprano
The High Priest (Speaker) . . . . Baritone
Sarastro . . . . Bass
An old woman, later Papagena . . . . Soprano

*The Story**

ACT I. The Prince Tamino is pursued by a serpent, while hunting in a wild rocky region, and falls unconscious. Three ladies, attendants on the Queen of the Night, kill the serpent and rush off to inform the Queen. Tamino awakens and hides on sight of Papageno, the birdcatcher, who tells of his lonely life (**Papageno:** *Der Vogelfänger bin ich ja*—I catch the birds) and then boasts that he has slain the serpent. The ladies return, punish Papageno for his lie about the serpent by locking his lips together, and then give Tamino a portrait of the Queen's daughter, Pamina, with which he instantly falls in love (**Tamino:** *Dies Bildnis ist bezaubernd schön*—O image, angel-like and fair).

The Queen appears and begs Tamino to save Pamina from the sorcerer Sarastro (**Queen of the Night:** *Zum Leiden bin ich auserkoren*—In lonely grief).

The ladies give Tamino a golden flute and present Papageno with a chime of bells, promising the help of three winged boys or genii to aid the prince and his new companion in their rescue of Pamina (**Quintet—Papageno:** *Hm, hm, hm . . .*; **Tamino:**

* The aria translations of *Die Zauberflöte* are those of the English version now sung at the Metropolitan. Copyright, 1941, 1951, by G. Schirmer, Inc., and printed by permission.

Der Arme kann von Strafe sagen—The poor young lad must surely suffer).

Three slaves herald the arrival of the cruel Monostatos, who brings Pamina to a room in Sarastro's exotic palace and forces his attentions on her until she swoons from fright. Papageno appears at the window, and he and Monostatos frighten each other away (**Monostatos, Pamina, Papageno:** *Du feines Täubchen, nur herein!*—My dainty lambkin, please come in). Papageno subsequently returns to console Pamina (**Papageno, Pamina:** *Bei Männern, welch Liebe fühlen*—The man who feels sweet love's emotion).

The three genii lead Tamino to the gates of three temples, where a priest tells him of the Queen's deception and Sarastro's virtue in protecting Pamina from her mother. Tamino expresses his relief by playing his flute (**Tamino:** *Wie stark ist nicht dein Zauberton*—How strong thy tone) and hurries away to follow the birdcatcher's bells. Pamina and Papageno run in, pursued by Monostatos and the slaves. Followed by his suite, Sarastro enters, reassuring Pamina that a man will free her. Monostatos brings back Pamina, but is punished by Sarastro for his cruelty. Sarastro leads Pamina away, while the priests veil Tamino and Papageno for their initiation.

ACT II. The priests march from their temple to a palm grove where Sarastro announces Tamino's candidacy for initiation. All pray to the gods (**Sarastro and Chorus:** *O Isis und Osiris*).

Two priests lead the veiled Tamino and Papageno into the dark temple court where the candidates are warned of the trials ahead. The three ladies tempt them from their purpose, but even the gibbering Papageno is firm (**Quintet:** *Wie, wie, wie? Ihr in diesem Schreckensort*—Ye? in this place of night and gloom?).

Monostatos finds Pamina asleep in the palace garden (**Monostatos:** *Alles fühlt der Liebe Freuden*—All who have a sweetheart), but is dismissed by the Queen who cries vengeance on Sarastro (**Queen of the Night:** *Der Hölle Rache kocht in meinem Herzen*—The wrath of hell within my breast) and vanishes. Pamina is now rescued from Monostatos by the intervention of Sarastro, who tells her he will forgive her mother (**Sarastro:** *In diesen heil'gen Hallen*—Within these holy portals).

Two priests lead Tamino and Papageno to the entrance of the temple crypt where they undergo the test of silence. An old woman claims Papageno as her lover, but disappears when he asks her name. Three boys bring food and drink (**Boys:** *Seid uns* *zum zweiten Mal willkommen*—Soon speeds the morning light). Pamina questions Tamino, disconsolate at his apparent indifference (**Pamina:** *Ach, ich fühl's, es ist verschwunden*—Ah, to grief and sadness).

Deep in the crypt of the pyramid, the priests tell of Tamino's courage. Sarastro summons the lovers and informs them they must be separated for a time (**Pamina, Sarastro, Tamino:** *Soll ich dich, Teurer, nicht mehr sehn*—Must I from thee forever part?). As both are led away, Papageno gropes his way in, to learn from the High Priest that he has failed in his initiation. The birdcatcher pleads for a mate (**Papageno:** *Ein Mädchen oder Weibchen*—A sweetheart or a maiden) and is rewarded by the old woman, who turns into the youthful Papagena.

In a palm garden beyond the temple, the three genii sing of the triumph of wisdom and save Pamina from suicide.

At the caverns of fire and water two armed guards warn Tamino of the trials to come (**Guards:** *Der, welcher wandert diese Strasse voll Beschwerden*—Man, wandering on his road). The lovers pass through fire and water to the flute's music.

In an exotic garden, Papageno whistles for the lost Papagena and is rescued from suicide by the three genii, who finally bring her back (**Papageno:** *Papagena*).

The Queen storms the temple walls with her ladies and Monostatos, but is driven back by thunder and lightning.

Sarastro and the united lovers are hailed by the multitude that throng the Temple of the Sun.

THE MAGIC FLUTE, it must be remembered, is not an outright opera but a *Singspiel.* The French equivalent of the *Singspiel* is the *opéra comique.* Neither the one nor the other is necessarily comic, as we may judge from the example of an *opéra comique* like *Carmen,* with its tragic outcome. *Carmen,* in its original state and as always given in France, has spoken dialogue in place of recitative. This substitution of the spoken word for recitative is the distinguishing feature of both *Singspiel* and *opéra comique.* And it is, of course, a hallmark of *The Magic Flute.*

Beethoven prized *The Magic Flute* above all other operas of Mozart not only because its plot, with its elevated, humanitarian sentiments, appealed to him far more than the morally questionable intrigues of *The Marriage of Figaro* and *Don Giovanni,* but because it contained the greatest variety of music—lofty and noble pages, such as the air of Sarastro, *Within These Holy Portals,* and *O Isis and Osiris;* the uplifting choruses of the priests, tender love songs, and duets, like the meltingly sentimental expressions of the lovers, Pamina and Tamino; songs of a popular, almost folklike character (Papageno's birdcatcher song and the pretty songs with an *obbligato* of tinkling bells); figurated chorale, dramatic bravura, and much else. The listener who hears *The Magic Flute* without being an actual spectator at the performance can scarcely fail to be struck by that extraordinary musical copiousness and diversity of content which caused Beethoven to value Mozart's last opera above all his others. Every scene may be said to have its typical frame and background, its characteristic color and matter.

The airs of Tamino, the cheery folk tunes of Papageno, the chatter of the Three Ladies, the first great aria of the Queen of the Night, the humors of the quintet with Papageno's now angry, now entreating "Hm, hm, hm" through padlocked lips—these things, each preciously different from the other, dominate the opening scene. The succeeding ones are no less generous, no less diverse. Close on the heels of the encounter of the birdman, Papageno, and the rascally blackamoor, Monostatos, in which the pair mutually frighten each other almost to death, comes the simple but meltingly lovely duet of Pamina and her would-be rescuer. The Three Genii address themselves to their charge, Tamino, in music which sounds like a luminous transfiguration. Then Tamino plays his flute, to the spell of which animals appear momentarily to listen with delight. On the heels of this follows one of the supreme passages of the opera, the colloquy of Tamino and the Speaker, in a warmly accompanied song-speech which reminds one of how much Wagner learned from Mozart in the way of fluid musical discourse. Then, directly after Papageno by means of his tinkling chimes has charmed into helplessness the little rout of black-skinned slaves, Mozart put into the mouths of Pamina and Papageno a delicious duet whose melody was remembered by Schubert when he wrote the song, *Hedgeroses,* and by Richard Strauss in the closing moments of the *Rosenkavalier.*

The same process continues through the numerous scenes of the second act, setting one apart from another. The March of the Priests (the last number Mozart composed for the opera), the hymnlike songs of Sarastro, the subsequent chorus to Isis and Osiris of the ecclesiastics are as grand as anything in music. But there is really no need of indulging in a mere catalogue of the pearls past all price which Mozart has so lavishly strewn. He himself loved the opera—"If only I could hear my *Magic Flute* once again," he exclaimed on his death bed. He realized, furthermore, that it was unlike anything he ever had done for the lyric stage. And indeed, this score has a glow, a warmth, an inwardness, a depth, and a variety of color that belong to the era of romantic music about to dawn.

Let us consider momentarily several things which stand apart even from the rest of the opera—the two tremendous arias of the Queen of the Night and the scene of the two Armored Men. Nothing could be more erroneous than to regard the arias of the Queen as technical show pieces. Their great range and difficulty of execution is only incidental: Mozart composed them for his sister-in-law, a singer noted for her "voluble throat." The far-darting coloratura which flashes and flames through both had for its primary purpose not display but a fierce intensity of dramatic expression; and the singer who, in her delivery of these numbers, fails to make this fundamentally expressive purpose of the composer clear has simply no true grasp of the part she has undertaken. Heartbreak and entreaty are in the first aria, red-eyed fury and burning thirst for vengeance fill the second. The artist unable to encompass these emotions is, therefore, no qualified exponent of this role. What it calls for is a voice of authentic dramatic timbre, schooled in the utmost flexibility of colorature.

At different periods of his career Mozart was profoundly influenced by the study of Bach and Handel. It was his deep understanding of these masters which lies at the base of that magnificent scene of the two Armed Watchers in the last act. The warders of the Gates of Terror here sing a stark old chorale, against which, in the orchestra, Mozart has set an elaborate figuration in the shape of a *fugato*. The darkly somber piece is a specimen of what students of Bach and his contemporaries know under the name of chorale-prelude. It is one of those pages in *The Magic Flute* which Beethoven held in particular veneration.

The Magic Flute is the seed from which grew the operas of Weber, of Wagner, and therefore some of the outstanding works of the modern lyric stage. And if we have primarily to give thanks to Mozart for this matchless treasure, his much abused librettist and instigator has a foothold of his own in the niche of fame.

HERBERT F. PEYSER

Supplement: Eight Additional Operas

GIUSEPPE VERDI (1813–1901)

Don Carlo

Libretto by Joseph Méry and Camille du Locle after the play by Friedrich Schiller. First performance in Paris, March 11, 1867.

Characters

A Friar . . . . Bass
Don Carlo, Crown Prince of Spain . . . . Tenor
Rodrigo, Marquis of Posa . . . . Baritone
Theobald, the Queen's Page . . . . Soprano
Princess Eboli . . . . Mezzo-soprano
The Countess of Aremberg . . . . Silent role
Elisabeth of Valois, wife of King Philip II . . . Soprano
Philip II, King of Spain . . . . Bass
Count Lerma . . . . Tenor
The Royal Herald . . . . Tenor
A Celestial Voice . . . . Soprano
The Grand Inquisitor . . . . Bass

The Story

ACT I. In the cloister of the Convent of St. Just, Don Carlo, Crown Prince of Spain, seeks consolation. He has fallen in love with Elisabeth of Valois, daughter of Henry II of France, to whom he declared himself in the Forest of Fontainebleau. (The French scene is usually omitted.) His father, however, has married the lady. As a friar proclaims the vanities of the world, the sensitive Carlo thinks he hears the voice of his grandfather, Charles V. Soon, however, he is encouraged by his friend Rodrigo, Marquis of Posa, who suggests that the prince depart to the Netherlands to cure himself of his infatuation and help protect the Flemings against the tyranny of Spain. The two men pledge friendship (**Rodrigo, Carlo:** *Dio, che nell'alma*—O Lord, unto our souls). King Philip and Queen Elisabeth approach the tomb of Charles V, kneel briefly, and proceed on their way.

In a garden near the convent the Princess Eboli and the Countess Aremberg entertain themselves with their ladies. Eboli sings a Moorish song to the accompaniment of Theobald's mandolin (**Eboli:** *Nei giardin*—In the gardens). As the Queen comes sadly from the convent, Rodrigo appears, hands her a letter from Carlo, and tells her that the prince longs to see her.

Elisabeth agrees to receive him, and the page leads Carlo to her side. The ladies retire. Carlo begs the Queen's help to obtain Philip's permission to travel to Flanders. His fervor rises to a passionate avowal (**Carlo:** *Perduto ben*—O treasure lost). She repulses him. The King and his suite interrupt them. Philip rebukes his wife for being unattended and banishes the Countess of Aremberg, who should have been in waiting. Elisabeth consoles her (**Elisabeth:** *Non pianger*—Ah, weep not!). The ladies depart, leaving Rodrigo to plead with Philip for mercy towards the Flemings (**Rodrigo:** *O Signor, di Fiandra*—Sire, from Flanders.) The King charges Rodrigo to watch the Queen and warns him of the Grand Inquisitor.

ACT II. At midnight Carlo awaits the Queen at a masked ball in the royal gardens in response to a letter he believes Elisabeth has written him. It was in fact penned by the amorous Eboli whom he now finds masked and veiled and whom he woos passionately, mistaking her for the Queen. When she unmasks, she is horrified to learn that Carlo's heart is elsewhere and furiously accuses him of loving Elisabeth. Rodrigo tries to protect his friend from Eboli's rage and, as a safety measure, takes from him certain incriminating papers (**Carlo, Rodrigo, Eboli:** *Al mio furor*—From my fury).

In the square before the Cathedral of Our Lady of Atocha, in Madrid, an immense crowd awaits the coronation of King Philip. The monarch emerges from the church and is greeted by six Flemish deputies, led by Carlo (**Deputies:** *Sire, no, l'ora estrema*—No Sire, our last hour). Prince, populace, and court plead for the King's mercy, but the friars insist on punishment for his rebellious subjects. Drawing his sword in defiance of his father, Carlo swears to champion the Flemish cause but is soon disarmed, surrendering his weapon to Rodrigo. While a group of heretics are burned at the stake, a celestial voice promises peace in the next world.

ACT III. In his private study Philip laments his wife's coldness (**Philip:** *Ella giammai m'amò*—She never loved me). The monarch consults the Grand Inquisitor as to a fitting punishment for Carlo but is told that Rodrigo too must die. As the old man leaves, the King muses regretfully that the throne must always yield to the church. Elisabeth bursts in, crying that her jewel casket has been stolen. Philip hands it to her, disclosing Carlo's portrait among the jewels, and accuses her of adultery. The Queen faints as Eboli and Rodrigo enter, the former confessing responsibility for Elisabeth's betrayal, the latter swearing to free

Spain from political oppression (**Quartet:** *Ah, Sii maledetto*—Ah, be cursed). When the men have left, Eboli reveals to the Queen that she gave the casket to Philip from jealousy over Carlo's love and that she has been the King's mistress. Dooming Eboli to a convent, Elisabeth leaves her. The penitent princess laments her fatal beauty and swears to save Carlo (**Eboli:** *O don fatale*—O fatal beauty).

Rodrigo visits Carlo in prison, telling that he has sacrificed himself for his friend (**Rodrigo:** *Per me giunto*—On your behalf). There is a shot, and Rodrigo falls, mortally wounded by an officer of the Guard. The prince then refuses to flee with Eboli but is given his liberty by his father as the furious mob storms into the cell to attack the monarch. Philip is protected by the Grand Inquisitor. The altar has saved the throne.

ACT IV. In the convent cloister Elisabeth bids farewell to Carlo (**Elisabeth:** *Tu che le vanità*—Thou who knowest our vanities). Philip again surprises the lovers with the Grand Inquisitor, but Carlo is protected from them both when the ghost of Charles V emerges from his tomb and drags his grandson into the cloister.

DON CARLO is one of those strange but indisputable psychological hurdles that creative artists, at some stage of their careers, have to surmount in order to progress. It was an obstacle of which Verdi had to clear his path in order to scale such summits as *Aïda,* the *Requiem,* and *Otello.* It was a necessity that had, in one way or another, to be circumvented, a problem which demanded to be solved. Only because *Don Carlo* is musically and dramatically what it is could *Aïda* achieve its proportions and its distinctive perfections. The Méry-du Locle libretto (fashioned more or less in the Meyerbeerian tradition) is only part of the difficulty. Much later the worthy Ghislanzoni helped patch it, but its defects are organic. It does not offer a sequence of deftly and subtly contrasted moments such as the composer, with the help of a more skillful poet, was to achieve in his old age.

. . . . .

Almost three decades ago I asked a noted Italian conductor, then associated with the Metropolitan, whether it should not be possible to revive *Don Carlo.* His answer was: "*Vous savez, c'est bien beau, mais, c'est gris!*" ("You know, it is quite beautiful, but it is gray!") There is unquestionable truth in this verdict; the opera is superb, but it has a certain uniformity of color and not a little of this grayness pervades some of the very finest pages of an unequal score. There are few greater flights in Verdi than the King's heart-shaking, nocturnal monologue in which he reflects that his young queen has never loved him and never will. Definitely, this is a "gray" page, as by all rules of the game it was bound to be! Still, one would not barter it for ten thousand spectacular ballets or smashing mob scenes. Eboli's aria of agitated penitence, *O don fatale,* in which she curses her fatal beauty, is unquestionably a fine and extremely effective page of its kind. Yet it is just one more popular dramatic aria, of the sort of which operatic literature is full, and not to be compared to the desolation, gloom, and boundless loneliness of these meditations of the King—music which forms one of the most drearily atmospheric pages that Verdi or any other composer has written. And the wonder of this scene is that the soliloquy is instantly followed by another episode, in its way even more overpowering—the mighty colloquy of the monarch and that blind old fanatic of ninety, the Grand Inquisitor. Here is a scene which for sheer terror is virtually without its fellow in the whole range of opera.

. . . . .

The first act, opening with a chorus of monks who invoke the spirit of Charles V, develops on broad melodic lines. The monks, their invocations ended, withdraw to a superb *cantabile* phrase previously sung by one of the friars to the words *Padre che arrida a' tuoi fedel. . . .*

Carlo, relieved for a moment of his monkish company, is suddenly overjoyed to stand face to face with his devoted friend, Rodrigo (Schiller's "Roderich"), Marquis of Posa. It is said that Verdi disliked his librettists' Rodrigo, who impressed him as no more than the stereotyped figure of that "faithful comrade" with whom dozens of operas are populated. As a matter of fact, the operatic Rodrigo is a far cry from Schiller's Posa. Yet the composer has given him some of the noblest lyrical music of the score.

Not invariably, however; and one of the sorriest blots on *Don Carlo* is that C major duet of Carlo and Rodrigo, *Dio che nell' alma infondere*. This recurs repeatedly in the ensuing scenes, either as a kind of leading motive or otherwise. It is Meyerbeer of the worst type and one blushes that Verdi, with all his detestation of the Paris Opera and its ways (he had reluctantly written *Don Carlo* for Paris), did not throw this deplorable tune on the scrap heap when he undertook to revise the opera.

The following scene opens gracefully enough, with the introductory chorus of ladies in waiting: *Sotto ai folti, immensi abeti.* This charming page owes a thing or two to *Les Huguenots*. The Princess Eboli, accompanied by a page on the mandolin, has a real operatic "specialty" number, a so-called *Canzone del Velo*, an *allegro brillante* in A major, peppered with coloraturas and cadenzas. It is a "Moorish love song," with a mildly exotic touch provided by a flattened leading note; but it would hardly have added to the value of the opera, much as the average audience may respond to its showy features.

The ensuing scene, the little "trio in dialogue" of the Queen, Eboli, and Rodrigo, is engrossing for the pretty rhythmic touches of characterization underlining the voice parts, particularly that of Eboli. Rodrigo has passages of smoother cantabile to sing.

The duet between Elisabeth and Don Carlo rises to a much higher and far more serious level than this plane of elegant converse which had prevailed in much of the preceding. It attains one of the lyrical high points to the opera, with Carlo's *dolce espressivo: Perduto ben, mio sol tesor.*

The melody expands and reaches a pitch of exaltation. The King arrives, finds Elisabeth unattended, and demands to know the whereabouts of her ladies in waiting. There follows the instant banishment of the Duchess of Aremberg. The moving episode which opens with Elisabeth's romanza, *Non pianger, mia compagna*, has an accompaniment in which a series of unchanging C's, in syncopated rhythms, are conspicuous. There follows a scene between Philip II and the Marquis of Posa, in which the latter vainly pleads for the oppressed Netherlands. The pages beginning with Posa's *O signor, di Fiandra arrivo* include *Ah! sia benedetto Iddio.*

These must be numbered among the great ones of the score. Most charming, likewise, is the orchestral prelude to the third act which repeats, enriched, some portions of the omitted Fontainebleau prologue.

Let us pass to the spectacular business of the auto-da-fé, which is not so horrific on the stage as one might expect. It is a scene rich in Meyerbeerian effects and, musically, it contains Meyerbeerisms that blemish the score. One of the grossest of these is a march, a *cantabile* in A major, full of melodic triplets and the customary Meyerbeerian baggage. Another, even if slightly better march is a kind of funeral processional, played as the monks lead the victims of the Inquisition to the stake. One thing must be said of this scene—despite its tinsel, its noise, its crowds, and its movement, the main personalities never forfeit their individual characters. And there is exceedingly clever ensemble writing; likewise a stage band, as in *Aïda*—but very different in what it plays. The "Heavenly Voice" promising the unfortunate heretics peace in a better world is merely sugary, what with its harp and its rocking arpeggios. Let us forget this over-dimensioned piece of stage upholstery and turn to where Verdi is at his indisputable greatest—in the following scenes of the King's great soliloquy and the episode of the Grand Inquisitor.

The tremendous scene in the King's cabinet opens darkly, with a short but powerful instrumental introduction. . . . After this the King begins his great *scena, Ella giammai m'amò!*, the orchestra reiterating, for a space, the material which preceded, with repetitions of the desolate knockings. The D minor *andante mosso cantabile* passage, *Dormirò sol nel manto mio regal,* is heart-shaking. . . .

Scarcely has the hearer managed to recall himself from the melancholy of the great and truly psychological soliloquy than he is confronted with the dread mood of the scene between the king and the awful, almost spectral figure of the Grand Inquisitor. This is one of those moments in which Verdi, freeing himself from all thought of trivial effects and operatic conventions, has risen to heights of pity and terror which are the essence of Greek tragedy. Led by two Dominican monks, the sightless old man, more terrible by the force of superstition which he embodies than by anything else, enters to a theme which exercises its menacing influence through the great part of this never-to-be-forgotten interchange, in which the King forcefully, yet in the end vainly, struggles against the blind might of intrenched religion. This motive (which establishes the mood of the scene in the truest Wagnerian sense) is wrought of no more than a stark figure in octaves and a few syncopated chords. . . .

The agitated, but less appalling scene of Philip, Elisabeth, the Princess Eboli, and the Marquis of Posa, admirable as it indisputably is, remains definitely on the plane of more conventional opera. Still, it is well devised "theatre." It contains the fine and exciting quartet, which closes with the Queen's surging melody, *Ah! sola, straniera in questo suolo.*

After Eboli has vainly implored the betrayed Elisabeth's forgiveness for her perfidious actions against her royal lady, she remains behind to voice her penitence in the aria, *O don fatale.*

This falls into three distinctive sections—a passionate, introductory *allegro giusto,* a lyrical central portion, *molto meno,* in A flat (*O mia Regina*), and ends dramatically, *allegro più mosso,* with the phrase, marked *con slancio, Sia benedetto il ciel.*

The last act, relatively short, contains little music that can be compared with what has preceded. The first of the two scenes, which takes place in the prison to which Don Carlo has been committed, opens darkly, with simple but melancholy chords. The appearance of Rodrigo, seeking to comfort and advise his friend, brings us one of the more notable lyrical effusions of the act, Rodrigo's E flat *cantabile, Per me giunto,* its fluent melody supported by a simple accompaniment.

Rodrigo's death recalls for the last time that wretched "friendship" melody, which we heard (and deplored) early in the opera. A final scene shows the sorrowful leave-taking of Carlo and Elisabeth. The farewell of the ill-starred lovers brings a *cantabile, Ma lassù ci vedremo,* which develops into a touching duet that ranks among the finer moments of the closing scene; a little earlier, unfortunately, this had also offered a wretched C major *marziale, Si l'eroismo è questo,* that stands among Verdi's darkest sins in a work which so often bestrides the sunlit peaks of inspiration.

HERBERT F. PEYSER

RICHARD STRAUSS (1864–1949)

Elektra

Libretto by Hugo von Hofmannsthal, after the drama of Sophocles. First performance in Dresden, January 25, 1909.

Characters

Five serving women
Three Mezzo-sopranos, two Sopranos
Overseer of the servants . . . . Soprano
Elektra . . . . Soprano
Chrysothemis, her sister . . . . Soprano
Klytemnestra, their mother . . . . Contralto
The Confidante . . . . Mezzo-soprano
Trainbearer . . . . Soprano
A Young Servant . . . . Tenor
An Old Servant . . . . Bass
Orestes, brother of Elektra and Chrysothemis
Baritone
Guardian of Orestes . . . . Bass
Aegisthus, paramour of Klytemnestra . . . . Tenor

The Story

In the inner courtyard of the palace of Agamemnon, the murdered king of Mycenae, five serving women chatter of the plight of Elektra, daughter of Agamemnon and Klytemnestra, who lives in squalor like a beast, exciting their derision. Only the fifth maid recognizes Elektra's regal spirit and pities her (**Fifth maid:** *Ich will vor ihr mich niederwerfen*—I would kneel before her). She is sent off by the overseer to be flogged. Elektra appears alone, raving of her father's murder by Klytemnestra and her paramour, Aegisthus. She invokes the apparition of Agamemnon (**Elektra:** *Wo bist du Vater?*—O, my father). The half-demented princess swears to avenge her father's death and dance the ritual of victory on his tomb.

Elektra's younger sister, Chrysothemis, comes to warn her that Klytemnestra and Aegisthus plan to imprison her more closely. The terrified girl begs Elektra to help her escape. She wishes for a woman's life. She longs for children (**Chrysothemis:** *Ich hab's wie Feuer in der Brust*—There's fire in my breast). Chrysothemis tells her sister that the Queen is haunted by a dream that her son Orestes, who has been rescued from death and lives in hiding, is pursuing her, and begs Elektra to keep out of their mother's way. She herself hurries off.

Heralded by a noisy procession of sacrificial animals, Klytemnestra enters with her confidante and trainbearer and describes her sleepless misery (**Klytemnestra:** *Ich habe keine guten Nächte*—No longer happy are my nights). Dismissing her attendants, she calls on Elektra to help banish her terrifying nightmares. Elektra retorts that a blood sacrifice is necessary and then questions her mother on the fate of Orestes. She prophesies that the Queen will find relief only in death at the hands of her avenging children. Klytemnestra's spasms of terror turn to wild rejoicing as the confidante and trainbearer return, whispering to the maids.

After they depart Chrysothemis returns and announces Orestes' death in a foreign land. Elektra refuses to believe the story. A young slave emerges from the palace, demanding a steed from an old slave to fetch Aegisthus home. Elektra realizes that the sisters must find the axe that slew Agamemnon and avenge their father's murder unaided. She urges Chrysothemis to help her (**Elektra:** *Wie stark du bist!*—How strong thou art!). Elektra even promises to serve her, but Chrysothemis will have none of it. She prefers to die in the palace rather than assist in the murder. Elektra, resolved to accomplish the deed alone, digs for the hidden axe beside the palace wall.

A stranger appears to bear witness to Orestes' death. Elektra is desolate. The stranger, at length convinced that he is speaking to his sister, whispers the truth: he is Orestes, returned to avenge their father's murder. Trembling, Elektra greets her brother (**Elektra:** *Orest!*—Orestes!). She blesses his resolve to do the deed.

Orestes' guardian arrives to caution the youth. Klytemnestra is alone in the palace. Now is the time. Orestes and his guardian enter the great portal. Elektra paces the courtyard alone. The axe has been forgotten.

A piercing scream announces Klytemnestra's death. Chrysothemis and the maids return, heralding the approach of Aegisthus, who demands lights. Elektra escorts him obsequiously to the palace, assuring him of Orestes' death. A moment later another shriek is heard. Aegisthus vainly cries for help.

Shouts disclose that the palace attendants have recognized their young master. Chrysothemis hurries to bear the tidings to Elektra. The sisters unite in their jubilations until Elektra, her ecstasy rising to delirium, performs a dance of frenzy. At its conclusion she falls lifeless.

WHEN *Elektra* was first given in New York, the late American composer and critic, Arthur Farwell, called it "the marriage of horror and beauty." The "horror" is still there, unmitigated by the passing of more than forty years. The "beauty" is another story. The intervening decades have enhanced and illuminated it from an architectural and lyrical standpoint that lends a rather absurd sound to all the earlier talk about cacophony, orchestral bewilderments, noise, and similar clichés of that remote and innocent period. . . .

One quality *Elektra* has indisputably preserved for well over a generation—its monumentality. The tragedy of Sophocles, as Hugo von Hofmannsthal remodeled it, is dramatically monumental, and monumental, no less, is the score of Strauss. . . . The *Elektra* music should not be compared with that of *Salome*, which is rather subtler and aims at something like the effects of changeable silk. There are few subtleties in the score of *Elektra*, which is bigger and vastly more terrible in its impact, more somber in its dark ecstasies, more grandiose and immense, so that even its essentially lyrical quality is shaped on a larger and bolder scale.

. . . . .

Like *Salome, Elektra* has no prelude, let alone any fully developed overture. The curtain rises immediately on the first measure, so that the prelude (if one insists on such a title) is that Cyclopean three-bar theme of Agamemnon, which is to all intents the rhythmic duplication of the name of the murdered king.

*

This mighty theme winds its way through the tragedy, appearing and reappearing in numberless permutations and combinations on page after page of score. . . . This primeval motive surmounts the drama like a gigantic coat of arms above a

* Courtesy of Boosey and Hawkes, Inc., Copyright Owners.

vast portal. It pervades in association with several other themes the sinister chatter of the serving maids of the dread palace, who anticipate the entrance of Elektra, the wild, ragged, scarcely human creature, beaten and unspeakably brutalized, to bemoan the doom of her father, slain by his wife, Klytemnestra, and her paramour, Aegisthus. Almost immediately, as the Second Maid speaks, one hears a kind of diminution of this heraldic theme, followed by a rapid fortissimo ascending scale leading to a new and terribly rhythmic figure—the symbol of the axe with which Agamemnon was done to death.

A two-note *sforzando* harmonic device then depicts Elektra's disgust and another forceful and powerful motive in the orchestra is associated with her undying hatred of her mother and Aegisthus.

A new theme enters the texture of the music as the First Maid observes: "Were she my child, I'd hold her. . . under lock and key." It is the theme of Orestes, and it has something of a similarity to the foregoing theme of the axe.

On the heels of this come tenderer measures, picturing Elektra in shameful degradation.

One of the maids, more sympathetic, speaks of her as, after all, a king's child; and the degradation theme is associated with the ensuing symbol of royalty:

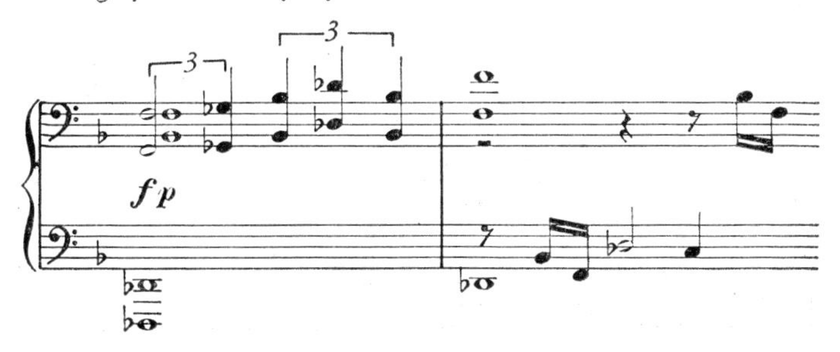

The opening scene of the maids may be described as a kind of prologue. The single long act which constitutes the work exhibits on closer structural analysis that the librettist's dramatic plan falls into seven distinct psychological stages "to each of which," as Ernest Newman says, "Strauss gives a different musical cast"; and the English critic enumerates these stages thus: (1) Elektra, (2) Chrysothemis, (3) Klytemnestra, (4) Elektra and Chrysothemis, (5) Orestes, (6) The Recognition, (7) The Vengeance. The delineation of Elektra herself actually takes place when the daughter of Agamemnon, the servants having returned to the palace, comes forward to launch her great monologue invoking her murdered father. It is a grandiose page in which mingle emotions of sorrow, ecstasy, and wild imagination, and musically it contains a number of the most memorable thematic and melodic elements of the score. Superbly, a great accented phase in octaves rises from the depths of the orchestra, towering above everything. It is a symbol of the shade of Agamemnon, Avenger of his own Wrongs. Newman likens it to "a great fist clenched above the house which was once the murdered king's."

Only a few measures further, after a series of themes already known to us, there enters, *molto espressivo,* the phrase of Agamemnon's children, which will accompany us through the

greater part of the tragedy and clings to our recollection as perhaps the most sweeping melody in the opera.

Toward the end of the scene we are brought a rhythmic element which underlies the idea of the dance of triumph Elektra envisions herself as performing once her deed of avenging sacrifice has been carried out.

At the close of the tremendous invocation, with Elektra's voice soaring to a sustained high C, the orchestra unites in a mighty tapestry of counterpoint the motive of Agamemnon's children and three other themes bound together by the beating rhythm of the dance of expiation.

Chrysothemis appears as the prodigious orchestral postlude to Elektra's monologue dies from its triple fortissimo to a mere whisper. Hofmannsthal's letters indicate that the dramatist planned the former as a foil to her terrible sister. Chrysothemis, as Mr. Newman has finely said, is "as weak through love as Elektra is strong through hate." Her chief wish is to escape the curse-laden palace, to become the wife of some worthy man—even if no more than a peasant—and to know the joys of motherhood. Strauss has, in reality, divined her dramatic unimportance, and her fluent, not to say mellifluous, music betrays her spiritual inferiority.

. . . . .

The interchange of the two sisters ends with Chrysothemis bursting into a fit of passionate weeping. She warns Elektra not to cross her mother this day, for she has dreamed that the avenging Orestes had returned, is mad with terror, and "when she trembles she is most terrible." Elektra, unmoved, says that more now than ever she wishes to confront her mother, and as Chrysothemis rushes out, appalled, there is a lurid glow of torches from within the palace, and one hears the noise of a procession of stumbling, hurrying animals making it plain that the guilty queen is attempting, once again, to propitiate the wrathful gods with a hecatomb. . . .

Finally, Klytemnestra appears, leaning on her confidante. She is a figure of horror, sallow, bloated, the paler for her scarlet robe and her numberless jewels and amulets to ward off evil. She seems to have trouble in keeping her eyelids open.

The music of the ensuing great scene is by turns dark, heavy, awesome, violent. . . . The succeeding dialogue between mother and daughter is one continual tissue of rapid and awful retorts filled with dark double meanings, hidden, to be sure, from the guilty queen but clear enough to the hearer who makes it his business to grasp the text. Musically the whole scene is one of mounting tension. Strauss' thematic invention is not, indeed, so memorable as Wagner's, but, as Ernest Newman notes, "opera with its leading motives that look before and after, and its capacity for supplementing, or even contradicting, in the orchestra what is being said on the stage, is incomparably more potent than any mere verbal drama can be in this regard." And the score of the Klytemnestra scene is a web of themes. One hears the rhythm of the dance of triumph, and a strongly accented five-note figure associated with the idea of Orestes, the Avenger, and, combined with it, a form of the noble melody of Agamemnon's children.

More and more deadly become Elektra's threats to her cowering mother till, growing steadily more threatening as well as monstrous in her tragic stature, she embarks on a merciless description of what Klytemnestra's end will be once "the hand of the hunter" reaches her and slits her throat. Shaken by speechless terror, the queen listens in horrible fascination, while the grisly music coils in serpentine patterns. . . .

Suddenly the musical and dramatic background changes. Chrysothemis enters, howling tidings of Orestes' death. The score is a welter of conflicting rhythms, dissonances, embattled themes. . . . Elektra, recovering instantly from the shock of the awful intelligence, resolves to take the bloody duty of the murder on herself. But as she cannot carry out the double business alone, she demands that Chrysothemis assist her. . . .

Chrysothemis, pictured by her music in characteristic 3-4 time, is naturally unequal to the task her sister asks of her, even though Elektra attempts by all sorts of appeals and beguilements to persuade her. She dashes away in horror followed by Elektra's reverberating curse. "Well then, alone!" Elektra cries with fierce determination, and she instantly sets about digging up by the wall of the palace the axe with which she intends to carry out the deed. Her action at the side of the threshold is carried out, according to the stage directions, "eagerly, without a sound, like an animal." . . .

She pauses a moment, gazes about her, then resumes her digging. One almost hears the scratching of nails. Suddenly the black-clad Orestes stands by the courtyard gate, silhouetted against the last rays of the sun, while the instruments play a succession of sighing motives in descending sequences. Elektra starts violently to a short, sharp dissonance.

It takes some time for her to learn the actual identity of the stranger. Orestes himself is slow to betray it, and, to make doubly sure that the worn and haggard creature before him is really his sister, he relates, posing as a messenger, the story of Orestes' supposed death under the hoofs of his steeds. At the words "We have been sent to the queen because we can give witness that her son is dead indeed!" the orchestra underlines the sombre fiction with a persistent wailing figure which rises and falls in desolate chromatics and shrouds itself in mourning harmonies.

Deviously at first and at length with cataclysmal impact, Elektra learns the truth. The stranger is no messenger, as she was led to believe, but Orestes himself. Servants have, meanwhile, appeared and kissed the black-garbed stranger's hands and the hem of his robe. "The hounds in the courtyard knew me well and my own sister not!" he exclaims in a heart-shaking passage.

"Orestes!" shrieks Elektra; and the orchestra dashes into a wild *vivace assai* of paroxysmal motives, rhythms, and dissonances that caused one American critic on first hearing it to think of a "murder scene in a Chinese theatre," but which suggests rather the suddenly liberated emotions of all the fury, insane joy of vengeance, and tigerish blood lust pent up in Elektra's soul all these black years. . . .

Then, with a mastery of emotional transition equalled by few but Wagner, the tension which has gradually been building up is relaxed in measures of subduing tenderness as the trembling Elektra stammers her brother's name. The quietly ecstatic A flat passage, flowing on for several pages and debouching with the utmost artistic naturalness in a duet is in a number of respects the lyrical peak of the opera. The flowing music originated unmistakably from the very source which fed Strauss' finest inspirations in certain of his most memorable *Lieder* and develops out of a theme accompanying the words *Lös' nicht in Luft dich auf* and symbolizes Elektra's joy:

Little by little the musical texture takes on a new complexity as further thematic elements associate themselves with the more facile mellifluousness; and when we come to Orestes' resolute *Lass zittern diesen Leib, er ahnt welchen Weg ich ihn führe,* there asserts itself a 6–4 phrase, of rather waltzlike character hinted at earlier but subsequently to reach its fullest development when Elektra, beside herself with joy, hurls herself like a maenad into her dance of triumph.

From here on the action, musical as well as dramatic, hastens on to its terrifying close. The Elektra-Orestes scene is the last lyrical point of repose this incandescent score will bring us. Now follows horror piled on horror. Orestes' tutor, a fierce old man with burning eyes, appears suddenly in the doorway and warns him to be silent lest his presence be discovered. Klytemnestra's treacherous confidante signs to the pair to follow her to the queen's chamber to carry out their bloody deed. The music evokes an atmosphere of nameless terror. By a superhuman effort Orestes has struggled to master his feelings at the mission which faces him. As he disappears into the palace, Elektra in horrid excitement runs about like a caged animal, then pauses for a moment crying that she has not been able to give her brother the sacrificial axe she had so carefully concealed against the hour of vengeance. As she runs back and forth, the orchestra in nightmare rushes of *pianissimo* scales establishes a nameless feeling of terror. . . .

From within comes a piercing shriek, followed by a demonic scream from Elektra to her brother, "Strike yet again!" After another and more bloodcurdling cry from the doomed Klytemnestra, the triple *fortissimo* with which Agamemnon's motive is sounded seems like a relief; and there is almost an effect of satanic irony and of gallows' humor in the words and the music of Chrysothemis and the terrified serving maids as they shout amid all these death shrieks and this tumult *Es muss etwas geschehen sein* and *Es müssen Männer drin sein*—"Something must have happened," "There must be men in the house!" And then, by a stroke of bitter comedy, there sounds from the orchestra *behaglich schlendernd*—"comfortable, as though strolling along"—the motive of the craven Aegisthus, all unknowingly hurrying to his doom. The dreadful little scene which ensues, with Elektra waving a burning brand and cynically inquiring, "May I not light thee," while she circles in a kind of diabolical torch dance around him, becomes a macabre *scherzetto.*

Aegisthus' murder, glimpsed through a window, lacks the awfulness and antique grandeur of Klytemnestra's, for all its implicit cruelty. And when with a last cry his slayers drag him away and dispatch him, the orchestra violently sounds the towering motive of Agamemnon, almost visibly present at the destruction of his foes.

Strauss, however, does not allow us a *detente* on the heels of all this frightfulness! What follows is, musically, a majestic sacrificial ceremony. The great motives tower upon one another cumulatively, like a vast statue of bronze. The melody of Agamemnon's children expands superbly, associated with the rhythm of the triumphal dance throbbing below. Here, too, we have that 6–4 melody, alluded to a little earlier and the grand duet of the two sisters. . . .

Elektra flings back her head like a maenad and momentarily eyes Chrysothemis, calling upon her and the awed torch-bearing throngs to be silent and join her in her indescribable dance of thanksgiving, shouting: "The burden of joy I carry and I will lead the sacred dance!" The music and the emotion of the scene have reached the point of saturation. All that is left is the alternative of living or dying; and as hatred has so long been Elektra's food she can have no choice. Her last steps of nameless ecstasy suddenly arrest the transfigured flow of the melodic tides. From a puissant 3–2 bar the music reverts to a tremendous 4–4 conjunction of the black themes of vengeance, hate, and the bloody axe. Then there is a stridulous tremolo on E flat and a long held E flat minor chord. Elektra falls inert. Chrysothemis rushes to her, bending over her sister's lifeless form. Several times more, with awe-stricken funereal harmonies intervening, the terrible three-note motto of Agamemnon sounds forth. Crysothemis batters wildly upon the palace door, shouting "Orestes." There is silence within the house and the curtain drops on a terrific reiteration of the Agamemnon motive.

HERBERT F. PEYSER

GAETANO DONIZETTI (1797–1848)

L'Elisir d'Amore

Libretto by Felice Romani, based upon *Le Philtre,* a play by Eugène Scribe. First performance in Milan, May 12, 1832.

Characters

Gianetta, a peasant girl . . . . Soprano
Nemorino, a young peasant . . . . Tenor
Adina, owner of a prosperous farm . . . . Soprano
Belcore, sergeant of the village garrison . . . . Baritone
Dr. Dulcamara, a travelling quack doctor . . . . . . Bass

The Story

ACT I. In the courtyard of a prosperous nineteenth-century Italian farm the peasants gather to rest from their labors in the fields. One of them, the lovesick Nemorino, gazes rapturously at Adina, the wealthy young owner of the farm, but her attention is concentrated on a book she is reading. This is the story of Tristan and the love potion which turned his beloved Isolde's indifference into eternal love (**Adina:** *Della crudele Isotta*—Beauteous but cruel Isotta). A detachment of soldiers is led in by Sergeant Belcore, who tries to flatter Adina with a bouquet of flowers (**Belcore:** *Come Paride vezzoso*—As the gay and gallant Paris). She coyly resists his advances and then, dismissing the peasants, turns her attention to Nemorino. It would be better for him to forget her, she insists, and hasten to the death-bed of his rich uncle. There is no hope for him to win such a frivolous creature as herself (**Adina:** *Chiedi all'aura*—Go demand of yon light zephyr).

ACT II. The villagers gather in the market place to welcome an itinerant quack, Dr. Dulcamara, who cries his wares from the steps of his carriage (**Dulcamara:** *Udite, udite o rustici*—Give ear now, ye rustic ones). Nemorino, who has been much impressed by Adina's story of Tristan's love potion, asks if the doctor can sell him a bottle. Dulcamara produces a flask of wine, vows the young man to secrecy, and accepts in payment the last coin in Nemorino's pocket (**Nemorino, Dulcamara:** *Obbligato*—Thank you kindly). A couple of drinks make Nemorino tipsy and he confronts Adina with a new bluff (**Nemorino,**

Adina: *Esulti per la barbara*—Though now the cruel one). Piqued by his apparent indifference, she welcomes the Sergeant and, learning from Gianetta that his company is to be moved to other quarters, promises to marry Belcore at once. Hoping that the elixir will eventually work, Nemorino implores her to wait (**Nemorino:** *Adina, credimi*—Adina, believe me), but she invites the crowd to her wedding while one and all jeer at the rejected suitor.

ACT III. The wedding feast has been prepared at an inn, where Belcore is the toast of the peasantry. Dr. Dulcamara offers to entertain them with a lively barcarolle from Venice, in which Adina joins him (**Dulcamara, Adina:** *Io son ricco e tu sei bella* —I have riches, you have beauty). The bride and groom withdraw with a notary to sign the contract of marriage, but Dulcamara remains to stuff himself at the dinner table. He is interrupted by the desperate Nemorino, who begs the quack for a second bottle of the potion but is refused—he has no money left to pay for it. Belcore returns—his marriage with Adina postponed till nightfall—and suggests to Nemorino that he enlist in the army for an advance payment of twenty crowns (**Nemorino, Belcore:** *Ai perigli della guerra*—I know full well the path of war). The young peasant signs away his liberty for the price of the potion.

Nemorino, unaware that his uncle has died, leaving him a considerable fortune, returns to Adina's farm with the fresh confidence he has found in the doctor's bottle (**Nemorino:** *Dell'elisir mirabile*—Of this miraculous elixir). The peasants now think him attractive, and when Adina learns from Dulcamara that the youth has sold his freedom to win her love, her heart is softened (**Adina, Dulcamara:** *Quanto amore*—What affection!). She will bring him to her feet with a tear, for the magic potion lies actually in her glance. Nemorino wanders in, hoping that the tear he has noticed in Adina's eye means that her heart belongs to him (**Nemorino:** *Una furtiva lagrima*—In her dark eye). Adina tells him that she has bought off his recruiting papers, and both joyously sign a marriage contract. Belcore takes his defeat with good humor: there are plenty of girls waiting to marry him. Dulcamara announces that Nemorino is now the richest man in the village: the magic potion has brought not only love but wealth. The villagers surround the quack, demanding samples for themselves. To the blare of trumpets and the cheers of the populace the doctor's chariot rolls away.

WHEN the final curtain falls on *L'Elisir d'Amore*, when the young lovers are at last united and the charlatan Dulcamara has departed in triumph for the next gullible village, one is left with the impression of a bright-colored necklace of characters and situations—alike only in their gay improbability —strung on a silken thread of light-hearted melody. Where but under the sun of Italy could so slight a tale have been set to music of such spontaneous charm!

After musing a bit along these lines, however, one is likely to wonder just how Italian audiences of Donizetti's time must have reacted to one more *opera buffa* in a tradition that even then was stereotyped. Like most of his operas after 1830, *L'Elisir d'Amore* achieved immediate and lasting popularity. Why? Whatever appeal it has for us today lies in its ingenious tunefulness; we approach it as a pleasant diversion from more substantial operatic fare, but it is a little difficult to understand the immense success it and its prototypes once enjoyed.

One explanation of this success may be that Donizetti was shrewd in his choice of book and librettist. Eugène Scribe, on whose *Le Philtre* the opera is based, was one of the leading French dramatists of the nineteenth century, a man whose fecundity and insight into the tastes of the day were equalled only by Donizetti himself. . . . Moreover, Donizetti's librettist was the foremost of his time, Felice Romani. Apart from its music, then, *L'Elisir d'Amore* holds together simply as a comedy.

But the score had its undeniable merits as well, despite what Grout calls "an almost inconceivable poverty of harmonic, rhythmic, and orchestral interest." Donizetti possessed a remarkable gift for contagious melody and also a knack for humorous musical characterization (*e.g.*, Doctor Dulcamara). Most importantly, he showed rare skill in writing for the voice, and in general the audiences of his era attended operas more to enjoy the singing than to enjoy "the art of drama intensified by its absorption of another art." For two centuries Italy had been the scene of the greatest cultivation of vocal technique; besides, it was (and still is) perhaps the only country in which opera was popular with all classes and not merely a diversion of the wealthy. The reasons for this dual phenomenon are not all clear. Two of the most plausible explanations point to the traditional use of song in Church services and to the "pure," musical quality of the Italian language, with its absence of diphthongs or final consonants. But at any rate the operagoer of the 1830's was infinitely more disposed to regard music as a vehicle for the display of *bel canto* than is his present-day counterpart. There is no doubt that the voice was the thing.

The emphasis on individual expressiveness appears to be just another manifestation of the prevailing Romanticism of the times. After all, the year of *L'Elisir's* first performance, 1832, saw the death of Goethe, who had just completed *Faust, Part II*, and of Scott, whose *Bride of Lammermoor* Donizetti was to turn into his most famous opera three years later; the young Tennyson published his first poems; Delacroix ruled French art, with the aging Ingres his only opponent; Mendelssohn was writing his *Italian* Symphony and Chopin gave his first concert in Paris. In Italy it was the period described with such gusto by Stendhal in *La Chartreuse de Parme*.

However, Alfred Einstein points out that "the Romantic movement was an essentially 'Northern' movement . . . a yearning for the warmth, naturalness, colorfulness, and freedom of the South"—qualities which are, of course, the birthright of every Italian—and goes on to say that Italy seems to have been the country least affected by the Romantic era. "There was here a musical self-sufficiency and seclusion, based not only upon the old tradition of the opera but also upon political conditions. The Hapsburgs in Lombardy and Venice . . . did not look with favor on an exceptionally lively intellectual exchange between their domains and the rest of Europe."

Indeed, Lombardy-Venetia, where Donizetti was born, grew up, and saw most of his earlier operas produced, suffered severely under the Austrian domination imposed by the Congress of Vienna. . . . In the face of this tyranny there arose in Italy the most fervent expression of that nationalistic sentiment which swept Europe on the heels of Romanticism and which was most effectively typified by the "Young Italy" society organized in Marseilles in 1831 by the patriot Mazzini. Like the other arts, music played a part in the struggle for freedom which led ultimately to the *Risorgimento* (1848 and after)—although with the notable exception of Verdi, most of the Italian composers deserved no credit for the revolutionary significance people persisted in finding in their operas. Neither Rossini nor Bellini, for instance, had any interest in politics, and yet on occasion *William Tell* and *The Puritans* roused imaginative audiences to a pitch of excitement the authorities found quite alarming. . . .

It is doubtful that Donizetti ever wore even this spurious halo of patriotism. He has been described as a careless worker, "without particular ambition, often driven to write by need," the success or failure of whose efforts was largely a matter of accident. Surely there is nothing in an opera like *L'Elisir d'Amore* into which even the most ardent patriot could have read a message. Its setting is not the real world but a conventional one of eternal sunshine, capricious love, and happy endings. And yet it seems probable that just this sort of pastoral idealization of their essential nature must have proved endlessly cheering to the Italian people during those long decades when they dreamed of national freedom—more cheering, indeed, than the more disturbing sort of utterance which could only engender feelings of frustration. Furthermore, *opera buffa* and the art of *bel canto* were indigenous creations, and they had been raised to the highest artistic level.

If we add to these sources of pride the solid stagecraft of *L'Elisir,* it becomes apparent why the work achieved the popularity it did. Such operas have seemed to distill some of the brightest aspects of Italian culture in a medium of effortless songs; *The Elixir of Love* must have been, in a very real sense, an Elixir of Hope in that unhappy period of oppression.

Besides, it was a mine of singable tunes—most of which stand up very well a century later, by the way—in a day that knew no radio or musical comedy. And how many songs from *South Pacific* will still be delighting audiences in 2049?

FRANK MERKLING

GIACOMO PUCCINI (1858–1924)

Gianni Schicchi

Libretto by Gioachino Forzano, based upon the story of a contemporary of Dante, mentioned in Canto XXX of the *Inferno*. First performance in New York, December 14, 1918.

Characters

Zita, the Old Woman, cousin of Buoso . . . Mezzo-soprano
Simone, cousin of Buoso . . . Bass
Rinuccio, Zita's nephew . . . Tenor
Marco, Simone's son . . . Baritone
Ciesca, Marco's wife . . . Soprano
Betto, Buoso's cousin . . . Baritone
Gherardo, Buoso's nephew . . . Tenor
Nella, Gherardo's wife . . . Soprano
Gherardino, son of Gherardo and Nella . . Boy soprano
Gianni Schicchi . . . Bass
Lauretta, his daughter . . . Soprano
Spinelloccio, a physician . . . Bass
Ser Amantio di Nicolao, a notary . . . Bass
Pinellino, a shoemaker . . . Baritone
Guccio, a dyer . . . Bass

The Story

The grasping relatives of the wealthy Buoso Donati gather about his deathbed in the Florence of 1299 to bewail his loss and investigate his bequests (**Relatives:** *Povero Buoso*—Poor Buoso). It is rumored by Betto, the poorest relative, that Buoso's fortune has been left to a monastery. If the will has not been filed, declares Simone, there is still hope for the relatives, who begin a frantic search for the document. Young Rinuccio finds it and exacts the promise of his aunt, Zita, to let him marry his beloved Lauretta if there is enough money. The will is read in silence. Their worst fears realized, the relatives now weep in earnest. But Rinuccio suggests that Lauretta's father, Gianni Schicchi, a shrewd, self-made man, can help them; his peasant stock will be the salvation of Florence, which the young man likens to a tree in flower (**Rinuccio:** *Firenze è come un albero fiorito*—Our Florence is a large, robust tree). Schicchi appears with Lauretta. Disgusted by the hypocrisy and avarice he finds at the deathbed, he starts to leave, but softens when his daughter begs permission to marry Rinuccio (**Lauretta:** *O mio babbino caro*—O my beloved daddy). Reluctantly reading the will, Schicchi conceives a plan to impersonate the dead man. He sends Lauretta out of the room and then orders the body removed from the bed. At this point the doctor Spinelloccio pays a call. The shutters are hurriedly closed, and in the darkness Schicchi manages to simulate Buoso's voice and convince the physician that his patient is better and does not need his help. Schicchi then tells the others to send for the notary (**Schicchi:** *Messer Notaio, presto*—Master Notary, quick!) and, donning Buoso's nightshirt and cap, promises to dictate a new will. One by one the relatives bribe him to leave the choicest items to them. He agrees but warns them all that they must keep his secret or be banished from Florence as accessories to a fraud (**Schicchi, Chorus:** *Addio Firenze*—Florence farewell). When the notary, Ser Amantio, arrives with his witnesses, Schicchi bequeaths some of the property to the relatives but reserves the best of it for himself. The notary is hardly out of the door when the relatives fall on Schicchi and pillage the house. He chases them away but returns to find the lovers on the terrace, gazing rapturously at their city (**Rinuccio:** *Lauretta, mia Lauretta*—Lauretta, my Lauretta). Schicchi, whose wits have provided his daughter with a dowry and a house, turns to the audience and asks for the verdict: not guilty!

WHEN Puccini's *Trittico* received its premiere, the composer stood high in popularity; but people had begun to speculate that he was slipping. Gone were the marshmallow sonorities of *Bohème* and *Butterfly*, the gaudy blood and gore of *Tosca*. Few operas could live up to the ballyhoo that anticipated *The Girl of the Golden West* in 1910; despite a brilliant premiere and a great deal of beautiful music, *The Girl* quickly slid from the repertory, donning a stepsister's drab cloak which enshrouds her still. *La Rondine* (1917) impressed a typical reviewer as "a series of familiar musical corpses floating out of a culvert." Had Puccini succumbed to his own success? What was happening to his style? . . .

The main thing that was happening to Puccini was his growth as an artist. He was becoming more of a composers' composer, and the public could not sense this without some resentment.

In his very first works, Puccini had formulated a style based on fluent melody and the exploitation of certain ripe harmonies—a style that without his uncanny theatrical instinct might seem less hypnotic. He had used exciting local color but had done relatively little to create real characterizations through music; his arias were appropriate but hardly profound. Now the twentieth century was starting to engulf him. His competitors were not only Italians of lesser gifts than his—Cilèa, Mascagni, Zandonai, Leoncavallo—but the supersophisticated Richard Strauss, whose orchestrations were every bit as slick as Puccini's and whose intellectual appeal was much more comprehensive. Puccini began to appraise the trends around him. French impressionism especially attracted him, because it expanded the frontiers of lush, sensuous sound and made subtlety possible without denying the precepts of his existing style.

Puccini's impulse further to refine his technique sprang from two origins: a desire to keep abreast of the times and the need to husband his natural melodic sources more providently. . . . Around 1910, Puccini's contemporaries were awakening not only to French impressionism, but to the discovery of Mussorgsky's *Boris Godunov* (largely a result of Debussy's youthful residence in Russia). Independent of these cosmopolitan trends, the Czech operatic master Leos Janáček had begun exhaustive research into the accents of natural speech and their relation to musical lines. Puccini was hardly the research type, but with customary facility he caught what was fresh in the air. So it is easy to figure the disappointment of a 1918 audience, confronted with a clipped conversational style, bordering on monotone, when they expected to savor in *Il Tabarro* another pungent plum from the supple branches of *verismo*. And we cannot picture the intense but almost ascetic tonal monochrome of *Suor Angelica* as a box-office nostrum.

Gianni Schicchi, concluding piece of the *Trittico*, was, however, an immediate success. To the chagrin of Puccini, who piously affected to prefer *Suor Angelica* (though he had rushed to complete the *Schicchi* music first), critics everywhere singled out *Gianni* as the best of the three one-act works. In terms of his growing style, *Gianni Schicchi* is the technical tour de force of Puccini's career, the most interesting and accomplished of his operas from a musician's viewpoint, his most polished artistic achievement.

Gianni Schicchi is a miniature. If only for this reason, it is an overstatement to call the piece a worthy successor to Verdi's *Falstaff* and the comedies of Rossini and Mozart. Yet a sequel it surely is, and a worthy one in that Puccini gave it the best of himself. . . .

What a shame, we may muse, that Puccini's instinct for comedy produced only one little masterpiece in this genre. But we must not overlook the salutary effect of comedy in his serious operas. The animated horseplay throughout *La Bohème,* the shruggings of the Sacristan in *Tosca,* the complaisant machinations of Goro in *Butterfly,* the pidgin Italian of the two redskins in *The Girl of the Golden West,* the Gilbert-and-Sullivan pontifications of the trio of mandarins in *Turandot,* all serve the function of ancient *commedia dell'arte* interludes: to divert the audience with some respite from the solemn doings of melodrama. . . .

Puccini was easygoing but capable of intense concentrations; he was full of wry humor, but he took sentimentality seriously. So in *Gianni Schicchi* he gives us music which flows as naturally as the Arno on its way through Florence but which craftily nurtures pungent, ardent little kernels of melody; music that cackles and grunts and glitters, only to lapse archly into premeditated charm. Perhaps sensing his limitations, Puccini gains a certain borrowed strength by weakening his audience, keeping us forever off guard against the buffets or blandishments of his next resource.

Puccini never characterized humanity so well as when he caricatured it. The limping, sobbing, sniffling motif which opens *Gianni Schicchi,* outrageously punctuated with the throbs of a muffled funeral drum, distills the very essence of crocodile tears. The desiccated slow-motion tango accompanying Gianni's description of his scheme to impersonate Buoso Donati is acid enough to pucker the ears with its mockery of obese stealth. As Gianni completes his costume, Puccini turns him into a grotesque Siegfried entreated by a trio of all-too-Wagnerian-looking Rhinemaidens (Zita, Ciesca, and Nella), the ravishing ensemble concluding with a flourish (*O Gianni Schicchi, nostro salvatore*) which aims a sharp sideways kick at Richard Strauss. The glowing music of the young lovers, with its overabundant innocence, lifts us with the same quick flush that typifies man's readiness to seize on rosy hopes which, like youth, come and go but create a wondrously restorative illusion.

. . . . .

The story of *Gianni Schicchi* is one of humanity's older quips. But the characters are not simply familiar puppets; the measure of Puccini's artistic stride is the length to which he overstepped this pitfall. Zita, the old woman, though evidently a cousin to Dame Quickly in Verdi's *Falstaff*, emerges as an unforgettable figure in her own obnoxious right. The other relatives are often differentiated in laconic twists of phrase. The chattering homogeneity of the ensembles, however, attains an opposite end: to emphasize the common vice which everyone shares, here sharpened to a peak of absurdity. Rinuccio and Lauretta, descendants of Verdi's Fenton and Anne, provide our means of detachment and escape from this den of vipers. As for Schicchi himself, he combines both the sly and the worthy qualities of humanity, emerging (to quote George Marek's biography, *Puccini*) "perhaps the only successful male character the composer put on the stage."

Thus a character who ran special danger of becoming a mere stereotype became, in Puccini's hands, a masterful portrait. And as we scrutinize this portrait, we begin to suspect that its authenticity lies in Puccini's ability (perhaps quite unconscious) to identify himself with Gianni Schicchi. For are not both men of rather weak character, but shrewd, ingenious, and charming? Did not Puccini see himself as part suave mountebank, part diligent entrepreneur, winking like a god while he wrested a treasure to leave us as his legacy?

JOHN W. FREEMAN

GIACOMO PUCCINI (1858–1924)

Manon Lescaut

Libretto by Marco Praga, Domenico Oliva, Giuseppe Giacosa, Luigi Illica, and Giulio Ricordi, after the novel by the Abbé Prévost. First performance in Turin, February 1, 1893.

Characters

Edmondo, a student	Tenor
The Chevalier des Grieux	Tenor
Lescaut, Sergeant of the Guards	Baritone
The Innkeeper	Baritone
Géronte de Ravoir, Treasurer General	Bass
Manon Lescaut, sister of Sergeant Lescaut	Soprano
A Singer	Mezzo-soprano
The Dancing Master	Tenor
A Sergeant of Archers	Baritone
A Lamplighter	Tenor
A Captain in the Navy	Baritone

The Story

ACT I. At an innyard in eighteenth-century Amiens, Edmondo, a student, is making merry with his companions. They taunt another student, Des Grieux, with his lack of success in love, but he retorts with a mocking serenade to all the ladies present (**Des Grieux:** *Tra voi, belle*—Now among you). A coach arrives, containing young Manon and her brother Lescaut, who is taking her to a convent. With them is the rich old Géronte. While the Innkeeper shows the men to their rooms, Des Grieux makes ardent love to Manon and, when she is called away by her brother, rhapsodizes over her beauty (**Des Grieux:** *Donna non vidi mai*—Never did I behold so fair a maiden). Géronte and Lescaut return, and, while the younger man joins the students at the gaming tables, the elder, encouraged by the brother's worldly ambitions for Manon, bribes the innkeeper to arrange for her abduction. He is overheard by Edmondo, who warns Des Grieux of the plot. The girl reappears, pointing out that she has kept her promise to return (**Manon, Des Grieux:** *Vedete? Io son fedele*—You see, I am faithful). The Chevalier tells her what is afoot and succeeds in persuading her to elope to Paris with him instead. Just as Géronte re-enters, the young lovers rush off in the carriage the roué had held in readiness for himself. His anger is calmed by Lescaut, who assures him that a girl who loves luxury will be easy to lure away from a poor student (**Lescaut:** *Parigi! È là Manon*—To Paris! Manon is there). While the onlookers laugh among themselves, the two men go in to supper.

ACT II. True to prediction, Manon has abandoned Des Grieux for the rich Géronte and receives her brother in her sumptuous Paris apartment, where the hairdressers assist at her toilette. Lescaut congratulates her on her beauty (**Lescaut:** *Sei splendida*—With beauty you're resplendent). Pensively she replies that her present luxury cannot compensate her for the loss of her young lover (**Manon:** *In quelle trine morbide*—In those soft, silken curtains). Although bored by musicians who arrive to sing a madrigal by Géronte (**Musicians:** *Sulla vetta tu del monte*—Speed o'er summit of the mountains), the frivolous girl is diverted when a group of her protector's friends arrive with him to sing her praises. A dancing master leads her in a minuet, to which Manon gaily adds a pastoral refrain as a greeting to Géronte (**Manon:** *L'ora, o Tirsi*—These are hours). Meanwhile Lescaut, who has heard that Des Grieux has been lucky at the gambling table, has summoned the youth to relieve Manon's boredom. The Chevalier appears the moment the company has left and reproaches the girl for her faithlessness, but under her allurements his bitterness soon turns to ardor (**Des Grieux, Manon:** *Vieni! Colle tue braccia*—I'm yours forever). Géronte, returning unexpectedly, surprises the couple in each other's arms. When Manon lightly dismisses him, the old man retires, furious, to arrange for her arrest. Lescaut rushes in with word that the police are at the door. Although Des Grieux berates her for her folly, the selfish Manon insists on gathering up her jewels before she leaves (**Des Grieux:** *Ah! Manon, mi tradisce*—Manon, the folly of your thoughts betrays me). The delay proves fatal. Led by a sergeant and the vindictive Géronte, soldiers break in, seize Manon and drag her away.

ACT III. After an orchestral intermezzo, suggesting Manon's regrets in prison and her journey to Le Havre, the curtains part on a corner of the barracks near the harbor quay. Des Grieux and Lescaut are waiting at dawn to abduct the girl before she is deported to America as an undesirable. When Manon appears at the barred window of her temporary prison, the chevalier passionately kisses her hands but hides as a lamplighter passes, singing a plaintive tune (**Lamplighter:** *Kate rispose al Re*—And

Kate replied to the King). Suddenly Lescaut runs in to report that the plot has been discovered and forces the unhappy young man to leave his beloved and take cover. Soldiers escort the deportees—some defiant, some in tears—to the ship; a sergeant calls the roll. Manon sobs farewell to her lover, and his anguish so moves the ship's captain that he permits Des Grieux to join the outcast on her journey (**Des Grieux:** *Guardate, pazzo son*—Behold me, I am mad).

ACT IV. Manon and Des Grieux reach a desolate plain in Louisiana, where they have fled after landing in New Orleans. Weary and ragged she implores Des Grieux to leave her alone to die, but he hurries off in search of help and shelter. As night falls, the miserable girl voices her terror and despair (**Manon:** *Sola, perduta, abbandonata*—Lonely, forsaken, and abandoned). When her lover returns, she declares her eternal love and dies in his arms.

IN *Manon Lescaut,* Giacomo Puccini came musically of age. His first two operas, *Le Villi* and *Edgar,* had not stamped him as a musical personality; his particular color, his individual flavor were still indistinct.

With the appearance of *Manon Lescaut* in 1893, Puccini emerged as a new and commanding voice in the operatic world, a sharply defined voice which has never yet left the consciousness of the opera-going public. . . . With *Manon Lescaut,* Puccini established himself, once and for all, as the intimate charmer, the sensuous melodist of the enveloping, soaring climax that today seems peculiarly his. This brand of musical outpouring was to last him through at least half a dozen more successes, which occupy a distinctive and enamoring niche in the annals of the lyric theatre.

Only a young man could have written the music with which Puccini served the Abbé Prévost's story. Youth, in all its divine belief in romantic ardor, is ever-present in *Manon Lescaut.* Only a Latin could have expressed himself in just this way, a Latin who was also a man of the world, with the sophisticated charm which such a term connotes.

When hearing the rare revivals of *Manon Lescaut,* people are apt to exclaim, "Why, it sounds just like *Bohème* and *Butterfly.*" They obviously forget that *Manon Lescaut* preceded *Bohème* by three years and *Butterfly* by eleven. Nor do they realize that in *Manon Lescaut* one can find Puccini's formula for success quite complete—all the musical features, all the stage-wise tricks, if you will, that were to appear refined and crystalized in his later operas.

. . . . . .

As in his later operas, Puccini blithely dispensed with any formal overture or prelude in *Manon Lescaut.* After twenty-eight measures of brisk, energetic music in the bright key of A major, *allegro brillante,* the curtain rises on the inn at Amiens, where the coach from Arras is awaited. Edmondo, a poet, is commenting on love, surrounded by a group of students and townsfolk. In his opening *Ave, sera gentile,* he speaks of stars and zephyrs, perfumes and swallows.

Des Grieux now appears and sings his opening *Tra voi, belle brune e bionde.* Immediately Puccini begins his sketch of a complete musical portrait with no little assurance in his touch. Through this brief and gay aria, you feel that Des Grieux has not yet met his fate and that under the semblance of gaiety he is a young man predisposed for a grand passion. The choral comments foreshadow the Café Momus scene in *Bohème* in their general musical structure.

A horn announces the arrival of the coach from Arras. The soldier, Lescaut, the elderly beau, Géronte, and finally, Manon descend from the conveyance. *Dio! Quanto e bella!* (Heavens! How beautiful she is!) exclaims Des Grieux, his eyes riveted on the exquisite bloom of the young girl. It is love at first sight. During the first meeting of the young people, Puccini employs the key of G major, as he ushers in for the first time the theme of the aria, *Donna non vidi mai,* which we will hear a few minutes later in its entirety and which symbolizes Des Grieux' tender awareness of Manon. The effect adds up to that peculiar brand of Puccini magic, the secret of which never forsook him, even in his final and wonderful *Turandot.*

As Manon leaves to go into the inn, we now hear Des Grieux pouring out his heart in the *Donna non vidi mai,* so effectively suggested just previously. . . .

Puccini again uses this beautiful theme (this time on the cellos) as Manon later descends the stairs of the inn to keep her first shadowy rendezvous with Des Grieux. *Vedete?* she says, *Io son fedele alla parola mia.* (You see? I am faithful to my word.)

Des Grieux is overcome with emotion, and, in the utterly charming scene that follows, discloses Puccini's own innate gallantry and awareness of women. For the first time, we now hear, timidly in the high voices of the orchestra, the theme that forms the basis for the love duet in the second act—first in the orchestra, then in Des Grieux' passionate avowal, and finally in a stretch of brief but soaring duet, which concludes with a typical Puccini climax.

Manon and Des Grieux, as in Massenet's opera, decide to fly to Paris, and thus thwart Lescaut's plan of putting his sister in a convent. When their flight is discovered, Lescaut has a hard time restraining the elderly Géronte from following them.

The dialogue between Lescaut and Géronte, is heard against a choral background based on Des Grieux' opening song, *Tra voi, belle,* sung in the sunny key of G major. With such a device Puccini points up the youth of the fleeing lovers, as against the materialism and the wrinkled age of the determined old fop.

The second act, which discovers Manon living in Paris in great luxury, is really the climax of the opera. Of the entire opera it contains the most typical of Puccini's music. Into the climactic scene between Manon and Des Grieux the composer poured all the concentrated essence of his youth.

Manon is at her dressing table. The silky atmosphere of the boudoir is depicted by Puccini in a little theme, which, curiously enough, has formed the middle portion of Des Grieux' opening song, *Tra voi, belle.* The flash of the curling iron, the flick of powder, the adjustment of a beauty spot have been cleverly suggested by the composer through deft touches of the triangle, flute, harp, and celesta.

Lescaut enters and Manon, who has fled from Des Grieux for the luxuries supplied by Géronte, asks for news of her lover. Lescaut says he has taken to gambling. Manon is overcome with remorse—*E ver! L'ho abbandonato senza un bacio* (It's true! I left him without a sign, a kiss). And now occurs Manon's best known aria, which still appears frequently on recital programs, *In quelle trine morbide,* in which, in true Puccini fashion, she recalls her young lover's caresses. . . .

The scene which follows is a sort of *grande levée,* like the Marschallin's in *Rosenkavalier,* only on a reduced scale and with none of the coarse humor of Hofmannsthal. Maids, flunkeys, hairdresser, and dancing-master, mingle with Géronte and a crowd of elderly admirers. A singer enters (again reminding us of *Rosenkavalier*) and sings a pastoral with choral accompaniment to an orchestration that cleverly simulates the lute. The gallantries, the little insincerities of the eighteenth century, are well realized by Puccini, whose scene hangs admirably together.

Manon's gavotte *L'ora, o Tirsi,* with its brilliant and culminating high C, might be said to be the peak of her worldly power. Never again will she reach such a pinnacle of mundane success.

The levee is over. Géronte and the elderly beaux withdraw. Des Grieux suddenly appears. The young people face each other and Massenet's scene at Saint Sulpice is almost duplicated, except that here Manon has a far easier time bending Des Grieux to her will than in the earlier opera.

The duet gains in momentum, and the soaring phrase, *Cedi, son tua . . . ah vieni colle tue braccia stringi Manon che t'ama* (Yield to me; I am yours! . . . Ah, come and take Manon, who loves you, in your arms) is the mainspring of the entire musical scene.

Nell'occhio tuo profondo io leggo il mio destin (In the depth of your eyes I read my fate) sings the young man on a series of strongly accented notes. One might be tempted to label this the "fate" motive, as Des Grieux' fate does hinge on his passion for Manon. We shall hear this phrase in subsequent portions of the score in moments of stress.

The rest of the act, which is concerned with the discovery of the lovers by the implacable Géronte and the subsequent arrest of Manon on a charge of moral turpitude, contains Des Grieux' celebrated passage, *Ah! Manon mi tradisce il tuo folle pensier*, as he chides the young girl for her insatiable craving for luxury.

The writing here is somber and straightforward, showing the basically serious and contemplative side of Des Grieux' nature. It rises to a dramatic climax of genuine and bitter passion. The act closes with Des Grieux' despairing cry—*Manon! O mia Manon!* twice ascending to a high A natural that must sound, if properly projected, like a lament wrenched from the human soul.

Preceding the third act Puccini has placed an intermezzo which he has labeled "The Journey to Havre." This music depicts the sorrows that have befallen the couple since Manon's arrest and imprisonment. Strings and harp work up an impassioned climax. This brief musical interlude is brought to a close with the "fate" motive reintroduced with an almost hymnlike solemnity. . . .

In the third act of *Manon Lescaut,* Puccini met his first test as a composer dealing with a complex and dramatic situation. His uncanny sense of theater, which was never to desert him, did not fail him here.

Somber orchestral chords are marked by the composer, *misterioso*. The feeling of the iron-grey city in the grip of pre-dawn chill, and the feverish impatience of Des Grieux, as he awaits a glimpse of Manon, who is incarcerated in the guardhouse, are admirably depicted in the music.

Finally a window in the guardhouse opens, and Manon appears at the iron grating. As Des Grieux rushes to her, Puccini creates a moment of great pathos by quoting the principal theme of the second-act love duet high on the strings—*dolcissimo.* It is the same effect of poignant reminiscence under tragic circumstances that he employed with such touching results in the final scenes of *Bohème.*

A lamplighter passes through the street; his grotesque song mingles with the sounds of morning church bells and other noises of the waking city, a forerunner of the shepherd who was to appear seven years later in the last act of *Tosca.*

During the dialogue between the lovers that follows, the fate motive is reintroduced, *animato,* to show the growing resolution of Manon and Des Grieux to keep together, no matter what the circumstances.

To a dolorous theme, the procession of fallen women on their way to deportation files past. The crowd comments as each name is called out: Rosetta! Madelon! Ninette! Claretta! and finally—Manon! This gives rise to a concerted scene—the first of the opera—in which the lovers' voices soar to altitudes of passionate despair over the military calls and commands, the comments of the crowds, and the massive orchestral chords that fall on the ear with the heavy and fateful thud of an axe.

As Manon is taken towards the gangplank for deportation to Louisiana, Des Grieux rushes forwards, confronting the ship's officers—*Ah! guai a chi la tocca! Manon, ti stringi a me!* (Beware, anyone who touches her. Manon, take hold of me!). The young man, reduced to tears, implores the captain to allow him to go on the ship even as a deckhand, if need be, and not to separate him from Manon. His plea takes the form of an impassioned *largo sostenuto* over insistent and accented triplets—*Guardate, pazzo son.* It is one of the most genuine scenes that Puccini ever wrote. Never in his later operas did he sound a note of truth more compelling than Des Grieux' appeal.

So eloquent is his grief, that the captain consents to take him on board. The fate motive is heard thundering triumphantly in the key of E major, *tutta forza.* The curtain descends.

The fourth and final act is a long and protracted duet between the lovers, who are discovered on a vast heath on the outskirts of New Orleans. Massenet was content to let his heroine die at Le Havre, but Puccini's librettists have seen fit to follow the Abbé Prévost to Louisiana.

Savage chords in the brass depict the arid, waterless plain in the New World. Manon is exhausted and can go no further. Des Grieux is distracted with grief as he looks at the limitless horizon. Their duet takes the form of a melody that was the main theme of the Intermezzo, "The Journey to Havre." Despite the heroine's pitiful state, she is able (through some operatic dispensation) to reach a high C of great power with her lover in the climax of the duet.

Manon, left alone, sings her long soliloquy, *Sola, perduta, abbandonata. Non voglio morir!* (I don't want to die!) exclaims Manon in the climax of the music.

Des Grieux returns. He has found nothing. Night descends. With the gathering of the shadows, Manon's strength fails her utterly, and to music suggestive of the death of Margherita in Boïto's *Mefistofele* Manon dies, murmuring *L'amor mio non muor* (My love does not die). The cruel and savage chords that describe the limitless plain reappear as the curtain falls on Des Grieux' despair.

MAX DE SCHAUENSEE

GIUSEPPE VERDI (1813–1901)

Simon Boccanegra

Libretto by Francesco Maria Piave and Arrigo Boïto, based upon a play by Antonio Garcia Gutierrez. First performance in Venice, March 12, 1857.

Characters

Paolo Albiani, gold-spinner, later courtier to the Doge . . . Baritone
Pietro, another Genoese commoner, later courtier . . . Bass
Simon Boccanegra, Genoese corsair, later Doge . . . Baritone
Jacopo Fiesco, Genoese nobleman, later known as Andrea . . . Bass
Maria Boccanegra, later known as Amelia Grimaldi . . . Soprano
Gabriele Adorno, her lover . . . Tenor
Amelia's maidservant . . . Soprano
Captain of the palace guard . . . Tenor

The Story

PROLOGUE. In a square of fourteenth-century Genoa, Paolo and Pietro, leaders of the people's party, plot to gain the power of the aristocracy by electing the popular corsair, Simon Boccanegra, as puppet Doge. Boccanegra accepts their proposal so that he may marry Maria, daughter of the noble Jacopo Fiesco, who has imprisoned her since she bore Boccanegra's child. After a mob of commoners, incited by Pietro, pledge support of the corsair's cause, Fiesco steps from the palace and mourns Maria's death (**Fiesco:** *Il lacerato spirito*—A wretched father's soul). Unaware of the tragedy, Boccanegra asks his friendship, but the implacable old man demands to be given Maria's daughter. Boccanegra laments that the child has disappeared (**Boccanegra:** *Del mar sul lido*—On foreign strand). Despairing of forgiveness for the dishonor he has brought to Fiesco's name, Boccanegra rushes into the deserted palace and is horrified to find Maria, lying in her coffin. As he emerges, a mob hails him as Doge.

ACT I. Twenty-five years have passed. In the garden of the Grimaldi palace, where the embittered Fiesco now lives in hiding under the pseudonym "Andrea," his ward Amelia awaits her lover, Gabriele Adorno (**Amelia**: *Come in quest'ora*—In this auroral hour). The youth has joined Fiesco in a plot to overthrow Boccanegra, and, when he learns from Amelia that the Doge wishes her to marry Paolo, he urges her to remain true to himself (**Gabriele, Amelia**: *Sì, dell'ara il giubilo*—The joy of the altar). When the girl withdraws, Gabriele begs Fiesco for her hand, unperturbed by the news that she is an orphan of unknown parentage. Fiesco bestows his blessing on the youth (**Fiesco, Gabriele**: *Vieni a me*—Come to me). Suddenly Boccanegra arrives and in an interview with Amelia learns that she is his daughter and in love with Gabriele (**Boccanegra, Amelia**: *Figlia! A tal nome palpito*—Daughter, at the name I thrill). Paolo refuses to renounce Amelia and plots with Pietro to abduct her.

While negotiating a treaty between Genoa and Venice in his ducal council room, Boccanegra is interrupted by rioting in the streets. Gabriele breaks into the chamber and demands vengeance for the abduction of Amelia. The girl flings herself between her father and her lover, maintaining that it was Paolo who tried to kidnap her (**Amelia**: *Nell'ora soave*—In the soft, quiet hour). The Doge pleads for peace (**Boccanegra**: *Fratricidi!*—Fratricides!) and bids Paolo curse the man who is guilty of Amelia's abduction.

ACT II. In a room adjoining the Doge's apartment Paolo empties a phial of poison into Boccanegra's cup (**Paolo**: *Me stesso ho maledetto*—Myself have I accursed). Next he tries to turn Fiesco and Gabriele from the Doge's side, suggesting to the former that he win power by murdering Boccanegra and insinuating to the latter that Amelia is being held in the palace for the Doge's pleasure. Gabriele is horrified by this suggestion (**Gabriele**: *O inferno! Amelia qui!*—O fury! My Amelia here!). Amelia enters, but, before she can explain to Gabriele that the Doge is her father, Boccanegra follows. Gabriele quickly hides in an alcove. Amelia asks her father to pardon her lover; he agrees on condition that the young man promise to desert the conspirators. Left alone, the weary ruler drinks Paolo's potion and falls asleep. Gabriele, who has heard nothing, emerges from hiding and draws his knife, but Amelia returns in time to stop him from murdering her father (**Gabriele**: *Suo padre sei tu!*—What, her father . . . thou?). When he learns the truth, Gabriele implores the Doge's forgiveness, and the two men rush off to defend the palace.

ACT III. Through the windows of the ducal palace can be heard the shouts celebrating Boccanegra's victory. Magnanimously he has set most of the rebel leaders free, including Fiesco, but the traitorous Paolo is condemned to death (**Paolo:** *All'estremo supplizio*—To my execution). On his way to the scaffold, tortured by the echoes of Amelia's wedding festivities, he tells Fiesco that he has managed to poison the Doge. A captain announces that revels must end in honor of the fallen heroes of the revolution. Boccanegra staggers in, gravely ill. Fiesco, still bent on revenge, reveals to the Doge his true identity, whereupon he learns who Amelia really is (**Fiesco:** *Delle faci festanti*—Where the torches are gleaming). Stunned, Fiesco tells Boccanegra that Paolo has poisoned him. As the Doge dies, he blesses the newly married Gabriele and Amelia, asking that the young man be proclaimed his successor as Doge (**Boccanegra:** *Gran Dio, il benedici*—From Thy celestial throne). Fiesco, grief-stricken, announces Boccanegra's death to the people.

WHEN Verdi was first meditating "the chocolate project," as he called *Otello*, he became engrossed in a scheme for retouching *Simon Boccanegra*. He had always felt an affection for the more than twenty-year-old work, fully as he recognized its crying defects. He had told Escudier, in Paris, some years earlier that it was monotonous and cold, and as late as November 20, 1880, he wrote Giulio Ricordi: "The score as it stands is impossible. It is too sad, too desolate." A month later he informed Boïto that probably the best thing for the opera would be to do "nothing at all." Nevertheless he went on to say that what he might call "professional reasons" kept him from abandoning the idea of putting *Boccanegra* in order, "without an effort at any rate." Boïto had criticized the piece from a number of angles and Verdi admitted the justness of his views. Yet he added: "You, absorbed in more elevated labors, and with *Otello* on your mind are laboring at a perfection that is here unobtainable. I do not aim so high and, more optimistic than you, refuse to despair. I admit that the table is shaky but, by putting a leg or two in order, I think it can be made to stand upright. I further admit that none of the characters . . . is of a kind to make anyone exclaim, 'What a masterpiece of delineation.' Nevertheless, I think something decent might be made of the personalities of Fiesco and Simon."

As usual, it was Verdi who saw deepest into the basic faults of the opera. These were primarily dramatic, and so far as they could be remedied the composer's stage instincts corrected them. In the pages of Francis Toye's sympathetic biography we read: "The crux of the revision lay in what is, in fact, the second act, the first being called a prologue. Verdi, inspired by some letters of Petrarch, wished to have a scene laid in the Council Chamber at Genoa, wherein the Doge should appeal to the Genoese to remember that both they and the Venetians were Italians. Boïto imagined a scene in the Church of San Siro, which aroused Verdi's warmest admiration but would, he thought, give him too much trouble. Finally, Boïto accepted Verdi's idea and made various slight changes throughout the rest of the libretto. Verdi's revision was far more drastic. Apart from the important new scene he rescored much of the opera and rewrote many passages throughout. These alterations . . . sufficed to assure to *Simon Boccanegra* a definite success . . ."

"Definite success," in the sense of an "enduring" one, is, perhaps, an overstatement. The truth seems to be that *Boccanegra* is one of those organically flawed masterpieces that crowd the pages of operatic literature and which cannot live and cannot die. Like *Macbeth*, like *Don Carlos* and several others, it leads an anomalous existence in a shadowy Verdian hinterland, from which it emerges now and then, only to relapse into obscurity. No doubt the opera is "gloomy" as the composer maintained, and surely Mr. Toye is right when he claims that Boccanegra is the "only interesting person in the opera" and that nobody can fail to appreciate the dark turbulence of much of the dramatic action. It is this which much of the music so faithfully reflects. . . . In short, *Simon Boccanegra* is never likely to be a very popular opera; but, of all the lesser-known operas by the composer, it is perhaps the one most worthy and most susceptible of resurrection." Speaking for myself, I can only say that I find its score incomparably finer than, shall we say, the far more popular and dramatically quite as scrambled *Forza del Destino*, which gained a genuine foothold among us a long time ago.

. . . . .

The *Simon Boccanegra* brought out in Venice in 1857 was a success with the critics and a failure with the public. The Venetian correspondent of the *Gazzetta Musicale* found in the score "something for every taste, beautiful melodies and profound philosophy." The public was abysmally bored, the story dull, gloomy, and confusing. The listeners were right. Verdi's wife wrote that the composer had worked "like a slave" over the score. The libretto this time was the handiwork of Francesco Maria Piave. The worthy but uninspired hack had gone to the Spanish writer, Gutierrez, for his dramatic material and turned out something still more tangled than the book of *Il Trovatore*, which also originated in the mind of that Hispanic dramatist. Whether Boïto would have had better luck with such a fiction had he come on the scene a couple of decades earlier is, of course, anyone's guess. Mr. Toye, at all events, discerns underneath the murky jumble "a noble, well-nigh Shakespearian conception that justifies Verdi's affection for the subject"; and he doubts whether Boïto, incomparably more gifted than Piave, would have fared much better with the material.

Scores of the 1857 version of *Boccanegra* do not grow on every bush, so that a comparative study of the two offers problems. One factor can be claimed for the renovated one: there are creative, technical, and psychological enhancements in the music that Verdi refashioned in 1881 which, compared with the cruder inspirations of 1857, bear certain analogies to what Wagner, in 1860, did in the Parisian *Tannhäuser* as against the Dresden versions of fifteen years earlier. "Throughout the score we find the orchestration changed," says Francis Toye, "sometimes only for a page, the vocal line of key altered, the harmony enriched, the accompaniment figures reworked, for anything from half-a-dozen to a couple of hundred bars. . . . It is obviously impossible to indicate here such minute details, as to the nature of which two examples, taken from the Prologue, will give some idea. They represent the reception by the crowd of Paolo's suggestion that Boccanegra be elected Doge." Here Mr. Toye reproduces five bars of music, from the old and the new editions. In both cases he gives the setting of the words *Simone? il corsaro?* In the former instance Verdi causes the crowds to sing *il corsaro?* in a strident *fortissimo*; in the latter, the *Simone* is shouted *fortissimo* and then, as the throng comes to realize that the new ruler is an ex-pirate, the shocked surprise is indicated by a psychologically subtle triple *pianissimo, sotto voce*, above a sustained G major chord instead of a noisy tremolo harmony as before. In the main Mr. Toye found it difficult to indicate the orchestral alterations made, "because it was Verdi's habit when he changed anything in a score to obliterate or destroy the original. But I was able to gather one characteristic instance where the original scoring was decipherable through the erasure-marks. Nothing could better illustrate than this one bar the general nature of the alterations or the progress made by the master in orchestration in twenty-four years." And the author reproduces in parallel columns a measure for full orchestra at Fiesco's *Simone! Tu!* with violins, flutes, and piccolo playing rising groups of two sixteenth notes and the later bar where these figures supplement enriching syncopations and strongly accented chromatic phrases in octaves and thirds in trumpets, trombones, tuba, and bassoons.

The opening page of the Prologue is, together with the short prelude to *Aïda,* possibly the most lovable introductory music in any of Verdi's operas.

The texture is characteristic mature Verdi, of the post-*Aïda* period, with the *Requiem* just behind the composer and *Otello* just ahead. It is a fluent, placid *Allegro moderato* in E major, with the part writing that distinguishes Verdi's late period, free from earlier commonplaces and vulgarisms. It has a fluidity which leads to the action with an effortless ease, which creates the proper mood of the scene yet is untouched by sinister intimations of conflict. Its tranquil idiom pervades the early pages of the scene. There is a lovely descent of soft chromatic harmony at Simone's first words, *Un amplesso. . . .*

On Fiesco's entrance from the palace, preceded by a noble if somber recitative, there comes the most familiar passage in the entire opera, the *Andante sostenuto, Il lacerato spirito.*

The number is frequently heard as a concert solo but loses much of its melancholy effectiveness when the poignant backstage choral lamentations, *È morta* and the whispered *Miserere,* are omitted. This is one of the pages which Verdi took over intact from the earlier version of the opera. Unaltered, likewise, save in a few details is the ensuing duet of Fiesco and Simon.

Fine pages follow up to the tumultuous chorus, *Viva Simon!* Here, unhappily, is an instance where the composer retained the original with the result that the last pages of the Prologue are rather blemished.

The first act begins charmingly with an orchestral prelude picturing daybreak, with pretty effects for woodwinds and strings. On the heels of this follows a cantabile for Amelia, *Come in questa ora bruna,* the most interesting portion of which is the orchestral accompaniment. The duet which follows between Amelia and Gabriele, her lover, Verdi improved by eliminating a *cabaletta* that originally weakened the musical interest and slowed up the pace of the scene. Amelia presently sings an Andantino in G, *Vieni a mirar la cella marina.* Gabriele has a phrase, *Angiol che dal empireo,* which marks one of Verdi's new additions to the opera. A little canon, *Si, dell'ara il giubilo,* is a shortened version of part of the old score, but its fascination has been heightened by a few shrewd retouches.

The duet of Fiesco and Gabriele is likewise new, though Mr. Toye believes the old one explains the action more clearly. At this point in the original occurred a change of scene. Another duet, this one between Amelia and Simone, is substantially unchanged up to the words, *Ah, se la speme,* where a new accompanying cello figure and a quantity of other retouches are to be heard. The second scene, culminating in the great finale, had originally been a wholly conventional festival scene, with noisy vengeance choruses and a grand ballet of African pirates. In the new edition this scene in the council chamber is, in its tumultuous splendor, probably the peak of the opera. Everything here is grandiose and powerful—the orchestral writing, the expressive silences, the declamation, the muttered curses, and Amelia's prayer for peace. Certainly the ensemble developed out of *Il suo commosso accento* is almost unsurpassed in the whole range of Verdi.

The second act is a more uneven performance. The third, on the other hand attains a higher level, though it has the earmarks of the composer's earlier rather than his later style. Yet the opening pages, up to the entrance of Boccanegra, are new, as is the wedding chorus. Boccanegra's 6–8 solo and his contemplations of the sea, *Il mare, il mare,* are strangely moving. Fiesco has a conspicuously effective solo, *Come un fantasima.* A final quartet for solo voices was one of the results of Verdi's revision; the composer seems to have been particularly eager to point up the phrase, *non morrai.* The concluding episode was greatly changed. The seven bars of soft descending chords and the last whisper for the peace of Simon's spirit make a heart-shaking close.

HERBERT F. PEYSER

GIACOMO PUCCINI (1858–1924)

Turandot

Libretto by Giuseppe Adami and Renato Simoni, based upon Schiller's version of a play by Carlo Gozzi. First performance in Milan, April 25, 1926.

Characters

A Mandarin	Baritone
Liù, a young slave girl	Soprano
The Unknown Prince, Calaf	Tenor
Timur, his father	Bass
Pu-Tin-Pao, the Executioner	
The Persian Prince	
Turandot, Princess of China	Soprano
Ping, the Grand Chancellor	Baritone
Pang, the General Purveyor	Tenor
Pong, the Chief Cook	Tenor
The Emperor Altoum, father of Turandot	Tenor

The Story

ACT I. A vast crowd of people has assembled at the walls of legendary Peking to hear the announcement of a Mandarin. The Prince of Persia is to be executed at the rising of the moon. As suitor of the princess Turandot he has failed to answer the three questions by which she tests her future consort. The people demand instant death and surge near the bastions, hurling to the ground the aged Timur. A young slave girl, Liù, tries vainly to protect him until a youth appears, an unknown prince who recognizes Timur as his father, the vanquished king of Tartary. Both men are in hiding, their throne occupied by a usurper. They stand aside as the crowd, moved to pity by the sight of the young Persian prince, begs Turandot for mercy. The princess appears radiant in the moonlight, and the Unknown Prince, Calaf, instantly falls in love with her. Vainly the three ministers of state, Ping, Pang, and Pong, try to dissuade him (**Ping, Pang, Pong:** *Notte senza un lumicino*—Dense night without light). Vainly Liù, who humbly loves Calaf, adds her plea. The prince begs her to care for his father should he be left alone (**Calaf:** *Non piangere, Liù!*—Weep not, Liù). Not even force can restrain Calaf's ardor. Three times he strikes the gong to signify his suit for the hand of Turandot.

ACT II. The three ministers furtively join forces in a pavilion of the palace to prepare for a future wedding or funeral. They lament the numerous executions under Turandot's reign (**Ping, Pang, Pong:** *Ho una casa*—I have a house). They pray that love may once more rule the country, but the approaching festivities for the contest call them back to harsh reality.

The court has gathered at the foot of a great staircase leading to the imperial palace. Here the ancient Emperor Altoum urges Calaf to withdraw, but the young man remains adamant. After the Mandarin announces the terms of the contest, Turandot mounts the throne. She describes how her ancestress, Princess Lou-Ling, was murdered by a conquering prince. In revenge she will deny herself to all men (**Turandot:** *In questa reggia*—Within this palace). But Calaf persists in his suit. Turandot proclaims the three enigmas: a phantom which is reborn daily in the heart of man, a fever which grows cold at death, the ice that fires its lover. One by one Calaf declares the answers: the phantom is hope, the fever is blood, the ice is herself, Turandot. The princess begs her father to save her from the victorious stranger, but the Emperor demands that she remain true to her oath. Furiously Turandot asks Calaf whether he will accept her, bitter as she is. His answer is magnanimous. He will free her by forfeiting his own life if she can answer one riddle before the dawn—she must tell his real name. Turandot consents and after the Emperor commends Calaf for his courage the people chant a hymn in praise of their ruler.

ACT III. In the gardens of the palace Calaf listens to the voices of the heralds: no one is to sleep that night in the city (**Calaf:** *Nessun dorma*—No one shall sleep). The ministers tempt the prince to reveal his identity, for Turandot has ordered that all must die unless she learns the name by dawn. The guards drag in Timur and Liù, whom they have seen with Calaf. Turandot comes from the palace. Ping suggests that torture will force the captives to speak. Liù cries out that she alone knows the prince's name but that even torture will not make her reveal it. Keeping the secret is the only offering she can make to show her love for him (**Liù:** *Principessa, l'Amore*—Princess, 'tis love). She snatches a dagger from a soldier and kills herself. Timur kneels despairing at her side until the girl is borne away. Turandot's attendants have veiled the princess, but now Calaf commands her to lift her veil and view the blood that was shed for her (**Calaf:** *Principessa di morte*—Princess of death). The princess still spurns her lover, but he is undeterred and clasps her in his arms. For the first time she feels emotion. Calaf has won. Secure in his love, he reveals his name. For a moment her pride returns, and she commands him to appear with her before the people.

Once more the court gathers before the Emperor at the foot of the imperial staircase. Turandot approaches and confesses she knows the name of the stranger: it is Love. Calaf rushes to embrace her as the populace rejoices in the new-found happiness of their country.

IT is often intriguing to speculate on what a composer might have written if he had lived longer, and this is especially tantalizing when the works of his last years show some striking change in style from the earlier ones. Was Schubert's real creativity only beginning? What might Beethoven have done with ten more years? And where was Puccini's musical thought leading him when he produced his last opera?

For *Turandot* is a new world for Puccini. The listener who expects a kinship with *Butterfly* will be startled; the composer does employ some of the same techniques to suggest an oriental atmosphere, but there is a new climate in both the music and the drama. Not since the youthful *Le Villi* had he treated a fantasy; now, after a succession of realistic and predominantly intimate works, he turned to a legendary extravaganza in which the hero and heroine are never alone together until fifteen minutes before the final curtain. The music reflects the grand scale of the plot as well as the fairy-tale stylization of the characters. Then, too, twenty years had passed since *Butterfly*, twenty years of rapid development in musical style, and Puccini had been quick to accept the new language and blend it with his own.

Many legendary themes are combined in the story of *Turandot*. The suitor who must solve three riddles in order to win his bride appears in old folk tales all around the world. The number is nearly always three; this may have to do as much with the satisfying dramatic rhythm of the number as with its mystical properties. The first problem creates the suspense, the second balances the first, and the third—usually the most difficult—resolves the tension and leads to success. There are other threesomes in *Turandot:* the trial of the three riddles is precipitated by Calaf's three strokes on the gong and preceded by the Emperor's three attempts to dissuade him from his purpose. Then there are the three ministers, Ping, Pang, and Pong, who provide the only light touch to remind us that this bloodthirsty episode is a fairy tale.

Another mythical theme in the plot is the search for the name of the unknown, the Rumpelstiltskin motif. This, too, is a very ancient story, closely connected with the belief that names in themselves had power and that knowledge of the name gave some magical control over the person. Name-magic was an important part of most primitive religions. An Egyptian legend, for example, tells how the sorceress Isis tricked the sun god Ra into revealing his name to her, thereby giving her mastery over him and all the other gods. If the true name of a god could not be found, all prayer was useless.

In addition, one finds a symbolic element in the libretto that is particularly interesting in connection with the Isis-Ra legend: the association of Turandot with the moon and Calaf with the sun. When the moon rises, the unsuccessful suitor must be beheaded; if Turandot cannot discover Calaf's name by dawn, he triumphs. Turandot first appears illuminated by moonlight, a vision of icy splendor, but after the kiss she weeps, "It is the dawn! Turandot's light is failing." Besides the legendary linking of the moon with chastity, and the consideration of what science tells us of the relative temperatures of the moon and sun, there is still another strain of legend here: the two "energy modes" of ancient Chinese belief, Yin and Yang. Yin is the force of the mysterious, cold, dark, destructive—and feminine. Yang is the masculine force, positive, warm, light- and life-giving. Evil spirits possess Yin; good ones, Yang. The two must exist together, balancing one another in the continual duality of life; night and day, ebb and flow, decay and growth. When Turandot cries out, "The enigmas are three, death is one!" and the prince answers, "The enigmas are three, *life* is one!" they bring Yin and Yang into direct conflict; yet they must exist together, their opposing natures necessary parts of a whole.

As usual when his libretto had a foreign setting, Puccini took care to become acquainted with some of the music of the country and to incorporate its characteristics into his work. Much of the oriental atmosphere is created through the orchestration, with the dry brilliance of piccolo and xylophone, the tinkle of glockenspiel and celesta, the shimmer of harps and the high violin harmonics cleverly suggesting the colors of Chinese instruments. The percussion section is considerably larger than usual, with such instruments as the Chinese gong and the tam-tam added to the customary ones. The result is a score of great tonal variety and breathtaking contrasts.

One easily recognized characteristic of oriental music is its pentatonic or five-note scale, equivalent in spacing to the black keys on the piano. Puccini used several authentic Chinese melodies of this type in his score, most prominently in the ceremonial scenes. For instance, the following melody recurs several times in the course of the opera, always in connection with Turandot herself—her appearance at the execution, the trial, and finally at the moment when she confesses that love has conquered her:

. . . . .

Puccini employs other unusual scales to suggest an exotic atmosphere, though one not specifically Chinese. An altered minor scale, containing an augmented second, has been a favorite with composers for evoking the mystic East. It is used in a poignant elegy as the Persian Prince is led to his execution.

Combined with modal harmonies and an occasional touch of the whole-tone scale, these devices lend a mysterious, otherworldly quality to many pages of the score. None of this was new to Puccini: all of it had been done in *Butterfly*. What could be added to catch the brutal spirit of *Turandot,* with its scenes of torture, its sadistic heroine, its crowd mad with joy at the prospect of a beheading?

Puccini found the answer in one of the many innovations that were revolutionizing the music of his time: polytonality, the combining of two keys to create a new and powerful effect. Charles Ives had experimented with this idea early in the century, and Stravinsky had brought it to world prominence, establishing it firmly as a new direction for music. Always curious about the works of his contemporaries, Puccini had followed these developments with alert interest. Although he had his reservations on first hearing *Le Sacre du Printemps,* he later spoke with great admiration of Stravinsky and acknowledged the younger composer's influence on his own style. Just as the harmonic mists of *Pelléas* had found their way into *Butterfly*, so the clashing tonalities and rhythms of *Le Sacre* provided the needed force for *Turandot*.

We hear the new language as the first curtain rises. The orchestra screams an angular theme, *fortissimo*, like an outcry of vengeance:

This motif, ambiguous as to key, seems to characterize the savagery of the executioner and the crowd waiting for him. In a quicker tempo, it becomes mocking laughter. Immediately a Mandarin begins to read the notice of the coming execution, accompanied by solemn repeated chords:

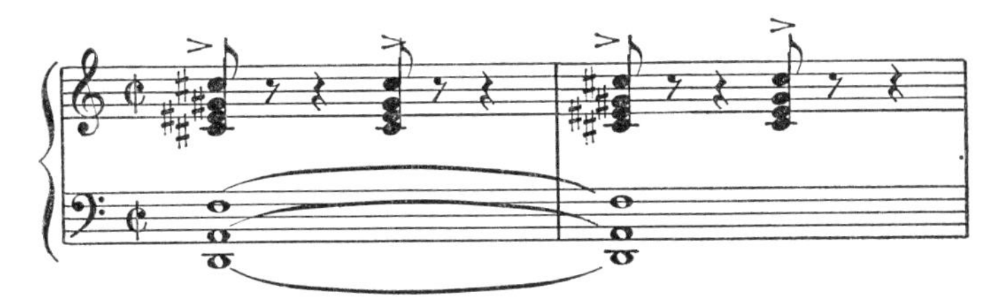

Here is the basic idea of polytonality—the tension of one chord against another, in this case C sharp major against D minor, A major against B flat minor. The fact that the tonic notes of each combination are only a half step apart—the greatest possible dissonance—intensifies the sting of the harmonies.

. . . . .

A polytonal passage can create a rich nocturnal effect, as in the opening measures of Act III:

. . . or, stripped down to two stark lines with no tones at all in common, it can emphasize the cruelty of Liù's torture:

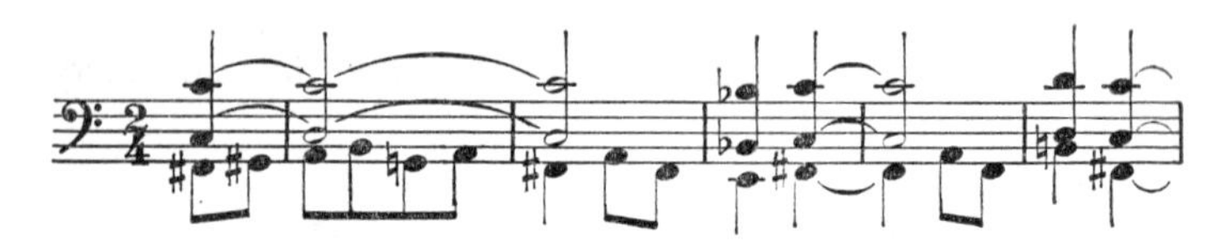

This is the most Stravinskian passage of all, strongly reminiscent of a page of *Le Sacre*. The lower line is the theme from the wild chorus of executioners in Act I; the upper one is a long-drawn *ostinato* figure that builds a sinister force through repetition.

For the most part, the barbaric elements appear in the great choral scenes, which dominate the first act and maintain unusually high importance through the rest of the opera. One might almost call *Turandot* a Chinese *Boris* in this respect; the emotion of an angry or frightened mob is often the composer's main concern. Indeed, there is a strong touch of Mussorgsky's technique in the handling of the choral voices and the gleaming crescendo of the processions.

Yet among all the influences and borrowings of exotic color, the more familiar Puccini style appears unmistakably. We hear his sweet, ardent melody in Calaf's *Nessun dorma* and the nostalgic moments of Ping, Pang, and Pong. We enjoy his gift for building suspense by economical means, as in the scene of the riddles. We see his fondness for bizarre contrast in one of the most magical passages of the score, the one in which the crowd awaits the rising of the moon, saluting it with such phrases as "O bloodless one! O lopped-off head!" to music of dreamy luminescence.

And for a characteristic Puccini heroine we turn not to Turandot but to the little slave, Liù. Here the composer is in his element, depicting a gentle and sympathetic girl whose music, from her first phrase onward, tells us that she is marked for disaster. She is rather like Butterfly in her youth, her devotion, and her readiness to die when necessary, and, though the libretto does not allow Puccini to develop her into a full-scale heroine, he does bestow upon her the most moving music of the score. There is little attempt at exoticism here. To be sure, her brief plea to Calaf in the first act is pentatonic, and her final aria is accompanied by delicate *chinoiserie* in the orchestra, but her language is pure operatic Italian. The artist of "the little things" was at his finest in these pages; few scenes in all opera convey as deep or true a pathos as old Timur's lament over Liù's body and the prayers of the people as she is carried away.

It is a pity, after all the care that Puccini put into choosing the text of the last duet between Turandot and Calaf, that he did not live to compose it. He set the icy princess to some of the most forbidding music ever required of a singer, but for the melting of the ice he left only sketches. What a challenge it would have been to him to show a sudden reversal of personality, to reveal a real woman, capable of warmth and suffering, emerging from her hard shell! Did Alfano come close to what was in the composer's mind, or would Puccini have expanded the duet in some other direction? Once the icy control was gone, what music might he have written for Turandot?

As usual, it is intriguing to speculate.

KATHERINE GRIFFITH McDONALD

ALBAN BERG (1885–1935)

Wozzeck

Libretto by the composer, after the drama by Georg Büchner. First performance in Berlin, December 14, 1925.

Characters

Captain	Tenor
Franz Wozzeck, a soldier	Baritone
Andres, his friend	Tenor
Marie, Wozzeck's mistress	Soprano
Margret, her neighbor	Mezzo-soprano
Marie's child	Speaking part
Drum major	Tenor
Doctor	Bass
First apprentice	Bass
Second apprentice	Baritone
Fool	Tenor
Soldier	Tenor
Townsman	Tenor

The Story

ACT I. A sadistic German captain is being shaved in his comfortable quarters by Franz Wozzeck, a simple-minded soldier whom the officer taunts with riddles about time and morality. Wozzeck replies to an attack on his unblessed union with Marie, who has borne him a child, by quoting the Gospel: "Suffer little children to come unto Me." Unprepared for such an answer, the captain demands an explanation. The soldier stammers that the poor cannot afford virtue; their lot is drudgery (**Wozzeck:** Poor folk like us). Disturbed, the officer admonishes him not to think too much.

Cutting sticks in an open field, Wozzeck is seized by weird hallucinations. While his friend Andres sings a song about the huntsman's life, Wozzeck imagines that the setting sun has kindled a fire through the world.

From the window of her wretched cottage Marie, her child in her arms, watches a military band led by the dashing drum major. Her neighbor Margret notes her intense interest and incurs her anger. Marie puts her child to sleep (**Marie:** Maiden, what song shall you sing?). Wozzeck pays her a brief visit and tells her of his fearful visions. She cannot seem to calm him and tries to follow as he rushes away.

To help support his family Wozzeck visits the laboratory of a doctor, who uses him as a guinea pig in unorthodox experiments. The short-tempered doctor exacts from his patient a tangled explanation of his behavior, at the end of which Wozzeck cries out desperately for Marie. Satisfied with Wozzeck's obedience, the doctor gloats that he will win immortality through his discoveries.

Marie admires the drum major, who struts before her in the street. Unable to resist his advances, she leads him into the house.

ACT II. Back at home, with her little boy in her lap, Marie tries on a pair of earrings given her by the drum major. When the child disturbs her reveries, she frightens him into silence. Wozzeck enters, and the guilty woman tries unsuccessfully to hide the earrings. She lies that she has found them, whereupon the man looks mournfully at the sleeping child and laments their fate. Wozzeck gives Marie his wages. After he has left she bitterly berates herself.

On the street the captain and doctor talk morbidly of sickness and death. Wozzeck, rushing past, is stopped by them and mocked with allusions to his wife's infidelity (**Doctor:** A fine, long beard). Wozzeck runs away in confusion.

Standing in front of her house, Marie is accused wildly by Wozzeck. When he starts to strike her, she tells him that she would rather have a knife-blade in her breast than his hand upon her. She goes into the house; Wozzeck staggers away, whispering, "Better a knife-blade."

Two drunken apprentices stumble about the dance floor of a beer garden, muttering foolishly. The band begins to play. Wozzeck sees Marie and the drum major passionately embracing in a lurid waltz and cries out to heaven for justice. Andres sings a folk song with a group of revellers (**Chorus:** A hunter from the South). He then joins Wozzeck, whom he tries to calm. One of the apprentices delivers a sermon, "Wherefore then is Man?", lapsing into stupor when the band strikes up again. An idiot tells Wozzeck that he smells blood. As Marie and her new lover whirl past, Wozzeck moans that everything seems to be twisting in a red mist.

Tossing fitfully in his bunk in the barracks, Wozzeck prays for deliverance from temptation. The drunken drum major lurches in, boasting of his conquest of Marie. Wozzeck whistles and turns away. Infuriated, the drum major beats him cruelly.

ACT III. In her shabby room the guilt-ridden Marie reads aloud from the Bible. Tenderly she takes her child into her arms and comforts him. Resuming her reading, she comes upon a passage dealing with Mary Magdalen. She sobs (**Marie:** Saviour! As Thou hadst mercy on her, have mercy on me, Lord).

At dusk Wozzeck leads Marie along a forest path beside a pond. They sit down to rest, and Wozzeck gently kisses her. When a red moon rises, he exclaims that it is the color of blood. Before Marie can escape, he draws his knife, murders her, and silently rushes off.

Seated upon a table in a tavern, Wozzeck applauds the dancing apprentices and their sweethearts. Margret begins a lusty refrain that enrages the soldier (**Margret:** To Swabia I will not go). Seeing blood on Wozzeck's hands, the apprentices question him but receive incoherent rebuffs.

Back at the pond Wozzeck searches desperately for the bloody knife. He finds it and wades into the water, hurling it as far as he can. The doctor and the captain pass by and hear him drown. They hurry away in fear.

In front of Marie's house a group of children play "Ring around the roses." Marie's child rides his hobbyhorse and does not understand when other children run in to tell him that his mother is dead. When they all rush off to see the body, he continues to play, notices that he is alone, and gallops after his friends (**Child:** Hop, hop!).

WE are amazed to learn that the intense, passionate, often wild music of Alban Berg's *Wozzeck* is highly organized in a complex of musical forms and procedures. The first scene is a suite containing a prelude, pavane, gigue, gavotte, and air, and the entire second act is a symphony in five movements with an appropriate formal organization for each movement or scene. Berg himself tells us that we should not be concerned with these formal intricacies while listening to the opera; yet in thinking back on a performance, or in studying the music or text, we cannot help wondering what purpose these devices serve. Do they give us special insights into the plot or the characters? With a little previous study, can they be "heard" in performance, as we hear the form of a Beethoven symphony?

It seems likely that these forms and procedures serve several purposes and thus establish several levels of interpretation in *Wozzeck*. The most immediate aspect of the opera to capture our attention is its atmosphere. The very opening chord, which slides into a tone-cluster with a soft roll on the snare drum, establishes a mood of dark, unstable foreboding. For the second scene, in which Wozzeck, cutting sticks in a field, is possessed by fearful hallucinations, Berg bases the musical material on three chords; these move back and forth from one to another, constantly changing their orchestral color—sometimes muted horns with clarinets, oboes, and bassoons, sometimes in the string section playing *col legno* (drawing the wood of the bow across the strings). In the fourth scene of Act III, when Wozzeck walks into the pond and drowns, a single chord is slid chromatically up the scale in overlapping waves, each at a slower tempo, as the poor, insane wretch is gradually covered by the waters.

But Berg was doing much more than creating an atmosphere for Büchner's dramatic fragments. . . . All the forces in *Wozzeck* sweep the listener and observer into the core of the matter and hurl him headlong into the tragedy of Wozzeck's madness and death. It is as if Berg were trying to make certain that no matter how many different people might approach his opera, they all would be carried along their various avenues toward the same end. The untutored observer will be overwhelmed by the sheer dramatic power of the action, coupled with the intense passion of the music. The Wagnerian will find an array of leitmotifs to mark characters and their emotions and thoughts. Those interested in psychological drama or social protest will find considerable meat in Büchner's grim fragments, made especially striking through Berg's music and stage directions. The exponent of abstract form in music can marvel over the structural intricacy of the work.

Questions of form and unity were foremost in Berg's thinking. The unity inherent in working with the twelve-tone system, rather than the dissolution of tonality or constant variation of pitches which the system claims, later led Berg to adopt it and ultimately to compose a vast operatic structure, *Lulu* (based on Frank Wedekind's two plays *Erdgeist* and *Die Büchse der Pandora*), in which all the musical material derives from a single basic twelve-note series. In *Wozzeck*, other methods achieve structural cohesion and unity. The forms used for each scene of *Wozzeck* supply a structural pattern that relates significantly to the stage action and dialogue, so as to marry the words and music more firmly than is usual in either through-composed or "number" operas. The fantasy and fugue of Act II, Scene 2, is an obvious example of this unity. Here three musical motives are used to designate three characters. The Captain and the Doctor meet in the street and discuss the Captain's ill health. Berg begins the scene with a counterpoint of two themes, the Captain's in the violin and the Doctor's in the bassoon:

*

Wozzeck soon enters, and the two tormentors hint of Marie's infidelity as they talk with him. Berg has arranged three fugal expositions as each of the men speaks in turn; when they speak, shout, or hum together, he develops a frenzied triple fugue on these motives. The result is an extension of the Wagnerian leitmotif technique. The motives are developed in an abstract musical design that parallels the increasing intensity of the dialogue, so that the ultimate climax is twofold: in musical counterpoint and in the counterpointing of personalities.

The previous scene, Act II, Scene 1, is more subtle in its organization. As the first movement in a five-movement symphony it is in sonata-allegro form, with an exposition and a varied repetition, a development section, and a recapitulation. Marie, gazing into the mirror, admires the gold earrings given her by the drum major. Her child is restless and repeatedly interrupts her musings. Wozzeck enters, angry and perplexed over the earrings, but, seeing the sleeping child covered with perspiration, he sorrows over the hardship of the poor. Then to the accompaniment of a long-held C-major triad in the strings—a stunning surprise after the dissonant harmony that has preceded it—Wozzeck gives Marie the money he has earned as a barber for the captain and as a guinea pig for the doctor and leaves the stage. The first theme accompanies not only Marie's musing over the earrings but her receiving of the money. The second theme, a variation of Marie's beautiful Act I lullaby, is used as she tries to quiet the child and again later to point up her feeling of remorse as the curtain falls. The frenzied closing theme, always heard in the brass, both marks the child's fear and restlessness and accompanies the arrival of Wozzeck.

This latter version played by three trombones with mutes outlines the beginning of the motive used in the next scene, played by one trombone, as the fugue subject for Wozzeck.

In *Lulu* Berg used forms as well as motives to mark characters in a kind of leitmotif technique, and the roots of this process can be found in *Wozzeck*. Many of the musical procedures in the opera consist of the elaboration of a single musical idea or "affection," as it is termed in relation to baroque music. They are used in scenes that show Wozzeck's growing madness. Appropriately the final act is a series of inventions, each on a single musical element. . . .

The scene of Wozzeck at the doctor's office is a *passacaglia*—twenty-one variations on a twelve-note bass theme—utilized to emphasize Wozzeck's own *idée fixe* as well as the doctor's theory. But in the final act the *idée fixe* permeates all the music. A single note (B natural) haunts the awful death scene of Marie by the pond, ending in one of the most terrifying crescendos in all music; a single rhythm constantly drives through the tavern scene as Wozzeck vainly attempts to forget his deed; finally, a single chord chases him back to the pond to fetch the knife and drown himself. No musical procedure could articulate more vividly the insanity that drives Wozzeck to murder and suicide. Even after his death, the bitter final scene of the children running off to see the body of Marie pulsates with a rhythmic perpetual motion that finally dissipates into silence.

Berg used these "single affection" processes most consistently in the first and last acts of the opera. Act I is an exposition of his drama and his musical material, wherein we are exposed to Wozzeck's growing insanity, his relation to his two tormentors and his mistress, and Marie's relation to the drum major; therefore the five distinct musical forms are not especially intertwined. For the second act, however—the development section of the drama—Berg uses the form of a symphony, in which the formal structure becomes more complex as the characters are juxtaposed and their relationships fully developed. The frenzied scene in the tavern garden is appropriately an extended scherzo form, its usual waltz rhythm interrupted by such trio-like sections as a drinking song, a hunting chorus, and a mock sermon. The symphonic structure generally tends to organize this act more tightly than the first, as the story draws its characters into closer contact with one another, leading to the final catastrophe of Act III.

How much of this vast ordering can be heard in performance, even after considerable study, is a difficult question. Certainly the motivic structure, with its similarity to Wagner, can be perceived—though many of the motives change throughout the opera as if they were living organisms. Certainly each scene is a structure as satisfying as a movement from a Mozart quartet, even though we cannot follow the details of the pattern. Above all, each performance or hearing reveals new details and thus a deeper sense of the power of the work. The music of Berg's *Wozzeck* is like the aural representation of the *Spiritus Mundi,* which within the bounds of a higher ordering contains the swirling passion, the horror, and the disintegration of the human tragedy.

BRUCE ARCHIBALD

A Guide to 48 Operas on Long-playing Records

by C. J. Luten

Record Critic, *The American Record Guide*, formerly of *Hi-Fi Music at Home* and *Musical America*

A Guide to 48 Operas on Long-playing Records

Since opera is seldom performed in most of the cities of this country, phonograph records will probably play a disproportionately large part in acquainting many readers with the music of the 48 operas covered in this book.

The long-playing record made its first appearance in America over a decade ago and brought with it a new era in opera-listening in the home. Because music in opera is more or less continuous during each act, eliminating side-break interruptions or reducing them, at the most, to one or two afforded an undeniable benefit.

The certain popularity of the long-playing record—both from the point of view of duration and of greater sonic fidelity—was obvious to most record manufacturers from the announcement of the first LP. For that reason and because it was easier and less expensive to record on tape and produce the disc from the tape than to record directly on the disc, manufacturers rushed to provide a new repertory on LP. The consequence of this hurry was a number of records which, for musical and mechanical reasons, are less than acceptable today but which at the time filled a need. A number of these recordings are, as one would expect, now out of print. Most of the recordings that have appeared since the original edition of this book have been prepared with greater care than many of the earlier ones discussed in the following pages. This is not to say that a number of the earlier ones were not done with the best available skills. Many were. Some, indeed, are unique, and we will undoubtedly be playing them for years to come.

The latest landmark in the history of the phonograph is stereophonic recording. The first stereo discs, in 1958, literally gave the listener a new dimension in sound. As against the flat perspective of even the best monophonic recording, a fine stereo record or 4-track stereo tape offers new depth and spaciousness, greater clarity of detail and differentiation of timbre, and a kind of "presence" that must be heard to be believed. Always the greatest challenge to recording engineers because of its large forces and enormous variety of vocal and instrumental combinations, opera is perhaps the major beneficiary of stereophonic recording. Not only does good stereo recording clarify the sound of even the largest forces, but it transmits the fixed positions and the very movement of characters in an opera. With stereo, it takes little imagination to see the movements of the opera's characters through the mind's eye.

The aim in this revised edition has been to cover all the complete or nearly complete recordings on disc and 4-track tape readily available in the United States in November, 1961 of the 48 operas covered in this volume. Recordings on certain labels, such as Cetra and Electrola, are listed and discussed only if they can be said to represent outstanding quality or when a certain recording is the only one or one of two renditions of a particular opera. I have not discussed recordings of excerpts for reasons of space, and because I feel that the only way to grasp the significance of even an aria is to discover and assimilate it in its context. This is, after all, what the composer intended one to do.

The reader will shortly become aware that in recorded opera, though I admire and enjoy splendid vocalism as much as the next singing enthusiast, I respect even more a performer's ability to make a character come to life. Recording an opera makes the singer's ability to act with his voice a requirement of the utmost importance. Opera is theater, and on records sound alone tells us what is going on. The rest is left to the imagination.

In the following section the material under each opera follows a definite form. Recordings are listed in order of preference. The first listing names the singers and the character each portrays. Subsequent listings give only the singers, but the roles taken are always given in the same order as in the first listing. Space limitations forbid the listing of any but principal singers in the opera and the name of the conductor, chorus, and orchestra. Each entry includes, of course, the name of the record manufacturer, the serial number of the recording, and its availability in a stereo edition. In parentheses is the number of records contained in the set. If a recording is available as a 4-track stereophonic tape, this fact is noted along with the serial number of the tape.

As for the engineering merits of each monophonic recording listed, I have called attention only to those recordings that have qualities that seem to me either outstanding or substandard. Where the engineering is not mentioned, it may be considered average and acceptable. The relative newness of stereophonic sound has caused me to describe the technical aspects of several such recordings in detail.

My gratitude is due to many of my friends and colleagues for help and encouragement in producing this discography. My first thanks go to my wife, who has given advice, editorial assistance, and sympathy all along the way. Among others, I must mention Peter Hugh Reed and James Lyons, in whose magazine, *The American Record Guide*, many of my reviews have appeared; also Will Lerner of the Music Masters record shop and Abner Levin of the Sam Goody record shop, both of whom lent me records I could not otherwise obtain. The cooperation of Jack Romann of Capitol and Angel Records, Bob Kotlowitz and John Kurland of RCA Victor, Jack Frizzell of Columbia Records, Leonard Marcus of London Records, and Bill Muster of United Stereo Tapes, has been indispensable in the preparation of this revision of my annotated list of recordings.

AÏDA. Zinka Milanov (Aïda), Fedora Barbieri (Amneris), Jussi Bjoerling (Radames), Leonard Warren (Amonasro), Rome Opera Chorus and Orchestra, Jonel Perlea; Victor LM-6122 (3).

Maria Callas, Fedora Barbieri, Richard Tucker, Tito Gobbi, La Scala Chorus and Orchestra, Tullio Serafin; Angel 3525 (3).

Renata Tebaldi, Giulietta Simionato, Carlo Bergonzi, Cornell MacNeil, Singverein der Gesellschaft der Musikfreunde and the Vienna Philharmonic Orchestra, Herbert von Karajan; London A-4345 or OSA-1313 (stereo) (3); LOR-90015 (4-track tape).

Herva Nelli, Eva Gustafson, Richard Tucker, Giuseppe Valdengo, Chorus and NBC Symphony Orchestra, Arturo Toscanini; Victor LM-6122 (3).

The Victor and Angel *Aïdas,* originally released in 1955, solved the old problem of finding a convincing LP performance of Verdi's brilliant theater piece. None of the recordings of *Aïda* released since the first edition of this book has been able to match them for over-all artistic merit, but the London effort offers quite the best monophonic engineering and, in its stereophonic registration, sets new standards in opera recording.

With this *Aïda,* and several other recent stereophonic operatic recordings commented on elsewhere in these pages, London has led its listeners to expect thorough musical preparation, exemplary mechanical polish, and thoughtful experimentation with dramatic effect. It is particularly in the latter area that London has piqued the interest of those who rightly view opera as something more than an extended vocal recital in costume. The listener in his home now begins to have the feeling of possessing an "opera house without walls" (to paraphrase Malraux's "museums without walls," his comment on the result of the wide distribution of high-grade prints). *Aïda* has, of course, provided ample opportunity for London and its performers to show off. This writer surveys the results with mixed feelings but admits that there are certain thrills to shake even the most sophisticated listener.

The stereo recording is a case in point. It has an extremely wide range and, for once, Verdi's pianissimi and fortissimi can be appreciated. Moreover, with the single exception of the Judgment Scene, where the use of an echo chamber is too much in evidence, all the unusual space effects—*e.g.,* the Temple Scene with the off-stage priestess, the victorious chorus overheard by Aïda and Amneris, the ensembles in the Triumphal Scene, the distant chorus at the magical opening of the third act—emerge in an imaginative and relevant manner, easy to accept. The recording gives a full measure of justice to the superb playing of the Vienna Philharmonic and the extraordinary singing of the Musikfreunde Singverein.

Where it seems to be less than ideal is in its too distant placement of solo singers. We have, of course, had our fill of "star recordings," in which the voice is exaggerated and the accompaniment minimized. The London recording, however, goes to the opposite extreme. Those who have heard Tebaldi's Aïda in the theater, for example, know that it is fuller and larger in sound than what we get here. Simionato's voice is even more gravely penalized. In the big opera house it is just large enough for Amneris. Here, her less than ideal vocal refulgence for the role is emphasized.

There are, in addition, orchestral passages, such as the first fortissimo in the overture, where the texture is somewhat smudged by what appears to be too much reverberation. Happily, there are few such incidents, and, all things considered, none of us has ever before heard this much of *Aïda* in our homes.

Herbert von Karajan, the guiding spirit of this performance, has rehearsed his forces to a fare-thee-well. One does not get such coherent sonorities, such fine internal balances, such precise attacks without special preparation and a thorough knowledge of the score. Yet, for all his skill, I cannot report that he really leaves me satisfied with this *Aïda.* His work is meticulous, astonishingly accurate in matters of attack and chording, frequently sensitive; but it is not consistently arresting. The pacing is sometimes too broadly conceived, and there are too many occasions—particularly in the first act—when Karajan fails to maintain consecutive tension. This manifests itself in some slack phrasing and in a long line that turns flabby, and there are moments that cry for an all-out approach, that extra excitement which, among conductors of recorded *Aïdas,* only Toscanini gives us.

Karajan's vocal associates are certainly among the best one could expect at the moment. Tebaldi sings with beautiful tone, though she is a trifle uncomfortable above the staff. On this occasion, she has curbed to some extent her tendency to distend many phrases inappropriately; and for this, I suspect we had better thank Karajan. She is a rather more dramatic Aïda than one had expected, though she is still outdistanced by Callas and Milanov. It may seem difficult to believe that Tebaldi can throw away such a line as *Imprecherò la morte a Radames* . . .

a lui ch'amo pur tanto in her first-act aria, but she manages to do so. I have already commented on the vocal attributes of Simionato as Amneris. I need now only give credit to her fine-grained characterization and her commendable restraint.

From the viewpoint of vocal size and brilliance, Bergonzi is hardly anyone's dream of Radames, but his musical taste is evident when he is not up against the terrors of the difficult passages in *Celeste Aïda* or when a line calls for nothing less than a tone of extreme power and tension. Cornell MacNeil is an acceptable Amonasro, and one suspects he will one day be a fine one. He is a sound musician. His voice is of good size, and it is firm and flexible. The tone is pleasing if not luxurious. His most serious fault at the moment lies in his inability to color many of the key words of his role.

To sum up, this is, all in all, a better than respectable *Aïda*, and that will be enough for those who love the work and want to hear it in stereo. Those whose paramount interest is in the best performance, however, will turn to the 1955 Victor set.

Though she was possibly past her vocal zenith at the time of this recording, Milanov presents an effective and believable Aïda with an authority gathered over the many years she has sung the role. Her voice, one of the most beautiful of our day, is manipulated with good musical taste and projected in what earlier generations would have called "the grand manner." Not quite so masterful but as successful in terms of natural vocal beauty, theatrical color, and personal enthusiasm is Barbieri's Amneris. The Radames of the late tenor Jussi Bjoerling is a phonographic curiosity. It is triumphant for musical distinction, dramatic intensity, and stylistic elegance; but it was not for the large opera house, for Bjoerling's voice was a small one when measured against Verdi's requirements for the role. Still the accomplishment is here on these tastefully recorded discs for one to enjoy at will. One of the late baritone Leonard Warren's chief glories was his ability to sing a broad cantilena with controlled fervor and beauty of tone, and he received a fine opportunity to display this skill in the second-act ensemble, which Amonasro dominates. In the third act, Warren manages an approximation of the requisite bravura style, but he lacks vocal poise in the more savage portions of his duet with Aïda. The supporting roles are well sung. Perlea paces his performance effectively; the chorus and orchestra are acceptable.

The Angel recording is excellent for clarity and resonance, but the voices are favored more than is ideal. Callas, aside from a few sustained high notes that are afflicted with a strong beat, is possibly the best Aïda on records. Her vocal coloring and flexibility are astonishing; her dramatic powers, notably persuasive. With engineering assistance, Tucker is close to the most satisfying phonographic Radames, and Barbieri is a more sensitive artist under Serafin than she was under Perlea. Gobbi does not have Warren's beauty of tone, but he is superior in the bravura passages. The secondary singers are not up to those in the Victor recording, but the chorus sings with precision and refinement. Serafin conducts with his usual authority; however, his performance catches fire but briefly until the latter half of the opera, from which point it burns with a steady glow.

The older Victor recording, which preserves the Toscanini-led *Aïda* broadcasts, dates back to 1949. The sound is as substandard as one would expect, and the vocalists, clearly nervous and on edge, are poorer than anyone has a right to expect. Be that as it may, this performance is memorable for the sheer incandescence of the late Maestro's effort. His masterful shaping of the score, his powerful phrasing that creates a rising curve of cumulative dramatic tension, the superb playing he drew from his orchestra—these are unique and unforgettable accomplishments.

UN BALLO IN MASCHERA. Herva Nelli (Amelia), Jan Peerce (Riccardo), Robert Merrill (Renato), Virginia Haskins (Oscar), Claramae Turner (Ulrica), Robert Shaw Chorale and NBC Symphony Orchestra, Arturo Toscanini; Victor LM-6112 (3).

Maria Callas, Giuseppe Di Stefano, Tito Gobbi, Eugenia Ratti, Fedora Barbieri, La Scala Chorus and Orchestra, Antonino Votto; Angel 3557 (3).

Antonietta Stella, Gianni Poggi, Ettore Bastianini, Giuliana Tavolaccini, Adriana Lazzarini, La Scala Chorus and Orchestra, Gianandrea Gavazzeni; Deutsche Grammophon LPM-18680/82 or SLPM-18680/82 (stereo) (3).

The last complete operatic broadcast Toscanini gave before his retirement took place on January 17 and 24, 1954. It was *A Masked Ball*, a wonderful score very near to his heart. This opera, like most of the others that he broadcast, has found its way to LP discs bearing many of his characteristic artistic thumbprints—the hair-raising intensity built up out of rhythmic alacrity and usually strict maintenance of tempi, the succession of sharply contoured phrases, each with its inner tensions building to and receding from climaxes of awesome fury. On this occasion he got spectacularly beautiful playing from his NBC Orchestra, vibrant singing from the Robert Shaw Chorale, and far above average performances from his vocal soloists. Peerce, for instance, though dry of voice, gave a fine performance in immaculate Italian style. The others were not far behind. Merrill, without all his original freshness of voice, sang well except for an overloud *Eri tu*. Although Nelli was vocally uneven, she rose to unexpected heights from time to time, particularly in the Love Duet. Haskins made a very light-voiced but high-spirited Oscar. Turner lacks the tonal impact to make the most of Ulrica's pronouncements, but she sang intelligently. The recording, then, is surely required listening for anyone interested in Italian opera. A word about the recording: the first act, which comprises the first broadcast, lacks the spaciousness and ring of the subsequent acts recorded the following week.

Better recorded and almost as arresting as the Victor set is the more recent Angel issue. Unlike its competitor, it is not quite a distinguished *tout ensemble*. Nevertheless, this performance boasts irresistible portraiture and some superb singing by Gobbi and Callas, as well as mostly firm, idiomatic support by Votto and La Scala's excellent forces. Insufficient grace and style mar the contributions of the vocally-well-endowed Di Stefano and Barbieri; Ratti, though musicianly, is rather shrill-voiced.

A superb recording, and the first stereo edition of *Ballo* we have had, comes from Deutsche Grammophon. It conveys with stunning realism a flickeringly effective performance, with outstanding dramatic singing from Bastianini (perhaps the most impressive he has offered on records). From the young soprano Tavolaccini comes the most persuasive Oscar this listener has encountered in two decades. Lazzarini makes a sinister and recognizably human Ulrica. Stella, in her best voice, presents a shadowy characterization, but here and there she does enter into the dramatic situation. Although Poggi has shown, for him, unusual musical care in his preparation of Riccardo, he communicates no knowledge of the character. The absence of brilliance at the top of his voice and his scooping attacks are other factors that mark Poggi as the chief weakness in the cast. Gavazzeni's conducting is curiously uneven. It has color and alacrity in the most dramatic pages of the opera, *e.g.*, the laughing ensemble that closes the second act and the episode of the drawing of lots. Elsewhere, it is often slack, and some of the tempi are often too deliberate.

IL BARBIERE DI SIVIGLIA. Robert Merrill (Figaro), Roberta Peters (Rosina), Cesare Valletti (Almaviva), Fernando Corena (Bartolo), Giorgio Tozzi (Basilio), Metropolitan Opera Chorus and Orchestra, Erich Leinsdorf; Victor LM-6143 or LSC-6143 (stereo) (4).

Tito Gobbi, Maria Callas, Luigi Alva, Fritz Ollendorff, Nicola Zaccaria, Philharmonia Chorus and Orchestra, Alceo Galliera; Angel 3559 or S-3559 (stereo) (3).

Renato Capecchi, Gianna D'Angelo, Nicola Monti, Giorgio Tadeo, Carlo Cava, Chorus and Bavarian Radio Orchestra, Bruno Bartoletti; Deutsche Grammophon LPM-138665/7 or SLPM-138665/7 (stereo) (3).

Ettore Bastianini, Giulietta Simionato, Alvinio Misciano, Fernando Corena, Cesare Siepi, Chorus and Orchestra of the Florence May Festival, Alberto Erede; London A-4327 (3).

Gino Bechi, Victoria de los Angeles, Nicola Monti, Melchiorre Luise, Nicola Rossi-Lemeni, Chorus and Milan Symphony Orchestra, Tullio Serafin; Capitol GCR-7138 (3).

The choice between the Victor and Angel recordings is difficult; one could take pleasure in either. The Victor is, however, a superb recording, whereas the Angel is unevenly engineered, and in the Victor stereo version, there are touches of theatrical realism not present in the Angel. Moreover, the Victor is the only nearly complete *Barber* (at last one can hear Almaviva's brilliant aria in the last act); all other sets, including the Angel, maintain most of the many traditional cuts.

On balance, Victor has the stronger cast. Merrill's handsome baritone is employed with a lightness and *brio* one does not usually associate with his work. Though tonally variable, Valletti has a command of legato style and a musical distinction that gives his Almaviva a degree of elegance unmatched by any of his rivals. Peters is in good voice and gives us a characterization that escapes dramatic monotony. Corena, of course, is in his element, and there is no other Bartolo who can challenge him (he is in the London set, too). Tozzi is a rich-voiced, stylish Basilio. Leinsdorf's direction is spirited; he draws from his forces the spontaneity vital to any representative disclosure of this ever-delightful score.

This spontaneity is missing at times in Angel's performance. Alva's Almaviva is colorless, and Galliera's direction, though frequently delightful, sacrifices its verve in some of the big ensembles in the interest of absolute clarity. For some listeners the singing of Callas and Gobbi will be the determining factor in choosing this set. Callas' Rosina is no stock ingenue—far from it. For once, this charming schemer comes to life in her opening *Una voce poco fà* just as Rossini meant her to; and vibrant she remains to the very end. No one can begin to describe how Callas has revitalized this role; one will have to sit down with a libretto and follow what she does line by line to find out. Unlike Merrill, Gobbi does not have the brilliant upper voice we want in a Figaro, but he has everything else; dramaticially viewed, here is the Barber of Seville with all his earthy gusto and shrewdness intact. The balance of the Angel cast is worthy, with Zaccaria particularly outstanding.

Somewhat less persuasive in totality than the two leading contenders is the Deutsche Grammophon set, although it boasts the neatest, most coherent musical direction to be found among the *Barbers* at hand. In Bartoletti, the young Italian conductor who is presently making La Scala pay attention, one has a leader who can transmit the mercurial qualities of Rossini's writing to any audience. His work, slightly less than powerful at this stage in his career, has a grace and a precision that are altogether uncommon; Bartoletti is clearly a young man to watch. The cast, excepting for D'Angelo, is short on vocal velvet. Though Capecchi performs with a certain dash easy to admire, the play, unfortunately, comes to life infrequently through the voices. Almost all the fun is in the orchestra.

The London and Capitol albums are notable for their Rosinas, both of whom sing their measures in the original mezzo key. Simionato has a warm voice with agility, range, and ample power for this role, and she does, if somewhat dimly, create a character. De los Angeles has even greater vocal suavity and tonal beauty and a livelier sense of Rosina's words. Both Almavivas are routine. Figaro requires a bravura style that Bastianini does not possess; but even so, his singing is much easier to take than the unsubtle bawling of Bechi. The remaining members of each cast are quite good, except for Nicola Rossi-Lemeni, who has neither the vocal nor the dramatic skills to justify his notion that he ought to play Basilio à la Chaliapin. Erede and Serafin employ several tempi of unorthodox deliberation, and, although the latter succeeds in making some of these acceptable, both miss too much of the music's sparkle.

LA BOHÈME. Licia Albanese (Mimi), Jan Peerce (Rodolfo), Francesco Valentino (Marcello), Anne McKnight (Musetta), Chorus and NBC Symphony Orchestra, Arturo Toscanini; Victor LM-6006 (2).

Maria Callas, Giuseppe Di Stefano, Rolando Panerai, Anna Moffo, La Scala Chorus and Orchestra, Antonino Votto; Angel 3560 (2).

Victoria de los Angeles, Jussi Bjoerling, Robert Merrill, Lucine Amara, RCA Victor Chorus and Orchestra, Sir Thomas Beecham; Victor LM-6042 (2).

Renata Tebaldi, Carlo Bergonzi, Ettore Bastianini, Gianna D'Angelo, Santa Cecilia Chorus and Orchestra, Tullio Serafin; London A-4236 or OSA-1208 (stereo) (2).

Bidú Sayão, Richard Tucker, Francesco Valentino, Mimi Benzell, Metropolitan Opera Chorus and Orchestra, Giuseppe Antonicelli; Columbia SL-101 (2).

Antonietta Stella, Gianni Poggi, Renato Capecchi, Bruna Rizzoli, San Carlo Chorus and Orchestra, Francesco Molinari-Pradelli; Columbia M2L-401 (2).

Though it is listed first, the Toscanini production (recorded from his 1946 broadcasts) is not the clearly superior choice in this competition. Its fidelity of sound is uneven, and many listeners will be unwilling to tolerate the Maestro's very audible humming of portions of their favorite arias. For hardier opera lovers there is the opportunity to study Puccini's orchestral framework in a manner seldom available and to hear what a truly integrated performance of this often-abused work can be. Toscanini lived with *Bohème* most of his life (he conducted its première in 1896), and he knew how to make the score move, sing, and soar. To help him, he had the excellent NBC Orchestra, an ensemble whose virtues surpassed even the better pit orchestras, and a very good cast. Although Albanese does not have quite the vocal amplitude Puccini wanted for Mimi, her tones are secure and appositely colored, and she brings us a convincing character of fragility and passion. Peerce is robust, intense, and stylish as Mimi's lover, but one would like a bit more of the tenderness and sweetness one expects from a romantic poet. McKnight makes small impression, but Valentino, especially, and the rest of the Bohemians, almost the same as in the older Columbia recording of a Metropolitan Opera production, are noteworthy.

Angel also offers an uncommonly lively version of this opera;

the male cast, in particular, crackles with vitality. Callas does not give us the consistently smooth vocalism one wants in a Mimi, but she does deliver many memorable phrases, and her attention to textual values is as impressive as usual. Moffo is a better-than-average Musetta. Votto and the La Scala ensemble offer able and alert support.

For sheer opulence of sound, some will prefer the more recent Victor release (LM-6042). The ear takes delight in the lovely singing and handsome musicality of the entire cast, and Beecham imparts a poetic glow to the proceedings. What is missing, at least for this writer, is sufficient theatrical urgency. No one seems actually involved in the drama; everyone seems concerned only with being beauteous. Each succeeds (no mean accomplishment, surely), and many will be satisfied with the results.

The style of the London presentation appears to be rather similar to that of the newer Victor. It does not make very lively theater. Moreover, this performance is not so glamorous as its rival, and the recording, especially in the stereo version, places the voices too far away from the ear. The star of the London recording is Tebaldi—golden-voiced, warm, very persuasive in the last act, but, to judge from most of her singing, innocent of strong feeling. Bergonzi is uneven—now faithful as can be to Puccini's requirements, a moment later aspirating and giving us an unnecessary catch in his throat. Corena, as Benoit and Alcindoro, gives the only performance among the other characters that makes a strong impression. Serafin, evidently not so sensitive as Beecham to the score's sonic values, provides a performance that is equally wanting in dramatic sinew.

The Columbia recording made in the Metropolitan Opera House soon after the war (SL-101) preserves, surprisingly enough (considering the age of the project), the clear, dry acoustics of the auditorium. This element will be of interest to those who have never attended an opera at the Metropolitan. The orchestral playing sounds uncommonly warm, but the conducting is lackluster. Sayão is a fine artist, but she has always seemed miscast as Mimi. Her voice is too light, and her characterization misses the intensity necessary in such places as the third-act duet with Marcello. Tucker, in fine voice, does not really create a character for all his musicianship; his Italian style seems quickly fabricated for the occasion.

The latest Columbia release has good conducting and a first-rate Marcello from Capecchi to recommend it. In the other leading role, Stella displays a voice of little color that is not always in focus. She is somewhat weak in temperament and cannot give us the pathos required of Mimi. Poggi has what I can only describe as a whiny voice. It is secure at the top, but it is employed with a limited dynamic scale in phrases that are untouched by any kind of vigorous thought.

BORIS GODUNOV. Boris Christoff (Boris, Pimen, Varlaam), Eugenia Zareska (Marina), Nicolai Gedda (Dimitri), Paris Opera Chorus and Orchestre National de la Radiodifusion Française, Issay Dobrowen; Capitol GDR-7164 (4).

Alexander Pirogov (Boris), Maxim Mikhailov (Pimen), Maria Maksakova, George Nelepp, Bolshoi Theater Chorus and Orchestra, Nicolai Golovanov; Period SPLP-554 (3).

Miro Changalovich, Branko Pivnichki, Melanie Bugarinovich, Miro Brajnik, Chorus and Orchestra of the National Opera, Belgrade, Kreshimir Baranovich; London A-4317 (3).

The Period issue presents a Bolshoi Theater performance of Mussorgsky's monumental music drama. The Russian tapes from which it derives are of poor quality and certainly no match for the luminous clarity of the Capitol sound. The Capitol issue, indeed, is the superior version on almost every count; but even the Period issue with its frequently strong dramatic power is far ahead of the inadequate London release.

Sung in Russian, all three performances use the familiar Rimsky-Korsakoff adaptation of Mussorgsky's original score, though the order of scenes is different in the Bolshoi presentation. This is no place to argue the respective merits of the Rimsky and the original version, but it would seem that the composer's conception deserves representation in the LP catalogue by more than a two-record set of excerpts (a souvenir of the Metropolitan Opera production of recent years, which is sung in English and conducted by the late Dimitri Mitropoulos: Victor LM-6063).

The Period recording includes the rarely performed scene before St. Basil's Cathedral; but in order to accommodate the opera to three discs, there is deleted a huge portion of the Polish scene (given intact in the Capitol set). Since *Boris* has no individual star (no character is on stage long enough to dominate the opera), the chorus representing the Russian people is of the utmost importance, and it is this element that is strongest in the Bolshoi performance; the chorus sings with electrifying vigor and dramatic fervor. Indeed, its performance of that most potent of operatic mob scenes—the revolutionary episode—is almost reason for acquiring the Period recording. Individual contributions of noteworthy character come from the rough but convincing Pirogov, from the masterful Mikhailov, and from

Kosslovsky, who sings the Simpleton's pathetic measures. Golovanov's direction is distinguished throughout by good pacing and firm control.

Capitol, whose cast is composed primarily of expatriate Russians, presents the Bulgarian bass Christoff in three roles. In this issue several other singers, for better or for worse, assume more than one role. The danger in this type of casting is demonstrated when Christoff as Boris replies to Christoff as Pimen in the Duma scene. Clearly the heir to Chaliapin, whom he sounds like more often than not, Christoff as Boris gives a superb portrayal that conveys an illusion of utter completeness in its revelation of the monarch's pride and guilt-haunted fear. Outstanding, too, is Zareska, who makes the most of her scenes with Rangoni and Dimitri. The remainder of the cast is uncommonly authoritative, and Dobrowen conducts the splendid French orchestra in an expressively flavorful and idiomatic manner.

However much good will and effort were expended by the forces responsible for the London set, the fact remains that the Belgrade company is not equal to its assignment. The orchestra is poor, the conducting is sluggish, and the only voices of sufficient strength and color are those of Bugarinovich and Brajnik. The Rangoni-Marina scene is cut. The recording is highly uneven; the pickup of sound varies from nearby to distant.

CARMEN. Victoria de los Angeles (Carmen), Nicolai Gedda (Don José), Janine Micheau (Micaela), Ernest Blanc (Escamillo), Choruses and Orchestre National of the Radiodiffusion Française, Sir Thomas Beecham; Capitol GCR-7207 or SGCR-7207 (stereo) (3).

Suzanne Juyol, Libero de Luca, Janine Micheau, Julien Giovannetti, Opéra-Comique Chorus and Orchestra, Albert Wolff; London A-4304 (3).

Risë Stevens, Jan Peerce, Licia Albanese, Robert Merrill, Robert Shaw Chorale and RCA Victor Orchestra, Fritz Reiner; Victor LM-6102 (3).

Consuelo Rubio, Léopold Simoneau, Pierrette Alarie, Heinz Rehfuss, Chorus and Orchestra of the Concerts de Paris, Pierre-Michel le Conte; Epic SC-603 or BSC-106 (stereo) (3).

By no means the worst but, rather, typical of the routine level of postwar exhibitions of *Carmen* is the one recorded by Epic. Its Carmen, Consuelo Rubio, has a voice of some beauty and amplitude, and it is produced with security except in such passages as those in *Les tringles des sistres tentaient* where brisk tempo, high *tessitura,* and the need for volume coincide. But a restricted range of dynamics makes her singing almost unrelievedly monotonous, and her characterization—if such it may be called—is virtually invisible. As you might expect, Léopold Simoneau is musically stylish and vocally equal to any passage that does not require sustained power. He is accordingly best in the first act before the *Seguidilla,* where he is effective in suggesting the weakness in Don José. Thereafter he fails dramatically because he is so often incapable of transmitting sufficient passion.

Unacceptable intensity and lack of complete smoothness of line prevent Pierrette Alarie from bringing off her all-important aria. With Simoneau, she makes a finer impression. Their first-act duet is very satisfying and altogether the only distinguished episode in the entire presentation. That estimable artist Heinz Rehfuss is miscast as Escamillo. Vocally, he simply does not have the high notes his role requires. Temperamentally, he seems several rods from the bravado of the fatuous toreador and, like his associates, does little to heighten the text. This weakness of dramatic projection extends to M. le Conte and the orchestra; time after time they fail to give significance even to key passages, not to mention secondary detail. Perhaps the somewhat muddy, strangely over-resonant recording abets the impression of restricted dynamics and of ensemble playing that is often anything but consistent. Whatever the ratio of fault, this performance is, at the least, dramatically undernourished and typical, alas, of many others all of us have heard.

Somewhat better, but nevertheless far from triumphant, are the London and Victor recordings. Juyol is the disappointment of the London recording, not for any breach of taste but for the lack of a more controlled voice and a more unified characterization. In the Victor set, Stevens displays a brilliant mezzo-soprano (particularly lovely and powerful at the top), and she shows that she has carefully studied her role; but her vocal and dramatic inspirations are too uneven to make a completely telling effect. Moreover, her French enunciation is by no means in the class of Juyol's.

This matter of enunciation, let it be said, does quite a bit to negate some of the Victor set's positive virtues. Listeners not concerned with such particulars of style may be content with the admirable musicianship of Peerce and Albanese and the luscious tones of Merrill. Others will prefer the good singing and stylistic refinement of De Luca (a sensitive Don José though he strays from pitch rather too often), Micheau, and Giovannetti. The conducting in both these performances is never less than efficient; Wolff indeed, is more than that. Reiner's poised work lacks the excitement I remember from his theater performances.

Entirely atypical is a presentation of *Carmen* recorded by Capitol that carries with it the shock of revelation. I do not think I have ever heard anything that quite equals it for completeness of dramatic expression and for musical precision. Its guiding hand is that of the late Sir Thomas Beecham, whose work in the last decade of his life has seemed to me uneven in the extreme. In this *Carmen*—a score known to be a favorite of his—Beecham has given us the best of which he is capable, and that is something to remember for a lifetime. Beecham has had no finer hour in the field of recorded opera, not even in his incandescent direction of Mozart's *Magic Flute*. Just as in the *Magic Flute*, he has first of all selected every tempo with uncanny taste. Further, he has galvanized the erratic Orchestre National into the noble instrument it can be with a conductor it admires and respects. Finally, he has drawn from his talented singers performances of which few would have dreamed they were capable.

Never in her recording career has Victoria de los Angeles left such an indelible imprint on an opera. Carmen is a new role for De los Angeles, but only in the final scene, which asks for greater urgency, and in the Gypsy Dance that begins the second act does she in any way reveal that she has just begun singing Carmen. In the latter, when Beecham urges her to accompany him in a properly wild accelerando, she demurs, the better to enunciate, it seems. De los Angeles has clearly made a special study of the text, and line after line she holds our attention in the web of Carmen's fascinating character. From her initial appearance she seizes the imagination and ravishes the ear. How long has it been since anyone has heard a *Habanera* of this quality? The variety of attack, of vocal color, of dynamics, of textual communication—all in the service of Bizet's thought—how far must one go back in time to find her equal? Then there's a *Seguidilla* fit to compare with Geraldine Farrar's recording, and a *Là-bas* that is quietly, devastatingly seductive, and a Card Scene so believable you can see Carmen stare into the eye of her destiny. Not only does De los Angeles do complete justice to her grand moments, but she works with equal persuasiveness on detail—her *Tralalala* in the first act, her one- and two-line conversational replies, and the like. Here is a musico-dramatic accomplishment of the highest order.

Memorable presentations of this opera need more than perceptive conducting and an excellent Carmen. One must have a fine Don José, and in Nicolai Gedda we have a completely believable José, one perhaps not so vocally opulent as a few others we have heard, but one who sings very well and who will challenge the memory of opera-goers to find his dramatic superior. It would take far too much space to detail the many instances of his sensitivity to the text in musical terms. Let me mention only the Flower Song, which in Gedda's rendition becomes not only a delectable musical episode but a touching revelation of human behavior in the difficult situation of declaring love while describing the emotion with precision and enforced brevity.

Janine Micheau, whose Micaela was admired in the London *Carmen,* is in good form and very stylish. Ernest Blanc, a singer new to me, makes an excellent contribution with his handsome baritone and his creation of a real Escamillo; *e.g.*, he makes his aria more than a musical goody—he shows *himself* in his description of a bullfight.

All the minor characters are unusually well presented. The chorus is quite good; and, indeed, the entire production says "thank you" for what must have been an extraordinary amount of rehearsal time. The recording, a bit too resonant for ideal clarity, is well balanced and almost always of good quality.

CAVALLERIA RUSTICANA. Maria Callas (Santuzza), Giuseppe Di Stefano (Turiddu), Rolando Panerai (Alfio), La Scala Chorus and Orchestra, Tullio Serafin; Angel 3509-3S (2, 3 sides; odd side blank).

Renata Tebaldi, Jussi Bjoerling, Ettore Bastianini, Chorus and Orchestra of the Florence May Festival, Alberto Erede; Victor LM-6059 or LSC-6059 (stereo) (2, odd side is Bjoerling Operatic Recital).

Zinka Milanov, Jussi Bjoerling, Robert Merrill, Robert Shaw Chorale and RCA Victor Orchestra, Renato Cellini; Victor LM-6106 (3, also includes *Pagliacci*).

Giulietta Simionato, Mario Del Monaco, Cornell MacNeil, Santa Cecilia Chorus and Orchestra, Tullio Serafin; London A-4240 or OSA-1213 (stereo) (2, odd side is Del Monaco Italian Song Recital); LOH-90032 (4-track tape).

Elena Nicolai, Mario Del Monaco, Aldo Protti, Milan Chorus and Orchestra, Franco Ghione; London A-4323 (3, also includes *Pagliacci*).

Margaret Harshaw, Richard Tucker, Frank Guarrera, Metropolitan Opera Chorus and Orchestra, Fausto Cleva; Columbia SL-123 (2, on 3 sides; odd side Verdi Overtures).

If you are tired of *Cavalleria* and think that it shows a lot of dull patches and offers no intellectual interest, try the Angel set and discover why the opera became famous in the first place and why it remains a hardy perennial in almost every opera house.

It is likely that since Rosa Ponselle essayed the role of Santuzza no one has given us such a complete view of the ill-starred peasant girl as Callas offers. She *is* Santuzza, from her questionings of Mamma Lucia, to her soaring participation in the Easter Hymn, to her heartfelt *Voi lo sapete,* and throughout her vibrant duets with Turiddu and Alfio. She compels you to feel Santuzza's anguish, her supplications, and her bitterness. No less striking a portrait is Di Stefano's Turiddu. He makes the most of every word, and his delivery of the Drinking Song is as sparkling as the wine of which he sings. His farewell is performed with restraint and in vivid tones. The other members of the cast are good, too, with Anna Maria Canali the most strikingly sensuous Lola I can recall. After a heavy start, Serafin is magnificent in support of the singers and outstanding in vouchsafing instrumental detail. The recording is not up to the highest standards, but it is pleasant enough when the soloists are not singing high and loud.

Almost as vital as the Angel set and certainly the pick of the stereo recordings is the latest Victor edition of *Cavalleria.* Renata Tebaldi is an excellent Santuzza, although the role is not one for which she is well known in the theater. She sings beautifully and strikes an appropriately pathetic note in her aria and in her scene with Turiddu. Bjoerling is not quite so expressive as Di Stefano, but his fine singing (decidedly better than his earlier effort as Turiddu) and impeccable musical manners are a pleasure. Bastianini is a peerless Alfio.

As for the earlier Victor release, I find Milanov's singing quite brilliant in spots, and she does create a character; but there are passages where her luscious voice is tremolo-ridden. Bjoerling lacks lyricism and forces his voice unduly, though he shows his usual mastery at shaping a phrase. Merrill is a fine Alfio and sings with handsome resonance and almost all the required abandon. The supporting forces are neat if nothing else; the chorus and orchestra under Cellini are brilliant but a bit hard-boiled in expression.

Like Victor, London is represented by two versions of this

opera. The newer one is the better, for it is particularly generous in the sound of three rich, healthy voices; but neither adds up to a vivid dramatic experience. None of these artists wholly wins our sympathy for the character he portrays. The quality of intense anxiety seldom comes through Simionato's tone and never through Nicolai's. Del Monaco's monotonously loud singing dissipates the humanity we expect in a Turiddu. MacNeil carries out his assignment well, and his duet with Santuzza turns out to be the best executed number in the new set.

Harshaw sang Santuzza for the first time for Columbia's recording. She does not get under the skin of the character by any means, and it seems to me she is miscast in a part so remote from her usual Wagnerian heroines. Tucker is in good voice, but he and the other singers would make more of an impression were they not rushed off their feet by Cleva's speedy tempi. The general impression of this recording, indeed, is that it is a patent-leather affair with no heart.

LES CONTES D'HOFFMANN. Léopold Simoneau (Hoffman), Mattiwilda Dobbs (Olympia and Antonia), Uta Graf (Giulietta), Heinz Rehfuss (Lindorf, Coppelius, Dappertutto, and Dr. Miracle); Chorus and Orchestra of the Concerts de Paris, Pierre-Michel le Conte; Epic SC-6028 or BSC-101 (stereo) (3).

Robert Rounseville, Dorothy Bond (Olympia), Margherita Grandi (Giulietta), Ann Ayars (Antonia), Bruce Dargavel, Sadler's Wells Chorus and Royal Philharmonic Orchestra, Sir Thomas Beecham; London A-4302 (3) (In English).

As a nearly complete recording of Offenbach's most serious work, the French performance has no competition, for the English presentation is cut somewhat severely in several places, and it is not so good a recording as the more recent Epic, particularly the stereo edition. The London set is the sound track of a film and, of course, had objectives rather different from an ordinary musical rendering. It deserves coverage here simply because Sir Thomas Beecham conducted it.

Offenbach's music was obviously close to the great English conductor's heart, and Beecham offers us a clear reading that is affectionate and lusty. His shaping of many phrases will give great pleasure, and his perfect support of his singers is the model of what good operatic conducting ought to be. Only two of the vocalists, however, are in any way memorable. Rounseville, a young American tenor, is ideally cast from the point of view of vocal weight and color, and he sings with admirable musical and dramatic intelligence. As early as the Kleinzach song in the Prologue one senses a keen awareness on the singer's part of Hoffmann's love-haunted melancholy and poetic sensibilities. The outstanding vocal honors in this performance, though, belong to Dargavel, who assumes all four of the villainous roles. His voice is big and dark and flexible, and one wonders why we have heard so little from him since this film was made.

Because it is a French production, the Epic set preserves the sound and general style the composer intended us to absorb, and on these grounds it is unique now that the excellent Columbia set (SL-106) has been withdrawn. The Epic set, though not the equal of the older rendition, has some merit. It sounds good; Simoneau, Dobbs, and Rehfuss head a vocally pleasing cast. Moreover, it is always a delight to hear even an average French orchestra (and that is what the Concerts de Paris ensemble is) play a score which was designed for the particular sonorities of French instruments.

What is lacking in this performance is dramatic atmosphere and a husbanding of theatrical values. Le Conte appears from this evidence to be no more than a dependable *routinier*. Simoneau as an almost passionless Hoffmann and Dobbs as Antonia miss the urgency and conviction that would give their characterizations vitality. Rehfuss, Graf, and the minor singers, however, give us some dramatic heat that proves a saving grace.

COSÌ FAN TUTTE. Lisa Della Casa (Fiordiligi), Christa Ludwig (Dorabella), Emmy Loose (Despina), Anton Dermota (Ferrando), Erich Kunz (Guglielmo), Paul Schoeffler (Don Alfonso), Vienna State Opera Chorus and Vienna Philharmonic Orchestra, Karl Böhm; London A-4318 or OSA-1312 (stereo) (3).

Elizabeth Schwarzkopf, Nan Merriman, Lisa Otto, Léopold Simoneau, Rolando Panerai, Sesto Bruscantini, Chorus and Philharmonia Orchestra, Herbert von Karajan; Angel 3522 (3).

Eleanor Steber, Blanche Thebom, Roberta Peters, Richard Tucker, Frank Guarrera, Lorenzo Alvary, Metropolitan Opera Chorus and Orchestra, Fritz Stiedry; Columbia SL-122 (3).

The standard for performing *Così Fan Tutte* in our day has been the Glyndebourne production recording, first issued in the United States over two decades ago and now, unhappily, no longer available. Today one has three sets from which to choose, and no one of them equals the out-of-print issue, though the London and Angel sets at least are at pains to demonstrate that *Così Fan Tutte* is no bedroom farce, that the opera is rather a touching and humane comment on young love, and that it is (not in spite of, but *because of*, its theatrical artifices) a perfect combination of comedy and pathos. Presented in English, the Columbia version is rather different in approach and must be accepted or rejected on its own terms. Those terms, it seems to me, are that *Così* be considered a highly stylized production played for laughs and sung with musical gusto.

One of the important keys to a successful rendering of this opera is the equilibration of the brilliant arias and the many intimate ensembles. Most of the big set pieces occur in the first act, and there is a grave danger in overemphasizing this facet of the work, for then the arias are apt to overshadow the muted tenderness and humanity of many of the second-act ensembles. The Columbia version does not, as an example, avoid this pitfall; but the London and Angel sets do. Nevertheless, a choice between the latter is difficult. One turns to London in the end for the superb playing of the Vienna Philharmonic and the full-throated singing of Della Casa and Ludwig, whose voices, incidentally, are particularly well matched. Dermota contributes a stylish and enjoyable performance. Kunz and Schoeffler, on the other hand, do not make the most of their roles, and Loose lacks the high spirit we expect from Despina. Böhm's pacing is often sluggish, but his beat is firm, and he clarifies much of the detail in Mozart's seemingly smooth but actually complex texture.

The cultivated singing of Schwarzkopf and Simoneau is a joy in the Angel set, however unspontaneous their characterizations may seem. Merriman sings with style and security, though she is not a vivid personality. Panerai pleasantly surprises by his judicious choice of tonal weights and his light-footed delivery of Guglielmo's second-act aria. Otto's Despina has personality, but Bruscantini strikes me as an over-refined Alfonso. No one can find fault with Karajan's selection of tempi, but he seems to me culpable in matters of proper emphasis and clarity, and there is a certain prissy quality in his work here that is not consonant with my ideas about *Così*.

In the Columbia recording we have an outstanding effort by Steber, who, when her voice is steady, sings with surpassing eloquence. Thebom is pleasing, but Peters' Despina is overly brassy. Tucker and Guarrera have excellent voices, but their style is not what one could call Mozartian. The Metropolitan Opera Orchestra plays well under Stiedry's less than lively direction.

DON CARLO. Maria Caniglia (Elisabeth), Ebe Stignani (Eboli), Nicola Rossi-Lemeni (Philip II), Mirto Picchi (Carlo), Paolo Silveri (Rodrigo), Radio Italiana Chorus and Orchestra, Fernando Previtali; Cetra 1234 (4).

Antonietta Stella, Elena Nicolai, Boris Christoff, Mario Fillipeschi, Tito Gobbi, Rome Opera Chorus and Orchestra, Gabriele Santini; Capitol GCR-7165 (3).

Despite certain vocal shortcomings, the Cetra set is consistently absorbing for its musical animation and for a degree of dramatic conviction decidedly rare. It displays Caniglia, Stignani, and Rossi-Lemeni bereft of much of their original vocal glory but using what they have left with stunning communicative power. There is a grandeur of style in Caniglia's delivery of *Tu che le vanità*, in Stignani's *O don fatale*, and in Rossi-Lemeni's contribution to the third act, particularly the harrowing episode with the Inquisitor, that one seems to encounter with diminishing frequency. Picchi, with his fresh tenor, and Silveri, reliable as ever, are also notably in the frame of Previtali's well-integrated and vigorous conception of this somber masterpiece.

In contrast to the teamwork of the Cetra forces, the Capitol set reveals an uneven cast which, for want of firm leadership, is forced to operate in a manner that can only be described as every man for himself. Gobbi and Christoff are the victors for our attention in this survival-of-the-fittest atmosphere. Gobbi, in particular, gives a perfect performance in which vocal resource and dramatic power are balanced to produce the nobility and sympathetic nature we expect in an ideal Rodrigo. Fillipeschi and Nicolai are inadequate in their roles. Stella, in good voice, needs the stylistic assurance that a more inspiring conductor than Santini might have provided for the occasion. The exceptionally clean and luminous Capitol recording is technically superior to the Cetra and represents a saving of one disc.

DON GIOVANNI. Suzanne Danco (Donna Anna), Lisa Della Casa (Donna Elvira), Hilde Gueden (Zerlina), Cesare Siepi (Don Giovanni), Anton Dermota (Don Ottavio), Fernando Corena (Leporello), Chorus of the Vienna State Opera and Vienna Philharmonic Orchestra, Josef Krips; London A-4406 or OSA-1401 (stereo) (4); LOV-90007 (4-track tape).

Birgit Nilsson, Leontyne Price, Eugenia Ratti, Cesare Siepi, Cesare Valletti, Fernando Corena, Chorus of the Vienna State Opera and Vienna Philharmonic Orchestra, Erich Leinsdorf; Victor LM-6410 or LSC-6410 (stereo) (4).

Sena Jurinac, Maria Stader, Irmgard Seefried, Dietrich Fischer-Dieskau, Ernst Häfliger, Karl Kohn, RIAS Chamber Choir and Berlin Radio Symphony Orchestra, Ferenc Fricsay; Deutsche Grammophon DGM-302 or DGS-7302 (stereo) (3).

Joan Sutherland, Elisabeth Schwarzkopf, Graziella Sciutti, Eberhard Wächter, Luigi Alva, Giuseppe Taddei, Philharmonia Chorus and Orchestra, Carlo Maria Giulini; Angel 3605 or S-3605 (stereo) (4).

Hilde Zadek, Sena Jurinac, Graziella Sciutti, George London, Léopold Simoneau, Walter Berry, Chamber Choir and Vienna Symphony Orchestra, Rudolf Moralt; Epic SC-6010 (3).

Viewed intellectually, musically, or dramatically, *Don Giovanni* is a work of incredible richness. One never tires of hearing it, thinking about it, or enjoying a new interpretation of any one of its many aspects by a different performer. There can never be too many recordings of *Don Giovanni* by skillful artists with serious intentions.

Over the years, there have been at least two presentations to stimulate the mind and gladden the ear. Who will ever forget the first recording of this masterwork on twenty-three 78 r.p.m. discs—the superb Glyndebourne Festival performance (later released on LP—Victor LCT-6102—and then withdrawn, but now available on special import order only—Electrola 80598/60)? And in the LP era, what pleasure the London recording has given! Here is an invigorating musical performance which often achieves dramatic power and is marvelously detailed. Inde d, if all the scores of *Don Giovanni* suddenly vanished, one feels confident that another could be reconstructed from this recording with almost every note in its proper place. This extraordinary clarity is due in no small measure to the precise, almost cool, direction of Krips and the transparency of the sounds he elicits from the admirable players of the Vienna Philharmonic.

For musical taste and precision, the singers also deserve commendation; in vocal and dramatic matters, though they tarry on a high level, they are, as one would expect, unequal. Let us consider Suzanne Danco, controversially cast as Donna Anna. Her light voice is certainly not up to required dramatic-soprano specifications, but aided by modern microphone techniques it communicates the complex emotions of Donna Anna amazingly well. Moreover, Danco seems to dominate every ensemble in which she takes part by her sturdy musicianship. Here is an example of inspired miscasting. The beautiful voice of Della Casa is ample compensation for her slightly timid characterization, and her vocal velvet enriches many of the ensembles. Gueden, though she has a bit of trouble with some of Zerlina's long-breathed phrases, sings with apt and touching expression. Her *Batti, batti* is assuredly a bit of magic. The long phrases in the famous tenor arias give Dermota some trouble, too; but he gets through them with poise, and elsewhere he is stylish indeed.

Perhaps the most brilliant dramatic performance is that offered by Corena. His Leporello is the real "common man" Mozart and his librettist Da Ponte would seem to have had in mind—an ambitious fellow with a zest for life and a clear-headed way of looking at and reacting to the behavior of people around him. Moreover, Corena sings with fine tone and admirable musical taste. Siepi has a somewhat mealy bass for the title role, and there are times when he fails to suggest the Don's aristocratic manner and passionate intensity. Nevertheless, he sings with authority and has done well to conquer so many of the problems associated with this enormously difficult role; he is especially persuasive in the recitatives.

It is the team of Corena and Siepi that makes the Victor set the second choice. They are the leading exponents of their respective roles before the public today, and their competition is far from matching them. The outstanding shortcoming of the Victor set is the work of its conductor, Erich Leinsdorf, who has failed to blend this unusually worthy group of vocalists and the Vienna Philharmonic into a durable musico-dramatic experience. Many numbers emerge with distinction, but as many others seem either superficial and insensitive or poorly rehearsed. There is, moreover, insufficient care for detailed characterization by several singers that betrays the absence of firm guidance. Even Siepi and Corena are rather more convincing in portraiture in the London album than here. Vocally, however, the cast has a number of delights. The full and brilliant, if slightly chilly, voice of Nilsson is well suited to the role of Donna Anna, but it is not sufficiently controlled to meet the formidable challenge of *Non mi dir*. The warmth and flexibility of Price's voice give considerable pleasure, but after a fine first act she lets us down, particularly with her rushed and graceless *Mi tradì*. Donna Elvira is, it must be understood, a difficult role and one new to Price, who has the equipment one day to make it her own. Ratti has a certain sparkle as Zerlina, but her voice is thin. Valletti's singing, although variable in purity of tone, is still something to hear; it is often ingratiating, particularly in *Dalla sua pace*. The Victor recording is uneven; now it is brilliant, now tainted by distortion. The stereo version gives a better sense of stage action than does any of the other sets, *e.g.*, the sword play in the opening scene, the noise of the crowd at the ball and of Masetto's comrades in the second act, and the clock in the cemetery. There is a musical bonus in the Victor set, too. For the first time the modern listener has an opportunity to hear the Zerlina-Leporello duet that Mozart wrote for the original production in Prague. It is scarcely one of the best numbers in the opera, and we may be thankful that Mozart later substituted *Il mio tesoro* for it; but it is good to hear it at last, and we may thank Victor for being so enterprising.

The fine conducting of Fricsay and the excellent performances of a strong female cast make the Deutsche Grammophon release a worthy rival to that of Victor. Jurinac, though a trifle light-voiced for Donna Anna, is superb, singing with brilliance, flexibility, color, and dramatic force. Stader warms up slowly, pushing a bit in her entrance aria, but thereafter she performs with fine musical style and secure tone. Seefried is a superb Zerlina; her finished phrasing and even scales are a special delight. The trouble with this recording (without elaborating upon the *qvestas* and *qvellas* and other vagaries of pronunciation one expects from German singers in Italian parts) is its two male leads. Fischer-Dieskau and Kohn have neither the style nor the temperament for the Don and Leporello. Häfliger makes a better impression, especially with his keen sense of rhythm, which is a particular joy in some of the ensembles.

The handsomely recorded Angel issue suffers from lack of dramatic impact. The conducting of Giulini can be faulted for favoring a richer tonal palette than is consistent with clarity and for lacking unanimity in much of the Philharmonia's playing. Then there is Wächter, a young artist with a fine voice, whose work testifies that Don Giovannis are not created overnight. His is a robust but hardly elegant Don, with such contrasts that the character seems more petulant than steadfastly willful.

Taddei, with his frequently toneless singing and hammy effects, and Alva, colorless in every way, complete a weak male cast. Dominating this performance is the completely finished portrait Schwarzkopf gives us, a notable achievement graced by commanding singing. The beautiful voice of Sutherland is also a blessing, but she generates little expressive force.

The Epic set, though well recorded, is something of a disappointment; it does not seem carefully prepared. Moralt has not given the production that sense of unity that attends effective renditions of this opera. Furthermore, the orchestra's playing lacks the polish and refinement of sound available in the other recordings. There are two outstanding performances, however, in Jurinac's convincing Donna Elvira and Ludwig Weber's authoritative Commendatore. On the other hand, Berry (the Masetto in the London version) is an adequate but by no means brilliant Leporello. The same may be said of Simoneau, who, on the basis of his fine work in the Angel *Così*, promised more than his Ottavio delivered. Zadek and Sciutti (the Zerlina in the Angel set) are not up to their competition: the former is vocally unstable; the latter, dramatically and musically colorless. These records indicate a shocking deterioration in the quality of London's singing. A few seasons ago I heard London give a commanding performance of the Don at the Metropolitan Opera House. Here he displays the same penetrating mind at work, but lapses of vocal control do much to diminish the force of his strong conception: his phrases are often explosive, his dynamics are often exaggerated, much of his singing is rushed, and he is guilty of some wayward rhythm.

DON PASQUALE. Sesto Bruscantini (Don Pasquale), Alda Noni (Norina), Cesare Valletti (Ernesto), Mario Borriello (Malatesta), Radio Italiana Chorus and Orchestra, Mario Rossi; Cetra 1242 (2).

Renato Capecchi, Bruna Rizzoli, Petre Munteanu, Giuseppe Valdengo, San Carlo Chorus and Orchestra, Francesco Molinari-Pradelli; Epic SC-6016 (2).

Donizetti's comic masterpiece is well served by the Cetra set. Rossi's light touch enables a nimble ensemble to perform with zest and a welcome dash. Particularly fresh and appealing are Noni and Valletti as the young lovers. Although he sounds too young for Don Pasquale, Bruscantini performs with grace and refinement, qualities that are in short supply in Borriello's spirited singing.

The Epic recording is clearly outclassed. Its sonics are frequently dim and lack sufficient bass; its singers are routine. Rizzoli has a flexible voice and a good trill, but her charm is vitiated by monotonous dynamics and a somewhat pinched tone. Munteanu's voice has little color and is strained at full stretch, though he manages *Sogno soave e casto* with considerable style. Don Pasquale is a richer character than Capecchi, in spite of careful enunciation and secure musicianship, makes him. A few good moments vocally help to make up for some careless phrasing and a general dramatic stiffness on the part of Valdengo.

ELEKTRA. Inge Borkh (Elektra), Jean Madeira (Klytemnestra), Marianne Schech (Chrysothemis), Dietrich Fischer-Dieskau (Orestes), Saxon State Opera Chorus and Orchestra (Dresden), Karl Böhm; Deutsche Grammophon LPM-138690/1 and SLPM-138690/1 (stereo) (2).

Anny Konetzni, Martha Mödl, Daniza Ilitsch, Hans Braun, Florence May Festival Chorus and Orchestra, Dimitri Mitropoulos; Cetra 1209 (2).

For a decade *Elektra* was represented by one inadequate recording which preserved a 1951 Florence May Festival stage presentation. A poor sonic approximation of the opera, this set fully demonstrates the problems inherent in recording "live" operatic events, *e.g.*, the movement of the singers, the catch-as-catch-can balances, and stage and audience noises. A stirring performance might have overcome one's resistance to the circumstances, but, with the exception of Mödl, no member of this cast can be said to have done anything above the routine. Most of the credit that can be claimed for the enterprise goes to the late Dimitri Mitropoulos, who drew from his orchestra playing notable for propulsion and effective nervous excitement.

The patience of those who were willing to wait for a suitable recorded *Elektra* has been amply rewarded with Deutsche Grammophon's outstanding performance. Superbly recorded within a broad dynamic range and balanced in a way that discloses the complex orchestral texture without ever obscuring the voices, this presentation strikes fire with the opening three-note motto and builds the music to a brilliant climax at the opera's conclusion.

The meticulous preparation of this production is manifested in every bar of the score. As director, Karl Böhm deserves the greatest praise for this accomplishment. He has also earned a special citation for the ease and lightness of tone he has secured in an opera which is as heavily scored as *Elektra*. All three of the female leads are to be congratulated on their intelligence, their respect for the music, and their vocal power and finesse. They are all in top form. If one is more skilled than the others, she would be Madeira, who projects a rare degree of torment and anguish through her tone and word-painting in the role of Klytemnestra. Fischer-Dieskau is a bit short of vocal weight for Orestes, but he conveys the nobility of his lines nonetheless.

L'ELISIR D'AMORE. Hilde Gueden (Adina), Giuseppe Di Stefano (Nemorino), Renato Capecchi (Belcore), Fernando Corena (Dulcamara), Florence May Festival Chorus and Orchestra, Francesco Molinari-Pradelli; London A-4321 or OSA-1311 (stereo) (3).

Alda Noni, Cesare Valletti, Afro Poli, Sesto Bruscantini, Radio Italiana Chorus and Orchestra, Gianandrea Gavazzeni; Cetra 1235 (3).

Rosanna Carteri, Luigi Alva, Rolando Panerai, Giuseppe Taddei, La Scala Chorus and Orchestra, Tullio Serafin; Angel 3594 or S-3594 (stereo) (2).

In my choice of the London over the worthy Cetra entry, the decisive factor has been the charm of Hilde Gueden. Her beauty of voice, her fine legato, and her neat phrasing are all requirements for depicting Adina's adorably feminine qualities. Well employed but with less guile is the bright, flexible soprano of Noni. Both tenors are pleasing, though Di Stefano's singing is a bit burly at times. Here, early in his career, Valletti shows occasional signs of immaturity but discloses the voice and style of the leading *tenore di grazia* he has become. Neither Belcore is quite satisfactory. Capecchi has, of course, the fresher voice, but Poli sings with more smoothness. Both avoid much of the ornamentation (trills, appoggiaturas) that Donizetti employed to give the role brilliance and vocal interest. Using his light voice with impressive art, Bruscantini makes a satisfying contribution; but Corena is the perfect Dulcamara, in tone, delivery, and effect. The conducting of both Molinari-Pradelli and Gavazzeni is animated and sufficiently graceful.

In the mediocre Angel recording, Carteri reveals a pleasing voice (other than at the top), but she does not have sufficient vocal agility and her expression is wooden. Alva is tidy but colorless. Panerai and Taddei lack elegance. The La Scala Orchestra plays beautifully, but Serafin's conducting is spiritless.

FALSTAFF. Herva Nelli (Mistress Ford), Nan Merriman (Mistress Page), Teresa Stich-Randall (Anne), Cloe Elmo (Dame Quickly), Giuseppe Valdengo (Falstaff), Frank Guarrera (Ford), Antonio Madasi (Fenton), Robert Shaw Chorale and NBC Symphony Orchestra, Arturo Toscanini; Victor LM-6111 (3).

Elisabeth Schwarzkopf, Nan Merriman, Anna Moffo, Fedora Barbieri, Tito Gobbi, Rolando Panerai, Luigi Alva, Philharmonia Chorus and Orchestra, Herbert von Karajan; Angel 3552 or S-3552 (stereo) (3).

Rosanna Carteri, Anna Maria Canali, Lina Pagliughi, Amalia Pini, Giuseppe Taddei, Saturno Meletti, Emilio Renzi, Radio Italiana Chorus and Orchestra, Mario Rossi; Cetra 1207 (3).

One of the outstanding achievements on LP is the Toscanini-directed *Falstaff*. Taken from the Maestro's famous broadcasts of April, 1950, the Victor set is a miracle for revelation of the vast detail of Verdi's wondrously light and fanciful invention. Such transparency of sound (even in the second-act nonette and the tremendous, complex finale); such exuberant, communicative impulse; such refinement of sonority; such buoyant rhythm are things one dreams about but hears only seldom. It is fortunate that by the season of 1949–1950 Victor had finally overcome the sonic challenge that the recalcitrant Studio 8H had posed ever since Toscanini began conducting his concerts there. Unlike the majority of operas that Toscanini has presented on records, this *Falstaff* sounds not only clear but also vibrant and acceptably spacious.

Let us be frank about the singing: it does not pretend to be of golden-age quality except for Elmo, but it is honest, forthright, and imbued with a sense of teamwork that is irresistible. Only Madasi is cast beyond his capabilities. As for Elmo, she gives a truly great singing-acting performance. Quickly's zest for life, her rough-and-tumble wit are apparent in every line; and her repetitions of *Reverenza* in the scenes with Falstaff are little comic master strokes. Valdengo sings with gratifying resonance and musical distinction, but he lacks the maturity and unction that an older-sounding voice might bring to Falstaff. Guarrera has never sung better in his life. To Ford's lines in the scene in which he impersonates Brook, the young singer brings a startling intensity and a revelation of the torments of the jealous man. Nelli and Merriman, tonally ingratiating, are at their best in the ensembles. Stich-Randall performs pleasingly, and her last-act aria is especially enchanting with its exquisite pianissimo singing.

There is, all told, even better singing in the Cetra production, which is far more than a respectable performance, if not up to that of the Victor release. For my taste, it is nearly Victor's equal in the first three scenes; but thereafter, in those scenes where rhythmic precision and ensemble niceties are so important, it is no match for what Toscanini and his forces have accomplished. The outstanding contribution is delivered by the Falstaff, Taddei. His delineation of the fat man's character is the work of a seasoned artist with a vivid theatrical imagination. Hear, for example, what meaning he imparts to each word in the first-act monologue, *L'onore, Ladri*. Meletti is a maturer Ford than Guarrera and perhaps more effective. The women, with the exception of Pagliughi, who has difficulty presenting a youthful Anne, are splendid vocalists and admirable stylists. Cetra's Fenton, Renzi, is, however, no improvement over Madasi. Rossi's conducting and the playing of his orchestra, though well out of the ordinary, are overshadowed by the incandescence created by Toscanini and the NBC.

Closely approaching the Toscanini standard, albeit in a different, lighter manner, is Karajan's direction of an impressive group of vocal artists and the Philharmonia Orchestra. Delicacy and refinement are the words for Angel's production, even to the very good engineering that allows us to hear so many pianissimo passages that the other recordings make too loud. The stereo version, incidentally, is a special delight. The grandest of all the Falstaffs is Gobbi, who makes the most of his every opportunity and gives us one of the great characterizations on records. It is all of a piece from Falstaff's blustering in the tavern; through his interviews first with Ford, then with Mistress Ford; his humiliation in the laundry basket; his recovery of spirit in the wonderful monologue which begins the third act; his swallowing of Quickly's final deception; his terror in the woods; and his merry display of pride in the face of defeat in the finale. Gobbi is supported by splendidly alert male artists (including the only acceptable Fenton) and a female cast of frequently exceptional quality. Schwarzkopf does not have the fullness of voice one longs for in a Mistress Ford, but she does have plentiful art, as she sometimes demonstrates too forcefully. Merriman, the Mistress Page in the Victor set, is again admirable. Barbieri is a vigorous but heavy-handed Quickly and no match for Elmo. Moffo is pert and charming as Anne.

FAUST. Victoria de los Angeles (Marguerite), Nicolai Gedda (Faust), Boris Christoff (Méphistophélès), Ernest Blanc (Valentin), Paris Opéra Chorus and Orchestra, André Cluytens; Capitol GDR-7154 or SGDR-7154 (stereo) (4).

Eleanor Steber, Eugene Conley, Cesare Siepi, Frank Guarrera, Metropolitan Opera Chorus and Orchestra, Fausto Cleva; Columbia SL-112 (3).

The Capitol entry is not to be confused with an earlier recording of *Faust* (now withdrawn) boasting almost the same cast listed above. This new version, which dates from 1958, is superior in a number of ways. First, De los Angeles has greatly improved her grasp of the text and sings Marguerite's music more beautifully than ever before. Indeed, her big scene in Act III is stated with the kind of ear-ravishing tone, dramatic understanding, and impeccable musicality that would qualify it as an accomplishment worthy of the "Golden Age." Gedda, too, has improved since his first recorded Faust; and, although he does not have the ideal brilliance of voice for the part, he manages a respectable characterization. Christoff, on the other hand, is still singing Méphistophélès à la Chaliapin with an explosive attack and the broad effects that recall Bernard Shaw's remark about the bass who craved "to mount the scarlet cock's feather and say to himself, like Barnaby Rudge's raven, 'I'm a devil, I'm a devil, I'm a devil!'." Christoff's devil confronts us with no suavity, no sophistication, no charm (imagine Satan without charm!), and he sings a language that seems to resemble Esperanto rather than French. Blanc, the new major singer in this *Faust*, is a capable Valentin but lacks the glamorous tone one associates with the former illustrious baritones who took this role. Cluytens conducts with a welcome, steady hand, and he invests some of the pages of this score with genuine poetic feeling. Unlike the Columbia set, Capitol's fine-sounding recording presents *Faust* complete, including even the Walpurgis Night scene with all the ballet music.

The participants in the Metropolitan Opera recording of *Faust*—an international cast—observe all musical amenities and deliver a moderately pleasing and well-routined performance, but they lack the feeling of dedicated music-making. Steber's voice, of course, is lovely when it is under control and does not flutter. Siepi, too, has an outstanding voice; but he would be more effective if he forced it to be more definite as to tonal center. Conley's tenor was fresh at the time of this recording and is pleasing below a forte; at full strength, the sound is apt to become a bit ugly. Cleva is not the equal of Cluytens in this opera. The recording shows its age, but the balance between voices and orchestra is uncommonly good.

FIDELIO. Martha Mödl (Leonore), Sena Jurinac (Marzelline), Wolfgang Windgassen (Florestan), Otto Edelmann (Pizarro), Gottlob Frick (Rocco), Vienna State Opera Chorus and Vienna Philharmonic Orchestra, Wilhelm Furtwängler; Electrola 90071/3 (3).

Rose Bampton, Eleanor Steber, Jan Peerce, Herbert Janssen, Sidor Belarsky, Chorus and NBC Symphony Orchestra, Arturo Toscanini; Victor LM-6025 (2).

Leonie Rysanek, Irmgard Seefried, Ernst Häfliger, Dietrich Fischer-Dieskau, Gottlob Frick, Bavarian State Opera Chorus and Orchestra, Ferenc Fricsay; Decca DX-147 (2).

Aside from the superiority of the Victor Leonore, the Electrola set is easily the more vocally accomplished; it also benefits from first-rate modern engineering. The Victor issue derives from two of Toscanini's broadcasts in December, 1944. Interest will doubtless center on the different approaches of the two great conductors—Toscanini and Furtwängler—to this noble score. Furtwängler's direction is exquisitely detailed both musically and expressively, and the lambent glow of the Vienna Philharmonic is a delight throughout. The tempi are, for the most part, more leisurely than Toscanini's, and as a result the sweet humanity of all the characters (except Pizarro) continually touches the heart. The Toscanini conception of *Fidelio* is intensely dramatic; the Maestro uses greater contrasts in tempi and dynamics and demands the crispest articulation from his fine orchestra. In those moments of great fury—Pizarro's *Ha! welch' ein' Augenblick*, Leonore's *Abscheulicher!*, the great second-act ensemble, *Er sterbe*—Toscanini is irresistible. The Italian also contributes a wonderfully proportioned and emotionally exciting *Leonore Overture No. 3*.

As for the singers: one must salute the impressive eloquence of Bampton's Leonore, the charm of Jurinac's Marzelline, and the fine contributions of Windgassen and Frick. The high reaches and long-breathed phrases of the title role tax Mödl, but she is dramatically convincing. Neither Janssen nor Edelmann (in splendid voice) manages to convey sufficiently the malignant character of Pizarro. Peerce gives a serious and respectable musical performance, but his voice does not possess the weight required for Florestan.

The Decca recording wilts before this competition, even though it offers the same fine Rocco as the Electrola recording and a Pizarro and a Marzelline of superior quality. Fischer-Dieskau, in particular, sings with exceptional control and understanding; his aria is delivered with a degree of power and malevolence not heard on discs since Friedrich Schorr presented it in the early years of electrical recording. The weakness of this performance exists in the work of its conductor, its Leonore, and its Florestan, the three places where greatest strength is needed. Fricsay's direction wants steadiness of pulse and a resolute feeling of inevitable movement. Rysanek's singing is often tremolo-ridden and weak in tone at the bottom of her register. Häfliger's voice requires more tone and his singing a firmer line to meet the demands of Florestan.

LA FORZA DEL DESTINO. Zinka Milanov (Leonora), Giuseppe Di Stefano (Alvaro), Leonard Warren (Carlo), Giorgio Tozzi (Guardiano), Santa Cecilia Chorus and Orchestra, Fernando Previtali; Victor LM-6406 or LSC-6406 (stereo) (4).

Renata Tebaldi, Mario Del Monaco, Ettore Bastianini, Cesare Siepi, Santa Cecilia Chorus and Orchestra, Francesco Molinari-Pradelli; London A-4408 or OSA-1405 (stereo) (4); LOV-90009 (4-track tape).

Maria Callas, Richard Tucker, Carlo Tagliabue, Nicola Rossi-Lemeni, La Scala Chorus and Orchestra, Tullio Serafin; Angel 3531 (3).

All three of these well-recorded sets score above average marks for vocal prowess and dramatic color; but Victor's, the most recent of the group, is outstanding for an extra measure of quality in engineering and in the balance of its cast. The Leonora in *Forza* is one of Milanov's "success" roles; its requirements of vocal generosity and grandeur of style fit her talents like a glove. It may be some time before we again hear anything to equal her incomparable, floated pianissimi in *Pace, pace* or the resonant tonal amplitude with which she concludes this aria. Don Carlo, one of the late Leonard Warren's triumphant parts, is the role in which the baritone made his final, tragic appearance at the Metropolitan Opera House on March 4, 1960. This recording is a faithful image of his powerful portrayal. It is, furthermore, a tribute to the ability of the other singers in this strong cast that they are not heavily overshadowed by Milanov and Warren. Tozzi, in particular, gives us singing of exceptional warmth and smoothness. The conducting of Previtali is notably efficient.

Much enjoyment can be had from the London performance. Tebaldi and Del Monaco, on his best musical behavior, are in splendid form and make telling contributions. Bastianini and Siepi sing well, but their counterparts in the Victor set outdistance them. Molinari-Pradelli directs his well-prepared forces with authority and taste, though not with consistent urgency.

The Angel set features a fine orchestral performance led by Serafin that does much to pull the uneven portions of this score together. It also has Callas—though in one of her less convincing roles (her *Madre, pietosa Vergine* is nonetheless something to hear)—and Tucker in one of his better roles (although he is inclined to exaggerate in his expression). Tagliabue is at least dramatically sound, but one will find little to please in the quavery singing of Rossi-Lemeni. The choral work is excellent. This recording does not include the first scene of Act IV, in which the acerbic Melitone dispenses soup to the beggars.

GIANNI SCHICCHI. Tito Gobbi (Schicchi), Victoria de los Angeles (Lauretta), Carlo Del Monte (Rinuccio), Rome Opera Orchestra, Gabriele Santini; Capitol GAR-7179 or SGAR-7179 (stereo) (1).

Giuseppe Taddei, Grete Rapisardi, Giuseppe Savio, Radio Italiana Orchestra, Alfredo Simonetto; Cetra 50028 (1).

The strong case that can be made for ranking this one-act comic masterpiece as Puccini's peak achievement during the last half of his career is supported by these two zestful, idiomatic presentations.

Though the newer Capitol set is the more smoothly recorded (there is, however, a good deal of surface noise in the stereo version), it is difficult to choose between two such persuasive performances. Capitol has the edge in polish and in the beauty of its voices. Del Monte's apostrophe to Florence and, of course, De los Angeles' lovely singing are well ahead of the offerings of Cetra's young lovers.

The older recording, however, has points of superiority. Impressive as is Gobbi's portrayal, it is not quite a match for Taddei's strong, brilliantly comic Schicchi. Simonetto, moreover, leads a firmer, more effectively paced performance than Santini. The minor parts, which add so much flavor to this opera, are vividly presented by both casts, particularly in the Cetra.

LA GIOCONDA. Zinka Milanov (Gioconda), Rosalind Elias (Laura), Belen Amparan (La Cieca), Giuseppe Di Stefano (Enzo), Leonard Warren (Barnaba), Plinio Clabassi (Alvise), Santa Cecilia Chorus and Orchestra, Fernando Previtali; Victor LM-6139 (3) or LSC-6139 (stereo) (4).

Anita Cerquetti, Giulietta Simionato, Franca Sacchi, Mario Del Monaco, Ettore Bastianini, Cesare Siepi, Chorus and Orchestra of the Florence May Festival, Gianandrea Gavazzeni; London A-4331 or OSA-1302 (stereo) (3); LOR-90004 (4-track tape).

Maria Callas, Fiorenze Cossotto, Irene Companeez, Pier Miranda Ferraro, Piero Cappuccilli, Ivo Vinco, La Scala Chorus and Orchestra, Antonino Votto; Angel 3606 or S-3606 (stereo) (3).

La Gioconda, the only durable composition of Amilcare Ponchielli, has recently been favored with three recordings, all of which are available in stereo. No one of them is ideal, nor should we expect the situation to be any better than it is. This opera requires *six* artists with grand dramatic temperaments and voices of power and flexibility. Such voices being in short supply today and recording contracts being what they are, a recorded version with an ideal cast is highly unlikely.

There are, however, outstanding singers in each of these three *Giocondas*, and any one of the recordings will give a degree of satisfaction. The Victor seems the best to this listener—but by a narrow margin. There is a thrilling Barnaba from Warren and a stylish Gioconda from Milanov, though her voice is frequently unsteady in loud and rapid passages. Di Stefano is in good voice, but his singing is often monotonously loud and insensitive. Elias, too, has a lovely voice, but it does not have the glint and impact for this role; her characterization, moreover, is rather colorless. The same may be said for Amparan's dramatic effect. Clabassi is a good Alvise but does not have the dash that sometimes rescues this ungrateful role from its expected pit of dullness. Previtali carries out his assignment with discipline and taste.

The London set is worthy of consideration and, indeed, may be your choice if raw vocal power is your special delight. Cerquetti, Simionato, Del Monaco, and Siepi sing with plentiful tone and enthusiasm, and the two ladies even get under the skins of their roles. It is they who contribute the greatest excitement. The conducting of Gavazzeni is, as usual, in need of tighter ensemble and a wider dynamic span, not to mention dramatic sensitivity.

The Angel set is the most recent *Gioconda*, as its full-bodied sonics will attest, although there is some wearying distortion in certain loud passages. Until the final act, the performance only fitfully rises above the level of good, big-opera-house routine. Indeed, the most compelling feature of the first three acts is the beautiful style and finished playing of the Scala Orchestra. The cast, headed by Maria Callas, is stocked with a number of live, young voices of pleasing amplitude. Those of Irene Companeez and Ivo Vinco are particularly persuasive. None of these voices, however, is manipulated with outstanding musical refinement, and the legato of Callas is something all of her associates could emulate with profit.

The news of this recording is what Callas accomplishes in the last act. Though her portraiture is consistent throughout the opera, it is only at the end that her vocal resources are consonant with her dramatic achievement. In the first act, for example, she is particularly futile in her effort to give us the purity of tone essential to the vital phrase, *Madre! Enzo adorato! Ah! come t'amo!*; and she misses the spontaneity requisite to Gioconda's scene with Laura in the second act. It is the finale where Callas makes the most of her powers and blots from memory anything she did in her earlier *Gioconda* recording for Cetra. Her *Suicidio* is a gripping episode and establishes the proper dramatic framework for the various currents of torment that rack the heroine during the course of this opera's grisly conclusion. Callas makes clear—as few have—the anguish, the hesitation Gioconda experiences while awaiting Enzo. Moreover, her acknowledgement of her beloved's arrival, *Enzo! . . . sei tu*, is a heart-stopping instant during which she reveals with stunning completeness her relief and apprehension. It is no wonder that Callas has inspired the rest of the cast to its best effort to produce the finest finale now available on records.

LOHENGRIN. Annelies Kupper (Elsa), Lorenz Fehenberger (Lohengrin), Helena Braun (Ortrud), Ferdinand Frantz (Telramund), Otto von Rohr (King Henry), Bavarian Radio Chorus and Orchestra, Eugen Jochum; Decca DX-131 (4).

Eleanor Steber, Wolfgang Windgassen, Astrid Varnay, Hermann Uhde, Josef Greindl, Bayreuth Festival Chorus and Orchestra, Joseph Keilberth; London A-4502 (5).

One can have little conviction about rating either of these *Lohengrins*, for neither is entirely effective. Indeed, it is doubtful whether this difficult opera can be satisfactorily cast today; certainly there will be many a season before we encounter any group equal to the Metropolitan Opera's prewar cast of Kirsten Flagstad, Lauritz Melchior, Karen Branzell, and Friedrich Schorr.

Each of the recordings in question has commendable traits, and even a moderately good *Lohengrin* is better than none at all. I prefer the Decca set for the incisive, well-paced conducting of Jochum, and the vigorous and convincing singing of Frantz and Rohr. Fehenberger does not have the power of an ideal Lohengrin, but he is exceptionally pleasing in the lyric passages and most particularly in his entrance. Even without the requisite vocal solidity, Braun manages a chillingly venomous account of Ortrud through the dramatic coloring of her words. There remains Kupper, who lacks absolute vocal steadiness, a ravishing legato style, and sufficient thrust in climactic moments. She contributes her best singing in the Bridal Chamber Scene. The Decca recording is good except that many of the fortissimi have been somewhat monitored.

The London issue was recorded at a public performance at Bayreuth in 1953. It retains the excitement of such affairs and admits such disadvantages as some "off-mike" singing and normal, unwanted stage and audience noises. The stars here are the extraordinarily brilliant chorus and the American soprano Steber, whose purity of tone and dedicated spirit amply make up for her moments of vocal unsteadiness. She is certainly the one Elsa on records who might occasionally be called rapturous. Windgassen seems to have had trouble getting warmed up, for he does not sing as he can until the third act. Varnay is a serious artist with a fine understanding of the Wagnerian roles she assumes, but here, as often, she seems to sing back in her throat. This allows her to get the power and tonal color she wants, but it causes her to sacrifice the amenity of crisp enunciation. Uhde sings satisfactorily and gets an interesting touch of paranoia into his characterization. The conducting is slack and nerveless.

LUCIA DI LAMMERMOOR. Renata Scotto (Lucia), Giuseppe Di Stefano (Edgardo), Ettore Bastianini (Enrico), La Scala Chorus and Orchestra, Nino Sanzogno; Mercury OL-2-108 or SR-2-9008 (stereo) (2).

Maria Callas, Ferruccio Tagliavini, Piero Cappuccilli, Philharmonia Chorus and Orchestra, Tullio Serafin; Angel 3601 or S-3601 (stereo) (2).

Joan Sutherland, Renato Cioni, Robert Merrill, Santa Cecilia Chorus and Orchestra, John Pritchard; London A-4355 or OSA-1327 (stereo) (3).

Lily Pons, Richard Tucker, Frank Guarrera, Metropolitan Opera Chorus and Orchestra, Fausto Cleva; Columbia SL-127 (2).

Roberta Peters, Jan Peerce, Philip Maero, Rome Opera Chorus and Orchestra, Erich Leinsdorf; Victor LM-6055 (2) or LSC-6141 (stereo) (3).

During the past decade, Maria Callas has inspired others to take seriously a number of early 19th-century operas—*Lucia* included—and to perform them as if they were newly composed and with the conviction that they were meant to push the emotions off center. The persistence and persuasiveness with which she has pleaded her cause has set in motion a desire to rehabilitate a rich treasure of stage pieces from one of Italy's notable periods of musical culture.

As sturdy as it is, *Lucia* needs performers who take a serious attitude about the severity of its tragedy, and this attitude must be reflected in the intentions of the majority of the performing group. A dedicated Lucia alone will not do, as Angel's recent recording of the opera makes clear. Callas, in this, her second recording of the role (her first, Angel 3503, is now withdrawn), reads her part with a mastery that challenges the memory to find an equal. Her phrasing, too, illuminates the vocal arabesques of Lucia in the white light of musical and dramatic purity. Callas's notes above the staff are not so steady as before, but one must praise the growth of her artistry while lamenting the decline of an important part of her vocal resource. The deterioration of Tagliavini's voice is also evident here. More and more the tenor resorts to crooning in soft passages, and his high, loud tones have lost their former lustrous quality. Tagliavini shows his sensitivity to the role on occasion, but he simply no longer has all the equipment necessary to carry out his assignment. Cappuccilli is too pale dramatically or vocally to make Enrico seem properly villainous. Serafin's support is sympathetic but somewhat nerveless.

The Columbia and Victor sets strain one's credibility in this opera's dramatics. Neither is poor musically, but then neither impels the listener to sympathize with the characters' distress; that would not seem to be either's real purpose. Of the two Lucias under consideration, the preference is for Pons, though she would have been more effective had she been recorded at an earlier date. Her fragile voice is appealing in this role, and it is tastefully recorded. Peters, with more vocal health, emerges as an automaton rather than as an unhappy woman; she has sung Lucia with more feeling in the opera house. Peerce, once a fine Edgardo, is now too dry of voice to fulfil his role; but one always appreciates his impeccable musical taste. Young Maero has a pleasing voice, but he does not yet have the command to make much of his part. The male roles are stronger in the Columbia set. Tucker sings very well indeed; few tenors can emulate his elegantly sustained vocalizing of the difficult *Verranno a te*. Guarrera is an acceptably menacing Ashton, if nothing else. The leadership of Cleva is more stylish than Leinsdorf's, though both maintain good discipline.

It is the Mercury set which makes this opera breathe again and restores to it a measure of the expressive alarm that stirred nineteenth-century audiences. Though this performance contains not one absolutely unforgettable portrayal, it seems to me an uncommonly fine *Lucia* and the best one we have ever had to hear at home. It has a consistent dramatic spirit that is apparent in the opening bars and is sustained by Maestro Sanzogno and his worthy associates. Sanzogno, hitherto known to gramophiles only for his splendid direction of Cimarosa's *Il Matrimonio Segreto*, emerges as an Italian operatic conductor to be reckoned with. His work is neat and very stylish, and he certainly knows how to put a singer at ease without getting himself pushed around.

Renata Scotto, making the most of her latest opportunity (this is only her third recording) sounds positively radiant. She has a well-schooled lyric soprano of good range and flexibility. She minds her musical manners and she pays attention to her text. If her high E flat tends to whiteness and if she does not phrase or paint her words like a Callas, one should not be dismayed. Scotto is, after all, very young; but, make no mistake, she is already capable of giving a great deal of pleasure.

Di Stefano may be at that point in his career when most of his Edgardos are behind him, but he has sung the role in this recording with almost all of his accustomed tonal splendor (some of his high tones reveal effort) and a welcome degree of dramatic participation. Is there any other Italian tenor singing Di Stefano's roles today who enunciates as well?

Enrico is tailor-made for Bastianini. The part does not require much subtlety, but it needs Bastianini's abundance of tone, good top, and his intense vitality. The remainder of the cast is always sufficiently capable. The orchestra and chorus are the best anywhere for this music.

In its recording Mercury has made little or no attempt to detail stage action, but, of its kind, this sound picture is of exceptional quality, except for an occasional pre-echo and an obtrusive sibilant. The sonics are live and natural, and the balance between voices and orchestra is first-rate. The surfaces are quiet, and, unlike many stereodiscs, these have not a trace of rumble.

Though this *Lucia*, like the others, does not present the scene between Edgardo and Enrico at the beginning of the third act, it does include a long passage in the Mad Scene that is usually cut and is missing from the other versions.

As these pages go to press, London has issued the first truly complete *Lucia*. Not only do these handsomely recorded discs let one hear the rarely performed first scene of the third act between Edgardo and Enrico, but, in addition, they offer the invariably cut episode in which Raimondo presents to Lucia further evidence of Edgardo's infidelity (first scene, second act) and the entire Mad Scene, including its quiet final pages in which Raimondo shames Normanno for precipitating the tragedy. The role of Lucia is used by Joan Sutherland as a vehicle to display the range and flexibility of her exceptionally beautiful voice. The soprano's point of view, as well as the conducting that gives her free reign to achieve her ends, however, vitiates the dramatic force latent in this opera. Cioni's scooping and Merrill's lack of vindictive fire are further deterrents to one's enjoyment of this performance. The remainder of the cast is stocked with opulent voices, even in the minor parts. Cesare Siepi, for example, is the Raimondo.

MADAMA BUTTERFLY. Victoria de los Angeles (Cio-Cio-San), Jussi Bjoerling (Pinkerton), Mario Sereni (Sharpless), Rome Opera Chorus and Orchestra, Gabriele Santini; Capitol GCR-7232 or SGCR-7232 (stereo) (3).

Clara Petrella, Ferruccio Tagliavini, Giuseppe Taddei, Radio Italiana Chorus and Orchestra, Angelo Questa; Cetra 1248 (3).

Toti Dal Monte, Beniamino Gigli, Mario Basiola, Rome Opera Chorus and Orchestra, Oliviero de Fabritiis; Angel GRB-4000 (2).

Victoria de los Angeles, Giuseppe Di Stefano, Tito Gobbi, Rome Opera Chorus and Orchestra, Gianandrea Gavazzeni; Capitol GCR-7137 (3).

Anna Moffo, Cesare Valletti, Renato Cesari, Rome Opera Chorus and Orchestra, Erich Leinsdorf; Victor LM-6135 or LSC-6135 (stereo) (3).

Renata Tebaldi, Carlo Bergonzi, Enzo Sordello, Santa Cecilia Chorus and Orchestra, Tullio Serafin; London A-4337 or OSA-1314 (stereo) (3); LOR-90010 (4-track tape).

Maria Callas, Nicolai Gedda, Mario Borriello, La Scala Opera Chorus and Orchestra, Herbert von Karajan; Angel 3523 (3).

Eleanor Steber, Richard Tucker, Giuseppe Valdengo, Metropolitan Opera Chorus and Orchestra, Max Rudolf; Columbia SL-104 (3).

For many the classic recording of Puccini's touching and evocative *Madama Butterfly* will always be the prewar Angel issue with Dal Monte and Gigli. Certainly Gigli never gave a keener dramatic or vocally smoother performance in any other role he recorded, and it is equally certain that the remainder of the cast was inspired on this occasion to give its very best. The controversial element in this brilliant ensemble is the Butterfly of Dal Monte. Past her vocal prime when this recording was made, she nevertheless used her aging but girlish-timbered voice with the skill and instinct of a great artist. It is not, perhaps, the voice Puccini had in mind for the role or one that the casual listener would associate with Butterfly; and for that reason and the fact that the recording, though surprisingly satisfactory, is naturally not up to present-day standards, you may prefer one of the modern issues.

Among these, the choice must be Capitol's second recording of this opera with Victoria de los Angeles—if you have the equipment, in the stereo edition. This fine artist's improvement in this role between her first and second effort is striking. Whereas before her chief accomplishment was a ravishingly lovely tone, we now have, in addition, a manifestation of her dramatic resource that makes poignant many passages (particularly the Love Duet and the scene with Sharpless) that were previously glossed over. In a few of Butterfly's most outspoken phrases, De los Angeles does not deliver quite the degree of intensity and tonal impact that seems apposite, but these moments cannot dull the otherwise brilliant impression she makes in the role. In the newer performance, which is much better prepared than the earlier one, De los Angeles also has much stronger support. The previous recording revealed an ensemble clearly underrehearsed and insensitively directed. Neither Di Stefano nor Gobbi, who often give pleasure, sang with the refinement and taste one has heard them exhibit on other occasions, and the minor parts were poorly presented. In the new recording De los Angeles is backed up by the sympathetic, if sometimes slack, direction of Santini, a knowing Sharpless in Sereni, who works well with her, and Bjoerling, who in this (his last) recording takes one's breath away with his vocal power and beauty and the grandeur of his musical style.

Almost as effective as the top-ranked recording is the version by Cetra with its well-balanced group of vocalists, its close-knit ensemble, and its appropriately idiomatic expression. Conductor Questa is to be praised for his carefully chosen tempi, which are largely responsible for the ease and spontaneity of this presentation. Without the vocal beauty of a number of her competitors, Petrella succeeds in using what she has in a way that makes us feel Butterfly's pathos. Tagliavini, despite certain vocal affectations, presents a credible Pinkerton, who seems hard-boiled and reckless enough to do what he did. Taddei is an outstandingly sympathetic Sharpless, the best I can remember for many years.

The artistic direction of the Victor presentation provides a degree of interest in an otherwise low-voltage performance. The idea here was to give *Butterfly* with the light touch. Puccini was said to have favored this approach instead of the heavy theatrics which we have all often encountered in presentations of this opera. So far, so good—but Victor has made the error of equating the light touch with light voices, and a cast of such voices, however skillful, cannot really do justice to the work. Leinsdorf, too, despite his care for clean musical execution, is something of a stylistic hindrance to entering the heart of *Madama Butterfly*.

The London set is the second London recording of the opera with Tebaldi. The first one, now unavailable, was more successful. Though she still offers much vocal beauty, a heavy, matronly quality has crept into Tebaldi's singing and characterization and erases any trace of girlishness it once had. The excessively expansive tempi of Serafin do not help matters either. The remainder of the cast performs in a routine fashion.

The well recorded Angel version represents a fascinating experiment and a noble failure. Karajan conducts a meticulously prepared performance that observes more of Puccini's printed directions than one is accustomed to. The pacing, however, is really too slow, and the dreamlike continuity Karajan tries to achieve does not come off. To be sure, the abundant detail in the instrumental performance and the delicate tonal coloring are uncommon pleasures; but they are not sufficient substitutes for the simple, direct expression that this opera demands. The only vocalist who makes an impression (most of the cast is either vocally weak or dramatically colorless) is Callas. This artist has apparently endorsed Karajan's delicate view of *Madama Butterfly*, and the result is that on two occasions only does her singing really burst into dramatic flame—when she is looking for the name of Pinkerton's ship and when she bids farewell to her child.

Almost as old as LP itself is the Columbia set, and its sound betrays its age. Here is a performance of some musical distinction but little dramatic fervor. After a slow start Steber warms up, and by the third act she performs with great conviction. Tucker and Valdengo sing with no more than good resonance, and the other participants are routine.

MANON. Victoria de los Angeles (Manon), Henri Legay (Des Grieux), Michel Dens (Lescaut), Opéra-Comique Chorus and Orchestra, Pierre Monteux; Capitol GDR-7171 (4).

Janine Micheau, Libero de Luca, Roger Bourdin, Opéra-Comique Chorus and Orchestra, Albert Wolff; London A-4305 (3).

London's recording of *Manon* could be considered an almost ideal version of the opera were there not so many cuts; *e.g.*, most of Act V has been eliminated. For smoother continuity, the recording employs a narrator to summarize what occurs during the cut portions, a procedure that will be of help only to those who understand French, for London has not provided a special libretto for the occasion. All the performers are unusually satisfying. Micheau may be a bit cool of temperament, but she sings with delectable lyricism and for the most part with consummate ease. De Luca makes an appropriately romantic Des Grieux, singing with warm tones and satisfying abandon, even though he occasionally loses some control of his voice in forte passages; his *Le Rêve* contains some truly exquisite pianissimo singing. Bourdin is a tower of strength as Lescaut; there are few today who could match his admirable singing-acting in this role. Also memorable is the stylish work of Wolff, who leads his forces with exceptional spirit and discipline.

As good as is the London recording, it must take second place to Capitol's entry, for Maître Monteux has, with the golden-voiced De los Angeles and an ensemble of French vocalists and instrumentalists, given us a *complete Manon* in every sense. *Manon* "plays" well in the theater, and here one senses this for the first time in a recording. The dramatic values are clear, as in the emphasis (with the help of Legay's fine singing-acting) given to Des Grieux, the pivot on which the play turns. Musically, furthermore, the performance has grace, vitality, and abundant style. A particular pleasure is Monteux's continual reminder of just how well Massenet orchestrated.

MANON LESCAUT. Licia Albanese (Manon), Jussi Bjoerling (Des Grieux), Robert Merrill (Lescaut), Rome Opera House Chorus and Orchestra, Jonel Perlea; Victor LM-6116 (3).

Renata Tebaldi, Mario Del Monaco, Mario Boriello, Santa Cecilia Chorus and Orchestra, Francesco Molinari-Pradelli; London A-4316 or OSA-1317 (stereo) (3).

Maria Callas, Giuseppe Di Stefano, Giulio Fioravanti, La Scala Chorus and Orchestra, Tullio Serafin; Angel 3564 (3).

The principals in the Victor set perform with a dramatic conviction rarely displayed by their rivals. Albanese no longer has all of her former vocal finesse, but nevertheless manages an acceptably youthful portrait with many telling expressive touches. Her contribution leads to our involvement with the drama and to the extraordinary impression made by Bjoerling and Merrill, both in splendid voice. Perlea's direction is firm and well-paced.

Tebaldi's and Di Stefano's richness of sound and Del Monaco's vocal gusto cannot be fully appreciated in productions so miserly in theatrical savor as the London and Angel recordings. The Angel recording, despite the high polish of its choral and orchestral work, is especially aloof. Harmed by Serafin's laggard tempi, it is irreparably damaged by Callas's overgenerous offering of unsteady tone and, surprisingly enough, her apparent unconcern for the vitality of her role.

DIE MEISTERSINGER VON NÜRNBERG. Ferdinand Frantz (Hans Sachs), Elisabeth Grümmer (Eva), Rudolf Schock (Walther), Marga Höffgen (Magdalene), Gerhard Unger (David), Gottlob Frick (Pogner), Chorus of the Municipal Opera and German State Opera, Berlin, and Choir of St. Hedwig's Cathedral and the Berlin Philharmonic Orchestra, Rudolf Kempe; Angel 3572 (5).

Paul Schoeffler, Hilde Gueden, Günther Treptow, Else Schürhoff, Anton Dermota, Otto Edelmann, Vienna State Opera Chorus and Vienna Philharmonic Orchestra, Hans Knappertsbusch; London A-4601 (6).

Otto Edelmann, Elisabeth Schwarzkopf, Hans Hopf, Ira Malaniuk, Gerhard Unger, Friedrich Dalberg, Bayreuth Festival Chorus and Orchestra, Herbert von Karajan; Electrola 90275/9.

These three recorded performances are a cut above what you are apt to run across in a casual tour of *Meistersingers* in the world's opera houses. In the first place, each is complete (most theater performances suffer from cuts) and each is unusual (especially the Angel and the London) for the obvious care expended in its preparation. The Angel is the most recent recording and has clearly the best sound. The Electrola set has the advantages and disadvantages that accrue from recording an actual performance. This one, accomplished at Wagner's own Bayreuth Festspielhaus, is notable for spirit and vitality but not for unfailing precision. Particularly in the first act, one is disappointed by poor balances and a certain lack of shipshapeness. The performance steadily improves, however, and the final scene is overwhelmingly grand and joyous. Throughout, one admires the superb Eva of Schwarzkopf and the Beckmesser of Erich Kunz. Edelmann, in the all-important role of Hans Sachs (he is a good Pogner in the London set), is a strong-voiced and serious musician; but, except in his final apostrophe to German art, he does not offer the richness of detail contributed by Frantz and Schoeffler. Hopf has the ideal voice for Walther, but it is not consistently under control. Unger is the David for two of the sets, satisfactory in the Electrola, and in the Angel set, superb and more than a match for London's elegant Dermota. Karajan is uneven in inspiration, but at his best he is exciting and compelling. The Bayreuth Chorus sings with uncommon excellence.

Schoeffler is the most tender of the Sachses, but he is not quite so steady vocally as Frantz, perhaps the best all-round cobbler-poet. Gueden is irresistibly charming, but her voice is a trifle light for such an outspoken passage as *O Sachs, mein Freund*. The over-brilliant tones of Treptow may not appeal to all listeners, but everyone will, I imagine, admire his steadiness and power. All others in the London cast are exceptional; Knappertsbusch leads a plodding but exquisitely detailed performance.

Frantz, as I have indicated, is a substantial Sachs. If his voice is not so rich as it was in the Urania *Meistersinger* (URLP-206, now withdrawn), it nevertheless remains satisfying; his gruff geniality is, moreover, very convincing. Grümmer has a lovely, silvery soprano which is just right for Eva, and she uses it with taste and vitality. Schock, like the other Walthers, is not ideal; but the timbre, weight, and relative flexibility of his voice make him the compromise choice in this difficult, vocally high-lying role. Frick is a capital Pogner.

The improvement in Kempe's conducting of this score will be readily apparent to those who own the old Urania set and compare it with the Angel. Here, he gives us a splendidly paced performance that is beautifully light and transparent in sonority. The Berlin Philharmonic plays magnificently, quite outclassing its rivals in this music.

NORMA. Maria Callas (Norma), Christa Ludwig (Adalgisa), Franco Corelli (Pollione), Nicola Zaccaria (Oroveso), La Scala Chorus and Orchestra, Tullio Serafin; Angel 3615 or S-3615 (stereo) (3).

Gina Cigna, Ebe Stignani, Giovanni Breviario, Tancredi Pasero, Chorus and EIAR Orchestra, Vittorio Gui; Cetra 1204 (3).

There is little to choose between these two performances; each has striking merits and flaws. The Angel will generally be given preference, however, since its engineering represents a technological advance of twenty years over the prewar Cetra recording.

Norma is one of the most taxing roles in the operatic repertory, demanding a powerful personality and a colorful voice of tremendous range capable of all kinds of dynamic contrasts. In addition, it requires a bravura style and, above all, a melting legato of the utmost smoothness. Callas comes closest of all contemporary singers to meeting these qualifications, but she is not ideal—even though she alone has recorded the role during the LP era. (She has recorded Norma twice, the first recording having been withdrawn upon the release of the second.) In her latest effort, Callas is inclined more than before to unsteadiness when sustaining high notes, and in long scale passages her voice is seldom even in weight and color. It is, of course, her imaginative projection of the text and her singing of Norma's reflective measures that is meritorious. Cigna is an intermittently exciting Norma; she has the required temperament and a voice of proper weight, but her singing needs more discipline and refinement.

Ludwig is a pleasing Adalgisa because of the warmth of her voice and her unfailing respect for the music and drama in her role. She does not, however, have the incomparable style and tonal impact of Stignani, whose voice can be heard at its zenith in the Cetra set. Corelli's handsome tenor is not matched by his musical deportment. His phrasing is frequently inelegant; moreover, his lack of an even scale, his aspirates and scoops are unfortunate in Bellini's music. Nevertheless, he is superior to his rival, Breviario, who bleats his way through Pollione's measures. Both Orovesos are splendid in voice and in dramatic effect. The conducting of Gui has the dramatic power that is missing in the graceful and affectionate work of Serafin.

LE NOZZE DI FIGARO. Lisa Della Casa (Countess Almaviva), Hilde Gueden (Susanna), Suzanne Danco (Cherubino), Cesare Siepi (Figaro), Alfred Poell (Count Almaviva), Vienna State Opera Chorus and Vienna Philharmonic Orchestra, Erich Kleiber; London A-4407 or OSA-1402 (stereo) (4).

Lisa Della Casa, Roberta Peters, Rosalind Elias, Giorgio Tozzi, George London, Vienna State Opera Chorus and Vienna Philharmonic Orchestra, Erich Leinsdorf; Victor LM-6408 or LSC-6408 (stereo) (4).

Elisabeth Schwarzkopf, Anna Moffo, Fiorenza Cossotto, Giuseppe Taddei, Eberhard Wächter, Philharmonia Chorus and Orchestra, Carlo Maria Giulini; Angel 3608 or S-3608 (stereo) (4.)

Sena Jurinac, Rita Streich, Christa Ludwig, Walter Berry,

Paul Schoeffler, Vienna State Opera Choir and Vienna Symphony Orchestra, Karl Böhm; Epic SC-6022 (3).

Perhaps, after all, *Le Nozze di Figaro* is Mozart's supreme operatic accomplishment as well as one of the greatest manifestations of human powers. Certainly while listening to the radiant London performance, one has little doubt about the superiority of this opera—brimful of brilliance, wit, and humanity.

The London issue is clearly the one to acquire. First of all, it is complete (we get all the recitatives and the seldom performed arias of Marcellina and Basilio). The recording, moreover, is clear, warm, and spacious; the balance between voices and orchestra, a model. Then there is the direction of Kleiber, who proves himself a Mozart conductor of rare ability, and, of course, there is the impeccable Vienna Philharmonic to attend his ministrations. Last, and by no means least, we have a group of vocalists whose work shows a distinction of musical style and, most particularly, an appreciation of the dramatic aspects of *Figaro* uncommon in any presentation. In the area of vocal beauty, only Poell's dry voice is shy of the best prevailing standards. The supporting roles are exceedingly well taken; one must cite the convincing bluster of Fernando Corena's Bartolo, the zest of Morgan Jones' spidery Basilio, and Anny Felbermayer's ingenuous Barbarina. Among the principals, Gueden is outstanding and the best Susanna on records; she seems to dominate the many ensembles in which she takes part. Dramatically, Siepi does not warm up until the close of the first act (where is the irony and the undercurrent of anger that should accompany *Se vuol ballare?*); but from his mock-heroic aria *Non più andrai* to the very end of the opera he is a satisfying Figaro indeed. There will be those who maintain that Cherubino ought to be sung by one who possesses a richer and darker voice than Danco. This group has a good argument, but I am bound to say that I have seldom heard anyone who brings Cherubino to life as Danco does immediately upon her entrance. Hers is an adorable page boy—ebullient in spirit and in love with love.

The Victor set has several elements in common with London's; the beautifully sung Countess of Lisa Della Casa, Corena's Bartolo, the Vienna State Opera Chorus, and the Vienna Philharmonic Orchestra. Moreover, it is, like the London, a complete *Figaro* (without the standard cuts that are maintained in the Angel and Epic versions). It cannot, however, command the degree of attention the London set demands, for it is rather shy of dramatic temperament. Leinsdorf's direction is neat and precise, but it reveals mainly the external beauties of the score. The same may be said of most of the vocalists. Tozzi and Elias, for example, have splendid voices and excellent musical taste, but they only fitfully get into the skins of their characters. Peters, too, sings well, but too often she is willing to give us routine ingenue archness instead of relevant details in portraiture. London, on the other hand, performs with a good deal of dramatic force; it is his legato singing that is often short of the best standards. To sum up, the Victor set is primarily a musical delight but only occasionally comes to grips with *Figaro's* theatrical problems.

Highly uneven is the Angel set—uneven in matters of musical style, in dramatic style, in emphasis, and in concentration. Giulini has not provided the kind of coherent direction that makes his associates pull together toward a common goal. Sometimes smoothness of execution seems to be the goal, then it seems to be dramatic revelation. When it is the latter, some of the vocalists sing out, others employ a kind of toneless speech. There are, happily, long passages when everyone performs the music in the same way, and these, of course, are gratifying. So, too, is the sense of aliveness that this splendid recording imparts, however inconsistent it may be. The outstanding performance is given by the young American soprano, Anna Moffo. Also satisfying, except in her arias where she is much too fussy, is Schwarzkopf. Taddei gives us a good idea of Figaro's spleen (too often overlooked by most performers of the part) but not such a good notion of Figaro's zest for life.

The Epic set is too often sluggish, both musically and dramatically. A heaviness of thought seems to pervade most of the cast and the conductor, Karl Böhm. Memorable are much of Jurinac's lovely singing and the forceful, manly characterization of Schoeffler.

ORFEO ED EURIDICE. Léopold Simoneau (Orfeo), Suzanne Danco (Euridice), Pierrette Alarie (Amore), Blanchard Ensemble and Lamoureux Orchestra, Hans Rosbaud; Epic SC-6019 (2) (In French).

Risë Stevens, Lisa Della Casa, Roberta Peters, Rome Opera Chorus and Orchestra, Pierre Monteux; Victor LM-6136 (3) (In Italian).

Dietrich Fischer-Dieskau, Maria Stader, Rita Streich, RIAS Chamber Choir, Berlin Motet Choir, and Berlin Radio Symphony Orchestra, Ferenc Fricsay; Decca DX-143 (2) (In German).

Gluck's original version of *Orfeo*, in Italian, was first presented on October 5, 1762, in Vienna. The title role was created for a male alto. Later, after Gluck had moved to Paris and taken the city by storm with his *Iphigénie en Aulide* (1774), he quickly followed up his success with a slightly revised version of *Orfeo*, the title role of which was designed for a tenor. This version in French, is the one that Epic has recorded. The best known version is the one prepared by Hector Berlioz from the Italian and French versions with the title role given to a contralto. This version has been recorded both by Victor and Decca. In the Decca recording, however, we find a baritone in the role of Orfeo. Hermann Abert, the editor of a full score of the original version, suggested that a baritone might be good in the main part. It was a poor suggestion, but we shall get to that in a moment. The Victor release, incidentally, is the only one that includes the complete ballet music that Gluck composed for the French version.

If the reader is not thoroughly confused by this time, I will continue by recommending the Epic performance as the most satisfactory of the three available. Simoneau sings with grace and refinement, if not with the ideal degree of force. Danco and Alarie perform well, and Rosbaud leads a precise, well-paced account of the score.

Though it is wanting in vitality, the Victor recording has the advantage of Monteux's authoritative direction and the lovely Euridice of Della Casa. Its serious weakness is the poor singing and style of Stevens. She cannot shape many of her lines properly, for her swollen and poorly focused tones and insufficient breath control make it impossible for her to phrase with the required smoothness. Peters, sounding shrill, was apparently not in good voice.

The tonal brilliance Gluck had in mind for Orfeo simply cannot be accomplished by a baritone, if one is to judge from Fischer-Dieskau's attempt in the Decca set. Moreover, the opera does not go well in German; the sounds of that language seem continually at odds with the flow of the music. No matter, for the performance is a sleepy one because of Fricsay's excessively deliberate tempi and the lack of dramatic involvement on the part of the cast.

OTELLO. Ramon Vinay (Otello), Herva Nelli (Desdemona), Giuseppe Valdengo (Iago), Chorus and NBC Symphony Orchestra, Arturo Toscanini; Victor LM-6107 (3).

Mario Del Monaco, Renata Tebaldi, Aldo Protti, Vienna Philharmonic Orchestra and Chorus, Herbert von Karajan; London A-4352 or OSA-1324 (stereo) (3).

Mario Del Monaco, Renata Tebaldi, Aldo Protti, Santa Cecilia Chorus and Orchestra, Alberto Erede; London A-4312 (3).

Jon Vickers, Leonie Rysanek, Tito Gobbi, Rome Opera Chorus and Orchestra, Tullio Serafin; Victor LD-6155 or LDS-6155 (stereo) (3).

Otello has finally been recorded in stereo—twice, in fact. Although one can be grateful for the opportunity of hearing this masterwork in one's home with a close approximation to its full sonic amplitude, and although at least the London stereo set offers a performance of unusual finish and certainly better-than-average dramatic vigor, one's reaction after investigating all the available sets is to turn to the incomparable Toscanini-directed *Otello*.

The Toscanini *Otello* is a miracle and a monument for relentless energy, irresistible passion, musical refinement, and control. Though it stems from December, 1947, broadcasts, it still is an acceptable recording. The chorus and the NBC Orchestra perform like demons, and their work is something you are unlikely to encounter again in this score. It is clear that Toscanini has inspired the vocal soloists to the performances of their lives. Certainly Vinay is not the *heldentenor* of Verdi's imagination; still he transmits a tragic dignity indispensable to his role. One would have to call Valdengo's Iago the big performance among the singing contributions. Dramatically, it is superbly articulated, grandly detailed, and altogether a complete study of the character's malevolence; vocally, it is supremely satisfying. Herva Nelli sings sweetly with musicianship, but she does not reveal the spunk that Verdi knew Shakespeare's Desdemona had.

It is to the credit of the newest London production that at times it banishes the memory of Toscanini's effort. Actually, this is an effective performance that has been well prepared by Karajan and frequently executed with uncommon skill by his associates. It begins impressively, rising to a particularly dazzling rendition of the *Fuoco di gioia* chorus. By the close of the first act, it is obvious that Del Monaco has seldom, if ever before, sung with such regard for Verdi's dynamics. As a result, he imparts a welcome degree of tenderness to his duet with Desdemona not to be found in his earlier recording. Even here, however, there are some awkward vocal moments, some coarse phrases.

some wayward rhythms that rob Del Monaco's singing of real distinction. And so it goes throughout the set. It is a good Otello and the best, very likely, that Del Monaco is apt to give us. It is crowded with the virtues of vocal health, tonal gleam, and dramatic participation; but the grand humanity of the role is not always apparent. Desdemona would seem to be Tebaldi's most congenial role; it suits her temperament, vocal quality, and technique as no other she has presented on records. As in her first recording of the part, Tebaldi is affecting in her every episode. Protti has improved his grasp of Iago's music considerably since his first recording, and his portrayal now has a definite profile. His voice, however, remains too light to cope with the passages that demand a strong, ringing tone. The remainder of the cast is of unusual merit, and it is seldom we hear the supporting roles handled with such skill. The Vienna Philharmonic plays with tonal luster and power, as well as with its usual finesse. Karajan once again demonstrates his considerable abilities as a conductor of Verdi's music, and he, above all, is largely responsible for the lift this presentation gives one. Certainly, his work is much superior to that of Erede and Serafin, and that alone would entitle the newest London set to its second rank.

Concerning the Victor set, it is difficult to write about a set that promised so much and has delivered so little. Serafin, with so many years of treasurable operatic conducting behind him, is never up to our best memories of his work. The Rome Opera Orchestra, on this occasion, cannot give him playing which is unfailingly unanimous. Vickers, one of the world's most promising tenors, has a number of successes to his credit, but this Otello cannot be counted among them. His voice, to begin, does not have the clarion ring essential to the part. Next, and most important, Vickers seems detached from the Moor's tragedy. Despite his musicality, the purity of his vowel sounds, and his careful attention to rhythmic pulse and required dynamics, he never for a moment makes you believe he is Otello. He has, of course, had little experience with this extremely arduous role; one day he may make us forget this initial attempt. Rysanek's voice is not sufficiently steady or so consistently pure in tone to give us a satisfying Desdemona, and nothing she is able to do can conceal this fact for long. Once a distinguished operatic portrait, Gobbi's Iago is now a remnant of its former glory. The perception is still there, but Iago's vocal demands are on a number of occasions too much for Gobbi's present resources. Outstanding among a generally good group of supporting singers is Glorindo Andreolli, an uncommonly fine Cassio.

PAGLIACCI. Franco Corelli (Canio), Lucine Amara (Nedda), Tito Gobbi (Tonio), Mario Zanasi (Silvio), La Scala Chorus and Orchestra, Lovro von Matacic. Angel 3618 or S-3618 (stereo) (2, 3 sides; odd side: Verdi Operatic Choruses).

Jussi Bjoerling, Victoria de los Angeles, Leonard Warren, Robert Merrill, Robert Shaw Chorale and RCA Victor Orchestra, Renato Cellini; Victor LM-6084 (2, on 3 sides; odd side: Operatic Choruses).

Mario Del Monaco, Clara Petrella, Afro Poli, Aldo Protti, Santa Cecilia Chorus and Orchestra, Alberto Erede; London A-4323 (3, includes *Cavalleria Rusticana*).

Mario Del Monaco, Gabriella Tucci, Cornell MacNeil, Renato Capecchi, Santa Cecilia Chorus and Orchestra, Francesco Molinari-Pradelli; London A-4237 or OSA-1212 (stereo) (2, on 3 sides; odd side is Del Monaco Italian Song Recital); LOH-90021 (4-track tape).

Giuseppe Di Stefano, Maria Callas, Tito Gobbi, Rolando Panerai, La Scala Chorus and Orchestra, Tullio Serafin; Angel 3527 (2, on 3 sides; odd side blank).

Richard Tucker, Lucine Amara, Giuseppe Valdengo, Clifford Harvuot, Metropolitan Opera Chorus and Orchestra, Fausto Cleva; Columbia SL-113 (2).

Lovro von Matacic has inspired the La Scala ensemble and a vocally well-endowed cast to its bravest offering, and the result is a *Pagliacci* that crackles with vitality. This outstanding performance, clearly and resonantly recorded (and with sufficient spread of sound in the stereo version), is unique among the many *Pagliaccis* that have achieved preservation by its unusually scrupulous musical preparation and its painstaking attention to dramatic detail.

In revivifying *Pagliacci's* simple, sturdy values, Matacic and his team have revealed its often-concealed strengths and made it clear that the opera is more than a vehicle for a *tenore robusto*, more than a homely dramatic exercise on the subject of illusion and reality. They have given *Pagliacci* the kind of realistic passion that suits it and, moreover, the picturesque quality appropriate to the provincial, itinerant Italian players of another day. Among the principal singers, it is perhaps Gobbi who contributes the most striking portrait. But Corelli, here performing up to his great promises as a singing actor, may strike you as equally effective by the plainness and honesty of his straightforward Canio. In such company, Amara, always the possessor of a lovely voice, gives us a persuasive characterization that entitles her at last to recognition as a theater artist. The remainder of the cast, the artists of La Scala, are unfailingly eloquent.

Victor holds a slight edge over the rest of its competition, though almost as good are the London recordings and the Angel release with Callas. Indeed, there is little to choose among all four versions. All are well recorded, particularly the London recording, available in stereo on tape and disc. All have their merits and a few shortcomings. Victor has the uncommon excellence of two rich-voiced baritones—Warren and Merrill—in superb voice and fine dramatic fettle. It also boasts the fervent expression and aristocratic phrasing of Bjoerling, not to mention the well-drilled Shaw Chorale and the fine RCA Victor Orchestra. Yet De los Angeles, for all her beautiful singing, does not create a character, and conductor Cellini pulls his singers about too much.

Both London versions star Del Monaco, whose big, ringing voice and secure top tones are ideal for Canio. His characterization, though lacking in pathos, has a compelling ferocity. Petrella is the reason for the earlier London set's higher rating. Unlike Tucci who is wanting in temperament and pale in dramatic color (she also needs a more poised tone, especially in the top of her range), Petrella is a vibrant Nedda, the best one on records, though she does stray from pitch on occasion. Poli is a fine actor, but it is the less-than-adequate Protti who sings Tonio's *Prologue* (in addition to his duties as Silvio). MacNeil, in the new London set, sings with fine musicianship, but his voice does not have Warren's opulence, and he could make more of Tonio's lines. Capecchi needs a warmer voice and more ardent expression to make him the properly romantic Silvio. Molinari-Pradelli's conducting is first-rate, and his pacing creates a more vital dramatic effect than does Erede's plodding direction.

The Angel issue offers Gobbi, who does more with his words than the other Tonios. Callas, as usual, is interesting dramatically; but here she is too sophisticated for the part. Serafin is magnificent and conducts with a style all his own. Far too light-voiced but still singing intelligently is Di Stefano. Acting persuasively, Panerai still cannot compete with the tones of a Merrill.

If it seems odd that the "official" Metropolitan Opera set is rated so low, do not be deceived. The Columbia version is but a small cut below all save one of its running mates. Richard Tucker is the star here, and it must be said that he gives as good an idea of the pathos in Canio as all but one of the other tenors under discussion. Cleva turns in a pleasing performance. Amara, on the other hand, sings well enough, but at the time of this recording she had not figured Nedda out. Valdengo lacks vitality and his rhythm is slack, and Harvuot's voice is not sensuous enough.

PELLÉAS ET MÉLISANDE. Suzanne Danco (Mélisande), Pierre Mollet (Pelléas), Heinz Rehfuss (Golaud), André Vessières (Arkel), Hélène Bouvier (Geneviève), Flore Wend (Yniold), Chorus and Orchestre de la Suisse Romande, Ernest Ansermet; London A-4401 (4).

Janine Micheau, Camille Maurane, Michel Roux, Xavier Depraz, Rita Gorr, Annik Simon, Elizabeth Brasseur Choir and Orchestre des Concerts Lamoureux, Jean Fournet; Epic SC-6003 (3).

Victoria de los Angeles, Jacques Jansen, Gérard Souzay, Pierre Froumenty, Jeannine Collard, Françoise Ogeas, Choeurs Raymond St. Paul and Orchestre National de la Radiodiffusion Française, André Cluytens; Angel 3561 (3).

Many ardent admirers of Debussy's magical and humane opera, including this writer, lament the withdrawal by RCA Victor of its LCT-6103, a dramatic performance of some inspired French singers and instrumentalists led by Roger Désormière during the German occupation of Paris. In spite of its mediocre recorded sound and some vocal inequalities, its characters spring to life and present a superior theatrical experience unchallenged by the later recordings. Of these three, I prefer the production directed by that prince of impressionists, Ernest Ansermet. As did Désormière, he weaves from his orchestra the luminous tonal fabric that properly sets off the words of the characters.

Fournet has the right idea and directs with style, but neither he nor the Lamoureux is quite capable of achieving the precise tonal blends and balances that are necessary for this score to make its greatest effect. The singing in both these sets is quite good—far above average, indeed. But in the London set, Danco is dramatically a wan Mélisande, and Micheau and Maurane in the Epic miss that touch of ecstasy especially essential in the last scene of the fourth act.

The Angel set is the most recently recorded *Pelléas,* but it is disappointing. Its principal advantages are the lovely singing of De los Angeles and the playing of the superb Orchestre National; its weaknesses are the no-longer-youthful voice of Jansen, the inappropriate lightness of Souzay's, and the mostly insensitive and sometimes imprecise conducting of Cluytens.

RIGOLETTO. Leonard Warren (Rigoletto), Erna Berger (Gilda), Jan Peerce (Duke of Mantua), Robert Shaw Chorale and RCA Victor Orchestra, Renato Cellini; Victor LM-6021 (2).

Giuseppe Taddei, Lina Pagliughi, Ferruccio Tagliavini, Cetra Chorus and Orchestra of Radiotelevisione Italiana, Turin, Angelo Questa; Cetra 1247 (3).

Tito Gobbi, Maria Callas, Giuseppe Di Stefano, La Scala Chorus and Orchestra, Tullio Serafin; Angel 3537 (3, 5 sides; odd side blank).

Ettore Bastianini, Renata Scotto, Alfredo Kraus, Florence May Festival Chorus and Orchestra, Gianandrea Gavazzeni; Mercury OL-3-112 or SR-3-9012 (stereo) (3).

Renato Capecchi, Gianna D'Angelo, Richard Tucker, San Carlo Chorus and Orchestra, Francesco Molinari-Pradelli; Columbia M2L-404 or M2S-901 (stereo) (2).

Robert Merrill, Roberta Peters, Jussi Bjoerling, Rome Opera Chorus and Orchestra, Jonel Perlea; Victor LM-6051 (2).

Aldo Protti, Hilde Gueden, Mario Del Monaco, Santa Cecilia Chorus and Orchestra, Alberto Erede; London A-4313 (3).

Oddly enough, the best version has an international cast; its nearest rival, an all-Italian one. Each is effective in its way; each will give satisfaction. Because the Cetra is more expensive by one record, many will prefer the Victor. The latter offers a good enough recording with a somewhat cavernous resonance and plenty of superior vocalism. Leonard Warren had one of the richest and smoothest baritones of the last twenty years, and Rigoletto was one of his finest roles dramatically. He does not give quite the sense of each individual word as Taddei does (with a fine but less resplendent voice), but he does communicate the overall expression of any given sequence. The great Erna Berger lacks Pagliughi's maidenly ecstasy, but her singing is consistent, her characterization believable, and her musical artistry, as usual, remarkable. Both Peerce and Tagliavini are inclined to miss the aristocratic elegance of the Duke. Peerce is the more stylish musically and sings with greater ardor. Tagliavini, however, offers greater tonal and expressive shading. The vigorous conducting of

Cellini is somewhat streamlined for my taste, and it lacks the ease and spontaneity of Questa's.

Another release with some fine moments to recommend it is Angel's. Gobbi and Callas may not be as consistent in vocal security as their rivals in the two top-rated albums, but they make handsome contributions from time to time. Gobbi reads his role with special sensitivity as does Callas at least in part, but she does not convince one with any regularity of the innocence and spontaneity expected in a Gilda. Di Stefano offers some good singing, but too much of his work is brash and anything but stylish. The Scala forces perform nobly under Serafin's frequently somnolent direction.

A resplendent recording, particularly persuasive in its stereo edition, is the decisive factor in awarding the Mercury entry a high rank. The performance it conveys is of the rough-and-ready variety, more notable for energy than for finesse. All of the principals display attractive voices, plentiful enthusiasm, but frequently untidy musical manners. Dynamic markings are frequently slighted, especially by conductor Gavazzeni, and the tempi are more than occasionally at odds with Verdi's indications. Like the London recording, the Mercury includes the tenor aria, *Possente amor,* omitted in all the other issues.

The Columbia *Rigoletto* is a well recorded performance of frequent merit. It offers in Tucker a rather graceful and notably well sung Duke of Mantua. D'Angelo's voice does not have the fullness one would like, but her delivery is disarmingly sweet and straightforward. Capecchi does not have the grand, solid baritone which is the foundation for Rigoletto's music; nevertheless, he colors his voice appositely—most effectively in his big scene with the courtiers. Molinari-Pradelli's conducting is better than routine, although it is difficult to praise any particular moment as being exceptional.

The latest Victor set sports three fine voices, but only Bjoerling's work is memorable. Peters' characterization is mechanical, and she wobbles on the sustained trills and the final note of *Caro nome.* Merrill misses the dramatic incisiveness one expects in this rich part, and his rhythm could be more secure.

A good cut below its competition is the London recording. The casting of the robust-voiced but unsubtle Del Monaco as the Duke, a role usually reserved for polished lyric tenors, was a mistake. He can sing all the notes, to be sure, but he is incapable of sustaining a smooth legato throughout so many phrases that demand nothing less. As a consequence, his Duke seems nothing more than a tough boor. Protti has neither sufficient vocal technique nor dramatic imagination to make much impression in the very difficult title role. Gueden's silvery soprano is an appropriate instrument for Gilda's music. But she seems vocally uncomfortable in the part, especially in long, high-lying phrases and in sustained notes above the staff. She also fails to convince that she is a complete mistress of the Italian style. The supporting cast is strong; it is a luxury to find such artists as Cesare Siepi, Giulietta Simionato, and Fernando Corena in what many opera companies consider *comprimario* parts. Erede disappoints once more; his conducting lacks rhythmic verve and dramatic color.

DER RING DES NIBELUNGEN

There is no sign as yet of a complete recording of *Siegfried*, which would give Wagner's tetralogy the permanence it so richly merits. During the LP era, no more worthy project has gone so long neglected, though I suppose we should be grateful for the *Götterdämmerung* and, most particularly, for the *Rheingold* that have been recorded since the first edition of this book. Like the *Walküre* commented on below, these are the first complete recordings of these operas.

DAS RHEINGOLD. George London (Wotan), Kirsten Flagstad (Fricka), Set Svanholm (Loge), Gustav Neidlinger (Alberich), Jean Madeira (Erda), Walter Kreppel (Fasolt), Kurt Böhme (Fafner), Eberhard Wächter (Donner), Waldemar Kmentt (Froh), Claire Watson (Freia), Vienna Philharmonic Orchestra, Georg Solti; London A-4340 or OSA-1309 (stereo) (3); LOR-90006 (4-track tape).

The first recording of this absorbing opera was in itself an event of uncommon significance. An engineering triumph of London's expert staff, the stereo edition was a history-making event and can be declared a milestone in the art of recording.

Das Rheingold, the prologue to Wagner's tetralogy, provided London's recording staff with manifold opportunities to demonstrate the wonder of hearing an operatic performance in three dimensions, including such special effects as the movement of the Rhinemaidens at the beginning of the opera, the sound of a full complement of anvils, the anguished cries of the Nibelungen, the stacking of gold in the Freia ransom scene, the shattering sound of Donner's hammer and the response of an immense clap of thunder, and the effect of distance and height in Erda's pronouncements and of depth in the Rhinemaidens' final lament.

What makes this technical *tour de force* meaningful, it must be emphasized, is that at all times it serves the musical performance. Such mechanical mastery and taste would be of no avail if the rendition it reproduced were not of sufficient quality. This performance, fortunately, is an outstanding one; it is seldom in a lifetime of operagoing that one encounters a *Rheingold* prepared with such meticulous care and executed with such brilliance.

The guiding spirit of this performance is the conductor Solti, who draws from the superb Vienna Philharmonic and his singers the finest work of which they are capable. Outstanding in this cast is the great Kirsten Flagstad, who is heard here, in the twilight of her career, singing her first Fricka with a grandeur and an authority one would expect of her hundredth. Equally impressive is Gustav Neidlinger as Alberich. He fully reveals every aspect of this complex character from the time we hear his frustrated attempt to seduce a Rhinemaiden, through his almost touching wails of self-pity over the loss of the gold, to his ringing curse.

The remainder of the cast, down to the third Rhinemaiden, must be cited not only for its contribution but for the spirit with which the performance was accomplished.

The only flaws in this performance are London's lack of a perfect legato, which robs his apostrophe, *Abendlich strahlt der Sonne Auge*, for instance, of just the proper sense of tender majesty, the want of greater solidity in Madeira's tones in *Weiche, Wotan*, and of sufficient atmosphere in the passages that open the opera.

These are, however, relatively insignificant details in a masterful production that will long serve as a fitting reminder of what recorded opera can be.

DIE WALKÜRE. Ludwig Suthaus (Siegmund), Leonie Rysanek (Sieglinde), Martha Mödl (Brünnhilde), Ferdinand Frantz (Wotan), Margarete Klose (Fricka), Gottlob Frick (Hunding), Vienna Philharmonic Orchestra, Wilhelm Furtwängler; Electrola 90100/4 (5).

The first complete phonographic presentation of Wagner's noble music drama is a good recording of what is in many ways a thrilling performance. It was, I believe, the very last recorded opera Furtwängler led before his death in 1954, and it will stand, along with his *Tristan und Isolde*, as an enduring memorial to perhaps the greatest Wagnerian conductor of our day. On this memorable occasion, the Vienna Philharmonic—one of the world's leading orchestras—has given of its best. So tasteful and harmonious is the playing that those who have complained that parts of the second act and the "Ride of the Valkyries" are noisy will have to revise their thinking; such is the power of a great conductor and orchestra to dispell barnacled fables. As for the singers: well, say what you will, they really sing Wagner. They do not shout and bluster, they really sing. Though Lauritz Melchior, the finest Wagnerian tenor of the past forty years, had a far superior voice than did Suthaus, it is difficult to recall his having found more song in Siegmund's music than Suthaus has conveyed on this occasion. Suthaus also reveals much in his delivery of the text that one had recently forgotten. If he does not sing with quite the unwonted abandon one would like at the end of the first act, his performance is nevertheless distinguished. Rysanek docs not give one the ecstasy of Sieglinde in the first act, but her reply to Brünnhilde in the last act is in every way exalted and touching. She is never less than acceptable in meeting the other demands of her role. Frick has a handsome bass voice and he, too, sings well; but he does not seem as sinister as Hunding ought to be.

Klose is, of course, a real professional, if an aged one; time has not robbed her of the ability to make the most of Fricka's shrewishness. Frantz is the finest Wotan since Friedrich Schorr. If he could give one a bit more tenderness in his farewell, I should have to rate him the equal of his great predecessor.

Mödl, I have saved for the last. What a curious artist she is! She is so very uneven vocally; she cannot invariably sing an even scale; her lower, middle, and upper registers are ever apparent in wide skips; yet she has considerable powers of expression. She always communicates the sense of her music and she shows imagination in coloring words. She is an appealing Brünnhilde—especially with Furtwängler supporting her glow with his unique radiance.

GÖTTERDÄMMERUNG. Kirsten Flagstad (Brünnhilde), Eva Gustavson (Waltraute), Ingrid Bjoner (Gutrune), Set Svanholm (Siegfried), Waldemar Johnsen (Gunther), Egil Nordsjø (Hagen), Per Grönneberg (Alberich), Oslo Philharmonic Orchestra, Norwegian State Radio Orchestra and Opera Chorus, Øivin Fjeldstad; London A-4603 (6).

These records stem from broadcasts especially arranged by the Norwegian State Radio System to present Kirsten Flagstad to her countrymen in her last performance as Brünnhilde in *Götterdämmerung*. The broadcasts took place in Oslo one act at a time on January 5, 8, and 10, 1956, a little over 32 years after Flagstad's debut in the same city; and one must be grateful for London's decision to preserve them on records.

Any performance of *Götterdämmerung* graced by Flagstad is, of course, something to cherish. Her portrayal of this noblest of the Brünnhildes is perhaps the most resplendent of her many triumphs. On this occasion, she is not up to the high-lying passages of the Prologue, but at her next entrance Flagstad begins to show us why she was the most accomplished soprano of her day. Then comes her fateful meeting with Waltraute. How she colors every word so fittingly! Next is her horror and terror as Siegfried tears the ring from her grasp, followed by her devastating denunciation of Siegfried, her floodtide of tone as she delivers her oath on spearpoint, and her bitter rejoinders to Hagen and Gunther in the marvelous scene that closes the second act. Finally, comes the Immolation Scene—full of firm resolve, tender reflection, and passionate decision.

Would that Flagstad's associates on this occasion had performed on a level near hers. Such was not to be. Svanholm, with his dry and aging voice, at least reads his part well. Gustavson and Grönneberg are good as less pivotal characters. We have, however, inadequate artists in the very important roles of Hagen and Gunther. Both Nordsjø and Johnsen lack anything like the requisite tonal volume and solidity and dramatic force.

Moreover, the conducting lacks firmness of line and inevitable forward progress. For one who remembers what Furtwängler did with this score, and what the late Artur Bodansky accomplished in innumerable performances with Flagstad at the Metropolitan Opera House during the thirties, Fjeldstad will not fill the bill. It is also deplorable that he has cut a passage out of Hagen's Watch in the first act.

DER ROSENKAVALIER. Elisabeth Schwarzkopf (Marschallin), Christa Ludwig (Octavian), Teresa Stich-Randall (Sophie), Otto Edelmann (Ochs), Philharmonia Chorus and Orchestra, Herbert von Karajan; Angel 3563 or S-3563 (stereo) (4).

Maria Reining, Sena Jurinac, Hilde Gueden, Ludwig Weber, Vienna State Opera Chorus and Vienna Philharmonic Orchestra, Erich Kleiber; London A-4404 (4).

Marianne Schech, Irmgard Seefried, Rita Streich, Kurt Böhme, Dresden State Opera Chorus and Saxon State Orchestra, Karl Böhm; Deutsche Grammophon DGM-301 or DGS-7301 (stereo) (4).

Because a convincing Marschallin is indispensable to a satisfying *Rosenkavalier*, the Angel set is the only possible choice among the three available versions. Schwarzkopf has a steady voice, even when employed at the full; her rivals do not. Moreover, her portraiture is outstanding, even if she does not have that art which invariably conceals art. Schwarzkopf is the star of this production, which has been meticulously prepared and ably directed by Karajan. It boasts a tight ensemble of very good supporting vocalists, who pay close attention to dramatic as well as to musical values, and of the members of the Philharmonia Orchestra, who play with zest and refinement of tone. The one keen disappointment (other than the rumble and rather noisy surfaces of the stereo edition) is the rendition of the Trio, which provides the expressive capstone to the opera. The pacing for this number is unusually slow, and the rhythm is insecure. The recording, elsewhere quite good, here makes a confusion of the sonorities and, to make matters worse, places the voices at such a distance that they have little impact even at the climax of the Trio.

The London album, adequately recorded, is graced by the firm leadership of Kleiber and by the lovely playing of the Vienna Philharmonic, as well as by Weber, the best of the Ochses. One would prefer (as in the Deutsche Grammophon set) a darker voice than Jurinac's disarmingly sweet one to contrast with Gueden's silvery soprano (the boy-girl relationship needs at least a rich mezzo in the Octavian part), but both are so intelligent and sing so attractively that it seems uncharitable to complain.

Almost as pleasing in the roles of the young lovers are Seefried and Streich in the Deutsche Grammophon set, but neither is quite so poetic as the London pair and neither is quite so scrupulous about Strauss' dynamic intentions. Böhm leads a lively, well-paced performance.

Though its inclusion in these pages may be questioned, I must mention the availability—once again—of the historic abridged performance of *Rosenkavalier* on two Angel LP's (set GRB-4001). It cannot give anyone a clear idea of the theater work Strauss intended, for some of the cuts are brutal (a great portion of the last act is missing); but it does contain some superb singing-acting by latter-day singers who were closely associated with the parts they portray. Lotte Lehmann is the Marschallin; Elisabeth Schumann, Sophie; Maria Olszewska, Octavian; Richard Mayr, Baron Ochs.

SALOME. Christel Goltz (Salome), Julius Patzak (Herod), Margareta Kenney (Herodias), Hans Braun (Jokanaan), Vienna Philharmonic Orchestra, Clemens Krauss; London A-4217 (2).

This London set is a triumph in almost every way. Goltz gives us a Salome of flaming intensity, highlighted by precise diction, care for dynamics, and vocal power, if not smoothness. Patzak is tremendous, revealing not only a being but the entire manner of that being; a more complete characterization I have yet to encounter. Hardly on the same level, but wholly agreeable is the dignified Jokanaan of Braun. Less effective is the rather strident, dramatically pale Herodias of Kenney.

Attention must be called to London's extraordinary casting of the minor roles. Anton Dermota, for example, is a capital Narraboth; and just imagine the luxury of a Ludwig Weber in the bit part of the First Nazarene!

The conducting of Clemens Krauss is something to treasure. A close friend of composer Richard Strauss, Krauss brought all his love and understanding of this music to his recording assignment. It was the last work he ever recorded, for he died shortly after its completion; and it endures as a worthy testament to his art and his friendship with Strauss. How fortunate that London's engineers have mirrored with uncommon fidelity the sound of this superb performance!

SIMON BOCCANEGRA. Tito Gobbi (Simon), Victoria de los Angeles (Maria), Giuseppe Campora (Gabriele), Boris

Christoff (Fiesco), Rome Opera Chorus and Orchestra, Gabriele Santini; Capitol GCR-7126 (3).

Paolo Silveri, Antonietta Stella, Carlo Bergonzi, Mario Petri, Radio Italiana Chorus and Orchestra, Francesco Molinari-Pradelli; Cetra 1231 (3).

Even if it is not an immediately appealing composition for many listeners, *Simon* is a noble opera with authentic quality, and we are fortunate that it is revived from time to time in the opera house and that it is available in two quite good complete recordings.

The Angel set, with its more recent recording and more vocally resplendent cast, is a shade more enjoyable than the better-integrated Cetra entry directed by Molinari-Pradelli. Both Gobbi and Silveri are sympathetic as the noble Simon, but Gobbi has more vocal and dramatic force in his big scenes. De los Angeles is wanting in dramatic intensity and sustained brilliance and power in her top register to make the ideal Maria; however, many of her lyrical passages are delivered with characteristically lovely tone and fine musical style. Stella made this recording early in her career, and the freshness and amplitude of her voice go far to make up for a certain indistinctness of dramatic profile. Bergonzi, with his passionate delivery and live, young tenor, is a fine Gabriele and one of Cetra's points of clear superiority. Campora sings well enough, but he cannot summon fire from tones that are not compact. The rich sound of Christoff's bass meets Fiesco's requirements better than does Petri's less vibrant one.

TANNHÄUSER. Marianne Schech (Elisabeth), August Seider (Tannhäuser), Margarete Bäumer (Venus), Karl Paul (Wolfram), Otto von Rohr (Landgrave), Munich State Opera Chorus and Orchestra, Robert Hager; Urania 211-4 or 5211-4 (stereo) (4).

Unless you feel you *must* have a recorded *Tannhäuser*, the advice here is to wait for a new performance that may be blessed with more virtues than this one. One can scarcely blame the work of the instrumentalists and chorus under the experienced, skillful, but not-quite-inspired hand of Heger or the dignified, sonorous singing of the two low-voiced principals—Paul and von Rohr. But surely one cannot be satisfied with a mediocre Tannhäuser or a Venus whose aged voice lacks any kind of sensuous appeal and furthermore is tremolo-ridden. Schech shows small soprano assets and hardly suggests the nobility and conviction of Elisabeth.

TOSCA. Maria Callas (Tosca), Giuseppe Di Stefano (Cavaradossi), Tito Gobbi (Scarpia), La Scala Chorus and Orchestra, Victor De Sabata; Angel 3508B (2).

Renata Tebaldi, Mario Del Monaco, George London, Santa Cecilia Chorus and Orchestra, Francesco Molinari-Pradelli; London A-4235 or OSA-1210 (stereo) (2).

Zinka Milanov, Jussi Bjoerling, Leonard Warren, Rome Opera Chorus and Orchestra, Erich Leinsdorf; Victor LM-6052 (2) or LSC-6052 (stereo) (3, odd side devoted to operatic arias).

Antonietta Stella, Gianni Poggi, Giuseppe Taddei, San Carlo Opera Chorus and Orchestra, Tullio Serafin; Columbia M2L-402 (2).

The importance of the conductor in Puccini's operas is minimized by many operagoers. All listeners who take the trouble to sample these four available recordings of *Tosca* will quickly see the error of this attitude. Though each set is stocked with at least two good voices, the only one that consistently grips the attention is the one that affords the virtue of superb dramatic and musical direction. In spite of stunning vocal performances in the Angel set, Sabata must be given acclaim equal to that of his singing artists.

This Angel recording of 1952 also gives us one of Callas' most affecting and strikingly detailed operatic portraits. Her imaginative singing, though not unfailingly smooth, nevertheless continually throws light on aspects of Tosca's character one seldom encounters. From her very entrance, she keeps preparing the listener by the expressive coloration of words in selected lines for what she will do later on in the opera. It is in every sense a distinguished, unified characterization, and Callas is supported by "singing-acting" almost up to her lofty standards. The role of Cavaradossi fits Di Stefano like a glove, and he is now its most distinguished exponent. Note his soft, intimately shaded singing in the first-act love duet and in *O dolci mani* in the last act, as well as his full-voiced, ringing *Vittoria* in the second-act torture scene. Gobbi is a masterful Scarpia; he gives us a fine balance of poise and passion in his richly voiced communication of the Roman police chief's insinuations, cruelty, and lust. The secondary singers are more than adequate in their parts, too. Over all, however, is the dominating spirit of Sabata—now cajoling tones of tenderness, now lashing his singers and instrumentalists to heights of awesome fury. It all adds up to one of the great performances of an Italian opera in today's LP catalogue.

London's second recording of *Tosca* with Tebaldi represents an improvement over its earlier effort (now out of print). Though hardly the equal of the burning-coal intensity of the Angel set, it is more than satisfactory; and the recording, particularly the stereo edition, lets you hear more of Puccini's score than you have ever heard before in your home. Tebaldi's mastery of the title role has grown since her first effort. Her voice is as outstanding as ever, and her grasp of the part is now firm and entirely her own. Some may not be able to accept a Tosca who is not really volatile, but others will be able to make a case for a Tosca whose character is generous and warm-hearted. One would not expect Del Monaco to be the ideal Cavaradossi, for the character requires a degree of tenderness that up to now has been alien to Del Monaco's manner of singing. He sings no differently here. But his strengths of vocal amplitude and enunciation are here allied with a pleasing measure of musical tension, and his contribution accordingly has a good deal of appeal. To my knowledge, London has never in the theater sung Scarpia so effectively as he does in this recording. He reads the part with persuasiveness, and his singing, if not the ultimate in polish, is more than adequate for Scarpia. The minor roles are in capable hands. The conducting is stylish and precise.

The Victor set is a mixed blessing. Though an all-star cast is on hand and the vocalizing of Bjoerling and Warren, in particular, is memorable, the production suffers from the frequently insensitive and unidiomatic conducting of Leinsdorf. Dramatically, it flickers fitfully. Milanov manages her role with a certain appealing grandeur, but she is not completely convincing. Moreover, she is not at many points in her best voice. The recording is clean, but in the stereo version the sound frequently lacks sufficient body. The monophonic edition is preferred.

The warmth and security of Serafin's conducting and the splendid acting of Taddei are the two recommendable qualities in the Columbia set. Poggi's singing is unmodulated and brutal. Stella's voice and characterization are somewhat cold.

LA TRAVIATA. Victoria de los Angeles (Violetta), Carlo Del Monte (Alfredo), Mario Sereni (Germont), Rome Opera House Chorus and Orchestra, Tullio Serafin; Capitol GCR-7221 or SGCR-7221 (stereo) (3).

Licia Albanese, Jan Peerce, Robert Merrill, Chorus and NBC Symphony Orchestra, Arturo Toscanini; Victor LM-6003 (2).

Anna Moffo, Richard Tucker, Robert Merrill, Rome Opera Chorus and Orchestra, Fernando Previtali; Victor LM-6154 or LSC-6154 (stereo) (3); FTC-8002 (4-track tape).

Renata Tebaldi, Gianni Poggi, Aldo Protti, Santa Cecilia Chorus and Orchestra, Francesco Molinari-Pradelli; London A-4314 (3).

Rosanna Carteri, Cesare Valletti, Leonard Warren, Rome Opera House Chorus and Orchestra, Pierre Monteux; Victor LM-6040 (3).

Antonietta Stella, Giuseppe Di Stefano, Tito Gobbi, La Scala Chorus and Orchestra, Tullio Serafin; Angel 3545 (2).

A completely outstanding *Traviata* for most tastes is yet to be recorded, though some will feel that the Capitol recording fills the bill. Certainly there are admirable elements in all of the other versions listed above, even if none of them is strong enough to provide in one recording the vocal finish and expressive potency one desires in this opera.

The Toscanini recording is his 1946 broadcast. Perhaps the demands of the radio time schedule upset everyone's equilibrium; whatever the reason, Toscanini conducts with more than a few unreasonably rapid tempi and with a nervousness that taxes his singers and makes them give less effective performances than they have been known to offer. Still, it is extraordinary to hear the orchestral framework so solid and gleaming; and the entire production reveals careful preparation and a dramatic power one will not find in the other recorded *Traviatas*.

The Capitol set is certainly the most stimulating *Traviata* on records since Toscanini's, and, all things considered, it deserves the top rating. It is a fine recording (particularly the stereo edition) of a somewhat unconventional presentation, but, because it does not violate what is inherent in the work, it cannot be considered eccentric.

Its viewpoint is one many keen observers have held about *Traviata:* that this composition is in reality a type of chamber opera that thrives on intimate projection. It is the recognition of this viewpoint by Maestro Serafin (taking into account his unfortunate use of several overdeliberate tempi) and Victoria de los Angeles that makes this performance so consistently fresh and ingenuous. The rest of the cast, not notable for vocal resplendence, is caught up in the spirit of the occasion and is more effective as participants in a living drama than the all-star, everyman-for-himself cast we sometimes hear. Working with Serafin, De los Angeles not only sings superbly but gives us a far more effective Violetta than the one she has previously displayed in America. This Violetta is shy, elegant, soft-spoken, and somewhat withdrawn in the social exchanges of the first act; and she maintains a degree of reserve even in the harrowing conversation with Germont in the second. Many will quarrel with this approach, for they will miss the expected broad contrast between one who must *show* her demon pleasure drive and one who hopefully dreams of a private love away from the crowd. They may also miss a Violetta who does not lose herself entirely in the scene with Germont. Their position commands respect; each listener will determine whether he can accept this interpretation of Violetta.

Though De los Angeles maintains her ladylike approach to her role to the end, the last two scenes will likely seem effective to those with a traditional Violetta in mind. Toward the end of the first of these scenes, De los Angeles shows us a Violetta who, after the strain of a continuous series of heart-tearing events, now humiliated personally and socially, afraid for her lover's life in an impending duel, is stripped at last of her reserve. Thus, De los Angeles has built her characterization in such a way that her last scene attains exceptional poignance. Such consistent portraiture betokens uncommon vocal resource and mental powers decidedly rare.

The newest Victor set, available on disc and tape, is a recording of considerable impact, despite some patches of distortion and occasional pre-echo. It serves as a suitable showcase for the talents of Anna Moffo, a young soprano whose career has just begun. Her youthful voice is colorful and flexible, and, if she does not have the power for Violetta's most outspoken feelings or the personality to give us a finished characterization, she nevertheless earns our respect for her usually enjoyable singing and the thought she has put into her dramatic effort. Incidentally, her whispering of Germont's letter in the last act is a novelty that should not become a practice in future recordings. Tucker discloses good vocal health and agreeable verve. Merrill's baritone is an asset, but his musical deportment here is frequently unbecoming.

Except for two elements, London offers no more than a comfortably routine performance of *Traviata,* but those two are important. Of first consideration is the Violetta of Tebaldi. Though she makes little impression in the first act, where her conversational passages are somewhat insensitively loud and her arias are rather disappointing, she is splendid throughout the remainder of the opera. The great final act finds her particularly touching. One must also admire fully half of Molinari-Pradelli's conducting (it is curiously matter-of-fact throughout certain episodes). The preludes especially are unusually well played.

The later monophonic Victor set is notable for Monteux's direction and the principals' voices. Carteri, unfortunately, does not have a sufficiently suave vocal delivery, and there are, in addition, some passages uneasily projected by Valletti and Warren. Neither this performance nor the one in the Angel release attains sufficient drama. The Angel set is graced by the dramatic perception of Gobbi and the conducting of Serafin, but Stella's voice is rather cold and too often quavery and Di Stefano's singing is decidedly inelegant in its monotonous loudness.

TRISTAN UND ISOLDE. Kirsten Flagstad (Isolde), Ludwig Suthaus (Tristan), Blanche Thebom (Brangäne), Dietrich Fischer-Dieskau (Kurvenal), Josef Greindl (King Marke), Chorus and Philharmonia Orchestra, Wilhelm Furtwängler; Angel 3588 (5).

Birgit Nilsson, Fritz Uhl, Regina Resnik, Tom Krause, Arnold van Mill, Singverein der Gesellschaft der Musikfreunde and the Vienna Philharmonic Orchestra, Georg Solti; London A-4506 or OSA-1502 (stereo) (5).

On its release in 1953, the Angel *Tristan und Isolde,* the first complete recording of Wagner's music drama, was clearly a landmark. Time, if anything, has simply enhanced its significance. True, we have now a much finer sounding *Tristan,* thanks to impeccable London engineering; but this newer version, while satisfying (particularly in the stereo edition), has no individual effort to match its counterpart in the older set.

The conducting of Furtwängler and the singing of the incomparable Flagstad, of course, are the stuff of which operatic dreams are made. Flagstad's Isolde—so musically stimulating, so apt in dramatic detail, so grand in sound, so complete in projection—is one of the most durable achievements in the lyric theater of our day, a measure by which other sopranos who assume this demanding role will surely be judged for many years. This recording has not captured the most radiant vocal performance Flagstad was capable of giving; it was made too late in her career for that. But it is close to her best singing, and, in expression, it reveals her highest dramatic powers.

Nothing in Suthaus' career had prepared one for his recorded Tristan. Here he sings—as few Tristans ever do—with plentiful tone and with a minimum of forcing to give us the letter as well as the spirit of the text. He is surpassingly fine in the last act, the most arduous portion of his assignment. The three major supporting vocalists all show care and understanding in their performances. Thebom's voice thins out at the top, but elsewhere it is equal to the considerable demands that the role of Brangäne makes on an artist. Greindl's voice lacks the weight and massive projection necessary to make of King Marke what a few other singers have accomplished with this intractable character, but it is certainly acceptable. Fischer-Dieskau has a similar problem. Though wonderfully sensitive in the quiet moments of the last act, he has not the heroic vocal resources to make Kurvenal's taunting reply to Brangäne in the first act, for example, as tough and hearty as it should be.

Furtwängler here is simply at his best, and we are rewarded with an ideally proportioned performance, one which—in the ebb and flow of its power and in its unyielding continuity—creates a thoroughly mesmerizing effect. Furtwängler must have made a special study of *Tristan* from an acoustical point of view, so transparent is the sound, so equilibrated are the strings, winds, and brass, so resolutely and with such rhythmic freedom does the music move.

It is precisely this miracle of motion that Solti, for all his sincerity and fastidiousness of detail, cannot duplicate. The grand line of *Tristan* is not always present in his performance, and the opera comes to us in a fragmented fashion. Some bits are full of excitement, others are either flat, fussy, or in some way unspontaneous. What never lets us down is the superlative playing of the Vienna Philharmonic Orchestra, the most impressive attraction of the London set. Closely competing for our admiration is Birgit Nilsson, the brilliant Swedish soprano who has by now assumed the roles associated with Flagstad in the world's leading opera houses. Nilsson brings to Isolde fine musical taste and a voice of considerable size and quality, particularly resplendent above the staff. Her portraiture is excellent in outline but something less than that in detail. Many touches that would fill out her characterization are missing because of the lack of impact in her lower register and the occasional impurity of tone which prevents her in several phrases from maintaining a smooth vocal line.

The remainder of the vocal cast is competent, but not what one could call "festival quality." The young tenor, Uhl, has been well coached; but his voice, though adequate in quiet expression, has neither enough resonance nor amplitude for Tristan's many outspoken passages. Resnik's voice is unsteady, and, for such a moment as Brangäne's warning in the second act, unacceptable, notwithstanding her sympathetic reading of much of her role. Krause is a sensitive Kurvenal, but he, like Fischer-Dieskau, needs more power for his heroic measures.

IL TROVATORE. Zinka Milanov (Leonora), Jussi Bjoerling (Manrico), Fedora Barbieri (Azucena), Leonard Warren (Count di Luna), Robert Shaw Chorale and RCA Victor Orchestra, Renato Cellini; Victor LM-6008 (2).

Maria Callas, Giuseppe Di Stefano, Fedora Barbieri, Rolando Panerai, La Scala Chorus and Orchestra, Herbert von Karajan; Angel 3554 (3, on 5 sides, odd side blank).

Leontyne Price, Richard Tucker, Rosalind Elias, Leonard Warren, Rome Opera Chorus and Orchestra, Arturo Basile; Victor LM-6150 or LSC-6150 (stereo) (3); FTC-8000 (4-track tape).

Renata Tebaldi, Mario Del Monaco, Giulietta Simionato, Ugo Savarese, Florence May Festival Chorus and L'Orchestre de la Suisse Romande, Alberto Erede; London A-4326 or OSA-1304 (stereo) (3); LOR-90005 (4-track tape).

Traditional cuts, such as Leonora's aria after the *Miserere* in the last act and the reprise of *Di quella pira* allow Victor to get its earliest *Trovatore* onto two discs, thereby making it the least expensive one now available. Happily, it offers an outstanding performance featuring a brilliant quartet of vocalists in top form. Milanov has given us few performances on records quite so appealing as this Leonora. In temperament and vocal velvet, it is a fitting reminder of the unique position Milanov held among Italianate dramatic sopranos in the decade following World War II. Manrico provided Bjoerling one of his finest roles, and it may be that the late tenor never sang the part more masterfully than on this occasion. Though he was not the ideal bravura singer, Warren sang Di Luna with ravishing beauty of tone and to thrilling effect in such a broad cantilena as *Il balen del suo sorriso*. His second recording of the role, Warren's last recording before his death, is perhaps a bit more polished, but it cannot outdo the vocal opulence of his first effort. Barbieri sings in her most hearty manner and is effective, even if she does not present the ultimate vocal refinements, *e.g.*, the trills and other ornaments in *Stride la vampa*. The vigorous conducting of Cellini, the fine contributions of the orchestra and chorus, and the warm, resonant recording are other factors that make this set memorable.

The electrifying playing of the La Scala Orchestra under Karajan's meticulous direction and the unequalled portraiture of Callas are enough reason for owning the Angel set, however crude some of the singing by Di Stefano, Panerai, and Barbieri may be.

Third place goes to the latest Victor set, which has two serious weaknesses. Elias has neither the temperament nor a voice of sufficient amplitude and impact to fit Azucena, and Basile conducts a performance flawed by many lapses from unanimity and some poorly chosen tempi. On the credit side is the work of Leonard Warren, already commented on, and the brilliance of Price's soprano. Price, however, needs more experience in this role to deliver it with grandeur and authority. Tucker's voice is cold, and his singing offers transparent, calculated intensity as a substitute for spontaneity of expression.

London's is the only absolutely complete *Trovatore*, and it earns respect for Simionato's vivid Azucena, Del Monaco's delivery of his heroic measures, the beauty of Tebaldi's voice, and Savarese's fine rhythm and all-around musicality. Shortcomings are Erede's nerveless direction; Tebaldi's difficulty in many rapid passages due to her failure to lighten her voice, her lack of a trill, and her inability to float her top tones in *D'amor sull' ali rosee*; Savarese's somewhat dry tone; and Del Monaco's conversational passages which are sung at a volume appropriate for communicating with someone hard of hearing across Grand Central Station during rush hour.

TURANDOT. Birgit Nilsson (Turandot), Jussi Bjoerling (Calaf), Renata Tebaldi (Liù), Rome Opera Chorus and Orchestra, Erich Leinsdorf; Victor LM-6149 or LSC-6149 (stereo) (3); FTC-8001 (4-track tape).

Maria Callas, Eugenio Fernandi, Elisabeth Schwarzkopf, La Scala Chorus and Orchestra, Tullio Serafin; Angel 3571 (3).

Inge Borkh, Mario Del Monaco, Renata Tebaldi; Santa Cecilia Chorus and Orchestra, Alberto Erede; London A-4320 or OSA-1308 (stereo) (3).

There is a ground swell of interest in *Turandot*, judging by the recent outbreak of revivals of the work here and abroad. Other evidence of increased interest is the recent appearance of three complete recordings of Puccini's last opera. Because *Turandot*, a work of imposing sonorities and bountiful spatial effects, is particularly suited to stereophonic registration, it is easy to make a choice between the two top-rated recordings. Despite some pre-echo, distortion, and the often annoyingly distant placement of its vocal soloists, the Victor stereo set gives much the best idea of the general effect this work makes in an opera house. The "mono" version, of course, cannot claim this advantage; and it is not, accordingly, notably superior to the Angel set.

Although her voice is basically unsuited in terms of amplitude to this gruelling, heavy-duty assignment, Callas is nevertheless musically stylish and temperamentally well endowed to perform the icy princess. She makes a great deal of the text—much more than do her competitors—notwithstanding some wobbly, strident tones above the staff. Nilsson, on the other hand, has the voice for Turandot; but dramatic mastery of the role is not yet hers. She, unfortunately, begins unsteadily, and her best singing occurs only after her big entrance aria. The outstanding individual contribution in either set is Bjoerling's superb Calaf. His exquisite shaping of phrases and the wide dynamic span and color of his singing are further evidence of his claim to having been the leading Italianate tenor of his day. Tebaldi, the persuasive Liù in the Victor as well as the London recording, is sympathetic and appealing in tone. Schwarzkopf, though she gives us some impressive vocal shading, does not provide the generous tone and character Liù demands. Fernandi is an adequate Calaf in every way, exciting neither disapproval nor enthusiasm. Serafin leads the superb La Scala forces in a firm, idiomatic manner. Leinsdorf is less stylish, but his work has ample spirit, and his orchestra plays with polish and precision.

The London recording, the earliest issue in this group, is an average recording of only a fair performance. Its chief defects are an uninspired and frequently insensitive direction and an unstylish and often tonally unsteady Turandot. Del Monaco makes the rafters ring with telling effect in the Riddle Scene, but elsewhere one wants at least an occasional touch of tenderness and elegance.

WOZZECK. Mack Harrell (Wozzeck), Eileen Farrell (Marie), Schola Cantorum Chorus and a children's chorus from High School of Music and Art, and New York Philharmonic, Dimitri Mitropoulos; Columbia SL–118 (2).

The postwar revival of interest in *Wozzeck* on this side of the Atlantic stems from the enthusiasm of the late Dimitri Mitropoulos. It was his exciting performances of Berg's moving and gloomy masterpiece with an impeccable, carefully trained cast and the New York Philharmonic in April, 1951, that paved the way for stage productions of *Wozzeck* first at the New York City Center and later at the Metropolitan Opera House. And it is a composite of the best of three of those 1951 renditions that we have as our only recording of this opera. The sound of these records is surprisingly good, considering their age. The vitality and dedication of the performers, particularly of the late Mack Harrell, are something special and are not likely to be duplicated soon.

DIE ZAUBERFLÖTE. Tiana Lemnitz (Pamina), Helge Roswänge (Tamino), Gerhard Hüsch (Papageno), Wilhelm Strienz (Sarastro), Erna Berger (Queen of the Night), Berlin Philharmonic Chorus and Orchestra, Sir Thomas Beecham; Electrola 80471/3S (3).

Hilde Gueden, Léopold Simoneau, Walter Berry, Kurt Böhme, Wilma Lipp, Vienna State Opera Chorus and Vienna Philharmonic Orchestra, Karl Böhm; London A-4319 (3).

Maria Stader, Ernst Häfliger, Dietrich Fischer-Dieskau, Josef Greindl, Rita Streich, RIAS Chorus and Orchestra, Ferenc Fricsay; Decca DX–134 (3).

Few operas have fared so well on records as Mozart's *The Magic Flute*. Certainly no other can boast *three* performances of such stature. In spite of its age, I must rate the still fine-sounding prewar Electrola set (which is available on order through most dealers) at the top of the list. Its singers—Lemnitz,

Roswänge, Hüsch, and Berger, who are among the outstanding vocal artists of the past thirty years—are, however, only slightly better in aggregate than those in the London and Decca issues. But there is Sir Thomas Beecham, and his accomplishment in 1938 still stands as monumental. Good as are Böhm and Fricsay, neither unfailingly gets that just-right tempo, that purity and transparency of tone, that sense of majesty, urgency, and momentum just when each of these qualities seems indispensable.

The London set (which includes the complete vocal score) is doubtless the best recording, and, for my taste, Gueden is the best of the Paminas. The other artists, with the exception of Böhme, who lacks tonal stability for Sarastro's serene passages, are excellent.

The Decca set has an advantage in dramatic coherence over its competition. It presents for the first time on records a good portion of the spoken text (read not by the singers, incidentally, but by professional actors) that one hears in actual performances of *The Magic Flute*. Among the vocalists, Streich is outstanding for her brilliant singing of the Queen of the Night's two extremely difficult arias. Häfliger makes a gallant, tender Tamino, but Stader is perhaps too light-voiced for Pamina, and Greindl needs a more even legato for Sarastro. This mostly good recording varies somewhat in quality and perspective.